W9-BVA-051

# THE COLLECTED
# WORKS OF
# JEREMY BENTHAM

*General Editors*
F. Rosen and P. Schofield

## POLITICAL WRITINGS

*Political Tactics*, composed for the Estates-General in the months just prior to the outbreak of the French Revolution, is one of Bentham's most original works. It contains the earliest and perhaps most important theoretical analysis of parliamentary procedure ever written. It was subsequently translated into many languages and has had a far-reaching influence—for instance, it provided the basis for the regulations adopted in the 1820s governing the procedure of the Buenos Aires assembly, and as recently as the early 1990s was reprinted by the Spanish Cortes. With typical thoroughness and insight, Bentham discusses such central themes as the publicity of proceedings, the rules of debate, the conduct of deputies, and the proper steps to be taken in composing, proposing, and voting on a motion. Even such relatively minor points as the size of the asembly room and the costume of the deputies are not overlooked. Throughout Bentham illustrates his points by reference to the actual practice of both the British Houses of Parliament and the French provincial assemblies.

### The Collected Works of Jeremy Bentham

The new critical edition of the works and correspondence of Jeremy Bentham (1748–1832) is being prepared and published under the supervision of the Bentham Committee of University College London. In spite of his importance as jurist, philosopher, and social scientist, and leader of the Utilitarian reformers, the only previous edition of his works was a poorly edited and incomplete one brought out within a decade or so of his death. The overall plan and principles of this edition are set out in the General Preface to *The Correspondence of Jeremy Bentham*, vol. 1 (Athlone Press), which was the first volume of the *Collected Works* to be published.

*Volumes published by Oxford University Press*

Constitutional Code
Volume 1
Edited by F. Rosen and J. H. Burns

*Deontology, together with A Table of the Springs of Action and Article on Utilitarianism*
Edited by Amnon Goldworth

Chrestomathia
Edited by M. J. Smith and W. H. Burston

*First Principles preparatory to Constitutional Code*
Edited by Philip Schofield

*Securities against Misrule and other Constitutional Writings for Tripoli and Greece*
Edited by Philip Schofield

*Official Aptitude Maximized; Expense Minimized*
Edited by Philip Schofield

*Colonies, Commerce, and Constitutional Law: Rid Yourselves of Ultramaria and other writings on Spain and Spanish America*
Edited by Philip Schofield

*'Legislator of the World': Writings on Codification, Law, and Education*
Edited by Philip Schofield and Jonathan Harris

*Correspondence, volume 6: January 1798 to December 1801*
Edited by J. R. Dinwiddy

*Correspondence, volume 7: January 1802 to December 1808*
Edited by J. R. Dinwiddy

*Correspondence, volume 8: January 1809 to December 1816*
Edited by Stephen Conway

*Correspondence, volume 9: January 1817 to June 1820*
Edited by Stephen Conway

*Correspondence, volume 10: July 1820 to December 1821*
Edited by Stephen Conway

# POLITICAL TACTICS

edited by
MICHAEL JAMES
CYPRIAN BLAMIRES
and
CATHERINE PEASE-WATKIN

CLARENDON PRESS · OXFORD
1999

146480

# OXFORD
UNIVERSITY PRESS

Great Clarendon Street, Oxford OX2 6DP

Oxford University Press is a department of the University of Oxford
and furthers the University's aim of excellence in research, scholarship,
and education by publishing worldwide in

Oxford New York

Athens Auckland Bangkok Bogotá Bombay Buenos Aires Calcutta
Cape Town Chennai Dar es Salaam Delhi Florence Hong Kong Istanbul
Karachi Kuala Lumpur Madras Melbourne Mexico City Mumbai
Nairobi Paris São Paulo Singapore Taipei Tokyo Toronto Warsaw

and associated companies in Berlin Ibadan

Oxford is a registered trade mark of Oxford University Press

Published in the United States
by Oxford University Press Inc., New York

© Oxford University Press 1999

The moral rights of the author have been asserted
Database right Oxford University Press (maker)

First published 1999

All rights reserved. No part of this publication may be reproduced,
stored in a retrieval system, or transmitted, in any form or by any means,
without the prior permission in writing of Oxford University Press,
or as expressly permitted by law, or under terms agreed with the appropriate
reprographics rights organizations. Enquiries concerning reproduction
outside the scope of the above should be sent to the Rights Department,
Oxford University Press, at the address above

You must not circulate this book in any other binding or cover
and you must impose the same conditions on any acquirer

British Library Cataloguing in Publication Data

Data available

Library of Congress Cataloging in Publication Data

Data applied for

ISBN 0-19-820772-7

1 3 5 7 9 10 8 6 4 2

Typeset by Joshua Associates Ltd., Oxford
Printed in Great Britain
on acid-free paper by
Biddles Ltd., Guildford & King's Lynn

# PREFACE

The Bentham Committee wishes to thank the Economic and Social Research Council, whose generous grant has made possible the completion of this volume. The Committee is also indebted to the British Academy and University College London for their continuing support, and to the Australian Research Grants Committee and La Trobe University for support for research visits by Dr James to the Bentham Project.

The editors wish to thank the following repositories for permission to quote from manuscripts held in their collections and for assistance in tracing rare volumes: the Bibliothèque Publique et Universitaire, Geneva; the British Library; the Bodleian Library; the London Library; and Cambridge University Library. Special thanks are due to the staff of University College London Library, and in particular to Ms Gill Furlong for her co-operation and assistance.

Many people have contributed to the production of this volume. In particular we would like to thank Mrs Katharine Barber, Professor J.H. Burns, Dr Stephen Conway, Mrs Claire Daunton, Dr Rosalind Davies, the late Professor John Dinwiddy, Dr Jane Haville, Professor Douglas Johnson, Dr Martin Smith, Dr Colin Tyler, and Mr Timothy Venning. For elucidation of particular references in the text we are grateful to Mr Andrew Lewis, Dr Alan Pitt, and Professor R.W. Sharples. Mrs Irena Nicoll has done sterling work at the final stages of checking the volume and preparing it for the press, and for this we are especially grateful. Other colleagues at the Bentham Project, Dr Tony Draper, Ms Catherine Fuller, Dr Jonathan Harris, Dr Luke O'Sullivan, and Dr Michael Quinn, with a characteristic spirit of collaboration have shared their knowledge and insight on countless occasions.

The General Editors, Professor Fred Rosen and Dr Philip Schofield, have read the whole of the text and have made numerous suggestions for improvement. The editors are particularly grateful to Dr Schofield for his invaluable criticism in the preparation of the Editorial Introduction, and his guidance in all other aspects of the volume.

# CONTENTS

CONTENTS

# SYMBOLS AND ABBREVIATIONS

Symbols

| |        Space left in manuscript.
[to]         Word(s) editorially supplied.
⟨ ... ⟩      Word(s) torn away.
⟨so⟩         Conjectural restoration of mutilated word.

Abbreviations

Apart from standard abbreviations the following should be noted:

Bowring         *The Works of Jeremy Bentham*, published under the superintendence of . . . John Bowring, 11 vols., Edinburgh, 1843.

UC              Bentham papers in the Library of University College London. Roman numerals refer to boxes in which the papers are placed, arabic to the leaves within each box.

BL Add. MS      British Library Additional Manuscript.

*CW*            This edition of *The Collected Works of Jeremy Bentham*.

Bentham 1791    Jeremy Bentham, 'Essay on Political Tactics: containing Six of the Principal Rules proper to be observed by a Political Assembly, In the Process of Forming a Decision: with the Reasons on which they are Grounded; And a Comparative Application of them to British and French Practice: Being a Fragment of a larger Work; a Sketch of which is subjoined', London, 1791.

Dumont MSS      Dumont MSS, Bibliothèque Publique et Universitaire, Geneva.

# EDITORIAL INTRODUCTION

Jeremy Bentham's 'Political Tactics', part of which was printed in 1791, was probably the first attempt ever made to theorize broadly about parliamentary procedure.[1] In spite of its title, it is not a treatise on political strategy and manoeuvre. In its strictest, most literal sense, the word 'tactics' means 'the art of setting in order'; thus, 'Political Tactics' is an exploration of the order to be observed in the proceedings of political assemblies. In other words, it is an analysis of parliamentary procedure, conceived in general, theoretical terms. The practice of the British Houses of Parliament is, however, often cited as a model of good procedure. As Bentham said, 'the very rules that suggested themselves as necessary to every assembly, turned out to be the very rules actually observed in both assemblies of the British Legislature.'[2]

The present text is, with a few small changes, the text of 'An Essay on Political Tactics' which appeared in the Bowring edition of *The Works of Jeremy Bentham*, published in 1838–43.[3]

## HISTORY OF THE WORK

There are three distinct versions of this work. The first version, printed in 1791, was a fragment, running to 64 pages plus two tables.[4] One of the tables was a detailed plan of the whole projected work, which was to bear the title 'Essays on Political Tactics'; ten essays were planned, each subdivided into chapters. The second table was a 'Tabula Ataxiologica' or 'Synoptical Table', which related the ends to be kept in view when framing regulations for a political assembly to the possible inconveniences which could arise from the proceedings of an assembly.[5]

The fragment was printed and circulated privately, and individual recipients of the printed sheets then had them bound. Thus of five copies

[1] See J.H. Burns, 'Bentham and the French Revolution', *Transactions of the Royal Historical Society*, 5th series, xvi (1966), 95–114.

[2] See the Preface, p. 1 below.

[3] See *The Works of Jeremy Bentham, published under the superintendence of . . . John Bowring*, 11 vols., Edinburgh, 1843, ii. 299–373. Sir John Bowring (1792–1872), merchant, radical MP, and diplomat, was Bentham's literary executor.

[4] 'Essay on Political Tactics: containing Six of the Principal Rules proper to be observed by a Political Assembly, In the Process of Forming a Decision: with the Reasons on which they are Grounded; And a Comparative Application of them to British and French Practice: Being a Fragment of a larger Work; a Sketch of which is subjoined.'

[5] For these tables see pp. 176–7 below.

of the 1791 fragment known to exist in England,[1] each is unique in terms of the binding, and indeed even the size of the pages is not uniform. Further, there were two distinct impressions of the text. One impression consisted solely of 'Essay VI', which became Chapter VI in the Bowring edition;[2] in the other, 'Essay VI' was preceded by a Preface, which Bowring appended as a footnote to Chapter VI, and part of 'Essay V', which was incorporated into Bowring's Chapter V.[3] Although only this fragment of the projected work was printed, the likelihood is that a large part of the work was written at this time.[4]

The second version of the work did not appear until 1816, when Étienne Dumont[5] published *Tactique des assemblées législatives, suivie d'un traité des sophismes politiques*. Dumont's recension of 'Essays on Political Tactics', entitled 'Tactique des assemblées politiques délibérantes', appeared in the first volume, followed by Dumont's own 'Règlement pour le conseil représentatif de la ville et république de Genève', and by 'Règlements observés dans la Chambre des Communes pour débattre les matières et pour voter', published anonymously but the work of Samuel Romilly.[6] The second volume contained 'Traité des sophismes politiques' and 'Sophismes anarchiques', two further works assembled from Bentham's manuscripts. In his introduction to the second volume, Dumont explained the reasoning behind the publication of this material together with the works on parliamentary procedure: while the works in the first volume gave rules regarding the *form* of debates, the second volume gave guidelines about their *substance*.[7] In the original plan of the whole work, Bentham had included six chapters on the fallacies and deceits employed in debating.[8]

'Tactique des assemblées politiques délibérantes' was prepared from Bentham's manuscripts. With the exception of a sequence of manuscripts

---

[1] Two copies in the library at UCL; two copies in the British Library and one copy in the Bodleian Library. See *A Bibliographical Catalogue of the Works of Jeremy Bentham*, Chuo University Library, Tokyo, 1989, p. 70, for full details.

[2] See pp. 72–109 below.    [3] See pp. 65–71 below.

[4] See the Preface to the 1791 fragment, p. 4 below: 'the remainder of the work . . . though considerably advanced, was not, even in manuscript, completed'; see in addition Bentham to James Madison, 30 October 1811, *The Correspondence of Jeremy Bentham*, vol. viii, ed. S. Conway, Oxford, 1988 (*CW*), p. 209: 'The printed but never published fragment on the subject of the *Art of Tactics* as applied to *Political Assemblies*, is but one Essay, out of some *thirty* or *forty*, which were at that time written and which, taken together, did not want much of having gone through the subject in its whole extent.' Presumably Bentham meant that thirty or forty of the chapters of his ten projected Essays were written at that time.

[5] Pierre Étienne Louis Dumont (1759–1829) was Bentham's Genevan editor and translator. *Tactique des assemblées législatives, suivie d'un traité des sophismes politiques*, 2 vols., Geneva and Paris, 1816. A second edition, with some revisions, was published in Paris in 1822. In the present volume all references to *Tactique des assemblées législatives* are to the 1816 edition, unless otherwise specified.

[6] Sir Samuel Romilly (1757–1818), lawyer and law reformer, Solicitor General 1806–7.

[7] See *Tactique des assemblées législatives*, ii. p.vii.    [8] See Table I, p. 176 below.

dealing with 'Motion Tables' (Bentham's term for large screens on which the motion under discussion in an assembly could be displayed by means of letters fixed up and taken down as required)[1] the original manuscripts are lost. Although it is probable that most of the work had been completed by Bentham, Dumont did find gaps which it was necessary to fill, and in other places he strayed from Bentham's plan and from his method. The order of chapters in 'Tactique des assemblées politiques délibérantes' does not follow Bentham's plan for the projected work; nor does Dumont use Bentham's 'interrogative method' of examining a subject by means of questions and answers.[2] The chapters of Dumont's recension which correspond to 'Essay on Political Tactics' by no means constitute a straightforward translation of the earlier work, and a comparison of the relevant chapters[3] shows how much Dumont has compressed Bentham's original text. Bentham's 'Essay VI' amounted to 64 pages, each with about 300 words; in Dumont's recension, this was reduced to four chapters covering 16 pages, each with about 220 words. A comparison of the original 'Motion Table' manuscript with Dumont's chapter on the same subject[4] provides further illustration of Dumont's compression of Bentham's text.

The third version of the work was the translation into English of Dumont's 'Tactique des assemblées politiques délibérantes' by Richard Smith, published in the Bowring edition with the title 'An Essay on Political Tactics'.[5] In a footnote the text is said to have been 'edited from the work of M. Dumont, and the papers of Bentham'.[6] It is not clear which 'papers of Bentham' are meant, although it seems possible that Smith used Bentham's plan of the projected work. Smith's edition follows the order of chapters in Bentham's original plan more closely than it follows the order of chapters in Dumont's recension, particularly in Chapters I-VI.[7] Essentially, however, Smith's 'An Essay on Political Tactics' constitutes a translation of Dumont's 'Tactique des assemblées politiques délibérantes', with the significant exceptions of Chapters V and VI. Smith's Chapter VI is a reproduction of 'Essay VI' printed in 1791, and does not draw on Dumont's work at all. Smith's Chapter V consists of the 1791 'Essay V', with paragraphs from Dumont's work interspersed.

Only a part of 'An Essay on Political Tactics'—most of Chapter V and

---

[1] Dumont MSS, 72. These manuscripts are published in the Appendix, pp. 157–75 below.
[2] See Dumont's 'Discours préliminaire', p. 10 below.
[3] 'Tactique des assemblées politiques délibérantes', Chapters X, XV, XVI, and XVII.
[4] Chapter XII.
[5] Bowring, ii. 299–373. Smith was a Collector of Stagecoach Duties at the Stamp and Taxes Office.
[6] Bowring, ii. 301.
[7] See pp. 217–26 below for a chart which compares the chapter headings of the three versions of the work.

all of Chapter VI—is certainly Bentham's authentic work. With regard to the rest of the text, it is impossible to know exactly what was contributed by Dumont and by Smith. However, this material printed by Bentham himself accounts for between a quarter and a third of the text, a substantial fraction. Furthermore, the inspiration and much of the execution of the work were Bentham's, and his peculiar genius for organization and classification still permeates the whole text, even if that text is not in exactly the form which Bentham envisaged.

## 'Essay on Political Tactics', 1791

Dumont stated in the introduction to 'Tactique des assemblées politiques délibérantes' that it was the *procès-verbaux* (proceedings) of the new French provincial assemblies, revealing the confusion and lack of internal discipline of those assemblies, which led Bentham to consider the principles of the art of parliamentary debate.[1] It was in 1778 that assemblies were first held in the provinces of Berry and Guyenne; these assemblies are extensively referred to in the 'Essay on Political Tactics.'[2] The earliest surviving reference made by Bentham to a work on the subject of parliamentary procedure occurs in a letter of 14 August 1778 to his younger brother Samuel.[3]

However, it was not until the autumn of 1788 that Bentham was prompted to take an active interest in French affairs by the news that Louis XVI intended to call a meeting of the Estates-General in May of the following year. In September 1788, the *parlement* of Paris, which had the task of registering the King's measures and the right to raise objections to those measures, decreed that the Estates-General should meet under its 1614 constitution, that is in three almost numerically equal but separately elected chambers, representing the orders of nobility, clergy, and third estate. One feature of the 1614 constitution, voting by order, meant that the third estate could be outvoted by the two higher orders. There was much debate and disagreement about the composition of the Estates-General, and in response to this, Jacques Necker,[4] at the head of the French administration, called an Assembly of the Notables for November 1788.[5]

---

[1] See pp. 8–9 below.　　　　　　　　　　[2] See pp. 76, 90–1, 95–7, 103–5 below.
[3] Bentham to Samuel Bentham, 14 August 1778, *The Correspondence of Jeremy Bentham*, vol. ii, ed. T.L.S. Sprigge, London, 1968 (*CW*), pp. 156–7. Samuel Bentham (1757–1831), naval architect and engineer.
[4] Jacques Necker (1732–1804), Swiss banker, Director-General of Finances in France 1777–81, 1788–90.
[5] The Assembly of the Notables was chosen by the King with no element of election; it had a consultative rather than a legislative function, and was called at irregular intervals in response to particular crises. A previous Assembly of the Notables had met in February 1787.

The purpose of the meeting was to consider the composition of the Estates-General and to advise the King on the matter; Necker was hoping to secure from the Notables a recommendation for double representation of the third estate. The Assembly of Notables met between 6 November and 12 December 1788; they rejected Necker's suggestion, but by December 1788 the King had bowed to intense public pressure and agreed to double the representation of the third estate.

During the 1780s Bentham had been closely involved with the Marquis of Lansdowne[1] and the circle, including Romilly and Dumont, which gathered around him at Bowood, his Wiltshire residence. Bentham had spent several weeks at Bowood in 1781, and his relationship with the Marquis continued throughout the 1780s, broken only by Bentham's long trip to see his brother Samuel in Russia between August 1785 and February 1788. Contact with Lansdowne was renewed in early summer 1788.[2] Romilly had been a part of Lansdowne's circle since 1784, at which time he was also introduced to Bentham.[3] Dumont had been a close friend of Romilly's since their first meeting in Geneva in 1781, and joined Lansdowne's household in January 1786, ostensibly as tutor to his younger son, Henry Petty.[4] In the summer of 1788, Dumont and Romilly made a visit of two months' duration to Paris, where Dumont first met Mirabeau.[5] Dumont recorded the 'fermentation' in Paris at that time, caused by the imminent meeting of the Estates-General;[6] it is possible that news he and Romilly carried back to England helped to kindle Bentham's interest in France.[7]

In the autumn of 1788, Bentham embarked upon several distinct works relating to France, not all of which were completed. Two of these were relatively short works, written in French: the first, an 'open letter' which Bentham sent to Mirabeau, criticized the decision to maintain the constitution of 1614;[8] the second was Bentham's critique of a publication, issued by the Breton nobility, in support of the 1614 constitution.[9] The latter piece was the occasion of Bentham's first collaboration with

---

[1] William Petty (1737–1805), second Earl of Shelburne, created first Marquis of Lansdowne in 1784.

[2] See *The Correspondence of Jeremy Bentham*, vol. iii, ed. I.R. Christie, London, 1971 (*CW*), pp. 617, 621–2.

[3] See *The Correspondence of Jeremy Bentham*, vol. iv, ed. A.T. Milne, London, 1981 (*CW*), p. 17.

[4] See Dumont, *Souvenirs sur Mirabeau et sur les deux premières assemblées législatives*, Paris, 1832, p.vii. Lord Henry Petty, later Petty-Fitzmaurice (1780–1863), was Lansdowne's son by his second wife, formerly Lady Louisa Fitzpatrick.

[5] Honoré Gabriel Riqueti, Comte de Mirabeau (1749–91), French politician; later to become member for Aix-en-Provence, and one of the leaders of the Third Estate, in the Estates-General.

[6] See Dumont, *Souvenirs sur Mirabeau*, p. 23.

[7] *Correspondence* (*CW*), iv. 17–18 n.

[8] 'A Mirabeau', UC clxx. 1–7.

[9] 'Observations d'un Anglois sur un Écrit intitulé *Arrêté de la Noblesse de Bretagne*', UC clxx. 122–33.

Dumont, to whom Romilly had passed the manuscript for the purpose of checking and correcting Bentham's French.[1]

A third piece of work which Bentham began in the autumn of 1788, in response to the situation in France, was that which in 1791 he eventually entitled 'Essay on Political Tactics', but which, while in progress, he referred to as 'Tactics'. In November 1788 Bentham received a letter from an unidentified French correspondent, who wrote: 'Our debates are carried on as barbarously as in the time of Charlemagne,—our national character seems opposed to sedate deliberation.'[2] The letter refers to the debates of the Notables rather than to the debates of a full parliamentary assembly, yet the information could have been further grist to Bentham's mill. Although the idea of a manual of parliamentary procedure had first occurred to Bentham ten years earlier, it was the situation in France in 1788 which provided him with a specific opportunity to supply some useful guidelines on the subject. He was also engaged simultaneously on another work in French, an 'essay on Representation', some of the subject-matter of which overlapped with that of 'Tactics'.[3]

In a letter of January 1789, Lansdowne invited Bentham to make use of the library at Lansdowne House, his London home.[4] One of the books specifically mentioned by Lansdowne was *Résultat des assemblées provinciales à l'usage des états d'une province*,[5] a work which Bentham cited in 'Essay on Political Tactics'.[6] In March 1789 Lansdowne once again arranged to supply Bentham with books, and on this occasion wrote: 'The King of Sweden is going on at a rare rate without making the least account of your Indignation or mine. I don't believe he knows it. I wish you would make him sensible of it, for which there is but one way, that of appealing to the Public opinion of Europe.'[7] Bentham was working, at this time, on material which was later printed as 'Essay on Political Tactics'; in that work, there is a long footnote on the contemporary situation of Sweden.[8]

Lansdowne's encouragement was not confined to the provision of books and the discussion of issues. In a letter of 3 February 1789 he introduced Bentham to Morellet.[9] Bentham himself wrote to Morellet on

[1] See Bentham to Romilly, 2 December 1788, *Correspondence (CW)*, iv. 17–18.
[2] Ibid. 13.
[3] UC clxx. 65–121. See Bentham to Morellet, 25 February 1789, *Correspondence (CW)*, iv. 31. André Morellet (1727–1819), writer on economics, published *Observations sur le projet de former une Assemblée Nationale sur le modèle des États-Généraux de 1614* [Paris?, 1788] as a contribution to the debate on the form which the revived Estates-General should take. He was a friend of Lansdowne.
[4] *Correspondence (CW)*, iv. 21–2.
[5] Charles Marie, Marquis de Créquy (1737–1801), *Résultat des assemblées provinciales, à l'usage des états d'une province* [i.e. Artois], Brussels, 1788.
[6] See pp. 86–90, 104, 108–9 below.
[7] Lansdowne to Bentham, 29 March 1789, *Correspondence (CW)*, iv. 44.
[8] See pp. 65–6n. below.        [9] See *Correspondence (CW)*, iv. 27 n.

25 February 1789; his letter, and some manuscripts (including those dealing with the Motion Tables)[1] were sent via Lansdowne's elder son Lord Wycombe.[2] Bentham told Morellet that 'Tactics' was written for the Estates-General:

What Lord Lansdowne attempts to trouble you with, is a Treatise on Political Tactics, containing principles relative to the conduct and discipline of Political Assemblies. It will be impossible for me to complete it [in] time enough to be published before the meeting of the Etats Generaux, for whose use it is principally designed: but I hope to be able to despatch, by that time, such parts as seem to be of most immediate and essential importance.[3]

Bentham asked Morellet if he could arrange for and oversee a translation, for although he had begun the work in French, he had subsequently decided to write it in English, probably on the advice of Lansdowne.[4] Bentham expressed the hope that, should he be able to send 100 or so pages to Morellet by the end of March 1789, Morellet might be able to translate and publish them by the time of the meeting of the Estates-General in May 1789. Bentham also proposed terms by which any putative profits would be shared between himself and the translator. To Wycombe, Bentham put a proposal that Wycombe should act as his 'ambassador' to Mme Necker, and present 'at the toilette of the said lady—not a pincushion, but a project of a pincushion of my invention for sticking motions on, for the entertainment of the Etats Generaux',[5] in other words, the 'Motion Table' manuscript.

Morellet, having seen Bentham's letter to Wycombe and the enclosed manuscript, replied in a complimentary way to Bentham on 25 March 1789: 'Votre tactique me paroit la seule à l'aide de laquelle nous puissions

---

[1] See pp. xiv–xv above.

[2] John Henry Petty (1765–1809), Lansdowne's son by his first marriage, had taken the title Lord Wycombe in 1784 when his father was made first Marquis of Lansdowne. On his father's death in 1805 he succeeded to the Marquisate.

[3] *Correspondence* (*CW*), iv. 30.

[4] See Bentham to Wycombe, 1 March 1789, ibid. 34; Lansdowne to Morellet, ibid., 27n. The manuscripts of the original French version have disappeared, but one sheet, probably dating from the 1780s (UC clxx. 191), contains some preliminary notes on the topic: 'Je n'ai point vu de livre où l'on recherche les règlements qu'il seroit à propos d'établir pour maintenir le bon ordre dans les délibérations des corps politiques. On en pourroit faire un très bon en prenant pour base celles qui s'observent communément en Angleterre. En voici un échantillon.' (Accents have been supplied). In the notes which follow, several topics which reappear in 'An Essay on Political Tactics' are touched upon: for example, the role of the president, the necessity of written motions, and the inconveniences arising from the absence of members. Bentham even uses the word 'tactique' in its specific sense: 'Il seroit curieux de suivre les règles de la tactique de toutes des assemblées dans tous les états policés.' The final paragraph contains a hint that Bentham envisaged organizing the rules of procedure in a systematic way: 'Elles sont simples ces règles là, claires et un petit nombre et si simples qu'en les regardant on se demande comment on a pu ne pas les avoir, et comment on a pu en avoir d'autres. Cependant il leur manque encore d'être redigées, corrigées peut être, motivées, réduites en système.'

[5] Bentham to Wycombe, 1 March 1789. Suzanne, née Curchod, had married Jacques Necker in 1764. She presided over a literary and political *salon*.

gagner la grande bataille que la raison et la liberté vont livrer à l'ignorance et à la tyrannie des mauvaises loix et d'une vicieuse constitution.'[1] Morellet, rather than Wycombe, presented Bentham's manuscript to Mme Necker, and together they spoke of it to Jacques Necker; according to Morellet, neither Necker nor his wife had had time actually to read it. As for the translation of the work, Morellet declined to undertake it, but he did suggest a candidate, Louis Joseph Faure.[2] He then explained at some length that it was vain to hope for any financial gain from the work, citing the sheer volume of literature on the Estates-General as the reason, and calling Paris 'notre *bibliopolium*'. Morellet's encouragement focused on Bentham's essay on representation. In Morellet's view, this was the most urgent issue to which Bentham could apply himself on France's behalf: 'Nous aurions bien besoin . . . d'une bonne theorie de la representation nationale . . . votre esprit me semble plus que celui d'aucun philosophe connû capable de voir et d'embrasser la question par toutes ses faces et de ne rien laisser à dire quand vous l'aurez traitée'.[3] Thus Morellet was flattering, but he did not offer Bentham very much practical assistance in disseminating his work in Paris.

On 28 April 1789 Bentham wrote again to Morellet, enclosing 'three sheets of my Tactics',[4] and hoping that Morellet could secure their translation in time for the meeting of the Estates-General in May. On 8 May 1789, three days after the first session of the Estates-General, Morellet wrote to Bentham with disappointing news: Faure had made no progress with the translation of 'Essay on Political Tactics'. Morellet pointed out that Bentham had missed the chance to bring out his work before the meeting of the Estates-General. He continued, however: 'comme je suis convaincu que les formes et le regime de l'assemblée elle même ne seront pas reglées d'icy à quelque tems vos recherches auront encore le tems de paroitre et de nous etre utiles'.[5] Morellet considered that the support of the Duc de la Rochefoucauld and the Marquis de la Fayette,[6] both of whom had received 'des exemplaires de l'original anglais', could speed publication of a translation of 'Tactics'. Once again Morellet pointed out the unlikelihood of Bentham's making any money out of such a work.

[1] *Correspondence (CW)*, iv. 39.

[2] Louis Joseph Faure (1760–1837), jurist and magistrate. *Recherches historiques et politiques sur les États-Unis de l'Amérique septentrionale*, 4 vols., Paris, 1788, was his translation of a work by Philip Mazzei, never published in English.

[3] This was a remark which Bentham clearly took to heart, as he was to quote it nearly 18 months later: see Bentham to Lansdowne, 24 August 1790, *Correspondence (CW)*, iv. 168.

[4] *Correspondence (CW)*, iv. 48.　　　　　　　　　　　　　　　　[5] Ibid. 55.

[6] Louis Alexandre, Duc de la Rochefoucauld d'Enville (1743–92) was elected as a representative of the *noblesse* of Paris to the Estates-General and was one of the first peers to join with the third estate in the National Assembly. He was stoned to death by a mob at Gisors in September 1792. Marie Joseph du Motier, Marquis de la Fayette (1757–1834) was also a prominent member of the Estates-General.

By June 1789, Morellet had ceased his efforts to secure a translation of 'Tactics'. He wrote to Lansdowne of 'la grande difficulté de faire cette traduction morceau à morceau sans connoitre l'ensemble et en recevant continuellement des additions et des changements'. Morellet had written to Dumont, asking him, in accordance with Bentham's wishes, to retrieve the manuscript of 'Tactics' from the Duc de la Rochefoucauld and to give it to Mirabeau, and that was 'tout ce que je puis faire pour remplir les intentions de Mr. Bentham'.[1]

Samuel Romilly, assisted by George Wilson[2] and James Trail,[3] had also written a work on parliamentary procedure, *Règlemens observés dans la Chambre des Communes, pour débattre les matières et pour voter*, which was published in Paris in June 1789 with a preface by Mirabeau.[4] Bentham's comment about this work illustrates the difference between his approach and Romilly's, in spite of the similarity of their subject-matter. He wrote:

An account has been sent from hence by some very intelligent people I know of the English practice, but not a syllable on the way of giving reasons and showing the inconveniences of any other mode, and without such explanation I should fear the naked exposition of the *little* that is useful and necessary, involved with the *much* that is either useless or mischievous, would afford but imperfect lights.[5]

This is an important criticism which reveals more about Bentham's own work than it does about Romilly's. First, Bentham criticized Romilly's work for not giving *reasons*; as the full title of 'Essay on Political Tactics' makes clear,[6] all the 'rules' of procedure discussed in that work are supported by 'reasons'.[7] Secondly, Bentham commented on the omission in Romilly's work of any discussion of the *inconveniences* of other modes of procedure; the relation of procedure and inconvenience was explored in Bentham's 'Tabula Ataxiologica', appended to 'Essay on Political Tactics'. Nonetheless, Bentham described his own work on Tactics as 'a sort of supplement' to the *Règlemens*.[8]

Reactions to 'Tactics' at this time were mixed. Morellet, in spite of his initial praise for the work, wrote:

---

[1] Morellet to Lansdowne, 22 June 1789, *Correspondence (CW)*, iv. 68 n.

[2] George Wilson (d. 1816), barrister, had known Bentham since 1776, and was a close friend of Romilly.

[3] James Trail (1750–1809), barrister, was later elected MP for Oxford 1802–6, and Under-Secretary for Ireland 1806–8.

[4] Romilly's work was translated into French by Dumont and Guy-Claude, Comte de Sarsfield (d. 1789). It was at Sarsfield's request that Romilly had written it. Note that when the work was reprinted in *Tactique des assemblées législatives* in 1816, the spelling of the title was slightly different.

[5] Bentham to Morellet, 28 April 1789, *Correspondence (CW)*, iv. 50.

[6] See p. xiii n. above.

[7] See pp. 77–82 below for examples of 'regulations' supported by 'reasons'.

[8] Bentham to the Duc de la Rochefoucauld[?], early May 1789[?], *Correspondence (CW)*, iv. 52.

Je trouve que vous vous arretez trop sur ce que vous appellez *les formes* ou *la pratique francoises*. Nous n'en avons point de fixes et de connues pour les assemblées nationales car les assemblées des etats de nos provinces[1] ne meritent vraiment pas ce nom et l'assemblée de guyenne que vous cîtez est de trop fraiche date et a trop peu d'autorité pour meriter qu'on discute les avantages et les inconveniens de ses formes.[2]

As the contrast between British practice and French practice was a central component of the structure of 'Essay on Political Tactics' (the full title refers to 'a Comparative Application . . . to British and French Practice') this was a significant comment.

George Wilson was both complimentary and critical. He wrote: 'There is much excellent matter in these sheets and often great happiness of expression'; but he wondered whether the terms 'discipline' and even 'tactics' itself were 'as dangerous to the liberty of the Assembly as the word Marshall which in your first note you are so afraid of'. Presumably Wilson saw inconsistency between Bentham's intolerance of the military word 'marshall' and his acceptance of the equally military words 'discipline' and 'tactics'. He thought some passages could be shortened, and found fault with 'a fondness for parentheses . . . a passion for Metaphor' and 'too much arrangement'. In contrast with Morellet, Wilson deemed the 'addition of the English and French practice . . . very entertaining and highly useful'.[3] Romilly also wrote a complimentary note to Bentham.[4]

In June 1789 Bentham sent Dumont 'a short view of the contents' of 'Tactics', although by this time work on it had lost momentum, due to a lack of encouragement from France, some 'private affairs, and the superior urgency of some calls of a public nature'.[5] During the spring and early summer of 1789, work on 'Tactics' was hampered by a lack of documentary evidence from France. In a draft letter Bentham asked Morellet for information about the French mode of proceeding;[6] he also made several other attempts to obtain information, both about French procedure and about the procedure of the British House of Commons.[7] In June 1789 Bentham wrote to Dumont: 'Mean time I see hints of things

---

[1] See pp. 75–6 below.

[2] Morellet to Bentham, 8 May 1789, *Correspondence* (*CW*), iv. 56.

[3] Wilson to Bentham, 12 May 1789, ibid. 59–60.

[4] Romilly to Bentham, *c*.12 May 1789, ibid. 61.

[5] Bentham to Dumont, 9 June 1789, ibid. 68. This was the first time Bentham wrote directly to Dumont, although they had met the previous year. By early June 1789, Bentham was writing the 'Anti-Machiavel' letters (Bowring, x. 201–11), which criticized the anti-Russian stance taken by the British ministry. See *Correspondence* (*CW*), iv. 69 n.

[6] Bentham to Morellet, 28 April 1789, ibid. 49 n.

[7] See Bentham to Wilson, 16 May 1789, ibid. 61; Bentham to Charles Butler, 3 June 1789, ibid. 67; Romilly to Bentham, 19 May 1789, ibid. 63; Wilson to Bentham, 21 May 1789, ibid. 64.

which make my mouth water every post, and none of them reach me.—
The Comte de Mirabeau's letters to his constituents, answering the
purpose of the suppressed Journal, etc. etc. I am in a rage with M.M.
with the Abbé M. with you, with Ld L., with R.[1] and in short with every
body through whose means I might hope to come in for a share of these
delicacies.'[2] Bentham confirmed in June 1789 that because of other
projects, 'Tactics have accordingly been suspended, spite of Mirabeau's
"*vive impatience*"'.[3]

Bentham's 'suspension' of 'Tactics' coincided with the publication in
June 1789 of six of his principles relating to debate, which appeared in
French translation, without acknowledgment of the author, in Mirabeau's
journal *Dixième lettre du Comte de Mirabeau à ses commettans*, with a
note to the effect that further discussion of the principles would appear in
subsequent issues of the journal.[4] Bentham was magnanimous about the
lack of acknowledgment: '[Mirabeau] could not with Dumont *en tête* mean
anything dishonourable'.[5] Thus, after many months of intense effort both
in the writing and in the attempts to publicize that writing, and at a time
when his own interest in the project was beginning to wane, a tiny
fragment of Bentham's output on the subject of parliamentary procedure
finally appeared in the *bibliopolium* that was Paris.

Bentham's interest in 'Tactics' having waned, it was Dumont who
appeared keen to rekindle enthusiasm. Writing to Bentham in September
1789, he praised the work and its author, and described the disarray of the
French National Assembly:

J'ai montré ce plan à M^r. De Mirabeau, au Duc de la Rochefoucault et quelques
autres personnes qui ont admiré cette conception vraiment philosophique et cet
ensemble qui forme le systeme d'un ouvrage absolument neuf et original; . . . je
puis vous dire qu'en achevant cet ouvrage projetté, vous remplirez une des
lacunes de la littérature politique, il n'y a que vous peut-être qui puissiez combler
ce déficit puisque vous seul en avez mesuré l'etendue et que vous avez jetté toute
la trame de l'ouvrage. Je ne vous promets pas un succès prompt. Les François
sont encore des enfants qui bégayent dans leur assemblée nationale: point
d'ordre, nul enchainement, nulle discussion, le hazard les entraine çà et là,
chacun joue le rôle du President, et ils ont la manie de tout faire.

---

[1] i.e. Mirabeau, Morellet, Lansdowne, and Romilly.
[2] *Correspondence* (*CW*), iv. 70. Mirabeau had issued two numbers of a journal called *Etats-Généraux* on 2 and 5 May 1789, ignoring the laws controlling the press. For nineteen issues, between 10 May 1789 and 9–24 July 1789, the journal was entitled *Lettre du Comte de Mirabeau à ses commettans*, and from the issue of 24–7 July 1789 onwards, it was entitled the *Courier de Provence*. Dumont became one of the editors of the journal in June 1789. See Dumont, *Souvenirs sur Mirabeau*, p. 89; C. Blount, 'Bentham, Dumont and Mirabeau', *University of Birmingham Historical Journal*, iii. (1951–2), 161 n., 162.
[3] Bentham to Lansdowne, 17 June 1789, *Correspondence* (*CW*), iv. 74.
[4] *Dixième lettre du Comte de Mirabeau à ses commettans*, 7–12 June 1789, pp. 8–9.
[5] Bentham to Wilson, 8 July 1789, *Correspondence* (*CW*), iv. 80.

Dumont also spoke of the disharmony between the three orders, and urged Bentham: 'Je vous presse donc Monsieur, au nom de votre philantropie, d'achever l'ouvrage que vous avez commencé, et s'il vous est possible de l'achever pour le commencement de la seconde legislature, vous rendrez à ce pays un service essentiel'. Dumont emphasized his point—'Je reviens à un objet qui m'occupe beaucoup plus fortement, c'est la Tactique parlementaire'—and offered to supply Bentham with information, should he be persuaded to continue with the work. He suggested that they should meet in London.[1]

Dumont's encouraging attitude is quite at variance with the impression of his position given to Lansdowne by Morellet, in a letter written at almost exactly the same time. By this stage Morellet's own opinion of Bentham's work was somewhat negative: 'son ouvrage, eût-il paru un an avant la convocation, on n'en auroit rien emprunté du tout à l'Assemblée Nationale. Au reste M. Dumont, qui s'étoit chargé de suivre la traduction et de se concerter avec M. le duc de La Rochefoucault pour cela, me paroit l'avoir abandonnée'.[2] Dumont's support and offer to supply information for 'Essay on Political Tactics' came too late; Bentham had already lost interest in the project, perhaps realizing that the moment had passed.

In the writing of a manual of parliamentary procedure for the Estates-General of France, Bentham's own particular circumstances may have occasionally been uppermost in his mind. He had been hoping that Lansdowne would secure a seat in Parliament for him, but in the summer of 1790 it became clear that this was not to be the case. Bentham wrote to Lansdowne:

You mentioned Parliament to me in the precisest terms: asking me whether I should like to have a seat there. My answer was in substance, 'that it was more than I could possibly assure myself, how far I might be able to do any thing in such a situation: that besides the want of fluency, the weakness of my voice might, for aught I knew be an insuperable bar to my being able to make myself *heard* in the literal sense of the word, in the House: but at any rate in Committees I flattered myself I might do as well as other people'.[3]

At the time when he thought he had some prospect of a parliamentary seat, Bentham had considered the problem of the weakness of his own voice. In the Bowring text of 'An Essay on Political Tactics' there are two references to the difficulty faced by a member of an assembly who has a

---

[1] Dumont to Bentham, 27 September 1789, *Correspondence* (*CW*), iv. 92–4.
[2] Morellet to Lord Lansdowne, 24 September 1789, published in *Lettres d'André Morellet*, ed. D. Medlin & J.-C. David, 3 vols., 1992–6, ii. 148.
[3] *Correspondence* (*CW*), iv. 146.

weak voice, one of which occurs in Chapter III, in the section entitled 'Of the Building suitable for a numerous Assembly', and there is a third reference in the manuscript material on the Motion Tables.[1] Although it is impossible to know how much of the text of his projected 'Essays on Political Tactics' Bentham himself completed, or exactly when he wrote that material, it is certain that the Motion Tables manuscript was written before February 1789, when it was sent to Morellet, and some material on the subject of the kind of room suitable for a political assembly was sent at the same time.[2] So rather than being merely examples of Bentham's attention to the most minor detail, the references in 'An Essay on Political Tactics' to vocal weakness could also have a particular personal relevance. Later Bentham was to link explicitly his work on parliamentary procedure with his 'prospects' of a seat in Parliament: 'The fragment has for its subject a situation I had once some prospects of which are now sunk by perfidy and oppression'.[3]

Bentham probably ceased work on 'Tactics' some time in June 1789; by early January 1791, however, the fragment which was printed as 'Essay on Political Tactics', the 'horn-book for infant members', was with the printer.[4] By late January 1791 it had been printed,[5] and by February 1791 it was being circulated.[6]

Lansdowne had attempted to publicize Bentham's work before it appeared in printed form, and once it had been printed, he continued to do so. In February 1791 Lansdowne received a list of questions on parliamentary matters from a Polish correspondent, Prince Adam Czartoryski (1731–1823), and suggested that Bentham might send a copy of 'Essay on Political Tactics' to the King of Poland[7] for his edification.[8] Bentham's response to this suggestion was somewhat sceptical. He said that the small part of his book which was printed did not touch upon the subjects of the questions, and continued:

As to the finishing my work on Tactics, and even drawing up a *Rituel* and applying it to the local circumstances of Poland, it is what I should have no

---

[1] See pp. 45, 62, 175 below.

[2] See Morellet to Bentham, 25 March 1789, *Correspondence* (*CW*), iv. 39. With reference to Bentham's Motion Table, Morellet suggested that a simple slate board on which the motion could be written in chalk would make a cheaper alternative.

[3] Bentham to Sir William Pulteney, 12 May 1802, *The Correspondence of Jeremy Bentham*, vol. vii, ed. J.R. Dinwiddy, Oxford, 1988 (*CW*), p. 22. Sir William Pulteney (1729–1805), Scottish advocate and MP.

[4] Bentham to Caroline Fox and Caroline and Elizabeth Vernon, 1790–91, *Correspondence* (*CW*), iv. 211; Bentham to Wilson, c.7 January 1791, ibid. 216.

[5] Bentham to Baron Grenville, late January 1791, ibid. 231.

[6] Benjamin Vaughan to Bentham, 2 February 1791, ibid. 236 & n.

[7] Stanislaus Poniatowski (1732–98), the last King of Poland, who reigned as Stanislaus Augustus 1764–95.

[8] Lansdowne to Bentham, 23 February 1791, *Correspondence* (*CW*), iv. 242.

objection to, if I saw any probability of its being made use of. But it is not the request of any individual howsoever distinguished, unless perhaps it were the King, that I should look upon as affording me any such probability.[1]

However, Bentham enclosed answers to Czartoryski's questions, some of which concerned the conflict between parliamentary and military duty, and others procedure in the House of Commons. In a note following his answers, he reverted to a theme which is of some importance in 'Essay on Political Tactics': the confusion generated in France by the lack of specific political nomenclature, and particularly the terms 'motion' and 'deliberation'. Bentham drew an analogy between political tactics and military tactics: 'la Tactique des Assemblees Politiques est au meme point de perfection a peu près en France, que le seroit la Tactique Militaire,[2] ou bien l'Anatomie, s'il n y avoit que deux mots pour expresser *front, flanc* et *derriere*'. Finally, he described his 'Essay on Political Tactics' as '[u]n petit Mappemonde de ce Chaos'.[3]

Although Bentham's efforts to disseminate 'Essay on Political Tactics' in France had largely failed, he did achieve more recognition from France for some of his other works. In October 1791 Jean Philippe Garran de Coulon[4] proposed that the National Assembly should make use of foreign, as well as French, experts in the drawing up of a code of laws. He cited Bentham's 'Draught of a New Plan for the Organisation of the Judicial Establishment in France',[5] praised it highly, and proposed that the Assembly give Bentham a vote of thanks. Further, Garran de Coulon proposed that Bentham should be invited to communicate his ideas on civil law to the Assembly, and suggested that a committee of the Assembly familiarize itself with the 'Draught'.[6] Garran de Coulon's proposals were reported in a French periodical, the *Journal logographique*. On reading this, Bentham wrote to him in October 1791. With a new opportunity to be of service to France, Bentham was once again concerned that he lacked the necessary documentation to proceed with his work. He suggested that, if the Assembly did 'commission' him, he should be furnished, 'from the bounty of the Assembly', with:

[1] Bentham to Lansdowne, 24 February 1791, ibid. 246.

[2] See p. 15 & n. below.

[3] *Correspondence (CW)*, iv. 254. On the lack of precise terms in France see pp. 86–92, 94, 95–7 below.

[4] Jean Philippe Garran de Coulon (1749–1816), lawyer, was a member of the Legislative Assembly in 1791.

[5] Bentham had written this text in early 1790, at Lansdowne House. It was printed in instalments, and extracts, translated into French by Dumont, had appeared in the *Courier de Provence* between March and May 1790. In April 1790, Bentham had sent 100 copies of the parts so far printed in England to Paris. See Bentham to the President of the National Assembly, 6 April 1790, *Correspondence (CW)*, iv. 124.

[6] See *Archives Parlementaires de 1787 à 1860, première série (1787 à 1799)*, Paris, 1879–1913, XXXIV. 251.

the Procès-Verbal of the late Assembly, the decrees of that Assembly in their systematic order, and the acts of the present Assembly as they came out: to which may be added the Logograph, as containing the fullest and exactest account of the debates—that is, of the reasons for and against every measure, without which, the bare acts would be but a very imperfect guide.[1]

Bentham also sent Garran de Coulon copies of some of his works, including 'Essay on Political Tactics'. An extract from 'Panopticon', translated into French,[2] a promise to send the English work, and an offer to establish a panopticon prison in France, followed in November 1791.[3] On 13 December 1791, Garran de Coulon showed Bentham's extract to the Assembly. The Assembly then voted to mention Bentham's offer in the *procès-verbal*, recommended that a committee should examine the extract, and ordered that it should be printed.[4]

Garran de Coulon then sent Bentham a copy of the *procès-verbal* in which he and his works were mentioned; nothing was said, however, about the documentary information sought by Bentham. He also reported that the *Comité de législation* had not had time to read those works of Bentham's which had been passed to them by the Assembly. However, he was still a keen student of Bentham's works, and promised to devote several days of spare time to their perusal, adding that Bentham's works 'ne sont pas faits pour être parcourus';[5] rather an understatement in the light of Bentham's 'faculty of exhausting what can be said on either side of any question'.[6] However, in spite of this admiration, there is no evidence in Bentham's correspondence until late in 1792 that any further progress was made in presenting Bentham's ideas to the National Assembly.

In October 1792, Bentham received a further token of appreciation from France: he was awarded honorary French citizenship.[7] Earlier that month a 'delegation' of French politicians visiting London, led by Jean Antoine Gauvain Gallois,[8] sought Bentham's acquaintance in most flattering terms. The party included a former president of the National Assembly,

---

[1] *Correspondence* (*CW*), iv. 336.

[2] 'Panopticon; or, the Inspection-House' was printed in Dublin and London in 1791. 'Panoptique' was edited and translated from Bentham's manuscripts by Dumont, and later reprinted in Dumont's recension of Bentham's writings, *Traités de législation civile et pénale*, 3 vols., Paris, 1802, iii. 209–72.

[3] See Bentham to Garran de Coulon, 25 November 1791, *Correspondence* (*CW*), iv. 340–1.

[4] See *Procès-Verbal de l'Assemblée Nationale; imprimé par son ordre*, 1791, Tome Second, p. 368 (13 December 1791).

[5] Garran de Coulon to Bentham, 22 December 1791, *Correspondence* (*CW*), iv. 352.

[6] Bentham to Lansdowne, 24 August 1790, ibid. 168.

[7] See Roland de la Platière to Bentham, 10 October 1792, ibid., 398. Jean Marie Roland de la Platière (1732–93) was French Minister of the Interior March–June 1792 and August 1792–January 1793.

[8] Jean Antoine Gauvain Gallois (1761–1828), politician and author. He was to become President of the Tribunat in 1802.

de Beaumez,[1] who had been a member of the *Comité de législation* and who 'a le plus grand désir de faire connaissance avec Monsieur Bentham dont il a été à portée de connaître particulièrement et d'estimer les travaux'.[2]

Between the early 1790s and 1808 there are very few references to 'Essay on Political Tactics' in Bentham's correspondence, although Bentham sent copies of the work at various times to several people, including Henry Dundas,[3] John Jay,[4] Charles Maurice de Talleyrand-Périgord,[5] and Sir William Pulteney.[6] As late as 1818, the work drew an admiring comment from William Plumer Junior, who wrote: 'Another work which I wish much to see completed is your Treatise on the "Tactics of Political Assemblies". To us in the United States, who have more than forty distinct legislative assemblies, . . . making in the whole probably not less than five thousand legislators, the mode of doing business in these Assemblies, is an object of the greatest importance.'[7]

### *'Tactique des assemblées politiques délibérantes', 1816*

In a letter to Romilly dated 1 August 1800, Dumont indicated that he had almost completed a French recension of 'Tactics' which was eventually published as 'Tactique des assemblées politiques délibérantes'.[8] However, nothing appears to have been done with this draft version until 1808. In August 1808, Dumont mentioned to Bentham the possibility of revising 'Tactique' (as they referred to the work while it was in progress) for use in Spain. Provincial committees were forming in Spain to organize resistance to French rule, and deputies from these committees had come to London in search of support. The principal supporter in London of Spanish

---

[1] Bon Albert Briois de Beaumez (1759–c.1801), was made President of the National Assembly in May 1790. He left France at the end of 1792 and became a sugar and spice merchant in India.

[2] Gallois to Bentham, 4 October 1792, *Correspondence (CW)*, iv. 397–8.

[3] See Bentham to Dundas, 20 May 1793, ibid. 430. Henry Dundas (1742–1811), later first Viscount Melville, was Home Secretary 1791–4.

[4] See Bentham to Jay, 8 April 1795, *The Correspondence of Jeremy Bentham*, vol. v, ed. A.T. Milne, London, 1981 (*CW*), p. 129. John Jay (1745–1829), American statesman and diplomat, was in England in 1794 negotiating the Jay Treaty with William Wyndham Grenville, Baron Grenville (1759–1834), Foreign Secretary 1791–1801.

[5] See Dumont to Bentham, 23 December 1801, *The Correspondence of Jeremy Bentham*, vol. vi, ed. J.R. Dinwiddy, Oxford, 1984 (*CW*), pp. 466–7, and Bentham to Dumont, 15 January 1802, ibid., vii. 5. Charles Maurice de Talleyrand-Périgord (1754–1838) was at this time French Foreign Minister.

[6] See Bentham to Sir William Pulteney, 12 May 1802, ibid. 22.

[7] Plumer to Bentham, 2 October 1818, *The Correspondence of Jeremy Bentham*, vol. ix, ed. S. Conway, Oxford, 1989 (*CW*), p. 278. William Plumer Junior (1789–1854), son of William Plumer (1759–1850), Governor of New Hampshire 1812–13, 1816–19.

[8] See Dumont MSS 17, fo. 144.

patriotism was Lord Holland,[1] from whom Dumont learned that the Spanish deputies were looking for a guide to parliamentary procedure. Lord Henry Petty suggested Romilly's *Règlemens*; Dumont mentioned 'Tactique'. Lord Henry was enthusiastic about 'Tactique': 'il a pris la chose avec intérêt—car votre ouvrage dit-il sera plus utile aux Espagnols, il leur faut des raisons'. Once again, a contrast was drawn between Bentham's work, which encompassed reasons, and Romilly's work, which did not.

Lord Henry Petty's opinion was that the French work should be printed immediately in London and dispatched to Spain as soon as possible. Dumont was inclined in favour of translation into Spanish; for the second time, the work was in the 'wrong' language. However, for Dumont the main thing was that the manuscript needed revision: 'but I must revise the MS. Eight years have passed since it was written.' This point was emphasized when Dumont wrote to Bentham again: 'Mais avant tout, il faut revoir ce manuscrit . . . je vous ecrirai . . . ce que j'en pense après le repos de neuf ans'.[2]

At the same period, Dumont met Aaron Burr, American politician and 'adventurer',[3] who had been familiar with Bentham's works for several years[4] and who became particularly involved with the attempt to supply a Spanish version of 'Tactique'. Burr expressed his admiration for Bentham's writings and asked Dumont whether he could arrange a meeting between himself and Bentham.[5] This was duly achieved and Burr spent a few days with Bentham at his summer residence at Godstone, and then moved into Bentham's London home at Queen's Square Place.[6] It was from Queen's Square Place that Burr wrote to Bentham (still at Godstone): 'My first work was to hunt for the "Tactics." The book was presently found; but my disappointment is very great that this volume contains only a part of the sixth essay.'[7] Burr asked a friend, David Mead Randolph,[8] to approach the Marqués de Casa Irujo, a Spanish diplomat then

---

[1] Henry Richard Vassall Fox (1773–1840), third Baron Holland. Having lost both his parents as a small child, he was brought up by his uncle Charles James Fox (1749–1806) and his maternal grandfather John, Earl of Upper Ossory. His mother, Lady Mary Fitzpatrick (d. 1778), was the sister of Lord Lansdowne's second wife; thus, Baron Holland and Lord Henry Petty were first cousins.

[2] Dumont to Bentham, *c*.20 August 1808; 26 August 1808, *Correspondence (CW)*, vii. 529, 532–3.

[3] Aaron Burr (1756–1836), soldier, lawyer, and statesman, Vice President of the United States 1801–5. Acquitted of treason in 1807, he travelled extensively in Europe, under the assumed name of H.E. Edwards, between 1808 and 1812.

[4] See *Political Correspondence and Public Papers of Aaron Burr*, ed. M.-J. Kline and J.W. Ryan, 2 vols., Princeton, 1983, ii. 767–8.

[5] See Dumont to Bentham, *Correspondence (CW)*, vii. 514–15.

[6] See Bentham to Dumont, 7 August 1808, ibid. 517; Burr to Bentham, 22 August 1808, ibid. 530–1.

[7] Burr to Bentham, 22 August 1808, ibid. 531.

[8] David Mead Randolph (1760–1830), a former United States Marshall for Virginia. He had befriended Burr during the latter's trial in 1807; later that year he had travelled to Europe in search of investors for his own inventions.

in London,[1] and to seek his support for the project.[2] Bentham said he would need Burr's help with the preparation of the text: 'I insisted on having the benefit of his annotations, with which he . . . agreed with equal readiness.'[3]

Bentham's prevailing inclination was to distance himself from 'Tactics', even to the extent of professing complete ignorance of the text: 'if it was really I that wrote what it seems is in my hand, I really and truly have no more recollection about it than the Pope of Rome who had not, I imagine any great hand in it'. He also expressed uncertainty about the relation between his own manuscripts and Dumont's evolving work, referring to the 'translation—abridgment—whatever it is to be called'. Bentham divided editorial responsibility for 'Tactique' between Dumont, Burr, and Irujo; he was not, however, averse to organizing their work, writing to Dumont:

Knowing nothing about the matter, I have no pretension to sit in judgment on it, along with the three great men whom it may be its destiny to have for censors. I have neither governed a legislative Assembly like Burr, nor attended the deliberations of one like Dumont; nor do I ⟨ . . .⟩ and write Spanish like Uruyo. . . . my conception of the most eligible course is this: 1. You to make your annotations, and then the Mss here to Burr, who will have the original if necessary and worth while, to confront them with. Burr to add his annotations, and then to put the Ms. in the hands of Uruyo, for him to cut and slash, and so far as concerns translation into Spanish to do with it as he pleases.

Furthermore, Bentham did offer some advice of an editorial kind:

Now, as to *stile* any time you were, on the present occasion, to bestow on the subject would be thrown away, since your French coat if it were covered all over with embroidery, would be to be stript off, and a Spanish one put on in the room of it. As to any parts which, it seemed to you, might be omitted to advantage, a note of yours, saying as much, and putting in brackets the part proposed to be omitted would be of great use: and so in regard to additions and alterations.[4]

In the event all attempts to enlist the help of Irujo in producing a Spanish version of 'Tactique' were to come to nothing. The obstacle was that the Spanish Cortes was reluctant to accept a foreign work as a guide to parliamentary procedure, a situation predicted by Dumont[5] and confirmed by Irujo himself via Burr.[6] A trace of the attempt to interest the Spanish Cortes in 'Tactique' may be seen in an issue of the journal *El Español* published on 30 September 1810.[7] Extracts from a Spanish

---

[1] Carlos Fernando Martínez de Irujo, Marqués de Casa Irujo (1763–1824), who had been the Spanish Minister to the United States 1796–1806.

[2] See *Political Correspondence and Public Papers of Aaron Burr*, ii. 1051.

[3] Bentham to Dumont, 26–8 August 1808, *Correspondence (CW)*, vii. 533.

[4] Ibid. 534.  [5] See Dumont to Bentham, *c.*29 August 1808, ibid. 537.

[6] Burr to Bentham, 1 September 1808, ibid. 539.

[7] *El Español*, 30 September 1810, vii. 411–37. The editor, Joseph Blanco White (1775–1841), came to England in 1809. He was an influential journalist and propagandist, and a protégé of Lord Holland.

version of Romilly's *Règlemens* appeared in this issue, followed by a 'Noticia de un obra inedita, intitulada "Tactique des Assemblées Politiques"'. The editor stated that he himself had been preparing to translate the *Règlemens* into Spanish when his friend Dumont told him about the other work still languishing in manuscript; and he added that in publishing the extracts his intention was to inform the Spanish about two works that would be useful for the Cortes.

Although nothing had come of the attempt to involve Irujo, Burr was still interested in proceeding with the work. He reported to Bentham that Dumont 'thinks his work so imperfect that some *months* will be necessary to complete it for translation'—an idea which drew from Burr the robust response, 'All nonsense'.[1] Bentham seemed to agree with Burr's assessment: 'Dumont's story, about the so many *months* for revisal, is a put-off'. He related that Dumont, when working previously on some chapters of Bentham's on religion for *Traités de législation*, had been reluctant for Bentham to look at the result: 'Put-offs various; and at last, upon my pressing and insisting, a peremptory refusal. I found out that is I divined what the cause was: I taxed him with it, and he confessed it. He had begotten upon his own brain a God of his own, and fathered the bastard upon me.'[2] This illustrates both that Dumont habitually diverged from Bentham's manuscript when preparing his recensions, and that Bentham accepted that this was the case and did not object. In the present instance, Bentham was tolerant of Dumont's protective attitude towards his work and acknowledged, albeit sparingly, Dumont's efforts: 'if he should not let you see his Translation of the Tactics . . . dont you trouble yourself to cut his throat, for he has drudged hard at it, and deserves whatever he has made of it for his pains'.[3]

The attitudes of Dumont and Burr towards 'Tactique' were very different. Dumont was cautious, anxious not to jeopardize the good reputation earned by *Traités de législation* by precipitate publication of 'Tactique'. He wrote to Bentham: 'il ne s'agit point de correction de stile, il s'agit du fonds des choses, de certaines questions à examiner de nouveau, de lacunes importantes à combler'. Dumont also listed some of the topics which had not been covered by Bentham in the manuscripts.[4] Thus it is clear that Dumont thought that there was still a lot of work to do on 'Tactique'. Burr, on the other hand, remained opposed to a long period of further work on the text and thought that the manuscript might be improved within a short time (he mentioned 'eight days' for supplying

---

[1] Burr to Bentham, 3 September 1808, *Correspondence* (*CW*), vii. 542.
[2] Bentham to Burr, 3 September 1808, ibid.
[3] Ibid. 542–3.
[4] Dumont to Bentham, 5 September 1808, ibid. 544. Of these topics, only one—exceptions to the rule of publicity—was actually to appear in 'Tactique des assemblées politiques délibérantes' and thence in 'An Essay on Political Tactics' in the Bowring edition. See §4, p. 39 below.

omissions). However, his eagerness to proceed in haste met with resistance from Dumont, who 'lectured' Burr 'on the folly of precipitation'.[1]

Dumont and Burr also had widely differing perceptions of their mutual relationship. Dumont thought that he had enlisted Burr in favour of delay—a significant ally in view of Burr's previous impatience: 'Mr Burr, que j'ai trouvé ardent pour la prompte execution, après deux heures d'examen avec moi, me paroit sentir la convenance d'un délai.'[2] Burr meanwhile clearly saw himself as Bentham's champion, in opposition to Dumont the cautious editor, who furthermore might try to infiltrate some of his own material into the manuscript: 'I engage to defend you, penna et pugnis,[3] against Dumont's gods'.[4] Burr's attitude towards Dumont seems rather harsh as there clearly were gaps in the manuscripts of 'Tactics', or 'Tactique', which Dumont had to fill; what is more, on the previous occasion when Dumont had 'begotten a God of his own', Bentham had taken it in good part.

The whereabouts of some of Bentham's 'Tactics' manuscripts was a subject of dispute in 1808, a dispute which was to continue even after Dumont's death.[5] Bentham wrote to Dumont: 'H. K.[6] and I have been rummaging over my Tactic Ms. for the use of B.[7] But he finds it in several places incompleat: viz. not merely whole titles untreated of, but sheets omitted (as appears by the paging) in those that are treated of. I have here but one bundle: were there not two? I have some notion there was: pray tell me by your next.'[8] The obvious conclusion is that part of this material had gone astray several years previously, when Dumont did his first stint of work on 'Tactique'. Dumont, however, firmly rejected the notion that he was responsible for losing any manuscripts, and pointed out that the text had always been incomplete: 'je ne puis rien dire de positif sur l'etat des Mss., je n'ai aucun souvenir des vôtres—je suis seulement très sur que tout vous est retourné dans l'etat où je l'avois reçu—les lacunes dans les paginations ne doivent pas vous surprendre, elles m'ont tourmente ⟨ . . .⟩nt fois là et ailleurs, me faisant chercher ce qui avoit existé et ⟨ . . .⟩ n'existoit plus.'[9]

In early 1809, Dumont's manuscript of 'Tactique' was also the object of some contention between Dumont and Bentham. In February 1809,

---

[1] Burr to Bentham, 7 September 1808, *Correspondence* (*CW*), vii. 546.
[2] Dumont to Bentham, 5 September 1808, ibid. 544.
[3] i.e. 'with pen and with fists'.
[4] Burr to Bentham, 7 September 1808, *Correspondence* (*CW*), vii. 546–7.
[5] See p. xxxviii below.
[6] i.e. John Herbert Koe (1783–1860), Bentham's secretary and protégé for some twenty years from about 1800.
[7] i.e. Burr.
[8] Bentham to Dumont, 26–8 August 1808, *Correspondence* (*CW*), vii. 535.
[9] Dumont to Bentham, 30 August 1808, ibid. 538.

Dumont asked Bentham to return the manuscript to him.[1] Bentham seems to have complied with Dumont's request, but a month later he wrote to Burr:

Dumont has been applied to, and has brought himself, though not without some reluctance, to part with *Tactique* out of his hands. The burthen which the shoulders of Etienne Dumont sunk under, and those of Jeremy Bentham shrunk from, is now waiting for those of Hercules Burr ... Meantime the midnight lamp is burning here in view, with the *Tactique* papers spread out before it. Say—tell us—what shall be done with them? Will the eye of Hercules vouchsafe to visit them? or shall they be consigned to the hands of the housemaid, to light fires?[2]

Burr replied to the first of these questions in the affirmative, but in a somewhat lukewarm manner: 'I will start myself off for eight days, and devote them to *Tactique*, but without the hope of adding one useful idea.'[3] In the event, neither severally nor collectively did Burr and Dumont manage to complete a version of 'Tactique' between autumn 1808 and spring 1809.

In May 1814, Dumont left London for Geneva which had been liberated in 1813 from French rule. He was elected to the Representative Council and appointed to a commission for drawing up a new procedural code for this council.[4] He was chosen for this committee and 'chargé du premier travail' as it was well known that he had long been interested in the subject of procedure. Dumont was delighted to have the chance to create a system of rules of procedure for a new assembly, and in this task he drew heavily on the rules of procedure observed in the British Houses of Parliament; of course these rules were to a great extent the model for the system of rules described in Bentham's 'Essay on Political Tactics' and thence in 'Tactique des assemblées politiques délibérantes'. Presumably the experience of drawing up a code of procedure for Geneva brought the subject once more to the forefront of Dumont's attention and gave him the necessary incentive to complete 'Tactique des assemblées politiques délibérantes'. Dumont thought that the text analysing the theory of parliamentary procedure ('Tactique') and the account of actual practice at Geneva (his own 'Règlement') could profitably be presented in conjunction: 'Après avoir lu cette théorie, on verra peut-être avec intérêt comment et avec quel succès elle a été mise en oeuvre dans le conseil représentatif de la république de Genève.'[5]

[1] See Dumont to Bentham, 6 February 1809, ibid., viii. 15.
[2] Bentham to Burr, 6 March 1809, ibid. 18.
[3] Burr to Bentham, 8 March 1809, ibid. 19.
[4] See François Ruchon, *Histoire politique de la République de Genève 1813–1907*, 2 vols., Geneva, 1953, i. 127 n.
[5] *Tactique des assemblées législatives*, i. 270. This introduction is entitled 'Exposé préliminaire' in the 1822 edition.

In June 1815, Bentham sent a copy of his original 1791 fragment 'Essay on Political Tactics' to the French Minister of the Interior, Lazare Carnot,[1] with a request that Carnot should pass the book on to the President of the Chamber of Deputies.[2] The gift of 'Essay on Political Tactics' was accompanied by an advance notice of the publication of Dumont's 'Tactique des assemblées politiques délibérantes'. Bentham wrote: 'Un ouvrage en François, extrait des Mss. dont cet Essai fait partie, doit paroître dans peu à Genève'. At this stage Bentham reported that Dumont had put the finishing touches to the work: 'Il y avoit "déjà mis" (disoit il) "la dernière main"' and spoke of Dumont's continuing efforts to publish 'Tactique des assemblées politiques délibérantes': 'S'il avoit raison d'en espérer quelque utilité pour la France, il n'est pas à douter, que M. Dumont ... trouveroit, dans cette espérance, un motif suffisant pour faire son possible pour hâter la publication de cet ouvrage.'[3] Bentham was optimistic about the usefulness of 'Tactique des assemblées politiques délibérantes'; a little under two months after the date when Bentham wrote the draft letter to Carnot, James Mill wrote to Dumont to inform him that Bentham 'had been frequently talking with some warmth about your proposed publication of Tactics, as promising to be of singular utility at the present moment, when so many of your continental governments are proposing to make trial of legislative assemblies'.[4]

*Tactique des assemblées législatives, suivie d'un traité des sophismes politiques* was published in Geneva and Paris in early 1816. In March 1816 Dumont reported from Geneva: 'Mad. de Staël has been reading in society the Book of Fallacies, and with great success'.[5] In August 1816 Bentham received a note about the work from Brougham,[6] who wrote: 'The Tactics are for foreign consumption rather than the home market.'[7] Perhaps as a consequence of its publication outside England, Bentham did not actually see *Tactique des assemblées législatives* until the following year:

About a fortnight ago, for the first time I got a peep at it ... If my time would, my eyes you know would not, admit of regular reading: but on dipping in here and

---

[1] Lazare Nicolas Marguerite Carnot (1753–1823), military engineer and statesman, was Minister of the Interior during the Hundred Days.

[2] Jean Denis, Comte Lanjuinais (1753–1827).

[3] Bentham to Carnot, 8 June 1815, *Correspondence* (*CW*), viii. 457.

[4] Mill to Dumont, 1 August 1815, Dumont MSS 33, fo. 38. James Mill (1773–1836), philosopher, economist, and historian, was one of Bentham's most influential followers.

[5] Dumont to Bentham, 23 March 1816, *Correspondence* (*CW*), viii. 518. Necker's daughter Anne Louise Germaine (1766–1817) had married Baron de Staël-Holstein, Swedish Ambassador to France, in 1786. She was a literary and political writer. In 1816 the title 'Book of Fallacies' was used to describe, in English, the 'Traité des sophismes politiques'. *The Book of Fallacies*, London, 1824, was a separate work, prepared directly from Bentham's MSS and edited by Peregrine Bingham (1788–1864).

[6] Henry Peter Brougham (1778–1868), created first Baron Brougham and Vaux in 1830, Lord Chancellor 1830–4.

[7] Quoted in Bentham to Koe, 1 August 1816, *Correspondence* (*CW*), viii. 539–40.

there, it seemed to me every where to read very prettily. I did not expect to find in it so much as I actually found: for as to the details, they were as compleatly out of my head as if they had never been in it.[1]

Bentham claimed to have revised neither 'Tactique des assemblées politiques délibérantes' nor Dumont's other recensions of his work: 'Cependant son extrait, tiré d'un tas de papiers, jamais complette, n'a pas été revû par l'*auteur*, non plus que les autres ouvrages qui portent les deux noms'.[2] In the autumn of 1817, Bentham still did not possess a copy of *Tactique*,[3] and indeed in 1818, he was to say that he had never read it.[4]

Nonetheless, after having 'a peep at it', Bentham asked Dumont: 'The *interrogative* method that method the utility of which is now so universally confessed and so extensively put to use ... why did you give it up in the Tactics? For no other purpose than to meet the lash and thereby gain the suffrages of a few superficial lawyers.'[5] In the 'Discours préliminaire' to 'Tactique des assemblées politiques délibérantes', Dumont explained his reasons for dispensing with the 'interrogative method'. He acknowledged the advantages of this method ('méthode excellente pour établir précisément quelle est la difficulté à résoudre, et pour mettre le lecteur en état de juger si la solution est satisfaisante') but was also aware of its limitations: 'cette forme de catéchisme, outre ses longueurs, a l'inconvénient de couper tous les sujets en petites parties, et d'éteindre l'intérêt par le défaut de liaison'. Therefore, Dumont decided 'd'abandonner ces questions et ces réponses, et d'y substituer la marche unie du discours'.[6] In support of the explanation in the preface to 'Tactique des assemblées politiques délibérantes', Dumont defended his decision: 'Quant à la Tactique, je n'ai aucun regret à n'avoir pas suivi la forme de Catéchisme, et considérez-moi à cet égard comme un pécheur en impénitence finale'.[7]

In November 1817 Dumont told Romilly that *Tactique des assemblées législatives* was very highly regarded, yet in the same letter he noted that the work remained virtually unknown among the wider public.[8] However, later that month Bentham reported to Dumont some more encouraging news: 'A friend of Mr. Mills brought him advice from Paris last year I think it was that just before the opening of the legislative assembly two

---

[1] Bentham to Dumont, 22 July 1817, *Correspondence (CW)*, ix. 22.
[2] Bentham to Carnot, 8 June 1815, ibid., viii. 457. Dumont's other recensions to date were *Traités de législation civile et pénale* and *Théorie des peines et des récompenses*, 2 vols., London, 1811.
[3] Bentham to Dumont, 3 November–14 December 1817, *Correspondence (CW)*, ix. 99.
[4] See Bentham to William Plumer Junior, December 1818, ibid. 307.
[5] Bentham to Dumont, 22 July 1817, ibid. 20.
[6] See p. 10 below.
[7] Dumont to Bentham, 12 August 1817, *Correspondence (CW)*, ix. 40.
[8] Dumont to Romilly, 9 November 1817, Dumont MSS 17, fos. 279–80.

hundred copies of Tactique having been sent to Paris they were all sold the first or second day of their appearance. I wonder whether any more have ever since been sent thither.'[1] By April 1818, supplies of *Tactique des assemblées législatives* were almost exhausted.[2]

In the years following publication, 'Tactique des assemblées politiques délibérantes' became widely known. Translations into German, Italian, Portuguese and Spanish appeared between 1817 and 1829.[3] The Argentine statesman Bernardino Rivadavia,[4] a particular admirer of Bentham, published another Spanish translation in 1824.[5] Bentham's influence in Spain was also demonstrated by two works based on Bentham's thought published in 1820 and 1821 by a Spanish disciple, Toribio Núñez.[6] He sent Bentham a copy of the first of these works which Bentham acknowledged in May 1821. The particular influence of 'Tactique des assemblées politiques délibérantes' on Núñez is evident from his remark to Bentham: 'I am wanting from you an opinion . . . on the volume of yours that I sent to you in a Spanish translation;[7] some have already baptized it here the *Manuel de Diputados a Cortes*—in deference to your *tactica de los congresos políticos*.'[8]

'Tactique des assemblées politiques délibérantes' was also well regarded in Portugal. Bentham had sent a number of his works to the Portuguese Cortes, and in April 1821 João Baptista Felgueiras, Secretary to the Cortes, sent a formal acknowledgement of receipt.[9] The Cortes had resolved to mention the gift in their Journals, and to translate and publish in Portugal the works in question. In July 1821 Bentham was shown some

---

[1] Bentham to Dumont, 3 November–14 December 1817, *Correspondence (CW)*, ix. 99.

[2] Dumont to Bentham, 13 April 1818, ibid. 192.

[3] *Tactik oder Theorie des Geschäftsganges in deliberirenden Volksständeversammlungen von Jeremias Bentham*, Erlangen, 1817; *Tattica delle Assemblee Legislative seguita da un Trattato di Sofismi Politici*, Naples, 1820; *Tactica das assembleas legislativas*, Lisbon, 1821; *Tactica de los congresos legislativos, seguida de un tratado de los sofismas politicas*, Guadalajara, 1823, *Táctica de las asambleas legislativas; por Jeremias Bentham. Nueva edicion revista y corregida*, Burdeos [Bordeaux], 1829.

[4] Bernardino de la Trinidad González Rivadavia (1780–1845) was in Europe between 1814 and 1818 attempting to negotiate Spanish recognition of Argentine independence. He was later to become chief minister of Buenos Aires 1821–5, and first President of the United Provinces of the Río de la Plata 1826–7.

[5] *Tactica de las asambleas legislativas*, Paris, 1824. See Rivadavia to Bentham, 25 August 1818, *Correspondence (CW)*, ix. 255.

[6] Toribio Núñez (1786–1834), Librarian of the University of Salamanca. The works were *Espiritu de Bentham ó sistéma de la ciencia social, ideado por Jeremías Bentham*, Salamanca, 1820, and *Principios de la ciencia social ó de las ciencias Morales y Políticas Por el Jurisconsulto Inglés Jeremías Bentham, ordenados conforme al sistema del autor original y aplicados á la Constitucion española*, Salamanca, 1821.          [7] i.e. *Espiritu de Bentham*.

[8] Núñez to Bentham, 20 December 1821, *The Correspondence of Jeremy Bentham*, vol. x, ed. S. Conway, Oxford, 1994 (*CW*), p. 474. A translation of 'Tactique' was published by the Spanish Cortes as recently as 1991.

[9] Felgueiras to Bentham, 24 April 1821, ibid. 322. João Baptista Felgueiras (1790–1848), lawyer and politician, elected to the Cortes in 1820.

extracts of a letter from José da Silva Carvalho,[1] a member of the Portuguese Regency government, to Dr Rocha,[2] a compatriot in London; one extract read as follows: 'I am very glad of what you told me about the illustrious Mr. Bentham. . . . I have only read his works as they were translated into French: but what I most admire, is the Tactics of Public Assemblies, where he shows his sound judgment, and the practical knowledge he possesses of mankind.'[3]

As early as April 1818, Dumont had considered a second edition of *Tactique des assemblées législatives*, to be distributed further afield: 'je reserverai pour la fin de l'année une autre edition de la Tactique . . . chose curieuse—un libraire de Naples vient de demander 24 exemplaires de la Tactique et ce livre n'est pas connu en Espagne, Bossange m'a dit qu'il y feroit passer une bonne partie de la seconde éd⟨ition⟩.'[4] However, by 1820–1, *Tactique des assemblées législatives* was well known in Naples and in Spain, and the bookseller in Naples was considering a second edition.[5] In August 1821, there was also demand in Paris for a second edition, and Dumont began work on it in the autumn.[6] He spent a month on revision, and the second edition was ready for the printers by November 1821;[7] it was due to appear in the spring of 1822, and by August of that year was almost sold out.[8]

In April 1824 Bentham received further confirmation of the success of *Tactique des assemblées législatives*. The work had finally been put to the practical use for which Bentham had originally envisaged it. From Buenos Aires, Rivadavia sent a copy of the rules of procedure of the chamber of deputies recently established there.[9] In an accompanying letter, Rivadavia wrote: 'le règlement de notre Chambre des Deputés . . . que j'ai eu l'honneur de lui proposer et qu'elle a sanctionné . . . est entièrement basé sur les incontestables et frappantes verités contenues dans votre ouvrage sur la Tactique des Assemblées Legislatives'. Rivadavia went on to seek Bentham's advice for the improvement of that 'règlement': 'vous me ferez le plus sensible plaisir si vous daigniez . . . me donner votre avis sur ce même reglement de la Chambre, et m'indiquer les changemens, additions, ou modifications qu'il vous paroîtroit

---

[1] José da Silva Carvalho (1782–1856).

[2] Dr João Baptista da Rocha (1778–1853), editor of *O Portuguez*, a monthly periodical published in London between 1814 and 1835.

[3] See Bentham to Bowring, 14 July 1821, *Correspondence (CW)*, x. 357.

[4] Dumont to Bentham, 13 April 1818, ibid., ix. 192.

[5] Dumont to Bentham, 27 September 1820, ibid., x. 106; Dumont to Bentham, 22 February 1821, ibid. 297.

[6] Dumont to Bentham, 10 August 1821, ibid. 379.

[7] Dumont to Bentham, 17 November 1821, ibid. 430.

[8] Dumont to Bentham, 15 January 1822, UC x. 127; Dumont to Bentham, 21 August 1822, UC x. 128.

[9] *Reglamento que establece el orden de las operaciones, y la policía de la Sala de Representantes de la Provincia de Buenos Aires. Sancionado por la Honorable Junta en 26 de julio de 1822.*

necessaire d'y faire.'[1] Bentham then sent the Buenos Aires procedural code on to the Greek provisional government in September 1824. Characteristically, Bentham said that he had not even read the Buenos Aires code, explaining with acute self-knowledge that were he to read it and find in it anything with which he could not agree, he would have to add 'a reservation', and such a reservation would necessitate the adducing of 'reasons, which would have drawn me into discussions of inconvenient length'.[2]

## 'An Essay on Political Tactics', 1843

In the preface to the version of the work which appears in the Bowring edition, edited by Richard Smith, 'An Essay on Political Tactics' is said to have been 'edited from the work of M. Dumont, and the papers of Bentham'.[3] However, as noted above, it is not known which, if any, 'papers of Bentham' were drawn upon. The mystery of these 'papers' is intensified by a remark in a letter which Bentham wrote to J.-L. Duval, Dumont's nephew, on 20 October 1829, on receipt of the news of Dumont's death. Bentham added a postscript: 'Manuscripts of the original on the subject of *Tactique des Assemblées politiques*. I know not by what fatality it has happened that, since their being placed in your Uncle's hands, I have never been able to find them in any part of my house. Should they be found in the possession of your family, I should be much obliged by the return of them.'[4] At least a part of this material had been in Bentham's possession in 1808 ('I have here but one bundle');[5] by 1829, it seems that all the manuscripts were missing. It is impossible to ascertain now which 'papers of Bentham' were used by Smith in the preparation of the text, which is essentially a translation of 'Tactique des assemblées politiques délibérantes'. The general difficulties of translating into English a French recension of his work, and the importance of the original manuscripts, had already been noted by Bentham in 1818, when he wrote: 'You see under what disadvantage a retranslation of the french works would be performed without the benefit of a recourse to the original Manuscripts: especially in such parts in which every thing depends upon the words'.[6] Smith's text, however, was not entirely translated from Dumont; Chapter VI is a complete reproduction of 'Essay VI' from the 1791 fragment,

---

[1] See Rivadavia to Bentham, 26 August 1822, *'Legislator of the World': Writings on Codification, Law, and Education*, ed. P. Schofield & J. Harris, Oxford, 1998 (*CW*), pp. 346–9.

[2] See Bentham to the Greek Provisional Government, 21 September 1824, draft at UC xii. 309–11.

[3] Bowring, ii. 301.

[4] Bentham to J.-L. Duval, 20 October 1829, Bibliothèque Publique et Universitaire, Geneva, MS. fr. 3787, fo. 6.　　　　　　　　　　　　　　　　　　　　　　　　　　[5] See p. xxx above.

[6] Bentham to William Plumer Junior, December 1818, *Correspondence* (*CW*), ix. 308.

'Essay on Political Tactics', and Chapter V intersperses Bentham's 1791 'Essay V' with sections from Dumont. Although the remainder of Smith's text is a fairly close translation of Dumont's 'Tactique des assemblées politiques délibérantes', the order of the chapters is quite different.[1] Furthermore, Smith occasionally summarized Dumont's text, or omitted sentences and footnotes wholly or in part, particularly footnotes composed by Dumont himself. On occasion he also added material of his own, some of it in the form of footnotes which he normally identified by appending the abbreviation '*Ed.*'

## PRESENTATION OF THE TEXT

It might be argued that Dumont's 'Tactique des assemblées politiques délibérantes', having been prepared directly from Bentham's manuscripts, is closer than Smith's 'An Essay on Political Tactics' to Bentham's original conception. The present edition, however, is based on the Smith text, on the grounds that this text incorporates the only printed material which can be identified with certainty as Bentham's unadulterated work. Bentham's original Preface to 'Essay on Political Tactics', which Smith included in a footnote at the beginning of Chapter VI, here precedes the text of 'Political Tactics', and serves as a Preface to the whole work.[2] It must be remembered, however, that originally it was the Preface to part of Essay V and Essay VI only. Dumont's 'Discours préliminaire' to the text of 'Tactique des assemblées politiques délibérantes' also precedes the text in the present edition, as it contains important information about the genesis of Bentham's original work and about the changes which Dumont made to that work in the preparation of the recension.[3]

The only surviving part of the manuscript of 'Political Tactics', on the Motion Tables, is reproduced in the Appendix. In August 1810 Morellet sent these sheets to Dumont with an accompanying letter, in which he described the Motion Tables as double doors 'sur lesquels on écriroit à la craye en grosses lettres la motion qui seroit ainsi présenté aux yeux de toute l'assemblée'.[4] This material is written on single sheets of foolscap ruled with a wide margin and with a double line at the top for the heading

---

[1] For the relation between the chapters of Bentham's original projected work, Dumont's 'Tactique des assemblées politiques délibérantes', and Smith's 'An Essay on Political Tactics', see the comparative chart, pp. 217–26 below.

[2] The Preface reproduces the original 1791 version. The Bowring edition (ii. 330–1) excludes the first paragraph and the last two, and incorporates a number of minor changes in punctuation which are not indicated here.

[3] The 'Discours' is from the first (1816) edition; variations in the 1822 edition are footnoted.

[4] Dumont MSS 72 fo. 1. Clearly Morellet still thought in 1810, as he had in 1789 (see p. xxv n. above) that chalk on a blackboard was a superior option.

and subheadings. In the margin are brief summaries of the contents; these marginal headings are reproduced in the text of the present edition. The manuscripts comprise six sections, numbered in the margin from 3 to 8. The first four sections correspond to Essay III, Chapters III–VI in Bentham's 1791 table of the contents of his projected 'Essays on Political Tactics' (Table I, p. 176 below). The final two sections are additional chapters which do not correspond to any references in the table of contents. Sections 3 and 8 are in Bentham's hand; the remainder are in the hand of a copyist.

Bentham's own footnotes and sub-footnotes to the text are indicated by superscript letters and editorial footnotes by superscript numerals, with a separate sequence for each page of the text. In addition to the editorial footnotes there is a separate sequence of endnotes, marked by the symbol [+], and compiled in a table at the end of the text. The endnotes draw attention to significant discrepancies between the 1816 edition of 'Tactique des assemblées politiques délibérantes' and the present text, although they are not intended to provide a full collation. The 1816 edition of 'Tactique' is used as the standard of comparison, as it seems likely that Smith used that edition; the few changes made in the 1822 edition do not seem to have been incorporated into Smith's text. The endnotes include omitted passages, material added by Smith, differences in the use of italics (other than instances where italics are used to distinguish headings), and mistaken or dubious translations. Dumont's additions to the 1822 edition are also reproduced. Not included, however, are minor differences between the 1816 and the 1822 editions, such as differences in the titles of chapters and differences in capitalization. Misspellings in the Dumont text have been corrected.

Otherwise, the present edition departs from the Bowring edition in the following respects. Bentham's 1791 outline of the entire work, which Smith did not reproduce, is included as Table I; and his 1791 Synoptical Table of Inconveniences, which Smith incorporated into the text of his edition, is included as Table II. Misspellings and minor printing errors (including those involving punctuation) have been corrected, although spelling has not been modernized; in the Appendix, punctuation marks have been supplied or adjusted where necessary; page numbers in cross-references have been amended to accord with the pagination of the present edition; and finally, in order to prevent confusion with editorial insertions, square brackets in Bentham's 1791 'Essay' and in the Bowring edition have been replaced by braces. The collation lists all the variants between this edition and the 1791 fragment 'Essay on Political Tactics', including the part of Essay V not printed in every copy.

# PREFACE[1]

THE present Essay[2] is, as the number subjoined to it imports, but a fragment of a much more extensive work, the design of which embraced the whole theory of the discipline and mode of procedure most proper to be observed in all sorts of political assemblies.

What gave rise to it was the notification that had been given of the then approaching meeting of the French States-General, since termed the National Assembly.

As to the particular matter of the present Essay, preceded, as it required to be, by several other matters, as well in respect to the chronological order of the subjects treated of, as in respect to the order that seemed most favourable to investigation, it presented itself as second to none in the order of importance.

What was more, the very rules that suggested themselves as necessary to every assembly, turned out to be the very rules actually observed in both assemblies of the British Legislature. What theory would have pitched upon as a model of perfection, practice presented as having been successfully pursued: never was the accord more perfect between reason and experience.

The conjuncture which gave rise to the publication seemed to be such as would give it its best chance of being of use. A political assembly, selected from the whole body of a great nation, were about to meet for the first time. Every thing that concerned them was as yet new to them: every thing was as yet to create. They were in the situation of a manufacturer, who, besides the work that was the object of his manufacture, should find himself under the necessity of making the very tools he was to work with. The presenting these new manufacturers with a new set of tools, with a description of their uses, tools whose temper had been so well tried, was the object of the present design.

The subject, however, taken in its full extent, and handled in the manner in which it was endeavoured to be handled, was far too extensive for the time. All that could be done at the moment, was to select for immediate publication what seemed to stand first in the order of importance. By forced exertions, the part now published was accordingly printed off; and, of a few copies that were sent to Paris, the last sheet reached that metropolis a day or two after the first formal meeting of the Assembly, and before any

---

[1] For details of this Preface, first printed in 1791, see the Editorial Introduction, p. xxxix.

[2] The 'present Essay', i.e. Chapter VI, pp. 72–109 below, was the sixth Essay in the projected work. See Table I, p. 176 below.

1

business was begun upon. Of these copies one having found its way into the hands of the Comte de Mirabeau, the sheets, as fast as they came over, had been honoured, as I afterwards learnt, with a translation, either by the pen of that distinguished member, or under his care.[1]

Congenial affections had happened about the same time to give birth, without my knowledge, to a little tract that promised to afford not only furtherance to the design, but assistance towards the execution of this larger enterprize. To deliver the theory of a copious and unattempted branch of political science, was necessarily a work not only of time, but of bulk, and would require more paper than could, at the ordinary rate of business, make its way, in the course of several months, through the press. Practice itself, stated simply and without reasoning, might be comprised within limits much less extensive. Moved by these considerations, a gentleman eminently qualified for the task, had undertaken, much about the same time, this philanthropic office. His valuable paper was sent over in manuscript: a translation of it was not only made, but soon after published, by the procurement of the celebrated Frenchman above spoken of, whose name stands in the title-page.[2]

To judge from the temper and modes of thinking that had so long appeared prevalent in the French nation, the larger of these works, if tolerably performed, and the other, almost at any rate, seemed to possess a fair chance of engaging some attention, and of being turned to some account in practice. The prepossession so generally entertained in favour

---

[1] Honoré Gabriel Riqueti, Comte de Mirabeau (1749–91), was member for Aix-en-Provence and one of the leaders of the Third Estate in the Estates-General and subsequently in the National Assembly. Mirabeau published many details of the proceedings of the assembly in a journal called, consecutively, *Etats-Généraux, Lettre du Comte de Mirabeau à ses commettans*, and *Courier de Provence*. The only part of Mirabeau's 'translation' of 'Essay on Political Tactics' to appear in print was the following passage in *Dixième lettre du Comte de Mirabeau à ses commettans*, 7–12 June 1789, p. 8:

En Angleterre, il y a dans le mode de délibérer, six principes qu'on regarde comme essentiels, et qu'il nous importe de connoître; ce sont:
1. L'identité des termes de la motion avec ceux de l'acte qu'on veut faire adopter.
2. Fixer les termes de la motion, en les donnant par écrit.
3. L'unité du sujet conservée inviolable dans le débat, et sur-tout lorsqu'on en vient à voter.
4. Distinction marquée entre l'opération du débat et celle d'opiner et de voter.
5. Point d'ordre fixe de préséance pour porter la parole dans un débat.
6. Les voix recueillies, non l'une après l'autre, mais toutes à la fois.

The six principles were not acknowledged as Bentham's. The journal in which they appeared was in Bentham's possession by 8 July 1789. See Bentham to George Wilson, *The Correspondence of Jeremy Bentham*, vol. iv, ed. A.T. Milne, London, 1981 (*CW*), p. 80, and the Editorial Introduction, p. xxiii above.

[2] Mirabeau provided the introduction to *Règlemens observés dans la Chambre des Communes pour débattre les matières et pour voter*, Paris, 1789, by Sir Samuel Romilly (1757–1818), lawyer and law reformer. The work had been translated into French by Pierre Etienne Louis Dumont (1759–1829), who became Bentham's translator and editor. Dumont's recension of Bentham's writings, *Tactique des assemblées législatives, suivie d'un traité des sophismes politiques*, 2 vols., Geneva and Paris, 1816, included Romilly's *Règlemens* (i. 301–61). See the Editorial Introduction, pp. xiv, xxi above.

of English law, had been no where more strenuous, more general, or more liberally avowed, than among our nearest neighbours. If such was the case with regard to points in relation to which both countries had possessed the advantage of practice, it seemed still more natural that it should be so with regard to points like these, in relation to which the whole stock of experience had fallen exclusively to the share of that country, to whose example the other had been used to look with so favourable an eye. To judge beforehand, the danger seemed to be, that English practice at least, whatever might become of English doctrine, so far from being slighted, should meet with an adoption rather too general and indiscriminate. What seemed to be apprehended, was rather that the dross should be taken up and employed, than that the sterling should be rejected. To make the distinction as plain as possible, was therefore all along one of the principal objects of my care.

With these expectations the event has, it must be confessed, but indifferently accorded. Howsoever it has happened, both these labours, for any good effect they seem to have had in the country to whose service they were dedicated, might as well have been spared. Of the theoretical essay the translation has not been so much as published: and the practical might as well not have been published, for any use that seems to have been made of it. Of the theoretical tract, the author was indeed given to understand at the time, that it had made as many proselytes as it had found readers. But this it might easily do, without having much success to boast of: for at that busy period, the time of the leading people in that country was, as it still continues to be, so fully occupied by the conversation which the topics of the day furnish in such abundance, that the faculty of reading, as to every thing but what absolute necessity forces into men's hands, seems almost laid aside.

Be that as it may, from any effect that has manifested itself, either in the rules or the practice of the French Assembly, few or no indications have appeared, from which it can be inferred that either British practice, or British reason, or both together, have met with that attention that either alone had some title to expect. A few English expressions, and some of them too misapplied, compose nearly the whole of what France has drawn upon us for, out of so large a fund.

Has she reason to congratulate herself on this neglect? On the contrary, scarce a day that she has not smarted for it. Nor has the wisdom of these rules received a farther, or more illustrious demonstration, from the beneficial consequences that have attended the observance of them in the one country, than from the bad effects that have resulted from the non-observance of them in the other. How often has the Assembly been at the eve of perishing, by the mere effect of the principles of dissolution, involved in its own undigested practice! What a profusion of useless

3

altercation, what a waste of precious time has been produced, by doubts started, and disputes carried on, concerning the terms of a decree, days after the decree has been supposed to have been framed! A sort of dispute which never has arisen for ages, nor ever can possibly arise under the British practice, the only practice on this head reconcileable to common sense. The minutes of the proceedings, a work performed with the utmost exactness and punctuality, in the House of Commons, by a single clerk, exercises the patience, and finds full employment for the time and ingenuity, of six members of the National Assembly of France. In London the publication of this work is as regular as that of a daily newspaper: while, in the corresponding work at Paris, the series of numbers has been commonly at least ten days or a fortnight in arrear, besides being broken by frequent gaps, and disturbed by second editions correcting and cancelling the first.

Little by little, the practice relative to these points has, it is true, already undergone some improvements. Well might it: for, if it had not, instead of going on ill as it does, it could not have gone on at all: and so far as, with relation to these same points, it has been altered and improved, so far has it been brought nearer and nearer to the British practice, as delineated and justified by the ensuing pages.

As to the present detached Essay, a natural question is, how it happens that being but a part, and that not the first, it comes now to be published separate from, and before the rest?—The answer is, that though but a part, it is, as far as it goes, complete within itself; and, as to every purpose of intelligibility, completely independent of every thing that was designed to precede or follow it. Observing it thus circumstanced, it has occurred to me that the sheets might as well be transferred to the booksellers, as remain any longer an incumbrance to the printer. Should it, in this country, be found to afford half an hour's amusement to half an hundred thinking individuals, the publication will have done its office.

As to the remainder of the work, which, though considerably advanced, was not, even in manuscript, completed, the occasion which called for it being over, and all chance of its being of any immediate use being at an end, it lies very quietly in a place where its quiet is not in any danger of being very speedily disturbed.

Mean time, a sketch of the principal divisions of it may, perhaps, be not unacceptable to such readers as may be curious to see before them, at one view, what the topics are that fall to be treated of under this head of legislation. At the conclusion of these sheets a slight sketch of this sort is accordingly subjoined:[1] though, until the work, thus analysed, be completed, every analysis that can be given of it must remain in an undetermined and unfinished state.

[1] See Table I, p. 176 below.

4

# DISCOURS PRÉLIMINAIRE DE L'ÉDITEUR[1]

Dés que le titre de cet ouvrage a été connu, il a trouvé des censeurs et des approbateurs. Le mot *Tactique*, me disoient les uns, est pris en mauvaise part; il implique quelque chose d'insidieux: on croira que vous enseignez l'art de manœuvrer dans une Assemblée politique, de la séduire ou de la faire servir aux vues d'un homme et d'un parti.—Conservez ce mot, me disoient les autres, puisque, dans son vrai sens, il exprime exactement ce que vous voulez dire. Son acception vulgaire ne doit pas vous faire peur. Elle piquera la curiosité d'un certain nombre de lecteurs qui croiront trouver le pendant du *Prince* de Machiavel.[2]

J'ai conservé le titre, mais ce n'est pas pour attirer ceux qui chercheroient ici l'art des stratagèmes politiques dans les Assemblées. Je les avertis que rien n'est plus contraire au but de cet ouvrage. La Tactique, prise dans leur sens, seroit l'art de former et de conduire un parti, d'employer habilement des moyens de corruption, de surprendre l'Assemblée par des propositions imprévues, de la mettre sous l'empire de la peur quand on veut emporter quelque chose d'assaut, de donner à ses antagonistes des couleurs odieuses par des imputations mensongères, de les entraîner à des excès pour profiter de leurs fautes, de ménager des diversions adroites quand on ne se sent pas les plus forts, de paroître disputer un point pour en obtenir un autre, et d'arriver à son but avec une parfaite indifférence sur le choix des moyens. C'est un composé de sophisme, de corruption, de violence et de fraude. Une pareille Tactique est à celle-ci ce que les poisons sont aux aliments.

Cet ouvrage doit être utile à tous les Gouvernements, même aux plus absolus, puisqu'il n'en est aucun où il n'y ait des Corps, des Conseils, des Compagnies qui s'assemblent pour former des résolutions et qui, par conséquent, ont besoin de connoître l'art de délibérer. Mais il est principalement destiné aux États mixtes ou républicains qui ont des Conseils représentatifs. C'est là surtout qu'il importe d'étudier l'art de conduire les opérations d'une nombreuse Assemblée.

Le Règlement interne d'une Assemblée politique est une branche de la législation, et même une branche essentielle. Jusqu'à présent, aucun écrivain politique ne s'en est expressément occupé. Ainsi, ce sujet est tout à-la-fois très-ancien et très-nouveau; très-ancien pour la pratique,

---

[1] For details of this 'Discours', first published 1816, see the Editorial Introduction, p. xxxix.

[2] Niccolò Machiavelli (1469–1527), Italian statesman and writer. *Il principe* was completed by 1513, but not published until 1532.

très-nouveau pour la théorie: si nouveau même à cet égard, qu'elle n'a point encore reçu de dénomination spéciale, et qu'il a fallu créer une expression pour la désigner.

Si cette branche de législation a été négligée, c'est qu'on n'a point connu son importance. On n'a pas assez compris quelle influence le mode adopté pour les opérations d'une Assemblée devoit exercer sur ces opérations mêmes. *Ce sont des formes*, a-t-on dit, et, pour les esprits superficiels, ce mot *forme* rabaisse aussitôt la dignité de l'objet. Des formes sont des minuties ou des pédanteries. Qui voit en grand, méprise les formes.

Si nous pouvions tracer exactement l'histoire de plusieurs Corps politiques, nous verrions que tel s'est conservé, tel autre s'est détruit par la seule différence de leurs modes de délibérer et d'agir.

Assurer la liberté de tous les Membres, protéger la minorité, disposer les questions qu'on traite dans un ordre convenable, produire une discussion méthodique, arriver, en dernier résultat, à l'expression fidelle de la volonté générale, persévérer dans ses entreprises, voilà les conditions nécessaires pour le maintien d'une Assemblée politique. Il faut qu'elle se préserve sans cesse de trois grands maux qui l'assiègent dans tout le cours de sa durée, la précipitation, la violence et la fraude. Deux grands ennemis sont toujours à ses portes, l'*Oligarchie*, par laquelle le petit nombre domine le vœu de la majorité, et l'*Anarchie*, dans laquelle chacun, jaloux de son indépendance, s'oppose à la formation d'un vœu général. Environnée de tous ces dangers, quels sont ses moyens de défense? Elle n'en a pas d'autre que son système interne, qui ne peut la sauver qu'autant qu'il impose habituellement au Corps entier la nécessité de la modération, de la réflexion et de la persévérance.

Si les anciens États-Généraux de France ont été si foibles et si impuissants, c'est qu'ils n'ont jamais su se donner une bonne discipline, une bonne forme de délibération, et qu'en conséquence, ils n'ont jamais pu parvenir à former une véritable volonté générale. A chaque nouveau rassemblement, les différents Ordres avoient tout à recommencer sur leurs prétentions opposées. Avec les meilleures intentions, leur désordre intérieur les auroit rendus incapables d'agir. C'étoit plutôt une cohue qu'un Corps politique; et leur véritable caractère peut s'exprimer en deux mots:—fougue pour le présent, et imprévoyance pour l'avenir. Sans une bonne discipline, le patriotisme a aussi peu de chance dans une Assemblée nombreuse, que la valeur sur un champ de bataille. Le courage suffit pour remporter un avantage momentané, mais il faut bien d'autres qualités pour s'assurer des succès permanents.

Le Parlement d'Angleterre, moins puissant dans son origine que les États-Généraux, mais plus régulier dans son institution, a su se maintenir au milieu des orages et sous les Princes les plus despotiques.

Ce système ne s'est pas trouvé dans les bois, comme le dit Montesquieu.[1] Il ne s'est pas formé tout d'un coup. Il a été le fruit de l'expérience. Il s'est perfectionné dans toutes les tentatives qu'on a faites pour le détruire.

Entre tant d'écrivains qui ont rendu compte de la Constitution Britannique et qui ne demandoient qu'à la vanter, il est étonnant qu'aucun d'eux n'ait pris pour sujet de ses éloges une de ses parties les moins connues et les plus estimables, le régime interne du Parlement, les règles auxquelles il s'est assujetti dans l'exercice de ses pouvoirs. Cependant ces formes ont eu la plus grande influence sur le maintien et l'accroissement de la liberté nationale. L'arbre entier, dans son développement, a frappé tous les regards; mais l'attention ne s'est point portée sur sa première culture dans l'enclos qui a servi à protéger sa foiblesse, jusqu'à ce qu'il eût jeté des racines assez profondes pour résister aux tempêtes.

Ce système de police interne n'est point renfermé dans un Code écrit. C'est une simple coutume qui s'est formée par l'usage, qui s'est conservée par tradition, et qui, depuis près d'un siècle, a très-peu varié.

L'ouvrage de M. Bentham est calqué en grande partie sur ce modèle. Il a observé ce qui se pratiquoit dans le Parlement d'Angleterre, et il en a déduit une théorie. Ce n'est donc pas ici un travail où l'invention ait eu beaucoup de part; mais moins il y a d'invention, plus il y a de sûreté. C'est une assez belle réponse à ceux qui ont accusé cet auteur de trop de penchant à l'innovation. Dès qu'il a trouvé un système établi qui répond pleinement au but, il en a fait la base de son travail avec autant de plaisir et plus de confiance que s'il en eût été l'inventeur.

Il est vrai toutefois qu'il s'est écarté, dans certains cas, de la méthode angloise: elle ne lui a pas toujours paru la meilleure possible, et surtout pour une Assemblée de création nouvelle. Pour transplanter un système entier avec succès, il faudroit transplanter en même temps beaucoup d'accessoires, et surtout des habitudes, qui servent de correctif à des imperfections. Il est tel usage, par exemple, qui ne produit pas des inconvénients sensibles en Angleterre, parce qu'il s'est formé une routine qui apprend à les éviter, ou qui les réduit presque à rien. Transportez le même usage dans une autre Assemblée dont la Constitution n'est pas la même ou qui est encore novice, vous aurez tout le mal de l'inconvénient sans connoître les moyens d'y remédier.

Combien n'évite-t-on pas de difficultés dans le Parlement Britannique par la réunion des Membres sous les bannières de deux partis! Cette division de l'Assemblée en partis est elle-même sujette à de grands inconvénients; mais il est incontestable qu'elle donne aux affaires une marche plus facile et qu'elle prévient une multitude de propositions

---

[1] See Charles Louis de Secondat, Baron de la Brède et de Montesquieu (1689–1755), *De l'esprit des loix*, 2 vols., Geneva, 1748, i.11.vi.

discordantes. Les Chefs des deux partis deviennent des surveillants plus actifs, qui s'observent mutuellement, qui mettent de la persévérance dans les mesures, et combinent les moyens de succès. Sous ce point de vue, l'absence habituelle des cinq sixièmes de l'Assemblée cesse d'être un mal. On les appelle quand on les juge nécessaires. Les conducteurs sont en sentinelle; les autres sont à leurs affaires ou à leurs plaisirs.

Mais dans une Assemblée qui n'auroit pas ces étendards de partis, il seroit bien à craindre qu'il n'y eût pas de suite et de régularité dans ses opérations: tantôt l'activité du grand nombre seroit nuisible par la confusion qu'elle apporteroit dans les travaux, tantôt le défaut de concert feroit avorter les meilleures mesures, ou donneroit lieu à des surprises funestes. Il faut donc que le Règlement fait pour une Assemblée novice prévoie beaucoup de difficultés qui ne se présentent jamais dans une vieille Assemblée.

Rien ne seroit plus mal jugé que d'attendre tous les effets salutaires du régime anglois de la seule adoption de ce régime. En politique, imitation n'est pas toujours ressemblance. Cette conformation extérieure de Gouvernement ne constitue qu'une machine qui ressemble aux yeux, et à laquelle manque le principe interne de vie.

Ceux qui parlent de la prospérité de l'Angleterre pour la proposer[1] comme un modèle universel, raisonnent très-mal. Ils supposent qu'elle n'auroit pas pu prospérer au même point sous un régime différent à mille égards; mais ils le supposent sans preuve. Pour tirer une conclusion légitime, il faut montrer qu'il existe une liaison nécessaire entre tel ou tel point de ce régime et la prospérité du pays. Hors de là, tout ce style d'admiration, si commun et si facile, n'est qu'une déclamation frivole et même nuisible. Ce ton d'enthousiasme et ces louanges absolues ne font que de mauvaises têtes et ne conduisent qu'à de mauvaises imitations.

Je dois ajouter ici que dans le petit nombre de cas où on désapprouve la pratique angloise, on est bien loin de conclure qu'il convînt aux Anglois de la changer.

Quand les choses ont pris une certaine routine, il sera plus convenable, en général, de la suivre que de la changer pour d'autres usages qui seroient préférables si on avoit à commencer. Mais quand tous les systèmes sont également nouveaux, il seroit absurde de ne pas choisir le meilleur.

Après ces observations générales, il me reste à rendre compte de l'occasion pour laquelle cet ouvrage avoit été entrepris, de l'état des manuscrits sur lesquels j'ai travaillé, et du mode particulier de mon travail.

Le premier dessein de ce Traité fut suggéré par les *procès-verbaux des Assemblées provinciales*. Les nombreuses questions qui s'élevèrent sur leur police intérieure,[2] et les embarras qui se manifestèrent dans leurs délibéra-

---

[1] 1822 'pour proposer ses institutions comme'.     [2] 1822 'police,'.

tions, conduisirent M.ʳ Bentham à méditer sur les principes de cet art. Il avoit commencé son travail à l'époque de la seconde convocation des Notables; il espéroit l'achever avant l'ouverture des États-Généraux, et se proposoit de leur en faire l'offrande; 'je rejeterois avec horreur l'imputation de patriotisme,' dit-il dans un projet de dédicace,[1] 'si, pour être l'ami de mon pays, il falloit être l'ennemi du genre humain. Les intérêts permanents de tous les peuples sont les mêmes. Je fais du bien à ma patrie si je puis contribuer à donner à la France une constitution plus libre et plus heureuse.'

Les États-Généraux étoient assemblés, et l'ouvrage de M.ʳ Bentham étoit encore loin d'être fini. Mais s'il l'avoit été, je ne sais quelle influence il auroit obtenue contre la jalousie de corps et la jalousie nationale. Une circonstance dont je fus témoin me fait présumer qu'il en auroit eu très-peu. L'Assemblée Nationale ayant reconnu par expérience l'impossibilité de marcher avec les vieilles formes, et la nécessité de se donner un règlement de police,[2] chargea un Comité de rédiger à la hâte cette législation qui devoit régler les procédés des législateurs eux-mêmes.

Le Comte de Mirabeau présenta à ce Comité un mémoire qu'on lui avoit envoyé de Londres. C'étoit un simple narré des faits, un simple exposé des formes suivies par le Parlement Britannique, sur la manière de proposer les motions, de les amender, de délibérer, de recueillir les votes, de créer des Comités, etc. etc.

Ce mémoire fut admis sur le bureau, mais un des Membres, croyant l'honneur national blessé par cette instruction étrangère, répondit à M.ʳ de Mirabeau: *Nous ne voulons rien des Anglois, nous ne devons imiter personne.*[3]

L'Assemblée Nationale n'eut jamais qu'une discipline irrégulière et informe. Son règlement étoit défectueux à mille égards. Tous ses Comités travailloient séparément sur des objets qui auroient exigé le plus parfait concert. Elle ne sut point se mettre à l'abri des surprises et de la précipitation. Il sembloit même que dans cette guerre tumultueuse de motions, on étoit jaloux de se réserver les victoires d'assaut et les coups de main nocturnes. La fatale nuit de 4 Août en fournit la preuve.[4] En un mot, tout se décidoit par une tactique bien différente de celle dont M.ʳ Bentham avoit tracé les règles. L'ascendant anarchique des galeries et du palais royal[5] fut soigneusement conservé pour faire plier la majorité de l'Assemblée sous le vœu d'une faction.

[1] The *projet de dédicace* may have been among the papers sent to Dumont by Bentham, but it does not form part of the text of 'Tactique des assemblées politiques délibérantes'.

[2] 1822 'règlement'.

[3] The *mémoire* was Romilly's *Règlemens*; see Dumont, *Souvenirs sur Mirabeau et sur les deux premières assemblées législatives*, Paris, 1832, pp. 164–5.

[4] On the night of 4 August 1789, sweeping decrees abolishing feudalism and its attendant privileges were passed by the National Assembly.

[5] The gardens of the Palais Royal were a centre of popular agitation during the Revolution.

Entre les journaux de cette époque, l'un des plus connus, *le Courrier de Provence*, publié sous le nom de Mirabeau, quoiqu'il n'y eût aucune part,[1] fut le seul dans lequel on prit à tâche de combattre les erreurs du régime de l'Assemblée, de lui faire sentir les vices de son règlement, et les inconvénients qui en résultoient chaque jour par l'immaturité des décisions, l'incohérence des decrets, le mauvais ordre des mesures, la rapidité à détruire avant qu'on eût pourvu aux moyens de remplacer. Ces observations déduites des faits, dans le moment même, et souvent répétées, furent toujours inutiles.

L'ouvrage de M.ʳ Bentham, abandonné sans être fini[2] dès qu'il ne vit plus l'occasion d'en faire un usage immédiat, n'étoit pas propre à une traduction. Non-seulement il est incomplet, mais, de plus, il paroîtroit suranné à plusieurs égards. Il étoit fait pour les circonstances. Le but qu'il[3] se proposoit l'engageoit à entrer dans beaucoup de discussions critiques sur les vices des anciennes formes adoptées en France; cette controverse étoit nécessaire alors, elle seroit aujourd'hui sans utilité et sans intérêt.[4]

La méthode qu'il avoit prise n'étoit pas certainement celle qu'on voudroit choisir pour l'agrément du lecteur, quelque instructive qu'elle soit. Cette méthode consiste à présenter un règlement tout fait, article par article, en forme de loi, en accompagnant chaque règle des raisons qui la justifient. Le texte de la loi qu'on a toujours devant les yeux pour l'expliquer, soumet l'écrivain au genre didactique le plus sévère, et ne lui permet pas le plus léger écart.

L'auteur s'étoit soumis à une gêne de plus, car il n'en craint aucune quand elle peut contribuer à l'instruction et à la clarté. Dans tout ce commentaire, il procède par questions et par réponses: méthode excellente pour établir précisément quelle est la difficulté à résoudre, et pour mettre le lecteur en état de juger si la solution est satisfaisante. Mais cette forme de catéchisme, outre ses longueurs, a l'inconvénient de couper tous les sujets en petites parties, et d'éteindre l'intérêt par le défaut de liaison.

Après bien des essais infructueux dont la sécheresse me rebutoit, j'ai pris le parti d'abandonner ces questions et ces réponses, et d'y substituer la marche unie du discours. En accompagnant chaque règle de ses raisons justificatives, je ne me suis pas attaché à les énumérer par 1., 2., 3. etc.: quand ces distinctions ne sont pas importantes, elles fatiguent la mémoire qui ne peut s'en charger; d'ailleurs il me semble que, sur la plupart des

---

[1] The *Courier de Provence* was written by a team which included Dumont himself. See the Editorial Introduction, p. xxiii above.

[2] 1822 'qu'il n'eut pas le courage de finir'.

[3] 1822 'que l'auteur'.

[4] In Dumont's 'Tactique des assemblées politiques délibérantes', to which this was the introduction, Bentham's original Essay VI, printed in 1791, was drastically altered and compressed, to become Chapters X, XV, XVI, and XVII. It was Bentham's 1791 Essay, Chapter VI of the present edition, which contained critical discussions of the procedure adopted by French institutions; see pp. 84–92, 94–101, 103–6, 108–9 below.

points, il n'y a qu'une raison essentielle qui frappe: on risque de l'affoiblir si on multiplie trop les considérations accessoires.

Accompagner chaque règle de ses raisons justificatives, c'est diminuer l'empire du hasard. Tout ce qui se fait de bon, sans qu'on puisse assigner le *pourquoi*, n'est bon que par hasard. Il n'y a que la raison connue d'un procédé qui puisse le soustraire au caprice, le fixer et le faire entrer dans le domaine de l'esprit humain, sous la sauve-garde de l'utilité.

Il faut convenir que l'on est souvent appelé à opter entre deux manières d'agir, sans trouver aucune raison bien forte de préférer l'une à l'autre: mais il y a mille points en législation sur lesquels il faut prendre un parti par pure nécessité. Dans ces cas où il faut se contenter d'une raison légère, on doit encore la tirer du bon principe, c'est-à-dire, d'un inconvénient à éviter. N'eût-on qu'un denier à offrir, il faut qu'il soit de bon alloi.

J'aurois bien désiré, à l'occasion de chaque règle, de présenter les divers usages des peuples qui ont eu des Assemblées délibérantes; j'aurois voulu transporter les lecteurs à Athènes, à Rome, à Venise et dans les autres républiques d'Italie. Mais nos connoissances sur leurs formes internes sont très-défectueuses. Les historiens ont négligé ces détails, soit qu'ils ne les crussent pas nécessaires pour les contemporains qui en étoient instruits, soit plutôt parce qu'ils n'en soupçonnoient pas l'importance.

Ceux qui conduisoient les affaires n'ignoroient pas l'influence de ces formes, ni l'usage qu'on en pouvoit tirer pour la domination. Le Sénat de Rome s'en servoit avec le plus grand art pour maintenir son pouvoir et pour l'étendre. Mais tout ce qu'on a pu recueillir de sa pratique est bien loin de former un système complet; et il y a dans le mode législatif de la république romaine des obscurités que les plus savantes recherches n'ont pu éclaircir.

L'éloquent et profond auteur de l'histoire de l'*Anarchie de Pologne*, M.ʳ Rulhiere,[1] ne doit pas être compris dans le reproche que nous faisons ici aux historiens. En étudiant les malheurs de cette république singulière, où il n'a manqué ni de grandes vertus, ni de grands caractères, ni d'habiles patriotes qui avoient prévu la ruine de l'État et conçu les moyens de le sauver, ce sage historien a été conduit à reconnoître que le principe de tous les maux étoit dans les formes mêmes de la délibération, dans ces formes vicieuses, qui empêchoient la création d'un vœu commun, et qui, dans quelque État libre qu'on les eût transplantées, y auroient bientôt naturalisé l'anarchie.

---

[1] Claude Carloman de Rulhière (1734–91), *Histoire de l'anarchie de Pologne, et du démembrement de cette république*, Paris, 1807.

11

# AN ESSAY

ON

# POLITICAL TACTICS,

OR

INQUIRIES CONCERNING THE
DISCIPLINE AND MODE OF PROCEEDING
PROPER TO BE OBSERVED

IN

# POLITICAL ASSEMBLIES:

PRINCIPALLY APPLIED TO THE PRACTICE
OF THE BRITISH PARLIAMENT,

AND TO

THE CONSTITUTION AND SITUATION OF
THE NATIONAL ASSEMBLY OF FRANCE.

# ESSAY ON POLITICAL TACTICS.[a]

## CHAPTER I.
## GENERAL CONSIDERATIONS.

### §1. *General view of the subject.*

THE word *tactics*, derived from the Greek, and rendered familiar by its application to one branch of the military art,[1] signifies, in general, *the art of setting in order*. It may serve to designate the art of conducting the operations of a political body, as well as the art of directing the evolutions of an army.

*Order* supposes an *end*. The tactics of political assemblies form the science, therefore, which teaches how to guide them to the end of their institution, by means of the order to be observed in their proceedings.

In this branch of government, as in many others, the end is, so to speak, of a *negative character*. The object is to avoid the inconveniences, to prevent the difficulties, which must result from a large assembly of men being called to deliberate in common. The art of the legislator is limited to the prevention of everything which might prevent[+] the development of their liberty and their intelligence.

The good or evil which an assembly may do depends upon two general causes:—The most palpable and the most powerful is its *composition;* the other is its *method of acting*. The latter of these two causes alone belongs to our subject. The composition of the assembly— the number and the quality of its members—the mode of its election— its relation to the citizens or to the government;—these things all belong to its political constitution.

Upon this great object, I shall confine myself to observing, that the composition of a legislative assembly will be the better in proportion with the greater number of the points of its contact with the nation;

---

[a] This work is now first published in English, being edited from the work of M. Dumont, and the papers of Bentham.

---

[1] The word *tactics* may have been 'rendered familiar' for instance by *Essai général de tactique, précédé d'un discours sur l'état actuel de la politique et de la science militaire en Europe; avec le plan d'un ouvrage intitulé: la France politique et militaire*, 2 vols., Liège, 1773, published anonymously but by Comte J.A.H de Guibert. The opening paragraph of this work also mentions the Greek derivation of the word (from τά τακτικά.) At the end of each volume are several fold-out diagrams showing various deployments of troops, two of which are entitled *'Ouverture d'une marche de front'* and *'Ouverture d'une marche de flanc'*. Bentham used the terms *'front'* and *'flanc'* when drawing an analogy between military and political tactics (see the Editorial Introduction, p. xxvi above.) A previous edition of Guibert's book had been published in London in 1772.

that is to say, in proportion as its interest is similar to that of the community.[a]

In a treatise on tactics, an assembly is supposed to be formed; and the subject under consideration is only the manner in which its operations ought to be conducted.

But there are points, with respect to which it may be a question whether they belong to constitutional law, or to tactics: for example, whether all the members should have the same rights, or whether these rights should be divided among them; so that some should have that of proposing—

[a] Four conditions are requisite to inspire a nation with permanent confidence in an assembly which is considered to represent it:—1. Direct election; 2. Amoveability; 3. Certain conditions for being an elector, or elected; 4. A number proportioned to the extent of the country. It is upon these points that questions of detail multiply.

The election ought to be *direct*. If it be made by more[+] steps, the people, who only elect the electors, cannot regard the deputies elected as their work; they are not connected with them by the affection of choice, nor by the feeling of power. The electors[+] are connected with the people neither by gratitude nor responsibility; there is no approximation of the superior and inferior classes, and the political bond continues imperfect.

*Amoveability* is absolutely necessary. What is an election? It is a solemn declaration that a certain man actually[+] enjoys the confidence of his constituents. But this declaration does not possess a miraculous virtue, which will guarantee the character and the future actions of this man. It is absurd to cause a whole nation to assert this grave foolery:—'We declare that these five hundred individuals, who now possess our confidence, will equally possess it whatever they do during all the rest of their lives.'

The conditions[+] to be required are of a more doubtful nature. Eligibility founded upon pecuniary conditions appears to turn upon a general distrust of individuals who cannot offer the pledge of property: they are considered as less attached to the established order,[+] or less secure from corruption. The conditions required to constitute an elector, have for their object the exclusion from political power of those who are considered incapable of exercising this power with intelligence or probity;—they are precautions against venality, ignorance, and intrigue.

*The number* is an important consideration: legislative functions demand qualities and virtues which are not common; there is no chance of finding them except in a large assembly of individuals.

Legislation requires a variety of local knowledge, which can only be obtained in a numerous body of deputies chosen from all parts of the empire. It is proper that all interests should be known and discussed.

Legislation is not susceptible of direct responsibility. A small *junta* of legislators may have particular interests in making laws opposed to the general interest.[+] It will be easy for the executive power to subject them[+] to its influence. But *number* is a preservative against this danger. A numerous body of amoveable legislators participate too strongly in the interest of the community to neglect it long. Oppressive laws would press upon themselves. Even the rivalries which are formed in a large assembly become the security of the people.

In conclusion, if the number of the deputies were too small, the extent of the electoral district would render the elections embarrassing; and by reducing the value of a vote almost to nothing, would proportionally diminish the authority of the electors,[+] at the same time that it augmented the relative value of the offices so much, as to expose the elections to the most violent contests and intrigues.[+]

16

others, that of deciding upon a proposition already made; some, that of deliberating without voting—others, that of voting without deliberating; whether their deliberations ought to be public; whether absence ought to be permitted—and in case of absence, whether the rights of an individual ought to be transmissible to another; whether the assembly ought always to remain entire, or whether it ought to be obliged or authorized to subdivide itself.

I shall consider these questions as part of my subject, because it appears to me that their examination is intimately connected with that of the best rules to be followed in deliberation;—it not being possible to treat well of the latter,[+] without referring to the others.

## §2. *Ends that ought to be kept in view in a code of regulations relative to this head.*

The tactics of deliberative assemblies, as well as every other branch of the science of government, ought to have reference to the greatest happiness[+] of society: this is the general end. But its particular object is to obviate the inconveniences to which a political assembly is exposed in the exercise of its functions. Each rule of this tactics can therefore have no justifying reason, except in the *prevention of an evil*. It is therefore with a distinct knowledge of these evils that we should proceed in search of remedies.

These inconveniences may be arranged under the ten following heads:—[a]

1. Inaction.
2. Useless decision.
3. Indecision.[+]
4. Delays.
5. Surprise or precipitation.
6. Fluctuations in measures.
7. Quarrels.
8. Falsehoods.
9. Decisions, vicious on account of form.
10. Decisions, vicious in respect of their foundation.[+]

We shall develop these different heads in a few words:—

1. *Inaction.*—This supposes that there are points which demand a decision, and which do not receive it, because the assembly is unemployed. The want of activity may arise from many causes; for example, if there be not sufficient motives to overcome natural indolence—if there be no pre-established arrangement for beginning business—if the assembly

---

[a] See also the Synoptical Table, page 177, in which these heads of inconvenience are differently arranged.

can only act upon propositions presented to it by the executive power. It may also remain inactive, as was often the case with the ancient States-General of France,[1] because there are preliminaries upon which it is not agreed, questions of etiquette or precedence, disputes concerning priority in the objects to be discussed, &c.

2. *Useless decision.*—This is an evil, not only on account of the loss of time, but also because every useless decision, by augmenting the mass of the laws, renders the whole more obscure, and more difficult to be retained and comprehended.

3. *Indecision.*[a]—Is the measure proposed a bad one? Indecision is not only an evil from the time lost, but it allows a state of dread to subsist in the public mind—the dread lest this measure should at last be adopted.

Is the measure proposed a good one? The evil which it would have caused to cease is prolonged, and the enjoyment of the good it would produce is retarded, so long as the indecision subsists.

4. *Delays.*[+]—This head may sometimes be confounded with the preceding, but at other times it differs from it: there may be occasion of complaining of indecision when there is no delay;[+] as if, after a single sitting, nothing is done. There may be ground for complaining of delay[+] in cases in which a decision has been formed. In matters of legislation, indecision corresponds to denial of justice, in affairs of justice.[+] Superfluous delays[+] in the deliberations, correspond with useless delays in procedure.

Under the head of delays may be ranked all vague and useless procedures—preliminaries which do not tend to a decision—questions badly propounded, or presented in a bad order—personal quarrels—witty speeches, and amusements suited to the amphitheatre or the playhouse.

5. *Surprises* or *precipitations.*—Surprises consist in precipitating a decision, either by taking advantage of the absence of many of the members, or by not allowing to the assembly either the time or the means of enlightening itself. The evil of precipitation lies in the danger lest it should be a cover for a surprise, or should give a suspicious character to a decision otherwise salutary.

6. *Fluctuation in measures.*—This inconvenience might be referred to the head of delays and lost time; but the evil which results is much greater. Fluctuations tend to diminish the confidence in the wisdom of the assembly, and in the duration of the measures it adopts.

7. *Quarrels.*—The time lost in these is the least evil. Animosities and

[a] I understand by this, the being in a state of irresolution in relation to questions upon which it is desirable to take one side.

---

[1] Bentham is presumably referring to the practice of the Estates-General prior to 1614, as there were no meetings between 1614 and 1789.

personalities in political assemblies produce dispositions most opposite to the search after truth; and have even too much tendency[+] to the formation of those violent parties which beget civil wars.

The histories of Rome and Poland furnish numerous examples. But war is an assemblage[+] of the most destructive acts; and the evil of civil war is never less than double that of a foreign war.

But before reaching this fatal term, the animosities of political assemblies substitute objects altogether foreign from those which ought to occupy them. A thousand incidents which daily arise, lead them to neglect what ought to be attended to. All who take any share in the assembly are in a state of suffering and agitation. An excessive distrust deceives more than an extreme credulity: the most certain result is loss of honour—disgrace for one of the parties engaged in the quarrel, and often for both.

8. *Falsehoods.*—I place under this general head, all acts opposed to the most perfect truth in the procedures of a political assembly. Honesty ought to be its animating principle. This maxim will not be contested even by those who are least observant of it: but those who are most enlightened upon the public interest will the most strongly feel its justice[+] and importance.

9. *Decisions, vicious on account of form.*—In French practice, the resolutions of the chamber are reduced into form after the sitting of the assembly. Hence the resolutions, as entered upon the journals, may err in form though not in substance;[+] that is, they may not entirely or not clearly express the intention of the legislature. They err by *excess*, when they contain anything superfluous; they err by *defect*, when they do not express all that is necessary; they are obscure, when they present a confused mixture of ideas; they are *ambiguous*, when they offer two or more meanings, in such sort that different individuals may find in them grounds for opposing decisions.[+]

10. *Decisions, vicious in their foundation.*[+]—Decisions opposed to what ought to be, in order to promote the welfare of the society.

All the inconveniences before enumerated, resolve themselves into this by lines more or less direct.

When an assembly forms an improper or hurtful decision, it may be supposed that this decision incorrectly represents its wishes. If the assembly be composed as it ought to be, its wish will be conformed to the decision of public utility;[+] and when it wanders from this, it will be from one or other of the following causes:—

1. *Absence.*—The general wish of the assembly is the wish of the majority of the total number of its members. But the greater the number of the members who have not been present at its formation, the more doubtful is it whether the wish which is announced as general be really so.

19

2. *Want of freedom.*—If any restraint have been exercised over the votes, they may not be conformable to the internal wishes of those who have given them.

3. *Seduction.*—If attractive means have been employed to act upon the wills of the members, it may be that the wish announced may not be conformable to their conscientious wish.

4. *Error.*—If they have not possessed the means of informing themselves—if false statements have been presented to them—their understandings may be deceived, and the wish which has been expressed, may not be that which they would have formed had they been better informed.

Such, then, are the inconveniences to which a political assembly may be exposed from the commencement to the termination of its labours;[+] and its system of tactics[+] will the more nearly approach perfection, the more completely it tends to prevent them, or to minimize or reduce them to their lowest term.

Every article of its rules ought therefore to have for its object the obviating either one or more of these inconveniences. But beside the particular advantage which ought to result from each rule taken separately, a good system of tactics will present a general advantage, which depends upon it as a whole. The more nearly it approaches perfection, the more completely will it facilitate to all the co-operators the exercise of their intelligence and the enjoyment of their liberty.

It is by this means that they will accomplish all that is in their power: instead of embarrassing each other by their number,[+] they will yield mutual assistance; they will be able to act without confusion; and they will advance with a regular progression towards a determinate object.

Every cause of disorder is a source of profit to undue influence, and prepares, in the long run, for the approach of tyranny or anarchy.[+] Are its forms vicious? The assembly is cramped in its action, always either too slow or too rapid; lingering among preliminaries, precipitate in reaching results. It will become necessary that one portion of its members submit to exist in a state of nullity, and renounce the independence of their opinions. From that time, strictly speaking, it is no longer a political body;—all its deliberations will be prepared in secret by a small number of individuals, who will become so much the more dangerous, because acting in the name of the assembly they will have no responsibility to fear.

### §3. *Of Political Bodies in general.*

The figurative expression of a body-politic[+] has produced a great number of false and extravagant ideas. An analogy, founded solely on this metaphor,[+] has furnished a foundation for pretended arguments, and poetry has invaded the dominion of reason.

An assembly or collection of individuals, inasmuch as they are found united together, in order to perform a common act, forms what may in certain respects be called a *body*.

But a body does not necessarily imply an assembly,[+] since many individuals may declare their concurrence in the same act without having assembled; for example, by signing the same writing. Nothing is more common in England, than *petitions* to parliament, by hundreds and thousands of individuals, who have separately signed them, without having formed any assembly.

A certain body has a permanent existence; a certain other may have only an occasional, or, so to speak, an ephemeral existence (as an English jury.)

A certain body may have an unlimited extent as to number; a certain other may be circumscribed within a fixed number.

A certain body may be privileged; a certain other, not: a privileged body is one of which the members, acting together under certain regulations, have received certain rights which the other citizens do not possess.

By *bodies-politic*, we generally understand privileged bodies, which have, under this name, an existence more or less permanent; they are often perpetual, and of a limited number.

A certain body is simple, another is compound. The British Parliament is a compound body, which is formed of two distinct assemblies, and of the supreme head of the State.

It may be easily conceived, that from the rest[+] of a great body already formed, it is possible momentarily to detach a less numerous body: this is what is called a *committee*.

That which constitutes a political body, is the concurrence of many members in the same act.[+] It is therefore clear, that the act of an assembly can only be a declarative act—an act announcing an *opinion* or a *will*.

Every act of an assembly must begin by being that of a single individual: but every declarative act, the expression of an opinion or of a will, beginning by being that of an individual, may finish by being that of a body. 'This,' says Titius, 'is what passes in my mind.' 'This is precisely what has passed in mine,' may Sempronius equally say.[1]

It is, therefore, the power[+] of agreeing in the same intellectual act which constitutes the principle of unity in a body.[a]

---

[a] It is in reality only an intellectual act which can be identical among many individuals, and constitute the principle of unity in a body. It cannot be a physical act: such an act, peculiar to the individual who exercises it, does not offer any foundation for this identity. When the Roman senate decided that the consul Opimius should put Tiberius Gracchus to death, this decision was literally, and without figure, the act of each senator who

---

[1] Titius and Sempronius were stock names in Roman legal discussion.

## §4. *Of Permanent Bodies.*

A permanent political body is a collection of individuals designed[+] to produce a train of actions relative to the object of their institution. These actions will be those of all, if they are unanimous; but as it is impossible that there should exist a perfect and constant identity of sentiment in a great assembly of individuals, it is generally the practice to give the same force to the act of the majority as to that of the total number.

The impossibility of an universal and constant concurrence of sentiments in an assembly, is demonstrated by the experience of all times and places. A government, in which the legislative body should be subject to the law of unanimity, is an extravagance so palpable, that without the example of Poland it would scarcely have been possible to believe that it had ever entered into the human mind; whilst the example of Poland equally shows, that if such a law were made, it could not be observed, and that in the case in which it should be observed, it would only produce the most frightful anarchy.[1]

When we consider the decision of a political body, what appears desirable in the first place, is to obtain the unanimous wish of its members:[+] what is desirable in the second place, is the will[+] which most nearly approaches it. This leads us to be contented with the will[+] of the simple majority; since, how far soever this may be from the really universal will,[+] it is nearer to it than the contrary will.[+]

Are the numbers found equal on each side? there results from it no general act—one will destroying the other; no conclusion is arrived at—things will remain as they were, unless there be a necessity[+] for giving a predominant voice to some person.

contributed to it by his vote. When Opimius in consequence slew Gracchus with his sword, the blow struck was the act of Opimius alone.[2] Jurists say that this act was no less the act of the senate than the other. *Qui facit per alium, facit per se.*[3] I am not examining whether this mode of expression, which tends to confound one person with another, may have any use; all that I intend to observe here is, that if, for the sake of abbreviation, or for greater emphasis, this stroke of the sword be represented as the act of the senate, it can only be so in a figurative sense.

---

[1] The Polish Diet had a unanimity rule, the *liberum veto*, which had medieval origins. Before the mid-seventeenth century the veto had not disrupted the proceedings of the Diet, but in 1652 the work of the whole session was deliberately nullified by an individual deputy's exercise of the veto. Henceforth Polish political life was progressively paralyzed by this means until the abolition of the veto in 1791.

[2] In 121 BC the Roman Senate passed the first *senatus consultum ultimum,* a decree granting emergency powers to consuls, and under which Lucius Opimius summarily executed thousands of supporters of the ex-tribune Gaius Sempronius Gracchus. Gaius himself avoided execution at the hands of Opimius by committing suicide. Bentham here confuses Gaius with his brother Tiberius who, with hundreds of his followers, was clubbed and stoned to death by a mob of hostile senators led by Publius Scipio Nasica in 133 BC.

[3] 'What a man does by the agency of another is his own act.' A Roman legal maxim.

# I. GENERAL CONSIDERATIONS

I have not as yet spoken of the case of absence, which continually changes the identity of the assembly. What shall be said of a will which is not declared? It does not belong either to one side or the other. It cannot be counted in the composition of the general will.

To annul the will of the assembly on account of absentees, would be to give to the wills of the absentees the same effect as if they had been declared for the party of the minority, which by the supposition has not been done. In the calculation of suffrages, the true value of an absent will, to speak mathematically, is *one less one;* that is, equal to zero. To give to it the value of *plus one*, or *minus one*, would be equally a false calculation.

But is it always necessary to have a decision? No; without doubt: there are many cases in which it would be too dangerous to permit a small portion of the assembly to act alone. It is better not to have any decision, than to have one which does not unite a certain proportion of the suffrages of the whole body. The number necessary for rendering any act of the assembly legal, should be fixed beforehand. This important question is only mentioned here—it will be discussed separately hereafter.[1]

It is enough to remark here, that the ordinary formula—*such has been the decision of the assembly*—announces some very different facts. With an assembly of which the numerical composition continually varies, the only identity which exists is the legal effect of its decisions.

This is too metaphysical, it may be said: but it may be replied, it is necessary, since it is wished to explain the nature of a political body,[+] without having recourse to figurative language. This expression has served as a pretext for allegories without end, which themselves have become the foundation of a multitude of puerile reasonings.

The imaginations of writers have been stretched to give to political bodies the properties of different kinds of bodies. Sometimes they are mechanical bodies; and then it is a question of levers and springs—of wheelwork—of shocks—of friction—of balancing—of preponderance.

Sometimes they are animated bodies;—and then they have borrowed all the language of physiology:—they speak of health—of sickness—of vigour—of imbecility—of corruption—of dissolution—of sleep—of death and resurrection. I cannot tell how many political works would be annihilated, if this poetical jargon were abstracted from them, with which their authors have thought to create ideas, when they have only combined words.

It is true, that for purposes of abbreviation,[+] it is lawful to borrow certain traits of figurative language, and that one is even obliged so to do;[+] since intellectual ideas can only be expressed by sensible images. But in this case there are two precautions to be observed: the one, never to lose sight of simple and rigorous truth—that is to say, to be always ready

---

[1] See p. 61 below.

mentally to translate the figurative into simple language; the other, not to found any conclusion upon a figurative expression, so far as it has anything incorrect[+] in it—that is to say, when it does not agree with[+] the real facts.

Figurative language is very useful for facilitating conception, when it follows in the train of simple language: it is mischievous when it occupies its place. It accustoms us to reason upon the most false analogies, and gathers round the truth, a mist which the most enlightened minds are scarcely able to penetrate.

§5. *Division of the Legislative Body into two assemblies.*

Is it desirable to have two assemblies, whose agreement should be rendered necessary to the authority[+] of a law?

There are reasons on both sides: let us review them.

The division of the legislative body appears subject to the following inconveniences:—

1. It will often have the effect of giving to the minority the effect of the majority. The unanimity even of one of the two assemblies would be defeated by a majority of a single vote in the other assembly.

2. This arrangement is calculated to favour two different intentions, according to the quality of the members thus distributed. If it be founded upon orders—for example, peers and commoners—the result is to favour an undue preponderance—to set the interests of a particular class in opposition to the interests of the nation itself. If there are two rival assemblies without distinctions,—the result is to favour corruption; since if a majority can be secured in the one, it is enough: the other may be neglected.

3. Each assembly would be deprived of a part of the knowledge it would have possessed in a state of union. The same reasons are not presented in the two houses with the same force. The arguments which have decided the votes in the one, may not be employed in the other. The proposer of the motion, who has made the subject a profound study, will not be present in the assembly in which objections are made against it. The cause is judged without hearing the principal party.[a]

4. This division necessarily produces useless delays. Two assemblies cannot be engaged at the same time upon the same matter—at least in all those cases in which there are original documents to be presented, or witnesses to be heard. Hence double labour—double delay.

Such assemblies cannot exist without opposite pretensions. There will arise questions of competency, which will lead to negotiations, and often

---

[a] This inconvenience will be lessened if the deliberations are public and successive. The reasons which have prevailed in one assembly will be known in the other.

to ruptures. These[+] disputes concerning powers or prerogatives, beside their own inconveniences, beside the loss of time they occasion, will often furnish the means of striking both assemblies with immovability. This continually happened in the ancient States-General of France. The court encouraged disunion between the different orders; it combated the one by the other, and always found in this discord a plausible pretext for dismissing them.

5. The final result of this division is to produce a distribution of powers, which gives to one of the assemblies the *initiative*, and reduces the other to a simple *negative*—a natural and fruitful source of undue opposition, of quarrels, of inaction, and of perpetuity for abuse.

Everything tends to produce a repartition of this nature. Two independent assemblies cannot long exist without measuring their strength. Besides, those who have the principal conduct of affairs cannot act without laying down a plan, and without securing the means of its execution. They must choose one of the assemblies in order to begin their operations there; if one appear to have more influence than the other, they will carry all important propositions thither. This alone would be sufficient entirely to destroy the balance. Thus would be established, not by right, but in fact, a distinction between the two powers, the one being endowed with the initiative, and the other with a simple negative.

But in reference to personal interest—the only motive upon which we can constantly reckon—that body which is reduced to a single negative,[+] will be opposed to everything. It can only show its power by rejecting: it appears as nothing when it accepts. To play the first part, is to govern;—to play the second, is to be governed.

Deprived of the motives of honour, this negative body will detach itself insensibly from the habits of business: business will be considered an ungrateful task. This body will reserve to itself the easiest part, that of opposing everything, except in those cases in which it fears to compromise itself with public opinion, and to lose its reputation by an odious resistance.

The following are the reasons which may be alleged in favour of this division:—[a]

{First advantage, *Maturity of discussion.*

---

[a] Mr. Bentham not having executed this labour, I have endeavoured to supply it.—*Dumont.*[1]

[1] In Bowring, the remainder of Chapter I was enclosed in brackets to indicate that it was not Bentham's work. In a letter to Bentham dated *c.*20 August 1808, Dumont wrote: 'I remember, that in a special chapter you attack the system of *two* deliberative chambers. My observations in France have not brought me to the same conclusion. I added a chapter in favour of the division of the Legislative body, and I think the balance was on the side of *two* Chambers'. See *The Correspondence of Jeremy Bentham*, vol. vii, ed. J.R. Dinwiddy, Oxford, 1988 (*CW*), p. 529; see also p. 10 above.

This division is a certain method of preventing precipitation and surprise.[+]

It is true, that in a single assembly, rules may be established which prescribe multiplied examinations, according to the importance of the business; and it is thus that we find in the House of Commons *three readings*, three discussions, at different intervals;—discussion in committee, article by article; report of the committee; examination of this report: petitions from all who are interested;[+] appointment of a day for considering these petitions. It is by these general precautions, and others like them, that the danger of surprise is obviated, and maturity of deliberation secured.

This is true: but a single assembly may have the best rules, and disregard them when it pleases. Experience proves that it is easy to lay them aside; and urgency of circumstances always furnishes a ready pretext, and a popular pretext, for doing what the dominant party desires.[+] If there are two assemblies, the forms will be observed; because if one violate them, it affords a legitimate reason to the other for rejection of everything presented to it after such suspicious innovation.

Besides, multiplied discussions in a single assembly do not present the same security as those which take place among different bodies. Diversity of interests, of views, of prejudices and habits, are absolutely necessary for the examination of objects under all their relations. Men who act long together contract the same connexions and modes of thinking, a spirit of routine and of party, which has its natural correction in another association.

A second assembly may therefore be considered as a tribunal of appeal from the judgment of the first.

Second advantage, *Restriction of the power of a single assembly.*

An assembly of deputies elected by the people, and removable, would from this cause be in a state of dependence, which would oblige them to consult the wishes of their constituents: but until a system of absolutely free election and removability is established, supposing such a system easy of establishment, and without inconvenience, it is no less true that a legislative assembly is only responsible to public opinion, from which a very imperfect security results against the abuse of power. If there be two assemblies differently constituted, the one naturally serves as a restraint to the other; the power of the demagogue[+] will be weakened; the same individual will scarcely be able to exercise the same influence in both assemblies. There will arise an emulation of credit and talents. Even the jealousy of one assembly would become in this case a safeguard against the usurpations of the other, and the constitution would be preserved by passions which operate in different directions.

Third advantage, *Separation of the nobility and the people.* If there be in a state certain powerful and privileged bodies, such as the nobility and clergy, it is better to give to their deputies a separate assembly, than to confound them with those of the people in one house. Why? In the *first*⁺ place, lest if their number were not determined, they should obtain, from the influence of their rank and fortune, a considerable preponderance in the elections.

*2dly,* If they act separately, the whole responsibility of opinion will rest upon their own heads: they cannot be ignorant that the public will explain their conduct by reference to their personal interests, and that the refusal of a popular law will expose them to the severity of the judgment of the whole nation. If they are confounded with the deputies of the people in one assembly, they will possess means of influence which will act secretly, and their peculiar votes will be hidden in the general vote.

*3dly,* If in a great state you have only a single assembly, it will be too numerous to act well, or it will be necessary to give to the people only such a number of deputies as will be insufficient to establish public confidence.

Of the five objections which have been presented against the division of the legislative power, the fifth is doubtless the strongest. One of the two assemblies will obtain the preponderance—it will have the initiation. There remains nothing for the other, in the majority of cases, but the negative. It appears sufficiently absurd to create a body of senators, or of nobles solely for the purpose of opposing the wishes of the deputies of the people. But in this manner of representing the matter, it is considered only in respect of its abuse, and there is a double departure from truth, in trusting more to an assembly called representative⁺ than ought to be trusted, and fearing more from an assembly of nobles than ought to be feared.[a]

It cannot be denied, that at all times⁺ the division of the legislative body, whatever may be the composition of the two houses, presents great obstacles to the reform of abuses. Such a system is less proper for creating than preserving. This shows that it is suitable to an established constitution. The vessel of the state, secured by these two anchors,

---

[a] To the reasons already given, for thinking that the nobility when united in one chamber are less to be feared than is commonly thought, it would be proper to add another, which is drawn from their character.

The nobility are naturally indolent; they dislike business,⁺ because, they are unaccustomed to it. Even in England, the House of Lords is extremely negligent of its senatorial functions. It is frequently necessary to recruit it, to maintain it in activity. They are like certain Indians, who allow themselves to be governed by men brought from another climate.

Those who have most to lose are in consequence most timid. Their rank makes them most prominent. They cannot escape in the crowd. If they render themselves unpopular, this unpopularity follows them everywhere.

possesses a power of resistance against the tempests, which could not be obtained by any other means.

But if the division of the legislative bodies, be extended to three or four assemblies, it will be seen to give birth to a complication of irremediable inconveniences:—not only are the delays, the rivalries, the obstacles to every species of improvement, multiplied, but a means is also given to the executive of stopping everything, by a superior influence over a single assembly, or of annihilating the power of one of these assemblies, if the concurrence of two others decides everything. There results from such a division, an illegal and fraudulent association, in which two of the associates have only to agree together, in order to leave the third only the semblance of power. It is thus that the nobility and clergy in Denmark held the commons in a condition of nearly absolute nullity; and it was thus also, that by a union between the commons and the clergy against the nobility, the States were destroyed, and absolute power bestowed on the King.[1] Sicily also had its parliament, in which the two superior orders having always agreed among themselves against the third estate, have reduced it to an existence purely nominal.[2]

Returning to the question of two assemblies: if it were asked what good has resulted in England from the House of Lords, it would not be easy to cite examples of bad laws which it has prevented by its negative; it is possible, on the contrary, by citing many good ones which it had rejected, to conclude that it was more hurtful than useful. But this conclusion would not be just; for in examining the effects of an institution, we ought to take account of what it does, without being perceived, by the simple faculty of hindering. An individual is not tempted to ask for what he is certain beforehand will be refused. No one undertakes an enterprise which is certain not to succeed. A constitution becomes stable, because there is a power established for its protection. If there were no positive proof of good which the House of Lords has done, we may in part attribute to it the moderation with which the House of Commons has used its power, the respect which it shows for the limits of its slightly determined authority,[+] and its constant subjection to the rules which it prescribes to itself.

I shall confine myself to a simple enumeration of several collateral advantages resulting from a superior chamber; such as the relief which it gives to the government in the eyes of the people; the greater force conferred on the laws, when the nobility[+] have concurred in sanctioning them; the emulation which diversity of ranks spreads among the different

---

[1] In 1660 the Danish clergy and burghers united in opposition against the nobility, and broke its power by offering the king an hereditary title.

[2] Sicilian constitutional practice remained essentially unchanged between the sixteenth and early nineteenth centuries. The first estate (the clergy) and the second estate (barons) both owned feudal lands. The third estate, representatives of the domanial or royal towns, were either nominated directly, or controlled through the patronage system, by the two higher orders.

classes of society; the advantage of presenting a fixed and precise career to ambition, in which a legitimate reward is worth more than the demagogue could promise himself from success; and the still greater advantage of retaining the nobility within certain limits, of rendering it hereditary only in the eldest son, and of connecting its interest with the general interest, by a continual transfusion of these noble families among the body of the nation. There is no ducal house in England which has not in its bosom a part more attached by interest to the liberty of the commons, than to the prerogatives of the peerage. This is the principle of stability. Each one in this beautiful political order, is more afraid of losing what he possesses, than desirous of what he has not.}

## CHAPTER II.
## OF PUBLICITY.

BEFORE entering into the detail of the operations of the assembly, let us place at the head of its regulations the fittest law for securing the public confidence, and causing it constantly to advance towards the end of its institution.

This law is that of *publicity*. The discussion of this subject may be divided into six parts:—1. Reasons for publicity; 2. Examination of objections to publicity; 3. The points to which publicity should extend; 4. Exceptions to be made; 5. The means of publicity; 6. Observations on the practice established in England.[1]

### §1. *Reasons for Publicity.*

1.[+] To constrain the members of the assembly to perform their duty.

The greater the number of temptations to which the exercise of political power is exposed, the more necessary is it to give to those who possess it, the most powerful reasons for resisting them. But there is no reason more constant and more universal than the superintendence of the public. The public compose a tribunal, which is more powerful than all the other tribunals together. An individual may pretend to disregard its decrees—to represent them as formed of fluctuating and opposite opinions, which destroy one another; but every one feels, that though this tribunal may err, it is incorruptible; that it continually tends to become enlightened; that it unites all the wisdom and all the justice of the nation; that it always decides the destiny of public men; and that the punishments which it pronounces are inevitable. Those who complain of its judgments, only

---

[1] Bowring lists parts 3 and 4 in the reverse order to that given here, thus perpetuating Dumont's mistake in the 1816 edition, which was corrected in the 1822 edition. On Bentham's 1791 plan of the projected work, 'Exceptions to the general Rule in favour of Publicity' preceded '*Points* to which the Rule of Publicity should extend'. See p. 176 below.

appeal to itself; and the man of virtue, in resisting the opinion of to-day—in rising above general clamour, counts and weighs in secret the suffrages of those who resemble himself.

If it were possible to abstract one's self from this tribunal, who would wish so to do? It without doubt would be neither the good nor the wise man, since in the long run these have nothing to fear, but everything to hope. The enemies of publicity may be collected into three classes: the malefactor, who seeks to escape the notice of the judge; the tyrant, who seeks to stifle public opinion, whilst he fears to hear its voice; the timid or indolent man, who complains of the general incapacity in order to screen his own.

It may perhaps be said, that an assembly, especially if numerous, forms an internal public, which serves as a restraint upon itself. I reply, that an assembly, how numerous soever, will never be sufficiently large to supply the place of the true public. It will be most frequently divided into two parties, which will not possess, in reference one to another, the qualities necessary for properly exercising the function of judges. They will not be impartial. Whatever the conduct of an individual may be, he will almost always be secure of the suffrages of one party, in opposition to the other. The internal censure will not be sufficient to secure probity, without the assistance of external censure. The reproaches of friends will be little dreaded, and the individual will become insensible to those of his enemies. The spirit of party shut up within narrow limits, equally strips both praise and blame of its nature.

2.[+] To secure the confidence of the people, and their assent to the measures of the legislature:—

Suspicion always attaches to mystery. It thinks it sees a crime where it beholds an affectation of secrecy; and it is rarely deceived. For why should we hide ourselves if we do not dread being seen? In proportion as it is desirable for improbity to shroud itself in darkness, in the same proportion is it desirable for innocence to walk in open day, for fear of being mistaken for her adversary. So clear a truth presents itself at once to the minds of the people, and if good sense had not suggested it, malignity would have sufficed to promulgate it. The best project prepared in darkness, would excite[+] more alarm than the worst, undertaken under the auspices of publicity.

But in an open and free policy, what confidence and security—I do not say for the people, but for the governors themselves! Let it be impossible that any thing should be done which is unknown to the nation—prove to it that you neither intend to deceive nor to surprise—you take away all the weapons of discontent.[+] The public will repay with usury the confidence you repose in it. Calumny will lose its force; it collects its venom in the caverns of obscurity, but it is destroyed by the light of day.[+]

30

LIBRARY
BRYAN COLLEGE
DAYTON, TENN. 37321

## II. OF PUBLICITY

That a secret policy saves itself from some inconveniences I will not deny; but I believe, that in the long run it creates more than it avoids; and that of two governments, one of which should be conducted secretly and the other openly, the latter would possess a strength, a hardihood, and a reputation which would render it superior to all the dissimulations of the other.

Consider, in particular, how much public deliberations respecting the laws, the measures, the taxes, the conduct of official persons,[+] ought to operate upon the general spirit of a nation in favour of its government. Objections have been refuted,—false reports confounded; the necessity for the sacrifices required of the people have been clearly proved. Opposition, with all its efforts, far from having been injurious to authority, will have essentially assisted it. It is in this sense that it has been well said, *that he[+] who resists, strengthens:*[1] for the government is much more assured of the general success of a measure, and of the public approbation, after it has been discussed by two parties,[+] whilst the whole nation has been spectators.

Among a people who have been long accustomed to public assemblies, the general feeling will be raised to a higher tone—sound opinions will be more common—hurtful prejudices, publicly combated, not by rhetoricians but by statesmen, will have less dominion. The multitude will be more secure from the tricks of demagogues, and the cheats of impostors; they will most highly esteem great talents, and the frivolities of wit will be reduced to their just value. A habit of reasoning and discussion will penetrate all classes of society. The passions, accustomed to a public struggle, will learn reciprocally to restrain themselves; they will lose that morbid sensibility, which among nations without liberty and without experience, renders them the sport of every alarm and every suspicion. Even in circumstances when discontent most strikingly exhibits itself, the signs of uneasiness will not be signs of revolt; the nation will rely upon those trustworthy individuals whom long use has taught them to know; and legal opposition to every unpopular measure, will prevent even the idea of illegal resistance. Even if the public wish be opposed by[+] too powerful a party, it will know that the cause is not decided without appeal:[+] hence persevering patience becomes one of the virtues of a free country.

The order which reigns in the discussion of a political assembly, will form by imitation the national spirit. This order will be reproduced in clubs and inferior assemblies,[+] in which the people will be pleased to find the regularity of which they had formed the idea from the greater model.

---

[1] This saying also occurs in the introduction to Dumont's 'Règlement pour le Conseil représentatif de la ville et république de Genève', which was published with his recension of Bentham's writings 'Tactique des assemblées politiques délibérantes'. See *Tactique des assemblées législatives*, i. 280; and the Editorial Introduction, p. xxxiii above.

How often, in London, amid the effervescence of a tumult, have not well-known orators obtained the same attention as if they had been in parliament? The crowd has ranged itself around them, has listened in silence, and acted with a degree of moderation which could not be conceived possible even in despotic states, in which the populace, arrogant and timid alternately, is equally contemptible in its transports and its subjection. Still, however, the régime of publicity—very imperfect as yet, and newly tolerated,—without being established by law, has not had time to produce all the good effects to which it will give birth. Hence have arisen riots, for which there was no other cause than the precipitation with which the government acted, without taking the precaution to enlighten the people.[a]

3. To enable the governors to know the wishes of the governed.[+]

In the same proportion as it is desirable for the governed to know the conduct of their governors, is it also important for the governors to know the real wishes of the governed. Under the guidance[+] of publicity, nothing is more easy. The public is placed in a situation to form an enlightened opinion, and the course of that opinion is easily marked. Under the contrary régime, what is it possible to know with certainty? The public will always proceed, speaking and judging of everything; but it judges without information, and even upon false information: its opinion, not being founded upon facts, is altogether different from what it ought to be, from what it would be, if it were founded in truth. It ought not to be believed that government can dissipate at pleasure, those errors which it would have been easy to prevent. Late illumination does not always repair the evil of a previously erroneous impression. Have the people, from the little which has transpired respecting a project, conceived sinister apprehensions? We will suppose them unfounded; but this does not alter the case, they become agitated; they murmur; alarm is propagated; resistance is prepared. Has the government nothing to do but to speak—to make known the truth, in order to change the current of the public mind? No; without doubt: confidence is of slow growth. The odious imputations exist; the explanations which are given of necessity,[+] are considered as the acknowledgements of weakness. Hence improvement itself produces a shock,[+] when improperly introduced, and when it is opposed to[+] the inclinations of the people. The history of the Emperor Joseph II would furnish a multitude of examples.[1]

[a] For example, the riots in London in 1780.[+2]

---

[1] Joseph II, Holy Roman Emperor 1765–90, promoted numerous radical reforms which generated much opposition.

[2] The 'Gordon riots' of 2–8 June 1780 occurred in response to legislation of 1778 that sought to release Roman Catholics from certain disabilities. The riots took their name from Lord George Gordon MP (1751–93), who was invited to become President of the London Protestant Association in 1779 in

To these major considerations may be joined others, which ought not to be neglected.[+]

4. In an assembly elected by the people, and renewed from time to time, publicity is absolutely necessary to enable the electors to act from knowledge.[+]

For what purpose renew the assembly, if the people are always obliged to choose from among men of whom they know nothing?

To conceal from the public the conduct of its representatives, is to add inconsistency to prevarication: it is to tell the constituents, 'You are to elect or reject such or such of your deputies without knowing why—you are forbidden the use of reason—you are to be guided in the exercise of your greatest powers only by hazard or caprice.'

5. Another reason in favour of publicity:[+]—To provide the assembly with the means of profiting by the information of the public.

A nation too numerous to act for itself, is doubtless obliged to entrust its powers to its deputies. But will they possess in concentration all the national intelligence? Is it even possible that the elected shall be in every respect the most enlightened, the most capable, the wisest persons in the nation?—that they will possess, among themselves alone, all the general and local knowledge which the function of governing[+] requires? This prodigy of election is a chimera. In peaceful times, wealth and distinguished rank will be always the most likely circumstances to conciliate the greatest number of votes. The men whose condition in life leads them to cultivate their minds, have rarely the opportunity of entering into the career of politics. Locke, Newton, Hume, Adam Smith,[1] and many other men of genius, never had a seat in parliament. The most useful plans have often been derived from private individuals. The establishment of the sinking fund by Mr. Pitt, it is well known, was the fruit of the calculations of Dr. Price, who would never have had the leisure requisite for such researches, if his mind had been distracted by political occupations.[2] The only public man, who from the beginning of the quarrel with the

recognition of his leadership of the movement to oppose Catholic relief. Bentham witnessed some of the rioting; see Bentham to Samuel Bentham, 5 June 1780, *The Correspondence of Jeremy Bentham*, vol. ii, ed T. L. S. Sprigge, London, 1968 (*CW*), p. 457.

[1] John Locke (1632–1704), philosopher; Sir Isaac Newton (1642–1727), scientist; David Hume (1711–76), philosopher and historian; Adam Smith (1723–90), political economist. In fact Sir Isaac Newton represented Cambridge University for a year in the Parliament of 1689, and again between November 1701 and July 1702.

[2] Richard Price (1723–91), nonconformist minister and writer on morals, politics, and economics. William Pitt (1759–1806) was Chancellor of the Exchequer July 1782 to April 1783, and then leader of the administration, combining the positions of First Lord of the Treasury and Chancellor of the Exchequer, from December 1783 to March 1801 and from May 1804 until 1806. He decided in 1786 to re-establish the Sinking Fund, with the purpose of reducing the national debt. Pitt was influenced by Price's *An Appeal to the Public, on the Subject of the National Debt*, London, 1772, and *The State of the Public Debts and Finances at signing the Preliminary Articles of Peace in January 1783; with a Plan for Raising Money by Public Loans and for Redeeming the Public Debts*, London, 1783.

American colonies had correct ideas upon the subject, and who would have saved the nation from war if he had been listened to, was a clergyman, excluded by this circumstance from the national representation.[a] But without entering into these details, it may easily be conceived how effective publicity is, as a means of collecting all the information in a nation, and consequently for giving birth to useful suggestions.

6. It may be thought descending from the serious consideration of this subject, to reckon among the advantages of publicity, *the amusement which results from it*. I say amusement by itself, separate from instruction, though it be, in fact, not possible to separate them.

But those who regard this consideration as frivolous, do not reason well. What they reckon *useful*, is what promises an advantage:[+]amusement is an advantage already realized;[+] and this kind of pleasure in particular, appears to me sufficient by itself to increase the happiness of any nation, which would enjoy much more than those nations who know it not.[+]

Memoirs are one of the most agreeable parts of French literature, and there are few books which are more profound:[+] but memoirs do not appear till long after the events which they record have happened, and they are not in the hands of every one. English newspapers are memoirs, published at the moment when the events occur; in which are found all the parliamentary discussions—everything which relates to the actors on the political theatre; in which all the facts are freely exhibited, and all opinions are freely debated. One of the Roman emperors proposed a reward for the individual who should invent a new pleasure:[1] no one has more richly deserved it, than the individual who first laid the transactions of a legislative assembly before the eyes of the public.[b]

## §2. *Objections to Publicity.*

If publicity be favourable in so many respects to the governors themselves—so proper for securing them against the injustice of the public, for procuring for them the sweetest reward of their labours—why are they so generally enemies of this régime? Must it be sought in their vices?[+] in the desire of the governors to act without responsibility—to withdraw their conduct from inspection—to impose upon the people—to

[a] Dean Tucker.[2]

[b] See Paley's Moral Philosophy, b. vi. ch. 6, in which this subject is treated in a manner to which there is nothing to add.[3]

---

[1] Suetonius records that Tiberius (42 BC–AD 37), Emperor from AD 14, established a new office, master of the imperial pleasures (*De vita Caesarum*, III. xlii. 2.)

[2] Josiah Tucker (1712–99), economist, clergyman, and sometime Dean of Gloucester, supported the demands of the American colonies for fair representation.

[3] William Paley (1743–1805), Archdeacon of Carlisle, devotes a paragraph to discussing 'The satisfaction which people in free goverments derive from the knowledge and discussion of political subjects . . .' in his *The Principles of Moral and Political Philosophy*, London, 1785, pp. 459–60.

keep them in subjection by their ignorance? Such motives may actuate some among them; but to attribute them to all, would be the language of satire. There may be unintentional errors in this respect, founded upon specious objections: let us endeavour to reduce them to their just value.

First objection—'The public is an incompetent judge of the proceedings of a political assembly, in consequence of the ignorance and passions of the majority of those who compose it.'

If I should concede, that in the mass of the public there may not be one individual in a hundred who is capable of forming an enlightened judgment upon the questions which are discussed in a political assembly, I shall not be accused of weakening the objection; and yet, even at this point, it would not appear to me to have any force against publicity.

This objection would have some solidity, if, when the means of judging correctly were taken from the popular tribunal, the inclination[+] to judge could be equally taken away: but the public do judge and will always judge. If it should refrain from judging, for fear of judging incorrectly, far from deserving to be charged with ignorance, its wisdom would deserve to be admired. A nation which could suspend its judgment, would not be composed of common men, but of philosophers.

But the increase of publications,[+] it will be said, will increase the number of bad judges in a much greater proportion than the good ones.

To this it may be replied,—that for this purpose it is necessary to distinguish the public into three classes: The first is composed of the most numerous party, who occupy themselves very little with public affairs— who have not time to read, nor leisure for reasoning. The second is composed of those who form a kind of judgment, but it is borrowed—a judgment founded upon the assertions of others, the parties neither taking the pains necessary, nor being able, to form an opinion of their own. The third is composed of those who judge for themselves, according to the information, whether more or less exact, which they are able to procure.

Which of these three classes of men would be injured by publicity?

It would not be the first; since, by the supposition, it would not affect them. It is only the third:[+] these judged before—they will still judge; but they judged ill upon imperfect information; they will judge better when they are in possession of the true documents.

Whilst in respect of the second class, we have said that their judgments are borrowed, they must therefore be the echo of those of the third class. But this class being better informed, and judging better, will furnish more correct opinions for those who receive them ready made. By rectifying these, you will have rectified the others; by purifying the fountain,[+] you will purify the streams.

In order to decide whether publicity will be injurious or beneficial, it is only necessary to consider the class which judges; because it is this alone which directs opinion. But if this class judge ill, it is because it is ignorant of the facts—because it does not possess the necessary particulars for forming a good judgment. This, then, is the reasoning of the partisans of mystery:—'You are incapable of judging, because you are ignorant; and you shall remain ignorant, that you may be incapable⁺ of judging.'

Second objection—'Publicity may expose to hatred a member of the assembly, for proceedings which deserve other treatment.'

This objection resolves itself into the first,—the incapacity of the people to distinguish between its friends and its enemies.

If a member of a political assembly have not sufficient firmness to brave a momentary injustice, he is wanting in the first quality of his office. It is the characteristic of error to possess only an accidental existence, which may terminate in a moment,⁺ whilst truth is indestructible. It requires only to be exhibited, and it is to effect this that everything in the region⁺ of publicity concurs. Is injustice discovered?—hatred is changed into esteem; and he who, at the expense of the credit of to-day, has dared to draw for reputation on the future, is paid with interest.

As regards reputation, publicity is much more useful to the members of an assembly than it can be hurtful: it is their security against malignant imputations and calumnies. It is not possible to attribute to them false discourses, nor to hide the good they have done, nor to give to their conduct an unfair colouring. Have their intentions been ill understood?—a public explanation overturns the false rumours, and leaves no hold for clandestine attacks.

Third objection—'The desire of popularity may suggest dangerous propositions to the members;—the eloquence which they will cultivate will be the eloquence of seduction, rather than the eloquence of reason;—they will become tribunes of the people, rather than legislators.'

This objection also resolves itself into the first,—that is, the incompetence of the people to judge of their true interests, to distinguish between their friends and their flatterers.

In a representative state, in which the people are not called upon to vote upon political measures, this danger is little to be apprehended. The speeches of the orators, which are known to them only through the newspapers, have not the influence of the passionate harangues of a seditious demagogue. They do not read them till after they have passed through a medium which cools them; and besides, they are accompanied by the opposite arguments, which, according to the supposition, would have all the natural advantage of the true over the false. The publicity of debates has ruined more demagogues than it has made. A popular favourite has only to enter parliament, and he ceases to be mischievous. Placed amid his equals or his superiors in talent, he can assert nothing which will not be combated: his exaggerations will be reduced within the limits of truth, his presumption humiliated, his desire of momentary popularity ridiculed; and the flatterer of the people will finish by disgusting the people themselves.

Fourth objection—'In a monarchy, the publicity of the proceedings of political assemblies, by exposing the members to the resentment of the head of the State, may obstruct the freedom of their decisions.'

This objection, more specious than the preceding, vanishes when it is examined, and even proves an argument in favour of publicity. If such an assembly be in danger from the sovereign,[+] it has no security except in the protection of the people.[+] The security arising from secret deliberations[+] is more specious than real. The proceedings of the assembly would always be known to the sovereign,[+] whilst they would always be unknown to those who would only seek to protect it, if the means were left to them.

If, then, a political assembly prefer the secret régime, by alleging the necessity of withdrawing itself from the inspection of the sovereign,[+] it need not thus deceive itself: this can only be a pretence.[+] The true motive of such conduct must rather be to subject itself to his influence, without too much exposing itself to public blame; for by excluding the public, it only frees itself from public inspection. The sovereign will not want his agents and his spies: though invisible, he will be, as it were, present in the midst of the assembly.

Is it objected against the régime of publicity, that it is a system of *distrust?* This is true; and every good political institution is founded upon this base. Whom ought we to distrust, if not those to whom is committed great authority, with great temptations to abuse it? Consider the objects of their duties: they are not their own affairs, but the affairs of others, comparatively indifferent to them, very difficult, very complicated,— which indolence alone would lead them to neglect, and which require the most laborious application. Consider their personal interests: you will often find them in opposition to the interests confided to them. They also possess all the means of serving themselves at the expense of the public, without the possibility of being convicted of it.[+] What remains, then, to overcome all these dangerous motives? what has created an interest of superior force?[+] and what can this interest be, if it be not respect for public opinion—dread of its judgments—desire of glory?—in one word, everything which results from publicity?

The efficacy of this great instrument extends to everything—legislation, administration, judicature. Without publicity, no good is permanent; under the auspices of publicity, no evil can continue.

### §3. *Objects to which Publicity ought to extend.*

The publication of what passes in a political assembly ought to embrace the following points:—

1. The tenor of every motion.

2. The tenor of the speeches or the arguments for and against each motion.

3. The issue of each motion.

4. The number of the votes on each side.

5. The names of the voters.

6. The reports, &c. which have served as the foundation of the decision.

I shall not stop to prove that the knowledge of all these points is necessary for putting the tribunal of the public in a condition for forming an enlightened judgment. But an objection may be made against the publicity of the respective number of the voters. By publishing these, it may be said, the authority of the acts of the assembly will be in danger of being weakened, and the opposition will be encouraged when the majority is small.

To this it may be replied, that it is proper to distinguish between illegal and legal opposition. The first is not to be presumed; the second is not an evil.

The first, I say, is not to be presumed. The existence of a government regulated by an assembly, is founded upon an habitual disposition to conformity with the wish of the majority: constant unanimity is not expected, because it is known to be impossible; and when a party is beaten by a small majority, far from finding in this circumstance a motive for illegal resistance, it only discovers a reason for hope of future[+] success.

If afterwards a legal opposition be established, it is no evil; for the comparative number of suffrages being the only measure of probability as to the correctness of its decisions, it follows that the legal opposition cannot be better founded than when guided by this probability. Let us suppose the case of a judicial decision;—that there have been two judgments, the one given by the smallest majority possible, the other by the greatest: would it not be more natural to provide an appeal against the first than against the second?

But the necessity of appeal in judicial matters is not nearly of the same importance as in matters of legislation. The decisions of the judges apply only to individual cases: the decisions of a legislative assembly regulate the interests of a whole nation, and have consequences which are continually renewed.

Do you expect that you will obtain greater submission by concealing from the public the different numbers of the votes? You will be mistaken.

The public, reduced to conjecture, will turn this mystery against you. It will be very easily misled by false reports. A small minority may represent itself as nearly equal to the majority, and may make use of a thousand insidious arts to deceive the public as to its real force.

The American Congress, during the war of independence, was accustomed, if I am not deceived, to represent all its resolutions as unanimous. Its enemies saw in this precaution the necessity of hiding an habitual discord. This assembly, in other respects so wise, chose rather to expose itself to this suspicion, than to allow the degrees of dissent to the measures which it took, to be known. But though this trick might succeed in this particular case, this does not prove its general utility. The Congress, secure of the confidence of its constituents, employed this stratagem with their approbation, for the purpose of disconcerting its enemies.

The names of the voters ought to be published, not only that the public may know the habitual principles of their deputies, and their assiduity in attending, but also for another reason. The quality of the votes has an influence upon opinion, as well as their number. To desire that they should all have the same value, is to desire that folly should have the same influence as wisdom, and that merit should exist without motive and without reward.

## §4. *Exceptions to the rule of Publicity.*

Publicity ought to be suspended in those cases in which it is calculated to produce the following effects:—

1. To favour the projects of an enemy.
2. Unnecessarily to injure innocent persons.
3. To inflict too severe a punishment upon the guilty.

It is not proper to make the law of publicity absolute, because it is impossible to foresee all the circumstances in which an assembly may find itself placed. Rules are made for a state of calm and security: they cannot be formed for a state of trouble and peril. Secresy is an instrument of conspiracy; it ought not, therefore, to be the system of a regular government.

## §5. *Means of Publicity.*

The following are the means of publicity which may be employed, either in whole or in part, according to the nature of the assembly, and the importance of its affairs.

1. Authentic publication of the transactions of the assembly upon a complete plan, including the six points laid down in the preceding article.

2. The employment of short-hand writers for the speeches; and in cases of examination, for the questions and answers.

3. Toleration of other non-authentic publications upon the same subject.

4. Admission of strangers to the sittings.

The employment of short-hand writers would be indispensable in those cases in which it would be desirable to have the entire tenor of the speech. But recourse need not be had to this instrument, except in discussions of sufficient importance to justify the expense. In England, in an ordinary trial, the parties are at liberty to employ them. In the solemn trial of Warren Hastings,[1] the House of Commons on the one side, and the accused on the other, had their short-hand writers;—the House of Lords, in character of judge, had also its own.[2]

With regard to non-authentic publications, it is necessary to tolerate them, either to prevent negligence and dishonesty on the part of the official reporters, or to prevent suspicion. An exclusive privilege would be regarded as a certificate of falsity. Besides, the authentic publication of the proceedings of the assembly could only be made with a slowness which would not give the public satisfaction, without reckoning the evil which would arise in the interval from false reports, before the authentic publication arrived to destroy them.

Non-official journals completely accomplish this object. Their success depends upon the avidity of the public, and their talent consists in satisfying it. This has in England reached such a point of celerity, that debates which have lasted till three or four o'clock in the morning, are printed[+] and distributed in the capital before mid-day.

The admission of the public to the sittings is a very important point; but this subject requires explanations, which would not here be in their place. It will be treated separately.

The principal reason for this admission is, that it tends to inspire confidence in the reports of the journals.[+] If the public were excluded, it would always be led to suppose[+] that the truth was not reported, or at least that part was suppressed, and that many things passed in the assembly[+] which it did not know. But independently of this guarantee, it is very useful for the reputation of the members of the assembly to be heard by impartial witnesses, and judged by a portion of the public which is changed every day. This presence of strangers is a powerful

---

[1] Warren Hastings (1732–1818), Governor-General of India. His impeachment for corruption was voted in the House of Commons on 3 April 1787. His trial before the House of Lords opened on 13 February 1788; Hastings was finally acquitted on 23 April 1795. See *Commons Journals*, xlii. 628; xxxviii. 76; xl. 388.

[2] Shorthand writers were employed in the trial of Warren Hastings on an *ad hoc* basis. It was not until 1813 that shorthand writers were officially appointed to attend sessions of both Houses whenever required. See *Commons Journals*, lxviii. 497; *Lords Journals*, xlix. 449, 482.

motive to emulation among them, at the same time that it is a salutary restraint upon the different passions to which the debates may give rise.[a]

## §6. *State of things in England.*

In order to form a just idea of the state of things in England relative to publicity, it is necessary to pay attention to two very different things—the rules, and the actual practice. The following are the rules:—

1. All strangers (that is to say, all who are not members of the assembly) are prohibited from entering, under pain of *immediate imprisonment.* Introduction by a member forms no exception to the prohibition, nor any ground of exemption from the punishment. This prohibition, established during the stormy times of the civil war in 1650,[1] has been renewed seven times, under circumstances which furnish[+] neither this excuse nor any other.[b]

2. Prohibition, as well of others as of the members themselves, to report anything that passes in the House,[+] or to publish anything on the subject without the authority of the House.

This regulation, which dates from the commencement of the civil war, has been renewed thirty[+] times, and for the last time in 1738, in an order in which passion appears carried to its greatest height.[2] The language of the proudest despots is gentle and moderate, in comparison with that of this popular assembly.

---

[a] In the Swiss cantons, no strangers are admitted to the debates in their representative councils, nor are any accounts of their proceedings published.[+]

[b] 26th Feb. 1688,     15th Nov. 1705,
21st Nov. 1689,     26th Jan. 1709,
2d April 1690,          and
31st Oct. 1705,     16th March 1719.[3]

---

[1] 20 December 1650: *Commons Journals*, vi. 512. In fact the first occurrence of the exclusion of a non-member from the House of Commons was recorded in the *Commons Journals* of 13 February 1575 (i. 105). There were seven further cases referred to in the Journals between 1575 and 1641; see *Commons Journals*, i. 105–6, 118–20, 417, 484, 878, 896; ii. 74, 433. On 15 November 1705 the prohibition became a Standing Order of the House (*Commons Journals*, xv. 26). See UC lxxxvii. 114–16 for further notes on the admission of strangers to the Houses of Parliament and the publication of parliamentary debates.

[2] The regulation dates from 28 March 1642: *Commons Journals*, ii. 501. The renewal of 13 April 1738 reads as follows: '*Resolved*, That it is an high Indignity to, and a notorious Breach of the Privilege of, this House, for any News Writer, in Letters, or other Papers (as Minutes, or under any other Denomination), or for any Printer or Publisher of any printed News Paper, of any Denomination, to presume to insert in the said Letters or Papers, or to give therein any Account of, the Debates, or other Proceedings, of this House, or any Committee thereof, as well during the Recess as the Sitting of Parliament; and that this House will proceed with the utmost Severity against such Offenders.' *Commons Journals*, xxiii. 148.

[3] See *Commons Journals*, x. 35, 291, 364; xv. 6, 26; xvi. 278; xix. 303.

3. Since 1722, there has been published by the House of Commons, what are called the Votes of the House;[+] that is, a kind of history of its proceedings, meagre and dry, containing the formal proceedings, with the motions and decisions; and in cases of division, the numbers for and against, but without any notice of the debates.

Before this period, this publication only took place occasionally.[1]

These votes, collected and republished at the end of the year, with an immense mass of public laws and private acts, form what are called the Journals of the House.[+] These journals were formerly given to each member, but not sold[+] to the public.[a]

4. Projects of laws before they are passed by parliament. These projects, called *bills*, are not printed under a general rule, but the printing is ordered upon special motion, and for the exclusive use of the members; so that no one can know what they contain, unless he obtain one of these privileged copies through a member.[+] It is, however, of more importance that the public should be made acquainted with these, than with the votes.

How singular soever it may be thus to see the deputies of the people withdrawing themselves with so much hauteur from the observation of their constituents, the principles of a free government[+] are as yet so little known, that there has been no general complaint against a conduct which tends to destroy[+] all responsibility on the part of the representatives, and all influence on the part of the nation.

But since public opinion, more enlightened, has had greater ascendency, and principally since the accession of George III,[2] though these anti-popular regulations are still the same,[+] a contrary practice has prevailed in many particulars. It is doubtless to be regretted, that whatever improvement has taken place in England has been accomplished through a continual violation of the laws; but it is gratifying to observe that these innovations insensibly[+] tend to the general perfection.

The House of Commons has allowed[+] a small portion of the public to be present at its sittings—about one hundred and fifty[+] strangers can be accommodated in a separate gallery. Unhappily, this indulgence is precarious. That the House ought to be able to exclude witnesses in the cases[+] of which we have spoken, is conceded; but at present it is only

---

[a] All the papers published by the House of Commons are now allowed to be sold (1838.)[3]—*Ed.*

---

[1] In fact the 'Votes' were first published in 1680 (*Commons Journals*, ix. 643). The 'Votes' were published regularly with very few breaks. F. Rodgers, *A Guide to British Government Publications*, New York, 1980, p. 76.

[2] George III (1738–1820), King of Great Britain from 1760.

[3] The Second Report of the Printed Papers Committee, presented to the House of Commons 16–17 July 1835, included a resolution that the Parliamentary Papers and Reports should be made available for sale to the public and that extra copies should be printed for that purpose. *Commons Journals*, xc. 462.

necessary that a single member should require the observation of the standing order, which being always in force, is irresistible.

As to the contents of the debates and the names of the voters, there are numerous periodical publications which give account of them. These publications are crimes; but it is to these fortunate crimes that England is indebted for her escape from an aristocratic government resembling that of Venice.[1]

These publications would not have obtained this degree of indulgence, if they had been more exact. At one time, if a stranger were discovered in the gallery with a pencil in his hand, a general cry was raised against him, and he was driven out without pity. But at present, connivance is more extended, and short-hand writers, employed by the editors of the public newspapers, are tolerated.[a]

Among the Lords, the regulations are nearly the same, but the tone is more moderate. No admission to strangers—(order 5th April 1707.) No publication of debates allowed—(order 27th February 1698.) It was, however, among them, that in our times the plan of indulgence which at present reigns was commenced.

This House has one custom, which gives to one set of its opinions a publicity of which no example is found in the other.

I refer to *protests*. These are declarations, made by one or many members of the minority, of the reasons for their dissent from the measures adopted by the majority, and inserted in the journals. These protests are printed and circulated, in opposition to the regulations. There results from this publication a singularity which ought to lead to consideration, if consideration were within the province of routine. It is, that the only reasons presented to the public in an authentic form, are those which are opposed to the laws.

The House of Lords, in permitting a portion of the public to attend its sittings, has rendered this favour as burthensome as possible. There are no seats. The first row of spectators intercepts the view, and injures the hearing of those who are behind. Some of the more popular members have

---

[a] They have in the present House of Commons a gallery appropriated to themselves (1838.)[2]—*Ed.*

---

[1] Bentham could have been thinking of a passage from John Moore, *A View of Society and Manners in Italy: with Anecdotes relating to some Eminent Characters*, 2 vols., London, 1781, i. 233–4: 'If all conversation on public affairs were forbid, under pain of death, and if the members of the British Parliament were liable to be seized in the night-time by general warrants, and hanged at Tyburn, or drowned in the Thames, at the pleasure of the Secretaries of State, I dare swear the world would know as little of what passes in either House of Parliament, as they do of what is transacted in the Senate of Venice.'

[2] Seats in the public gallery of the House of Commons were first reserved for reporters in 1803, and the press gallery was first used on 19 February 1835. M. Macdonagh, *The Reporters' Gallery*, London, 1913, pp. 311, 358.

at different times proposed to give the public more accommodation;[+] but the proposition has always been refused by the majority of their colleagues, either from considering that a painful attitude is more respectful, or from an absolute horror of all change.[a]

## CHAPTER III.
## OF THE PLACE OF MEETING AND ITS DEPENDENCIES.

### §1. *Of the Building suitable for a numerous assembly.*

MAGNIFICENCE of architecture in a building intended for a large political assembly, would be almost always injurious with regard to its utility. The essential points to be considered are—
1. Facility of hearing for the members.
2. Facility of seeing for the president.

[a] By the French constitution of the year 1814, it was directed,[+] that 'all the deliberations of the Chamber of Peers should be secret.'[1]

I can discover no good reason for this secresy. If publicity be dangerous, it appears to me that there is least danger for the peers, who are the least exposed to the danger of popular ambition.

Non-publicity[+] appears to me particularly disadvantageous to the peers. They require publicity[+] as a bridle and a spur; as a bridle, because in virtue of their situation they are thought to have interests separate from the body of the people—as a spur, because their immoveability weakens the motives of emulation, and gives them an absolute independence.

I suppose that the Chamber of Peers is considered as being, or about to become,[+] eminently monarchical, as being the bulwark of royalty against the attacks[+] of the deputies of the people. But in this point of view, is not the secresy of their deliberations a political blunder?[+] Public discussion is allowed to those who by the supposition are enemies of the royal authority, or at least too much inclined to democracy; and those who are considered the hereditary defenders of the king and his dominion,[+] are shut up to secret discussion. Is not this in some manner to presume that their cause is too feeble to sustain the observation of the nation, and that to preserve the individuals from general disapprobation, it is necessary they should vote in secret?

When a proposition in the Chamber of Deputies has obtained great popular favour, is it not desirable that the arguments by which it has been opposed should be known? that the body which has rejected it should have the right of publicly justifying its refusal? that it should not be exposed to the injurious suspicion of acting only with a view to its own interest? that it ought not to be placed in so disadvantageous a position in the struggle which it has to sustain? The body which speaks in public, and whose debates are published, possesses all the means of conciliating to itself numerous partisans, whilst those who deliberate in secret can only influence themselves. It would therefore seem that this secresy, so flattering to them,[+] had been invented as a means of taking from their influence over opinion, more than was given to them in superiority of rank.[+]

[1] *Charte constitutionnelle présentée par Louis XVIII au Sénat et au Corps législatif*, Paris, 1814, art. 32: 'Toutes les délibérations de la Chambre des Pairs sont secrètes.'

3. Personal convenience for the individuals;

And lastly, Fitness for the service.[+]

If any of the seats are so distant that the voice with difficulty reaches them, attention being rendered painful, will not be long sustained. The same distance will deprive one part of the assembly of the inspection of its president, and from this cause alone may give rise to habitual disorder.

Besides, those who do not hear are obliged to decide upon a borrowed opinion. It was thus that the great popular assemblies, in the ancient republics, were necessarily subjected to the direction of two or three demagogues.

The difficulty of making themselves heard may also drive from the service the individuals of greatest ability, if the strength of their lungs be not proportioned to the space that their voice is required to fill. Demosthenes might have been[+] obliged to give way to Stentor.[1] The first quality required would no longer be mental superiority, but a physical advantage, which, without being incompatible with talent, does not necessarily imply it. The presumption is even on the other side, and in favour of the feeble and valetudinary individual,—inaptitude for corporeal exercises being partly the cause and partly the effect of a studious disposition.

A form nearly circular, seats rising amphitheatrically above each other—the seat of the president so placed that he may see all the assembly[+]—a central space for the secretaries and papers—contiguous rooms for committees—a gallery for auditors—a separate box for the reporters for the public papers;—such are the most important points. I do not enter into detail respecting the salubrity of the hall and its adaptation for the service.[+] I only add, that a hall well adapted to all these objects would have more influence than would at first be suspected, in securing the assiduity of the members, and facilitating the exercise of their functions.

## §2. *Table of Motions.*[2]

Reference is here made to a very simple mechanical apparatus for exhibiting to the eyes of the assembly[+] the motion on which they are deliberating. The mere reading of a motion can only impart an imperfect and fugitive acquaintance with it. There is no other method for really presenting it to the minds of the members of an assembly,[+] beside that of presenting it to their eyes.

A general idea of this table only will be presented here.[+] We may

[1] Demosthenes (384–322 BC) was the greatest Athenian orator. Stentor, herald of the Greeks in the Trojan War, had a voice as loud as that of fifty men together (*Iliad*, v. 785–6.)

[2] See Appendix, p. 157 below, which contains Bentham's original material on the subject of 'Motion-Tables'.

suppose a gallery above the president's chair, which presents a front consisting of two frames, nine feet high by six feet wide, filled with black canvas, made to open like folding doors;—that this canvas is regularly pierced for the reception of letters of so large a size as to be legible in every part of the place of meeting. These letters might be attached by an iron hook, in such manner that they could not be deranged. When a motion is about to become the object of debate, it would be given to the compositors, who would transcribe it upon the table, and by closing the gallery, exhibit it[+] like a placard to the eyes of the whole assembly.

The utility of this invention, in its most general point of view, consists in so arranging matters that no one could avoid knowing upon what motion he ought to vote.

It is true, that what is of most importance to be known, is the *sense* of a proposition, and not its *tenor*—the spirit rather than the letter. But it is only by a knowledge of the letter that we can be sure of the spirit—a mistake in only a single word may entirely change the purport of a discourse: when the words are no longer present to the memory, we are in danger of falling into mistakes—a danger which it is a folly to incur, when it may be avoided by so simple and infallible a method.

There is not a moment in the course of a debate, in which each member has not occasion to know the motion,[+] and to be able to consult it, either for making a correct application of what he hears, or for the purpose of taking an active part in the discussion. This knowledge is of the first importance to him, whether he act as a judge, by giving his vote—or as an advocate, by speaking for or against it.

In the first place, with respect to those who listen, nothing could be more agreeable and useful to them than this table of motions. Everything which relieves the memory, facilitates the understanding—there is much less doubt about the meaning, when there is none about the words. Upon the simple enunciation or reading of a motion—all those who have been distracted—all those who readily forget—all those who are slow in understanding,[+]—are necessarily ignorant of the subject of debate, or obliged to apply to others for information. Hence arise irregular movements, reciprocal interruptions, confusion, and noise.

In the next place, as to those who speak, the utility of this table is still more clear. If the motion be of a certain length, it requires for its recollection an effort of memory, which distracts the attention at a moment in which there is a necessity for employing it altogether in another manner. There ought not to be a necessity of seeking for words when there is already too much to do in seeking for arguments: the hesitation occasioned by such a search, disturbs the current of the thoughts.

But besides, this effort of memory is often inefficacious. Nothing is more common than to see orators, and even practised orators, falling into involuntary errors with respect to the precise terms of a motion. If this be not perceived, an incorrect judgment is the result of the error: if it be perceived, the protests against it produce either apologies or disputes, and thence loss of time in accusations and defences.

The table of motions would contribute in many respects to the perfection of the debate. We have seen that it would preserve the orators from involuntary errors: it would be no less serviceable to the assembly as a security against intentional false misrepresentations—against insidious representations, by which sentiments are imputed to an antagonist which do not belong to him. This defect of candour springs from the same principle as calumny, which hopes that some portion of the reproach with which it asperses will not be wiped away. The individual who practises this meanness is screened by the difficulty of distinguishing his false representation from involuntary error. Remove this difficulty, and the temptation to be guilty of the meanness will be removed also.

Digressions are another inconvenience in debates: they often arise from the weakness of the mind, which without intending it, loses sight of the point with which it ought to be engaged. But when the orator forgets his subject, and begins to wander, a table of motions offers the readiest means for recalling him. Under the present régime, how is this evil remedied? It is necessary for a member to rise, to interrupt the speaker, and call him to order. This is a provocation—it is a reproach—it wounds his self-love. The orator attacked, defends himself; there is no longer a debate upon the motion, but a discussion respecting the application of his arguments.[+] The unpleasantness of these scenes, when they are not animated by the spirit of party, leads to the toleration of a multitude of digressions, experience having proved that the remedy is worse than the disease; whilst as to the president, although it be his duty to prevent these wanderings, his prudence leads him to avoid giving frequent and disagreeable admonitions,[+] and entering into altercations which might compromise his dignity or his impartiality.

But if we suppose the table of motions placed above him, the case would be very different. He might, without interrupting the speaker, warn him by a simple gesture; and this quiet sign would not be accompanied by the danger of a personal appeal.[+] It would be a sedative, and not a stimulant—a suggestion, and not an accusation; it would be the act, not of an adversary, but of a judge. The member would not be called upon to stop—would not be required to make a painful submission and avowal of error; he would only have, in continuing his speech, to return to the subject of discussion; and he could not be ignorant that the sign of the president was an appeal to the assembly, the attention of which had been directed to him.

In conclusion, it may be observed that this table[+] would give great facility in the production of good amendments. If a simple reading be sufficient for correctly seizing the spirit of a motion, it is not sufficient for giving attention to all its terms.[+] When observations are to be made upon style, we must not trust to memory: it is desirable that the writing should be under the eye—that it may be considered in many points of view[+]— that the microscope of attention may be applied to all its parts; and there is no other method of discovering the imperfections of detail. This kind of criticism is a peculiar talent, in which individuals are formed to excel who often do not possess any of the gifts of oratory. The profound grammarian is more useful than is generally thought to the legislator.

This table would possess a further merit, if it should only procure for the assembly the services of one clever man, who had been discouraged by a defect of memory, and retained by this defect in a state of inaction. It is well known that the two most important faculties of the mind— judgment and invention—are often very strong in those individuals who have very weak memories, especially with regard to words. With respect to talent, as well as virtue, the smaller the service required, the less the danger of its being wanting.[+]

It may perhaps be said, that the printing of the motions before the debate, would nearly accomplish the same object, and would supply the place of this table.

But in the course of a debate, how many accidental and unforeseen motions may be made!—how many amendments which there is not time to print! It may also be observed, that a paper to be read, to be consulted, does not afford to the hearers, or the speaker, the same facility as a table which remains immovably before their eyes. It is not necessary continually to stoop for the purpose of listening or speaking,[+] but the eye glances over the lines of the table without interruption. And besides this, the great utility of the table, the strength which it gives to the regulation against useless digressions simply by means of an admonitory sign, is an advantage not to be obtained by printing the motion.[a]

---

[a] I proposed this plan of Mr. Bentham's to many of the members of the Constituent Assembly of France. They considered it very ingenious, and even very useful, but that it could not be carried into effect, because of the rapidity of the motions and operations of the assembly. During many months I attended all its sittings with the greatest assiduity; and I cannot forget how often I have experienced difficulty in ascertaining what was the subject of deliberation: I have asked many members who were not able to inform me. When even the motion was known, it was only in its general object—never in all its details and in its precise terms. There were consequently continual disputes about words: a momentary absence, a momentary abstraction, a late entry, were sufficient to produce entire ignorance of the subject of debate. Individuals sought to instruct themselves by conversations, which formed the assembly into groupes, and gave rise to little particular debates. A multitude of motions thus presented passed as spectres, and were only half known. Hence the indolent

## §3. *Description of a Table of Motions.*

The plan here pointed out may serve for a first attempt: but the easier the mode of execution, the less important are the details.

*Frames.*—They may be made like two folding doors. They should be filled with canvas, stretched so as to present an even surface, not sinking in the middle.

*Size of the letters.*—This would depend upon the size of the place of meeting;—a black ground, the letters gilt;—a strong light thrown upon the table;—the form of the letter rather oblong than square.

*Method of fixing them.*—The letters being made like a button, should have a hook, by means of which they might be fixed with the greatest ease. The regularity of the lines might be secured by a thread in the cloth.

*Composition of the table.*—The two folding leaves turn upon their hinges like a door. The compositors whilst at work are visible to the assembly (which will secure their diligence and emulation.) The two leaves closed together, will present the appearance of two pages of an open book.

*Amendments.*—These might be exhibited upon a separate table, placed immediately beside the others,[+] with a reference which would direct the eye to the part of the original motion which it was wished to amend, and a word at the top of the table, which should simply indicate that[+] the amendment is *suppressive, additive,* or *substitutive.*

*Multiplication of tables.*—There might be an assortment of tables, upon which all the known motions might be previously prepared, and thus be made to succeed each other rapidly.

## *Contents of the Table of Motions.*

Suppose that each frame is nine feet high by six wide, and the letters one and a half inch by three quarters of an inch, the two leaves of the table would contain more than four ordinary octavo printed pages. This may be ascertained by calculation.[+]

At fifty-two feet distant, I have found in a church that the table of the decalogue was perfectly legible for ordinary eyes, when the letters were three quarters of an inch high.

*Composition.*—The labours of the compositors may perhaps be accelerated by what is called[+] the *logographical* principle, which consists in composing not with letters, but with entire words.

members either went away without voting, or voted upon trust; that is to say, not being able to form an opinion, they abandoned themselves to that of their party.

These observations may appear but trifles, but the sum of these trifles produces great effects. A torrent is composed of drops of water, and a mountain of grains of sand.—*Note by Dumont.*

By the multiplication of tables, a composition which was too long to be presented all at once to the eyes of the assembly, might be presented in parts. A project of a law, for example, whatever was its extent, might be previously prepared, and the tables shifted, without suspending the labours of the assembly.

But this plan has its limits;—that is to say, there are cases and circumstances which would prevent its being employed on account of time and space: these limits do not, however, furnish any argument against its utility upon all occasions on which it can be employed. This utility is so great—the inconveniences of the present plan are so manifest, that one might be astonished that this method had not been thought of before: but in these affairs it is not proper to be astonished at anything. Under the auspices of routine, barbarism gives law to civilization, and ignorance[+] prevails over experience.

### §4. *On a Table of Regulations.*

When good rules are established, it still remains to make arrangements for facilitating their execution—for making them known. A law can have no effect except as it is known.

The regulations of the assembly, reduced into the form of a table, and readable from all parts of the place of assembly, ought to be placed by the side of the president.

If they are too voluminous, the tables ought to be multiplied; but the essential points ought to be collected together in the principal table.

In every large political assembly, nothing is more frequent than an appeal to the regulations, either for attack or for defence. The contravention consumes time—the correction consumes still more. The rules are always as if they were non-existing for one part of the assembly. The new members are but little acquainted with them; and they are not always present to the minds of the most experienced veterans. Such, at least, is the state of things in the British parliament;—and it cannot be otherwise, because the regulations, far from being exposed to the eyes, only exist by tradition, and are confided only to the keeping of a treacherous memory.

A small table would not answer the end: a large table is an object of study in every moment when the attention is vacant. The least deviation becomes sensible; and hence deviations become rare; for rules are rarely transgressed when they cannot be transgressed with impunity,—when the law which condemns is before your eyes, and the tribunal which judges you at the same moment, no one will be more tempted to violate it than he would be tempted to steal[+] red-hot iron. Procedure, which moves on other occasions with the pace of the tortoise, is in this case rapid as the lightning.

General laws, whatever may be done for their promulgation, cannot be made universally notorious. But particular laws made for one assembly may be constantly visible within it. The method is so easy, it cannot be said to be unknown. There is not a club in England which has not its regulations exhibited in its place of meeting. There is the same foresight in gaming-houses. But the bitter reflection often recurs, that the wisdom displayed in the conduct of human affairs is often in the inverse proportion of their importance. Governments have great progress to make before they will have attained, in the management of public matters, to the prudence which commonly conducts private affairs. The cause[+] may be easily pointed out, but not the remedy.

# CHAPTER IV.
## OF WHAT CONCERNS THE MEMBERS PRESENT AT A LEGISLATIVE ASSEMBLY.

### §1. *Of the utility of a Distinctive Dress for Members.*

THE establishment of a particular dress[+] for the members during the hours of sitting, is one of those points upon which it would not be proper to wound national customs. The object, however, is not altogether so unimportant as might be thought at the first glance.

1. A particular dress serves to distinguish the members from the spectators: it may prevent the usurpation of their privilege.

2. Such a dress might attain the end of a sumptuary law, without having its rigour. This apparent equality would defend the poor man of merit from a disadvantageous comparison with the pride of fortune.

3. Such a dress tends in another manner to place the individuals upon a level, by diminishing the disadvantages of those who have to strive against any bodily defect.

4. It produces a certain impression of respect upon the spectators, and places the members themselves in a more distinguished situation—two causes which equally tend to the maintenance of order, and the preservation of decency.

5. In the course of a debate, when parties are nearly balanced, and when intrigue or corruption may be apprehended, the peculiar dress may serve to detect[+] the proceedings of the members, and to signalize what passes among them.[+] Every communication among them becomes more manifest, and attracts the public attention.

This method, I allow, is not of great force; but if it be possible, without inconvenience, to throw one additional grain into the scale of probity, it ought not to be neglected.

6. In a popular tumult, such as every political assembly is exposed to

see arise around it, a dress which announces the dignity of him who wears it, may dispose the people to respect, and give the members more influence in calming the storm.

7. If the tumult runs so high as personally to menace certain members of the assembly, the simple act of laying aside their peculiar dress would favour their retreat. The Chancellor Jefferies, so noted[+] under James II for his bloody decisions, succeeded, by laying aside the marks of his dignity, in eluding for a time the fury of the populace.[1]

These different reasons are not equally applicable to all political assemblies.

§2. *Of the manner of placing the Members, and of a Rostrum for the Orators.*

In a numerous deliberative assembly, there ought not to be any pre-determinate places. Every one ought to take his place[+] as he arrives.

This free arrangement is preferable to a fixed order, for many reasons; and first, because it tends to produce a debate of a better kind.

The members of the same party ought to possess every facility for concerting their operations and distributing their parts. Without this concert, it is impossible that the arguments should be presented in the most suitable order, and placed in the most advantageous light. It is only by a continual correspondence among the members themselves, that they can prevent a multitude of useless operations, delays,[+] contradictions, repetitions, inconsistencies, and other incidents, of which the common tendency is to interrupt that unity of plan which is necessary in conducting business to its termination. In this respect, party interests are the same as those of the public. It is necessary for the public good that each party should plead its cause with all its force—should employ all its resources; since truth only has everything to gain in the concussion.[+]

Consultations held previous to the assembly, cannot supply these little consultations at the moment. One particular observation, one new proposition, may give a new aspect to affairs, and render necessary a change of measures. The most consummate foresight cannot anticipate all the incidents which may arise in the course of a discussion. It is here as in a battle,—the best plan previously formed cannot supersede the necessity of occasional orders suggested at the instant by the events of the day.

The English practice is conformable to this theory. The arrangement being free, the two parties naturally place themselves[+] upon the two sides of the House. The first bench upon the right of the Speaker, which is called the Treasury Bench,[+] is occupied by the ministers and other official

---

[1] George Jeffreys (1648–89), first Baron Jeffreys of Wem. John Dunton, *The Merciful Assizes: or, a Panegyric on the Late Lord Jeffreys*, London, 1701, p. 344, notes that 'my Lord *Chancellor* betook himself to *Wapping*, disguised in a *Collier's Coat*'.

persons; but this is a matter of courtesy, and not of right. The first bench on the Speaker's left, is that occupied by the principal persons of the opposition party.

There is one single exception to this freedom of places—an exception, honourable in principle, but too rare in practice to be productive of inconvenience. 'It is commonly understood,' says Mr. Hatsell, (Vol.II. p. 94) 'that members who have received the thanks of the House in their place, are entitled to that place whenever they come to the House, at least during that parliament;+ and it is generally allowed them by the courtesy of the House.'[1]

In the House of Lords, different benches are appropriated of right to the different orders,—one to the Bishops, another to the Dukes, &c.; but these appropriations are but slightly observed.

The States of Holland and West Friesland used to assemble in a hall, in which, to judge from appearances,+ the fixation of places was most strict. Each town had its bench, or its part of a bench. The places being all occupied, no one could change without occasioning some derangement. Whether any inconveniences were the result or not, is a matter of conjecture, and nothing more. Since everything passed in secresy in these Dutch assemblies, they never understood the essential connexion between liberty and publicity which support each other.

This free arrangement is favourable to equality, in a case in which equality, not being hurtful to any one, is justice. To prevent disputes concerning precedence, those vain contests of etiquette which have so often been the principal object of attention in great political assemblies,+ would be in itself a great good. To correct the disposition itself which attaches importance to these distinctions, is a still greater advantage. The mode by which this scheme of graduated injuries is carried into effect, is begun by supposing that one place is preferable to every other, and that the occupation of it is a mark of superiority. This system of insults, which goes on regularly increasing from the last to the first place, is what is called *order, subordination, harmony;* and these honorary distinctions— that is to say, these gradations of affronts—given and received with privilege, are commonly regarded with more respect, and defended with more obstinacy, than the most important laws.

This, then, is one cause of contention and trifling, which ought to be excluded from a political assembly. Distinction of places, and disputes concerning rank, ought to be unknown there. *Merita sua teneant auctores, nec ultra progrediatur honos quam reperiatur virtus.*[2]

---

[1] John Hatsell, *Precedents of Proceedings in the House of Commons under separate titles, with observations*, 4th edn., 4 vols., London, 1818. Dumont has 'Hatsell 67', i.e. *Precedents of Proceedings*, 2nd edn., 4 vols., London, 1785–96, ii. 67.

[2] 'Let authors have their deserts, and let not honour advance beyond the entitlement of virtue.'

In England, a quarrel respecting precedence is sometimes heard of, but it is only in assemblies for amusement; most generally among females, and only among themselves. If these disputes reach the men, they treat them as a joke.

Ought there to be a place assigned for those who speak?

Before answering this question, two points ought to be determined,—the form and size of the place of meeting, and the number of members.

In a numerous assembly, the speaker is best heard when he speaks from a tribune, placed near the centre and visible to all. The debate, more easily followed, causes less fatigue. Those who have weak voices, are not obliged to strain themselves that they may make themselves heard at the extremities; and this is a consideration which ought not to be disregarded in a political assembly, in which there ought to be a large proportion of aged and studious men.

Regularity is better preserved. If every member may speak from his place, there is at least a danger of confusion, and it is more difficult for the president to prevent irregular interruptions. The necessity of going to the tribune, stops a crowd of insignificant and precipitate proposals. It is a deliberate act, which an individual will hardly perform without having first considered what he intends to say: it makes him conspicuous, and he must feel that it is ridiculous to fix attention upon himself, when he has nothing to say wherewith to repay that attention.

Besides, when a tribune is established as the place from which to speak, all the rest of the assembly ought to[+] be obliged to be silent. If any one speak out of the privileged place, he commits an obvious irregularity, and may[+] immediately be called to order.

The tribune presents also a certain advantage connected with impartiality. If the assembly, according to the disposition of all political bodies, form itself into two parties, each naturally tends to station itself in a certain portion of the place of meeting; and if each one speak from the midst of his party, it is known beforehand on which side he is going to speak: but there are always some men more or less impartial and independent. It is well, therefore, to require all the members to speak from a tribune, which being the same for all, relieves the individual from the association of ideas which would connect him with a given party. It must, however, be acknowledged, that this method is not perfectly effectual, because all the members know each other; but it is well calculated to have this effect with the public who listen to him, and who would be thus called upon to judge[+] the speaker by what he says, and not by the place from which he speaks.

It may be objected, that this is a restraint, and that this restraint may deprive the assembly of the information possessed by a timid individual, who would fear to push himself forward upon the scene in too marked a manner.

It may be said, that a loss of time would result from it, if, for a single word, a short explanation, a call to order, it were necessary to cross the house, and to ascend the tribune.

These two objections are of very little value. The first supposes a degree of timidity which is soon overcome by use: a practised speaker will speak from one place as well as another; but he will speak best when[+] he is best heard: he will speak more freely, or[+] he will speak with less effort.

As to short explanations, the president might permit a member to make them without quitting his place. These are minutiæ, with respect to which a routine of detail will readily be formed.[+]

The two houses of the British parliament have no tribune, and no great inconvenience results from the want. It must be observed at all times,[+] that these assemblies are rarely numerous, that there are few habitual orators, and that those almost always occupy the same places. But when a member speaks from a distant seat, he speaks under manifest disadvantage. He is less heard by the assembly, and often not heard at all in the gallery. There are few important debates in which the reporters for the public papers are not obliged to omit certain speeches, of which only scattered sounds and broken phrases have reached them.

§3. *Of the hours of business, fixed or free.*

It is very necessary to have a fixed hour for the commencement of business.

But is it proper to have a fixed hour for breaking up the sitting, although in the middle of a debate? There ought to be a fixed hour, or very nearly so; but it should be admissible to finish a speech which is begun.[+]

This regulation appears to me very reasonable, and more important than would be imagined at the first glance.

With reference to the personal convenience of individuals, this fixation of the hour is useful to all, and necessary for the infirm and the aged. An inconvenience which may deter feeble and delicate persons from this national service, is worthy of consideration.

But the principal reason is, that there is no other method of securing to each subject a degree of discussion proportioned to its importance. When the duration of the debate is unlimited, the impatience of those who feel themselves the strongest, will lead them to prolong the sitting beyond the term in which the faculties of the human mind can exercise themselves without weakness. The end of the debate will often be precipitated, if it be only from that feeling of uneasiness which results from fatigue and ennui.

In those circumstances in which parties are most excited—in which each of them, awaiting the decision,[+] would be most desirous of exceeding the ordinary time—it is then that the rule would be particularly useful: by interrupting the debate, it favours reflection, it diminishes the influence of eloquence, it gives to the result a character of dignity and moderation.

1. But it will be said, delay results from it. Those who dread being found in a minority will prolong the debates, in the hope that another day may give them some advantage.

I think that a systematic plan of delay, founded upon this law, is but slightly probable. The individual who should speak merely to consume the time, would do too much injury to himself. To talk to no purpose, in an assembly in which are heard the murmurs of indignation, and before the public which judges you, is a part which demands a rare degree of impudence; and, moreover, it would be necessary to suppose that a great number of individuals should enter into this disgraceful conspiracy, in order to make it succeed.

2. It may perhaps be said, that it opens a door to intrigue—to that kind of intrigue which consists in personal solicitations to the members, in the interval between two sittings.

But this objection amounts to nothing. There is no greater facility for solicitation after the first debate, than there was before it: there is even less; for those who have announced their opinions, would fear to render themselves suspected by so sudden a change of opinion.

If this objection were solid, it would lead to the conclusion that everything should be unpremeditated in political assemblies—that the object of deliberations should not be previously known, and that the only mode of guaranteeing their integrity is to take them unawares, and to separate them from all communication from without.

### English practice.

There is a fixed hour for beginning the sittings; there is none for their termination. Hence, debates which excite great interest have sometimes lasted from twelve to fifteen hours, and even beyond that.

The inconveniences which result from this practice are sufficiently numerous; but there is no danger, at least with regard to *projects of laws*, because the regulations secure certain delays. Every bill must be read three times, besides being discussed in committee. Two adjournments are therefore necessary, and there may be a greater number.[a]

---

[a] The Roman senate could not begin any business before the rising of the sun, nor conclude any after its setting. This was a precaution against surprises; but the English method is much preferable. Demosthenes caused a decree to be passed by surprise, after the party opposed to his had retired, believing the sitting finished.[1] Such an event could not have happened in the British senate.

---

[1] In this way Demosthenes in 339 BC prevented the Athenians from joining a campaign against Amphissa. See Aeschines, *Against Ctesiphon*, cxxxvi.

The sittings do not generally commence before four o'clock, and even later. This arises from the composition of the assembly. The ministers are engaged in the morning in their offices; the judges and lawyers in the courts of justice; a great number of merchants are necessarily occupied with their business. The different committees of the house require the attendance of a multitude of persons, and this service, in a large city, can only be conveniently rendered during the day.

These circumstances have caused evening sittings to be preferred, notwithstanding the inconvenience of prolonging the debates far into the night—of often producing precipitation, from the desire of concluding them—of affecting the health of delicate persons, and of exposing this public service to the formidable concurrence of all the dissipations of a large city. If the ancient usage of assembling in the morning were re-established, this change alone would necessarily change the composition of the House of Commons.

§4. *Duty of attendance—Mischiefs resulting from non-attendance.*

I begin with two propositions:—the first, that in every legislative assembly the absence[+] of the members is an evil;—the other, that this evil is sufficiently great to justify a law of constraint.

The inconveniences may be ranged under six heads:—

1. Facility of prevarication.
2. Occasion of negligence.
3. Admission of less capable individuals.
4. Inaction of the assembly, when the number requisite for the validity of its acts is not present.
5. Danger of surprises.
6. Diminution of the popular influence of the assembly.

1. *Facility of prevarication.*—There is more than facility—there is entire security, not for complete prevarication, but for demi-prevarication. Suppose a measure so bad that a deputy, if he were present, could not in honour refrain from voting against[+] it. Does he fear to offend a protector, a minister, or a friend? He absents himself: his duty is betrayed, but his reputation is not compromised.

Every voter produces by his vote two equal and distinct effects: he deprives one party of his vote, and gives it to the other. The absent produces only one of these effects, but there is always half the mischief.

2. *Negligence.*—Is one obliged to vote upon all questions? It is natural to pay some attention to them, to make one's self acquainted with them,[+] lest we become absolute ciphers in the assembly. But this feeling of honour does not exist when individuals may freely absent themselves. They will abandon their duty, rather than compromise themselves—they

will give themselves up to indolence; and the more they neglect their business, the less will they be qualified to engage in it.

3. *Admission of less capable individuals.*—So soon as an employment becomes a source of consideration and of power, without imposing any restraint, it will be sought after—will be bought and sold, by men who have neither inclination nor power to render themselves useful in it.

Such places will often become the appanage of fortune and dignity; but if it be requisite assiduously to discharge their functions, the little motives of vanity will not outweigh the bonds of labour. We shall only find among the candidates those who discover, in these public duties, some particular attractions;—and though inclination for an employment does not prove talent for its discharge, there is no better pledge of aptitude for the labour than the pleasure which accompanies it.

4. *Inaction for want of the number required.*—This evil is connected with the preceding. So soon as the places are occupied by men who only love the decorations they afford, they will neglect to attend, at least upon ordinary occasions. It will become necessary to fix a quota$^+$ for forming an assembly, and this expedient will itself produce many days of inaction.

5. *Danger of surprises.*—We may consider as a surprise, every proposition the success of which has resulted from absence, and which would have been rejected in the full assembly.

6. *Diminution of influence.*—Public opinion in a representative government is naturally disposed to conform itself to the wish of the assembly, and requires only to know it. But will the wish of the whole assembly be the wish of that portion from which the decision emanates? It is this which becomes more problematical, in proportion as this part is less than the whole. Is the part absent greater than that which is present? The public knows not to which to adhere. In every state of the case, the incomplete assembly will have less influence than the complete assembly.

## §5. *Means of insuring attendance.*$^+$

I confine myself here to the general idea. The first of these means would consist in requiring of each member a deposit, at the commencement of each quarter, of a certain sum$^+$ for each day of sitting in the quarter; this deposit to be returned to him at the end of the term, deduction being made of the amount$^+$ deposited for each day for every day he was absent.

If the members receive a salary, this salary should be placed in deposit, subject to being retained in the same manner.

This retention should always take place without exception, even in those cases in which there are the most legitimate excuses for absence.

This plan may at first appear singular, but this is only because it is new. This, however, is not a feasible objection$^+$ to it, if it be particularly efficacious. It belongs to that class of laws which[+] execute themselves.[a] If instead of this retention you establish an equal fine—there then becomes necessary an accuser—a process, a judgment; on the other hand, the deduction is not liable to uncertainty—it operates after a simple calculation, and does not bear the character of a penal law.

Emoluments are the price of service,—Is there any ground of complaint, if they are attached to the rendering of service?

If the employment be of a kind to be undertaken without salary, the chance of losing a part of the deposit ought to be regarded as the price of the place.

To admit any cases of exception, would be to alter the nature of this instrument. Its essence consists in its inflexibility—admit excuses, you admit fraud, you admit favour; refusal to receive them would become an affront,—you would substitute a penal for a remuneratory arrangement. But it may be said, in case of sickness, is it right to add to this natural misfortune, another factitious evil? Yes, upon so important an occasion. The professional man, the artisan, are subject to the same losses. At the price of this single inconvenience, contraventions without end are prevented, the public service is secured, which could not be secured by any means more easy and manageable.[+]

This expedient itself will not suffice.[+] It is necessary to add to it a coercive punishment; for it is always necessary to come to this, to give effect to the laws. I only propose one day of arrest for each contravention, it being always understood that every legitimate excuse for absence is admissible as a ground of exemption from this punishment.

This is necessary for constraining a class of persons upon whom the loss of the deposit would have only an uncertain influence.

The rich are often led by vanity to make pecuniary sacrifices: they would not be indisposed to acquire an honourable office, even though it were expensive, provided they were not compelled to attend to its duties; they might even glory in the infraction of a rule when the punishment was only a pecuniary fine. Hence there would perhaps be formed two classes in the assembly—those who were paid for their functions, and those who paid for not fulfilling them; and as wealth sets the fashion, it might happen that a kind of degradation would be reflected upon the useful and laborious class.

A punishment is therefore necessary, which should be the same for everybody—a slight but inevitable punishment. It is true that excuses would be admissible; but it is not to be expected that, for the purpose of

---

[a] See *Rationale of Reward*, Book I. Ch. IV.[+] p. 198.[1]

[1] *The Rationale of Reward*, London, 1825 (Bowring, ii. 189–266) was prepared by Richard Smith from Bentham's manuscripts and from the second volume of Dumont's recension *Théorie des peines et des récompenses*, 2 vols., London, 1811.

avoiding the inconvenience of one day's arrest, any one would compromise his honour by a lie.

These means should also be strengthened by a register, in which every case of absence should be specified. The name of the absent member should be inscribed therein, with the date of his absence, in order to indicate the sitting or sittings from which he was absent, the excuses he has made, or the days during which, he was subject to arrest. This memorial should be printed at the end of every session.

The power of granting leave ought not to exist. This power would soon reduce the demand which was made of it to a mere formality.

If this regulation had existed in the Roman senate, the letters of Cicero would not have contained so many bitter complaints against those senators, who left him to strive alone[+] against corruption and intrigue, that they might enjoy their pleasures in voluptuous repose, or rather that they might avoid compromising themselves, and might prevaricate without danger.[1]

### §6. *British practice in relation to attendance.*

In order to perceive how far this abuse of absenting themselves may be carried, it is only necessary to consider what happens in England.

In the House of Commons, out of 658 members, the presence of 40 is required to constitute a house, and often this number is not found. Its annals offer few examples of a sitting in which one-fifth of the whole number was not wanting. An opinion may hence be formed of the ordinary attendance. The two parties in this assembly[+] are composed of persons to whom their parliamentary functions are only a secondary object. Setting aside the official personages, and the heads of the opposition who seek to succeed them, there remain lawyers, merchants, and men of the world, who, unless they have a particular interest in the question, only attend the house as a show, for the purpose of varying their amusements. At the invitation of the slightest pleasure they leave the house. It is these persons who in general compose the class whose votes are the object of dispute to the two parties, and to whom they address their pleadings.

Is this the fault of individuals? No; since in this respect as well as in every other, men are what the laws make them to be.

The laws which exist for the prevention of this abuse are well calculated to be inefficacious. In ancient times there was a statute of fines: first, five pounds; afterwards ten, and afterwards forty, &c. [2] This

---

[1] Marcus Tullius Cicero (106–43 BC), orator, politician and writer. Bentham may have been thinking of a number of passages in Cicero's letters, such as *Epistulae ad Atticum*, I. xviii. 6, xix. 6, xx. 3; II. i. 7.

[2] An Act of 1382 (5 Rich. II, c.4) directed that members of the House of Commons who absented themselves should be punished; the Act did not specify fines. On 18 March 1580 it was ordered by the

mode is gone by—there remains only imprisonment in the custody of the sergeant-at-arms[1] (this implies a sufficiently heavy ransom under the name of fees.) But even this punishment scarcely exists except as a threat. It cannot take place but upon a call of the house,[+] as if a constant duty ought only to be performed at certain periods; and in the case of a call of the house, any excuse, solid or frivolous, vague or particular, is sufficient to prevent the infliction of this punishment. It is not possible to expect that the tribunal will be severe, when all the judges are interested in the contravention of the laws. Neither can it be expected that a political body will make efficacious laws for the prevention of abuses, in the continuance of which each member finds his account, unless compelled to do so by the force of public opinion.[+]

It must be acknowledged, that this habitual negligence, which has destroyed every other assembly,[+] has its palliatives, which diminish its evil effects, and which are peculiar to the parliamentary régime.

The division into two parties, has insensibly led them to allow themselves to be represented by a certain portion of each. Each portion is as the whole. In questions of importance—that is to say, of an importance relative to the party—the chiefs give the signal, and the members come up in mass.

There is little danger of surprise, because the principal motions are announced beforehand, and because all the ministerial measures pass through many stages, upon different days. If the decision taken by the small number be contrary to the wish of the majority, they assemble in force the day following, and abrogate the work of the previous day.

§7. *Of the practice of requiring a certain number to form a House.*

With good regulations against absence, there would be no necessity for a recurrence to this instrument.

Its principal use is to contribute indirectly to the compelling an appearance. Is the fixed number deficient? Business is retarded; public opinion is thought of; an uproar is dreaded. Those who direct the assembly are obliged to take pains to obtain the attendance of the requisite number, and rigorous methods have an excuse if the negligence becomes extreme.

This fixed quota is the last expedient to which recourse should be had with this view; since the suspension of business oftentimes produced by

House of Commons that such members as departed without licence should be fined over and above the loss of wages. *Commons Journals*, i. 136.

[1] On 27 February 1606 it was resolved that the House be called over, and that any who absented themselves without leave, or just cause of excuse, should be sent for by the serjeant, and answer as in breach of privilege. On 11 December 1678, 14 members were taken into custody for the offence of departing without leave. *Commons Journals*, i. 344; ix. 556.

it, is nothing more than a punishment inflicted[+] upon the constituents, when the representatives only are in fault.

It appears at first extremely singular, that the power of the whole assembly should be thus transferred to so small a portion. It arises from the circumstance, that abstraction made of intentional surprise, nothing more is to be feared from a fraction of the assembly than from the total number. Allowances being made for the differences of individual talents,—as is the whole, so is each part.

If there be no disposition on the part of the whole to prevaricate, there is no reason to attribute this disposition to any portions of the whole. Besides, responsibility with regard to the public is always the same.

It might be apprehended, that where parties existed, those who found themselves one day in superior force, would abuse this superiority to the production of a decree contrary to the will[+] of the majority. But this danger is not great; for the majority of to-morrow would reverse the decree of the past day, and the victory usurped by the weaker party would be changed into a disgraceful defeat.

The general advantage, in case of absence, is altogether on the side of the executive power. It is this which is always in activity—it is this which has all the particular means[+] of influence for securing the assiduity of its partisans.

§8. *Visitors—mode of admission.*

We have seen, in the chapter on *Publicity,* the reasons for admitting a certain portion of the public to the sittings of the assembly, and we have pointed out the cases of exception. The number admitted ought to be as great as possible, without injury to the facility of speaking and hearing— a principal consideration, which reduces the size of the place of assembly to dimensions much less than those of an ordinary theatre; since there ought not to be required of a deputy of the people, the strength of voice and the declamation of an actor.

The experience of France has shown other dangers, arising from the number of spectators equalling or exceeding that of the assembly. It is true, that these dangers might have been prevented by a severe police; but this police is more difficult to be maintained, in proportion as the number is large. Besides, there are some men, who, surrounded with the popularity of the moment,[+] would be more engaged with the audience than with the assembly; and the discussion would take a turn more favourable to the excitements of oratory, than to logical proofs.

It would be proper, in the distribution of these places, to allow a particular seat for the short-hand writers; another to students of the laws, who would find there a school and models; another for magistrates, whose presence would be doubly useful. It would be proper also to keep certain places in reserve, at the disposal of the president, for ambassadors and strangers, who would carry from this exhibition advantageous impressions respecting the nation, which would fructify in noble minds.[+] Cyneas left Rome more impressed with respect by his view of the senate, than by[+] all the magnificence of the court of Persia.[1]

With regard to places in the public seats, they should be paid for. This arrangement is most favourable to equality, in a case where equality is justice. If you allow them to be taken by the first comers; when there is a large concourse, many persons will be disappointed. The strongest and the rudest will have all the advantage in the struggle.[a] The gallery would be filled with spectators, who would be the least profited by the debates, and who have the most to lose by the cessation of their labours. Their number, and their want of education, would[+] often lead them to brave the anger of the assembly, and to disturb its deliberations by their approbations or their murmurs.

If the granting of tickets of admission were in the hands of the government, there would not be persons wanting who would accuse it of partiality and dangerous intention. There! they would say, the ministers have surrounded us with their creatures, in order to restrain our deliberations, &c.

This subject of discontent would be removed, by giving the tickets of admission to the members themselves; and I see only one objection to this: it would restrict the prerogative of publicity, instead of extending it, by making a common right degenerate into a personal favour, and thus opposing the principle of equality without any advantage.[b]

A price of admission unites all the conditions. It is an imperfect measure, it is true, but it is the only possible one, of the value attached to this enjoyment. It is also a proof of a condition in life which guarantees a respectable class of spectators.

This plan, I acknowledge, is not a noble one; but the employment of the

---

[a] It was for a long time a trade among the common people, to seize at an early hour upon places in the gallery of the National Assembly, for the purpose of selling them.

[b] All this is reconciled in England by an unauthorized but established custom. A small sum given to the doorkeeper of the gallery, introduces you into the gallery, as well as the order of a member.[a]

---

[a] This practice is now prohibited, by an order dated July 2, 1836, and no person is now admitted without a member's order.—*Ed.*[2]

---

[1] Cineas, orator and diplomat of Pyrrhus, King of Epirus, was sent as ambassador to Rome, with proposals of peace from Pyrrhus, after the Battle of Heraclea in 280 BC. While at Rome, Cineas was most impressed by the Senate, which he likened to 'a council of many kings'. Plutarch, *Life of Pyrrhus*, xix.5.

[2] It was resolved on 29 June 1836 that all officers of the House should be prohibited from receiving any emolument for admission into the gallery. *Commons Journals*, xci. 585.

produce may ennoble it; whilst, as respects those witticisms which may be borrowed from the language of the theatre, they must be expected, and disregarded.

Ought females to be admitted? No. I have hesitated, I have weighed the reasons for and against. I would[+] repudiate a separation, which appears an act of injustice and of contempt. But to fear is not to despise them. Removing them from an assembly where tranquil and cool reason ought alone to reign, is avowing their influence, and it ought[+] not to wound their pride.

The seductions of eloquence and ridicule are most dangerous instruments in a political assembly. Admit females—you add new force to these seductions; and before this dramatic and impassioned tribunal, a discussion which only possessed the merits of depth and justice,[+] would yield to its learned author only the reputation of a wearisome lecturer. All the passions touch and enkindle each other reciprocally. The right of speaking would often be employed only as a means of pleasing; but the direct[+] method of pleasing female sensibility consists in showing a mind susceptible of emotion and enthusiasm. Everything would take an exalted tone, brilliant or tragical—excitement[+] and tropes would be scattered everywhere; it would be necessary to speak of liberty in lyric strains, and to be poetic with regard to those great events which require the greatest calmness. No value would be put but upon those things which are bold and strong; that is, but upon imprudent resolutions and extreme measures.

Among the English, where females have so little influence in political affairs—where they seek so little to meddle with them—where the two sexes are accustomed to separate for a time, even after familiar repasts,—females are not permitted to be present at the parliamentary debates. They have been excluded from the House of Commons, after the experiment has been tried, and for weighty reasons.[1] It has been found[+] that their presence gave a particular turn to the deliberations—that self-love played too conspicuous a part—that personalities were more lively—and that too much was sacrificed to vanity and wit.

---

[1] Women began attending sittings of the House of Commons during the reign of George II (1683–1760), King of Great Britain from 1727. In 1778, after disturbances following an order to remove strangers, the Speaker, Sir Fletcher Norton (1716–89), ruled that women would in future be excluded from the gallery.

## CHAPTER V.[1]
## OF THE PRESIDENTS AND VICE-PRESIDENTS
## BELONGING TO POLITICAL ASSEMBLIES.

+§1. *Of the office of President.*[a]

*Rules.*

Rule 1. IN every political assembly, there ought at all times to be some *one* person to preside.

[a] The word *President*, I employ in preference to any other term which the English or any other European language offers as capable of being made to express the function I have in view.

To an Englishman, whose view was confined to his own island, and to the chief governing bodies in that island, *Speaker* is the word which would naturally first present itself. But the term Speaker exhibits the office of president no otherwise than as an appendage to a very different, and now frivolous function, of which hereafter, and of which latter only an intimation is given by this name;—and in relation to the business of debate, it has an incorrigible tendency to produce confusion: it confounds the president with any member whom there is occasion to mention as *speaking*. In the instance in which it is most used, viz. to denote the president in ordinary of the House of Commons, it involves a contradiction; the original propriety of the appellation having in this instance slipped away, and left absurdity in its place. In that House the Speaker, while he officiates as such, is the only person present who neither makes those speeches which all the other members make, nor has any right to do so. In this point of view, it lends countenance to a principle of etymology, generally cited as a whimsical one: *Speaker*, from not speaking; *ut lucus a non lucendo.*[2]

Orator (orateur) is the word by which the English word *speaker* has been usually rendered in the general language of Europe. It is by the same word that the presidency of the three inferior orders of the Swedish diet is rendered in the same language. To the innocent improprieties chargeable on the word speaker, this adds a dangerous one. Oration means supplication;—supplication implies pliancy as towards the person to be addressed: the pliancy of the Swedish presidents as towards the person they had to address, has just[a] consummated the ruin of everything that ought to be dear to Sweden.[3]

The word Chairman is free from the inconvenience attached to the use of the words

---

[a] Published 1791.[4]

---

[1] In the Bowring edition, this chapter is based on two sources: the fragment of Essay V included in at least one copy of Bentham's 'Essay on Political Tactics', printed in 1791 (see the Editorial Introduction, p. xiv above); and Chapter VI of Dumont's 'Tactique des assemblées politiques délibérantes'. Editorial footnotes indicate those passages derived solely from Dumont; while the endnotes, pp. 179–98 below, marked with the symbol + in the text, reproduce material from Dumont which is not incorporated into Bowring. Significant differences between the Bowring edition and the 1791 fragment are indicated in editorial footnotes. A complete account of the differences between the two editions is given in the Collation, pp. 199–215 below.

[2] i.e. 'as a grove from not being light'. Bentham is referring to the naming of objects by qualities they do not possess. See Quintilian, *Institutio Oratoria* I.vi.34: 'lucus, quia umbra opacus parum luceat'.

[3] Gustavus III (1746–92), King of Sweden from 1771, declared war on Russia in 1788, in contravention of the Swedish Constitution which stated that the king could not attack a foreign power without the consent of the Estates. A new constitution, the Act of Union and Security, drawn up by the King in

 [*See p. 66 for n. 3 cont. and n. 4.*]

Rule 2. In a permanent assembly, that function is best provided for by a permanent president in chief, with substitutes of equal permanency, in such number, that in case of absence or disability, the place of the chief may at the instant be supplied.

The[1] president[+] ought to be permanent, not only that the embarrassment arising from multiplied elections may be avoided, but especially for the good of his office. If permanent, he will possess more experience, he

---

*speaker* and orator; but it draws the attention to an idea too confined; as if it were necessary to the function that the person who performs it should sit in a chair, and that nobody else should. At times it may even bring up an improper and ignoble idea: several committees being about to sit, a voice is heard in the purlieus of the House of Commons, *Gentlemen, your chairmen wait for you.* Does *chairmen* here mean *presidents* or *porters*?

*Marshal* is the appellation by which the president is designated[2] in the Polish diet; in one of the four orders which compose the Swedish body of that name; and in the provincial assemblies of the noblesse, instituted within these few years, throughout the Russian empire. This term, besides being unexpressive, is liable to objections of a much more serious nature. In the original German, it signified neither more nor less than what we call a hostler or groom—a servant having horses under his care. A horse being an animal of great importance to a barbarian king, to have the care of the king's horses was to be a great man. When not to be military was to be nobody, to be a man in the service of the king was to have a[3] military command. Thus, by degrees, a command over horses has involved, as a matter of inferior consequence, a command over their riders; till at length the title of *marshal,* superior even to that of *general,* is come to denote, in most countries of Europe, the chief military command. But to command militarily, is to command despotically. Accordingly, in the Swedish diet, the nobles, sitting under the command of their marshal named by the king,[4] are to speak or to hold their tongues, as a soldier is to turn to the right or to the left as the commander gives the word. Thus, as will be seen below, ordained Gustavus Adolphus a military king.[5]

Hence, of all the words which ever were, or ever could be devised, to denote the president of an assembly, which is not meant for an army or a puppet-show, the word *marshal* is that which ought most studiously to be proscribed. France, therefore, in giving to the presidents of her national assemblies this simple and expressive name, instead of the swelling and so much coveted title of marshal, has had a fortunate escape.

The length of this note may demand justification, but needs no apology. While minds are led by sounds, and modes of thinking depend on association, names of office will never be of light importance. A king of Poland or Sweden looks upon himself as an injured being, so long as his will meets with any resistance that would not have been made to a king of Prussia or Denmark: and because a president is termed marshal, Sweden is destroyed.[6]

---

1789, led to an unprecedented degree of royal absolutism which allowed the King to continue the war unchecked. Cf. 'A Plan for an Universal and Perpetual Peace', Bowring, ii. 554, written in 1789.

[4] Note added in Bowring. In fact the Chapter was privately printed but not published.

[1] This paragraph from Dumont.　　　　　　　　　　　　[2] Bentham 1791 'denoted'.
[3] Bentham 1791 'a great military'.　　　　　　　　　　[4] Bentham 1791 'Crown'.
[5] Gustavus II Adolphus (1594–1632), King of Sweden from 1611, reformed the Swedish Estates by an Ordinance of 1617. While the Ordinance fixed the number of Estates at four, laid down rules for the conduct of their business and made them an integral part of the constitution, it nevertheless placed the king in a strong position to exercise a personal influence on political proceedings.

[6] Another allusion to the ease with which Gustavus III was able to ignore the Swedish constitution in his attack on Russia.

will know the assembly better, he will be more conversant with business, and will feel more interested in managing it well, than an occasional president. The occasional president, whether he execute his office well or ill, must lose it. The permanent president, who will only lose his office if he discharge it ill, has an additional motive for performing all his duties well.[+]

Rule 3. In the character of president, no more than *one* person ought to officiate at a time.

If[+] there are two, whenever there arises any difference of opinion between them, there will be no decision. If there are more than two, they will form a little assembly, which will have its debates, which will uselessly prolong the business in hand.[1]

Rule 4. But *two* persons at least, capable of officiating, *ought* to be present at *once*.[2]

This[3] rule is necessary, in order to prevent the assembly from being reduced to a state of inaction from the sickness, death, or absence of its president. The omission of so simple and important a precaution, announces so great a want of foresight, that it could hardly be thought that men would be guilty of it, if a striking example were not exhibited by one of the greatest and most ancient of political assemblies.[+]

### §2. *Functions, competent and incompetent.*

Rule 5. The functions that belong properly to a president, belong to him in one or other of two capacities: that of a *judge*, as between individual members; or that of *agent* of the whole assembly:—as judge,[+] when there is a dispute for him to decide upon; as agent,[+] where there is anything for him to do[+] without dispute.[a]

Rule 6. As judge, a president ought in every instance, to be subordinate, in the way of appeal to the assembly itself, sitting under another presidence.

Rule 7. As agent, he ought in every instance to be subject to the *controul* of the assembly, and that *instanter*, as to everything transacted in the face of the assembly.

Rule 8. In neither capacity ought he to possess any power, the effect of which would be to give him a controul in any degree over the will of the assembly.

[a] For instance, putting the question; declaring the decision from the number of the votes; giving orders to subordinates; giving thanks or reprimands to individuals; or, in short, using, in the name of the assembly, any other discourse of any kind which is not deemed of sufficient importance to be penned by the assembly itself.

---

[1] This paragraph from Dumont.
[2] Bentham 1791 'at a time'.
[3] This paragraph from Dumont.

Rule 9. In a numerous assembly,[a] and in particular in a numerous legislative assembly, a president ought not to be a member; that is, he ought not to possess a right either to make motions, to take part in a debate, or to give a vote.

This[1] exclusion is as much for his advantage as for that of the body over which he presides:—

1. It leaves him entirely at liberty to attend to his duties, and the cultivation of the particular talents which they require. If he be called to sustain the character and reputation of a member of the assembly, he will be often distracted from his principal occupation, and he will have a different kind of ambition from that which belongs to his office, without reckoning the danger of not succeeding, of offending, and of weakening his personal consideration by ill-sustained pretensions.

2. This exclusion is founded upon reasons of an elevated nature; it is designed to guarantee him from the seductions of partiality, and to raise him even above suspicion, by never exhibiting him as a *partisan* in the midst of the debates in which he is required to interfere as a *judge*—to leave him in possession of that consideration and confidence[+] which alone can secure to his decisions the respect[+] of all parties.

But it may be said, that the president, no more than any one else, can remain neuter[+] with regard to questions which interest the whole nation—obliged especially as he is to be continually occupied with them, even as matter of duty;[+] that it would therefore be better that he should be obliged to declare himself, and make known his real sentiments, and thus put the assembly upon its guard, rather than that he should enjoy, under a false appearance of impartiality, a confidence which he does not merit.

To this objection there is more than one answer: First, It cannot be denied, that so long as his internal sentiments have no undue influence upon his external conduct, they are of no consequence to the assembly, but that he cannot declare them without becoming less agreeable to one party—without exposing himself to a suspicion of partiality, which always more or less alters the degree of confidence.

Secondly, If you permit him to remain impartial, he will be so more easily than any one else. He will regard the debates under altogether a different point of view from that of the debaters themselves. His attention,

---

[a] An assembly may in this point of view be deemed too numerous, when it is too numerous for the opinion of each member to be recorded distinctly in his own terms. This takes out of the rule such assemblies, for instance, as the boards of administration, and the principal courts of justice in Great Britain, and the boards established in the dominions of the English East-India Company.

---

[1] Remainder of this section from Dumont.

principally directed to the maintenance of form and order, will be withdrawn from the principal subject. The ideas which occupy his mind during a debate, may differ from those which occupy the actors in it, as much as the thoughts of a botanist who looks at a field may differ from those of its owner.

Habit facilitates these sorts of abstraction. If it were not so, how could judges, full of humanity, fix their attention with a perfect impartiality upon a point of law, whilst a trembling family stood waiting beneath their eyes the issue of their judgment.

It follows from what has been said, that in a numerous political assembly, in which it is to be expected that passion and animosity may arise, that he who is called upon to moderate them, ought not to be obliged to enrol himself under the banners of a party, to make himself friends and enemies, to pass from the character of a combatant to that of an arbitrator, and to compromise by these opposite functions the respect due to his public character.

There have been assemblies which have only given a vote to the president when the votes have been found equal. This mode is more opposed to impartiality than that of allowing him to vote in all cases, and there is no reason which can be assigned in its favour. The most simple and natural plan to adopt in case of equality, is to consider that the proposition which has not had the majority of votes is rejected. In matters of election, it would be better to resort to lot, than to give the preponderant voice to the president. The lot offends nobody.

### §3. Sequel. Choice.

Rule 10. In a legislative assembly, or any other free and numerous political assembly, a president ought in every case to be chosen freely and exclusively by the assembly over which he is to preside.

Rule 11. In the choice of a president, the votes ought to be taken in the secret way, and the majority ought to be an absolute one.[a]

Rule 12. A president ought ever to remain removable by the assembly at its free pleasure, but not by any other authority.

Rule 13. In a permanent assembly, on the occasion of choosing a permanent president, if there be no other president in office, it may be

---

[a] In contradistinction to a comparative one: *i. e.* if there be a number of candidates, the having more votes than any other candidate ought not to determine the election, unless he who possesses such comparative majority have a majority of the whole number of the votes.[1]

---

[1] Bentham 1791 continues: 'For the method of reducing a comparative majority to an absolute one, see Essay VI.' Bentham did not in fact provide a method for reducing a comparative majority to an absolute one; but see p. 77 n. below.

better to accept a president *pro re natâ* from without doors, upon the ground of any claim, however slight, if single, than to stand in that instance upon its liberty of choice.[a]

Rule 14. So for all kinds of business in an assembly, which, however free, is but occasional.[b]

## §4. *General Observations.*

A very simple observation will furnish a clue to all the reasons that can be produced or required in support of the propositions above laid down. Throughout the whole business, the grand problem is to obtain, in its most genuine purity, the real and enlightened will of the assembly. The solution of this problem is the end that ought everywhere to be had in view. To this end, everything that concerns the president ought of course to be subservient. It is for the sake of the assembly, and for their use alone, that the institution of this office is either necessary or proper. The duty and art of the president of a political assembly, is the duty and art of the *accoucheur: ars obstetrix animorum*, to use an expression of the first Encyclopedist and his not unworthy successors;[1]—to assist *nature*, and not to force her—to soothe, upon occasion, the pangs of parturition—to produce, in the shortest time, the genuine offspring; but never to stifle it, much less to substitute a changeling in its room. It is only in as far as it may be conformable to the will of the assembly, that the will of this officer can, as such, have any claim to regard. If, in any instance, a person dignified with any such title as that of president of such or such an assembly, possess any independent influence, such influence, proper or improper, belongs to him, not in his quality of president, but in some foreign character. Any influence whatever that he possesses over the acts of the assembly, otherwise than subject to the immediate controul of the assembly, is just so much power taken from the assembly and thrown into the lap of this single individual.

It follows, that nothing ought to be permitted by the assembly to be

---

[a] For instance, where a king or other chief magistrate in any state institutes a new assembly, or convokes one not already provided with one by ancient designation, it might be of use that he should name a president for this purpose only.

[b] Thus, in an English county meeting, it may be better to accept of the presidency of the sheriff, though an officer of the king's appointment, than to consume the time in debating who shall fill the chair.

---

[1] 'The skill of being a midwife of souls' was attributed to Socrates by Plato in *Theaetetus*, cl. The 'Prospectus' to *Encyclopédie, ou dictionnaire raisonné des sciences, des arts et des métiers, recueilli des meilleurs auteurs*, 10 vols., Paris, 1751, edited by Denis Diderot (1713–84) and Jean le Rond d'Alembert (1717–83) alluded to Socrates as *obstetrix animorum*. The phrase *ars obstetrix animorum* appeared on the title page of Volume I of the first, though not the second, edition of *Tactique des assemblées législatives*.

done by a president, that the assembly itself could do in the same space of time.

In the case of an assembly and its president, we see judicial power in the simplest form in which it can exist, and in the simplest set of circumstances in which it can be placed. The judge single: the parties acting all the while under his eye. Complaint, judgment, execution, treading with instantaneous rapidity on the heels of contravention. Happy the suitor, if, in the other cases of procedure, instead of complication and delay, this simplicity of situation and celerity of dispatch had been taken for the standard of comparison[1] and model of imitation, by the founders and expositors of law.

The[2] regulations[+] which have been proposed above appear so simple and so suitable, that it is natural to suppose that they would have presented themselves to all political assemblies.

But if we proceed to consider what has been practised among different nations, we shall find that almost all these rules have been forgotten.[+] The English system, which most nearly approaches to them, differs in an essential point. It allows the president to deliberate and vote. All establishments have commenced in the times of ignorance: the first institutions could only be attempts more or less defective; but when experience renders their inconveniences sensible, the spirit of routine opposes itself to reform, and also prevents our perceiving the true sources of the evil.[3]

---

[1] Bentham 1791 'observation'.

[2] Remainder of the chapter from Dumont.

[3] Neither Dumont nor Bowring reproduces the following continuation of Essay V, which appears in some copies of Bentham 1791. The text breaks off in mid-sentence on the page preceding the beginning of Essay VI:

'CHAPTER II.

Of the Office of President.—*Number and Supply.*

*Questions, with Answers exhibiting Reasons.*

QUESTION 1. WHY always a person to preside?

ANSWER. 1. In order to collect the votes, on the proportionable numbers of which depends the genuineness of whatever may be given as the general will.

2. In order to apply, in less time than it would take for the Assembly at large to apply them, all such *remedies* as the laws of the Assembly have provided or allowed to be applied in case of any act done by any individual in *contravention* to those laws. The Assembly cannot act but by voting: voting, if according to knowledge, supposes debate; or at least the faculty of having recourse to debate, in proportion as it is thought needful; and voting'.

On the same page is a footnote, without a marker in the text, which reads: 'Whatever may be the advantages obtainable from the institution of a political Assembly, that of promptitude of action is certainly not of the number. The action of such an Assembly depends, in each instance, upon the reduction of many particular wills to one general one. But this reduction is a work of time; of which the greater quantity may naturally become requisite, the greater the number is of the objects upon which the process is to be performed.'

71

# CHAPTER VI.[a]
# OF THE MODE OF PROCEEDING IN A POLITICAL ASSEMBLY IN THE FORMATION OF ITS DECISIONS.

## §1. *Introductory Observations.*

T HE subject we are now about to engage in, is in its own nature abstract, intricate, and obscure. Of these undesirable qualities in the subject, but too strong a tincture must inevitably be imbibed by the work. To judge by the celerity with which a *motion* is oftentimes made, and an order framed in consequence, the path may at first glance appear short and simple. But, in this as in other instances, practice may be short and simple, where description and discussion are tedious and involved. To put in action the whole muscular system, is the work but of an instant; but to describe the parts concerned in that action, and the different modifications it admits of, is to exhaust the stores of a copious and recondite science.

For affording a clue to this labyrinth at the first entrance, no expedient seemed to promise better, than that of singling out, and laying before the reader at one view, the essential points upon which the due conduct of the business seemed principally to turn; suggesting at the same time such regulations as the dictates of utility seemed to prescribe in relation to those points. Chronological order, the order of the incidents, has for this purpose been broken in upon, lest these points of primary importance should have been lost, as it were, in the multitude of less essential details. But though broken in upon, it is not anywhere reversed: and, in the subsequent discussions, strict order will reassume its empire.[b]

On these few points turn the essential differences between the British and (what, as far as I have been able to learn, has been) the French practice in this line. In these points, too, if the reasoning which the reader will find as he advances be not erroneous, resides the singular excellence, or rather exclusive fitness, of the former mode.

---

[a] This chapter was originally published in 4to, in the year 1791.[1]

[b] Order, useful as it is in general to facilitate conception, and necessary as is the assistance it affords to the weakness of the human faculties, is good for nothing else: so that in the few cases where instruction can be administered to more advantage by dispensing with the laws of order than by the observance of them, to adhere to those laws with an inflexible pertinacity would be to sacrifice the end to the means.

---

[1] It was in fact not published but privately printed to form the bulk of 'Essay on Political Tactics'. In Bowring this footnote continued with a reproduction of the Preface to that work (see p. 1 above). Chapter VI in Bowring was based entirely on Bentham 1791, and made no use of the four chapters of Dumont (Chapters X, XV, XVI, and XVII) derived from the same source. As with Chapter V, significant differences between Bowring and Bentham 1791 are indicated in editorial footnotes. The Collation provides a complete account of the differences between the two editions.

In matters of inferior importance, invention has been set to work; in these, though equally disposed to have hazarded invention, I have found nothing to do but to copy.[a]

In this bye-corner, an observing eye may trace the original seed-plot of English liberty: it is in this hitherto neglected spot that the seeds of that invaluable production have germinated and grown up to their present maturity, scarce noticed by the husbandman, and unsuspected by the destroyer.

The importance of these uninviting forms is no fine-spun speculation— no fanciful conceit. Political liberty depends everywhere upon the free action and frequent and genuine manifestation of the public will: but the free action and genuine manifestation of that will, depend upon the mode of proceeding observed in going through the several steps that must be taken before any such result can be produced.

Without any such regulations as those here insisted on—in short, without any regulations at all—a general will, or pretended general will, may come now and then to be declared. But of what sort? Such an one as the will of him who gives his purse to save his life, or signs a deed he never read, or takes an oath with an *et cætera* at the end of it, is to the free and enlightened will of the individual. Without rules, the power of the assembly either evaporates in ineffectual struggles, or becomes a prey to the obstinate and overbearing: *Detur fortiori*, or rather *robustiori*,[1] would be its proper motto. Unanimity may glitter on the surface: but it is such unanimity as famine and imprisonment extort from an English jury. In a system of well-digested rules, such as the English practice, with little improvement, would supply, will be found the only buckler of defence that reflection can have against precipitancy, moderation against violence, modesty against arrogance, veracity against falsehood, simplicity against deception and intrigue.

Without discipline, public spirit stands as poor a chance in a numerous assembly, as valour in the field.

Happily the peaceful branch, though hitherto less understood than the military, is neither quite so difficult to learn nor quite so burthensome to

---

[a] I speak of the regulations themselves: for, as to the principles by which the propriety of regulations is to be tried, and the particular reasons on both sides deducible from those principles, these are matters which lie still open to the researches of invention in every province of the demesnes of law.

Considerations of expediency may have influenced practice long before they have found their way into books, or even into discourse. But, where this is the case, to report is to invent; for reason, till clothed in words, is scarce deserving of the name: it is but the embryo of reason, scarce distinguishable from instinct.

---

[1] 'Let it be given to the stronger' or 'the more robust'. A play on the phrase *detur digniori*—'let it be given to the more deserving', a variant of the traditional last words of Alexander the Great.

practise. The essential articles of it will be found comprised within the compass of a page.

It is the want of such a general will, the natural effect of the total want of discipline, that has been the great cause of the inefficiency and inutility so justly imputed to all former assemblies of the States-General of France; or, to speak correctly, it is in the non-formation of such will—in the perpetual failure of whatever efforts have been excited by the desire of forming one, that this inefficiency has consisted. But a political body lives only by the manifestation of its will. Here, then, intelligence is power; and to administer intelligence, is to give life.

The spirit of the people, the generosity of its superior classes, the unexampled virtue of the Sovereign, and the wisdom of the minister, all concur in promising to France a constitution which may soon be an object of envy, if it is not of imitation, to Great Britain. But inestimable as such a blessing would be, the benefit derivable from it will be found to hang upon so slender, and to many an eye imperceptible a thread, as the system of tactics, or the no-system, which in the form of their proceedings the regenerated assembly may happen to embrace. The pains employed in the construction of this great instrument of public felicity will prove but lost labour, if the only true method of working with it remains unpractised.

Powerful talents, and public-spirited dispositions, comprise the utmost good which the best possible constitution can produce. But of what avail are talents and dispositions, so long as either no decision is formed, or none that answers to its name?

Considerations of such essential importance as I shall have occasion to bring to view, can scarcely indeed at this interesting crisis, and at this era of inquiry, have escaped altogether the researches of an acute and ingenious nation; and the labours of many a pen better suited to the task have probably been employed ere now upon this great object. But as the success with which the public is served, depends upon the use which each man makes of his own powers, and not upon the reliance he places on those of other men—as this, like any other subject, may profit by being exhibited by different writers in different points of view—and as the mention of these more striking articles would be necessary, were it only to save the chain of reasoning that connects the whole, from appearing broken and obscure, the importance of them did not seem a sufficient warrant for the omission either of the provisions themselves, or of any part of the reasoning by which that importance is holden up to view.

In my endeavours to communicate such lights as my researches may be able to throw upon the subject, the following is, in general, the method I pursue:—In the first place are exhibited such *regulations*, relative to each head, as the dictates of utility appear to recommend; in the next place are subjoined, in the way of question and answer, the *reasons* by which such provisions came recommended to my notice.[a] After that, follows a view of the *British practice*, relative to the points in question; after that again, a view of what I have been able to collect relative to the *French practice*, the justification and confirmation of which, where it appears right—the correction of it, where it appears wrong—and the completion of it, where it appears deficient, is the principal object of the present work. Lastly, where occasion seemed to require, a few general *observations* are subjoined, containing such remarks as could not conveniently be brought under any of the former heads; particularly for the sake of placing different branches of the subject in a comprehensive and comparative point of view.

For the purpose of giving an idea of the French practice relative to these points, the fairest specimen, and that which would have rendered every other of small importance, would have been that of the States-General of France. But of this practice, it seems to be agreed that no documents are to be found. One may even see *a priori*, that nothing of the kind could well have had existence. Between the want of efficiency and the want of form, the connexion is in this instance so natural, that, in default of positive proofs, either of those circumstances might serve as a presumptive evidence of the other. If their proceedings had been attended with any effect, we should have seen the mode in which they proceeded: if their mode of proceeding had been in any tolerable degree suited to the purpose of giving birth to a general will, a general will would at times have been formed; and, being formed, would have been productive of some effect. *Nihil fecit* is the phrase in which some of the monkish historians have comprised the history of several of their kings.[b] The same history, with a small addition, may serve for all their national assemblies: *nihil fecerunt* gives the catalogue of their acts; *nullo modo*,[1] the form of their procedure.

Failing this source of intelligence, the next one should naturally turn to, is the practice of the few provincial states of ancient institution still subsisting in that great empire.[c] From the journals of these assemblies, if

---

[a] These reasons bear each of them a relation to some particular principle of the number of those laid down in Chapter I.[2] This will account for their being conceived in a form not always the most natural, and which consequently, were it not for the advantages dependent upon this sort of symmetry, would not have been the most eligible.

[b] Meaning by *nothing*, the foundation of no monasteries.

[c] *Viz.* Brittany, Languedoc, and Burgundy.[3]

---

[1] *Nihil fecit*, 'he did nothing'; *nihil fecerunt*, 'they did nothing'; *nullo modo*, 'with no method'.

[2] Bentham 1791 'Essay I'. For Dumont's remarks on Bentham's method, see p. 10 above.

[3] Prior to the Revolution, in approximately two-thirds of the territory of France, Crown officials were responsible for the collection of taxes. However, several large provinces, including Brittany,

made public, intelligence more or less satisfactory relative to this head could not but be afforded; but unfortunately I have not been able to hear of any such publication, and from circumstances I am strongly led to think no such publication has ever been made.

The only remaining source is that afforded by the modern provincial assemblies, instituted at first in two provinces only,[a] by way of experiment, in the years 1778 and 1779, and at length in the year 1787 communicated to the whole kingdom.[1] The regimen established in these assemblies, if it does not give the most ancient mode of proceeding known in France, gives, what for the purposes of instruction is much more valuable, the latest.

It is more so, in as much as through this medium may be obtained some sort of oblique view of the mode of proceeding observed in the old established provincial states. For, in drawing up a code of regulations for the first instituted of the provincial assemblies, those established for the provincial states compose the model which the committee employed on that business expressly declare themselves to have taken for the basis of their work.[b] In this code, adding to it the materials furnished by the succeeding establishments of the same kind, we may therefore view the quintessence of that part of the national stock of wisdom which has applied itself to this important subject.

Partly for shortness, partly for precision's sake, I have chosen all along, as far as the nature of the case would give leave, to exhibit the proposed regulations in the very words in which they might be couched. This practice, which in all authoritative compositions of this nature will be seen to be absolutely necessary, is, in unauthoritative ones, highly useful at least, and convenient. By specification, description is saved, attention

[a] Berry and Haute Guyenne.

[b] Procès-Verbal de l'Assemblée Provinciale de Berri, 23 November 1778.[2] The declaration here spoken of does not, it is true, in express terms comprise any other regulations than those relative to the '*convocation* and the *formation*' of the assemblies in question; but, as the committee who on that day presented a code of regulations relative to those two heads, are the same also who, three days afterwards, present another code relative to the *mode of proceeding* to be observed, it cannot be supposed that the documents, which had been taken for a model on the first of those occasions, were neglected on the second.

Burgundy, and Languedoc, maintained Provincial Estates, representative bodies which retained the right of consent to royal taxation and negotiated directly with the King. The Provincial Estates performed various administrative tasks in addition to their fiscal role.

[1] In 1778 Jacques Necker (1732–1804), Swiss banker, Director General of Finances 1777–81 and 1788–90, put forward plans for four experimental provincial assemblies, in Berry, Haute-Guyenne, Dauphiné, and the Bourbonnais. However, only the first two of these assemblies came into being, in 1778 and 1779 respectively. A royal edict of June 1787 announced the extension of provincial assemblies throughout France; provincial assemblies met in nineteen regions in November 1787, but not one lasted for more than a month and they were not reconvened.

[2] *Collection des procès-verbaux de l'Assemblée provinciale du Berri*, 3 vols., Bourges, 1787, i. 27–51.

arrested, and expectation satisfied: description, however well performed, leaves the main work still undone.

§2. *Principal points to be attended to in the mode of proceeding relative to the formation of the acts*[a] *of a political assembly.*

1. IDENTITY of the terms of the *proposition*[b] with those of the *act* proposed.
2. FIXATION of the terms of the proposition by *writing.*
3. UNITY of the subject of debate kept inviolate.
4. DISTINCTNESS of the process of *debating* from that of *voting.*
5. In *debating,* NO FIXED ORDER of pre-audience.
6. The *votes* given not one after another, but ALL AT ONCE.[c]

*Regulations proposed relative to the above points.*

ARTICLE I. Nothing shall be deemed to be the act of the assembly, that has not been proposed in and to the assembly by a motion made for that purpose,[d] put to the vote, and adopted by the majority of the votes.[e]

ART. II. Every proposition, designed to give birth to an act of the assembly, shall be exhibited in *writing* by the mover, and conceived in the

---

[a] *i. e.* as well momentary and particular *orders* and *resolutions* as permanent and general *laws;* so likewise *addresses,* declarations of *opinion* (termed also *resolutions* in the British practice,) and *reports.*

[b] *i. e.* whether *motion* or *bill,* or draught of any other sort of act of assembly, not comprised under the name of *motion.*[1]

[c] This last point is not altogether of equal importance with the preceding ones: but as it is so naturally connected with the 4th and 5th, and concurs with them in marking the opposition between the French and British practice, it was not thought worth while to separate it from them.

[d] This is according to the British practice. In two subsequent chapters relative to the previous promulgation of motions and bills, I shall have occasion to propose an additional mode of introducing propositions;[2] which mode, if adopted, would require an alteration to be made in the penning of this article: but, however different from this in other respects, it is, with respect to the points here noted, grounded on the same principles.

[e] *i. e.* by at least a *comparative* majority of the number of voters *present.*[3] Shall the majority of the voters *present* be sufficient, if it falls short of amounting to a majority of the whole number of persons entitled to vote?[4]

---

[1] Bentham 1791 continues: 'See Essay I.' This subject is not discussed in Chap. I above.

[2] A reference to two uncompleted chapters (Essay VI, Chapters XII, 'Of the *extemporaneous* Promulgation of *Motions*', and XIII, 'Of the *extemporaneous* Promulgation of *Amendments*'), which appear on Bentham's plan of the contents of his projected 'Essays on Political Tactics'. See the Table at p. 176 below.

[3] Bentham 1791 continues: 'Of the difference between a *comparative* and an *absolute* majority, see *infra,* Ch. . . .' In fact see p. 69 n. above.

[4] Bentham 1791 continues: 'See this question discussed in Essay IV.' This question is not discussed in Chap. IV above.

very terms, neither more nor fewer, by which it is designed such act should stand expressed.[a]

ART. III. A proposition of any kind having been once received,—until that proposition has been disposed of, no other motion shall be made, unless for one or other of three purposes:—

1. To offer an *amendment* to the proposition already on the carpet;

2. To propose a mode of putting an end to the business without decision; or

3. To reclaim the execution of some law of order at the instant of its infringement.

ART. IV. The process of *debating* and that of *voting* are distinct processes; nor shall the latter be entered upon till after the former is gone through.

ART. V. In debating, no member, after the author of the motion, shall have the right of speaking before any other,[b] but {he who first offers himself shall be first heard,[c] or else} the competition for pre-audience shall be decided by lot.[d]

ART. VI. Votes, when given openly, shall be given, not one after another, but as near as may be, all together.

§3. —POINTS I. and II. *Motion written, and in terminis.*[1]

*Questions, with Answers exhibiting reasons.*

Question I. Why nothing to be given as the act of the assembly that has not been put to the vote, and carried in the assembly?

Answer: This is only saying in other words that no act of the assembly shall be forged.

*British practice.*—From several orders of the House of Lords, made

[a] Form for a motion; *i. e.* for the introducing of a proposition:—'I, the undersigned, propose the Draught following, to be made an Act of the Assembly.' (Signed) 'A. M.'

*N.B.*—Then give the order, resolution, address, report, bill, or whatever other act it be, *in terminis*, whether it consist of six words or six hundred pages, beginning with its title, when it has one.

[b] In a subsequent chapter, I endeavour to show that the author of a motion ought to be heard in support of it, immediately *after*, but not, as is the British practice, *before* he makes it.[2]

[c,d] The passage in brackets expresses the British practice; the remainder, an operation which I have ventured to recommend as a preferable one in a succeeding chapter, in which I propose an instantaneous mode of performing it:[3] but the main point, as will be seen, is the putting a negative upon all fixed order; and in that respect both methods agree.

[1] Dumont Chapter X, 'Motion écrite d'avance', is based on this section.

[2] See pp. 125–6 below.

[3] Probably a reference to the uncompleted chapter (Essay VI, Chapter XXVII, 'On the Election of *Speakers* in debate, in case of *competition*') which appears on Bentham's plan of the contents of his projected 'Essays on Political Tactics'. See the Table at p. 176 below.

towards the beginning of the last century, it should seem, that about that period attempts to commit such forgeries had been made.[a] A counter-faction of this kind could not well have had for its author any other person than either the ministerial officer (the clerk) who has the penning of the journals, or the presiding officer (the Speaker), under whose authority and command the other acts.

The practice of the House of Commons furnishes two examples, and, as far as appears, but two, of an incongruity, the notice of which may serve by way of illustration to this rule.

One is that of a memorandum on the journals, that 'the Speaker, by leave of the House, declared it to be their sense,' so and so.[b] Was a motion in those words made, put to the vote, and carried? If not, no leave of the House was given, no sense of the House was taken: in the other supposition, the history given in this memorandum, which is a long and rather a perplexed one, was of no use. The usual introduction, the word *ordered*, or the word *resolved*, would have been a much more intelligible one, and just as proper in this case as in any other.

2. As to the other instance. At the commencement of every session, immediately upon the return of the Commons from the House of Lords, where they have been all hearing the king's speech in a place not big enough to hold a quarter of their number, before any other business is done, a bill, in pursuance of ancient orders, is read by the clerk, by direction of the Speaker, for form's sake.[c]

'This custom,' says Mr. Hatsell,[d] 'I understand to be nothing more than a claim of right of the Commons, that they are at liberty to proceed in the first place, upon any thing they think material, without being limited to give a preference to the subjects contained in the king's speech.' That such was the reason, may be, and upon the strength of such respectable authority, I suppose is, very true. But such a form is as absurd in itself as incompetent to the end. This thing called a *bill*, what title can it be said to

---

[a] Lords' Orders, Art. 45. Lords' Journals, 14th December 1621; 23d February 1623; 20th May 1626.[1]

[b] Commons' Journals, 27th January 1697.

[c] Commons' Journals, 22d March 1603; 7th April 1614; 3d February 1620; 21st February 1623.

[d] Precedents of Proceedings in the House of Commons, with Observations, by John Hatsell, Esq., First Clerk of the House, 1785. Vol. I. p. 59.[2]

---

[1] The orders referred to stipulate that no order should be entered in the Journals of the House of Lords without the assent of the House.

[2] The passage quoted is from the second edition, ii. 59 (not i. 59). It should read: 'I understand the custom of reading a Bill immediately on the return from the House of Lords, to be nothing more than a claim of right of the Commons, that they are at liberty to proceed, in the first place, upon any matter which they think material, without being limited to give a preference to the subjects contained in the King's speech.'

have to that name? The clerk reads it, because the Speaker orders him: whence comes it? From the Lords? Not so: for as yet they have done nothing, any more than the Commons. From the Speaker? But he has no right to make so much as a motion for leave to bring in a bill, much less to bring in a bill without leave. A bill is a composition presented by some member: the thing here called a bill, is a child without a father, born, like Melchisedec, in the way of equivocal generation.[1] The case seems to be, that at the time this order was established, no clear idea of the mode of generation of an act of the House seems to have been as yet formed. It was not as yet understood, that a composition, to be an act of the House—that is, of all, or a majority of the members—must, if it took its rise in the House, have begun by being the act of some one member. But to appear to be the act of some member, it must have been exhibited by him as such; and to make such exhibition, is to make a motion.

Years after this period, or these periods (take any of them) in the House of Lords, as we have just been seeing, things would be starting up, pretending to be acts of the House—orders, resolutions, rules—nobody knew how. There seems to be but too much ground for apprehending that this may still be liable to be the case in the French practice. But of this a little further on.

Make what one will of it, being no act of the House, it is no exertion of any right of the House: it answers not that purpose, any more than any other.

The right in question, so far from receiving any support from this futile form, neither requires nor admits of any support whatever. It exists of necessity in the first instance: it follows from the very constitution of that and every other political assembly. Nothing can be done—nothing can be expressed by the House, without being done, without being expressed, at some time or other, by some member of the House: expressed either *viva voce* or by writing, or in some other mode, no matter what—say, for instance, *viva voce*, by speaking. But when a man is up to speak, who shall say what it is he will speak, abstraction made of any antecedent rule? He speaks not to the business offered to the House by the king, but to that or any other business, as he thinks fit. For the House therefore to be in possession of this right, there can need nothing but the non-existence of a rule to the contrary.

The futility of this form appeared on the same recent occasion on which the establishment of it was recognised. On the 15th of November 1763, before this pretended bill was read, Mr. Wilkes and Mr. George Grenville start up together—Mr. Wilkes, to tell his own story about a breach of privilege, and Mr. Grenville (then minister) with a message on the same

---

[1] Melchizedek is described thus in Hebrews 7: 3: 'Without father, without mother, without descent, having neither beginning of days nor end of life'.

subject from the king. Great debates which should be heard first—Mr. Wilkes's speech, Mr. Grenville's speech, or the bill: it was carried at last in favour of the bill.[a] What was got by this? The House had the pleasure of hearing this bill; and then there was the same matter to settle—who should be heard first,—Mr. Wilkes, or Mr. Grenville, as before.[1]

Question II. Why in writing?

Answer: 1. Because it is only by writing that the tenor of any discourse can be fixed for any length of time.

2. It is only by such fixation that it can be ascertained that the draught exhibited is capable of standing as a resolution of the assembly, in the very words in which it is proposed.

Question III. Why put into writing by him who makes it, and not by any one else?

Answer: 1. Because no third person can so well tell what it is a man means as he himself can. If the words of it, as committed to writing, are chosen by anybody else, the utmost accuracy it can aspire to in the hands of such third person is, the being as exactly representative of the meaning of the avowed author of the motion, as if he himself had chosen them. But the chances are rather against its possessing that extreme degree of accuracy; and were they ever so much in favour of it, yet so long as there is the smallest chance on the other side, such chance will form a conclusive reason against the committing the business of penning the motion to anybody else.

2. To save time. Between the penner and the author, where they are different persons, a conversation of some sort must be carried on. This conversation may, and frequently must, occasion discussions and disputes. The sense of the author may be perverted by accident or design: or, where no such perversion takes place or was intended, it may be suspected. All this while, business must be at a stand, and the assembly sitting to no purpose.

Let it be of the mover's penning; and while he is about it, no part of the assembly's time is taken up. He may have penned it out of the house, and ought so to do (as will be seen farther on) whenever it can be done.

3. To promote maturity of composition.—If the author of a motion is permitted to rely on a third person for the penning of it, such permission will be liable to produce hasty indigested motions, the impropriety of which the author himself, had he been obliged to put them to writing, might have discovered. Writing summons up the attention to apply itself to the

[a] II. Hatsell, 59.

---

[1] On 15 November 1763 the House of Commons passed a motion claiming that a publication by John Wilkes (1727–97), MP, was a seditious libel. George Grenville (1712–70), First Lord of the Treasury, led the attack on Wilkes. It appears from the *Commons Journals*, xxix. 667–8 that Grenville spoke first.

discourse written, and furnishes it with a fixed subject. Whoever, in any instance, has corrected what he had once written, may find, in that single instance, a reason fully sufficient to justify the establishment of this rule.

Question IV. Why in the very words in which, when made an act of the assembly, it is proposed to stand?

Answer: 1. Because no other terms can express, with the certainty of being accurate, the object which the author of the motion proposes to the House. The composition given as the act of the assembly, is not really its act, any otherwise than as far as it is the very composition which those, whose votes form the decision of the assembly, have given their votes in favour of. If the discourse they had voted for differs, in a single word for example, from the discourse exhibited by the author of the motion, then, as to such word, it is not of his penning; which, as has just been proved, it ought to be. The only discourse they can have meant to adopt, the only discourse they can all of them, and from the beginning, have had under view, is, to a word, the very discourse presented to them by the mover: if the resolution given in their name by any one else—the secretary, for instance, or the president—differs from that original in a single word, it is, *pro tanto*, a forgery.

I say, in a *single word:* for every one knows, that in a single word may be comprised the most important alterations: take, for instance, the word *not*.[a]

*British practice.*—In every art, the proper mode, how simple soever, and how incontestably soever, when once hit upon and clearly stated, it appears to be a proper one, and even the only proper one, is seldom the one pitched upon at first.

In the British House of Commons it was the ancient practice, we are informed by Mr. Hatsell,[b] 'for the Speaker to collect the sense of the House from the debate, and from thence to form a question, on which to take the opinion of the House; but this,' adds he, 'has been long discontinued; and at present the usual, and *almost* universal method is, for the member who moves a question to put it into writing, and deliver it to the Speaker; who, when it has been seconded, proposes it to the House, and then the House are said to be in possession of the question.'[1]

---

[a] I lay out of consideration at present the case of an *amendment*: of which hereafter.[2] If an amendment is proposed, it is by some other member, who has the same right to propose the alteration, as the author of the original motion had to propose such motion. The amendment being carried, the amended motion comes instead of the original motion; and the resolution passed by the assembly has two authors—two equally known and avowed authors, instead of one.

[b] II. Hatsell, 81.

---

[1] The passage in fact appears at pp. 81–2. The word 'almost' is not italicized in Hatsell.
[2] See Chapter XII, p. 138 below.

From Lord Clarendon's account of his exploits in the character of chairman of a committee,[a] there appears some reason to suspect, that at that time the practice spoken of in the above passage still subsisted:[1] otherwise it is not easy to conceive how that able statesman could have done so much mischief as he boasts of.

The way he took was, amongst other things, to report, which he says he frequently did, two or three votes directly contrary to each other. He must therefore have contributed, more or less, to the making of them so, or the '*entanglement*' he speaks of would not in any degree have been, what he boasts of its being, his work. Whatever had been their contrariety, had they been moved *in terminis*, and in writing, by their respective authors, it would not have been in his power to have had any share in it.

That such, at any rate, was the practice in the year 1620, two or three and twenty years before the period Lord Clarendon speaks of, appears from the Commons' journal of that year: in which, on an occasion where the Speaker's conduct had been the subject of animadversion, in the course of the debates, amongst other charges is that of a practice he was in, of '*intricating the question*,' and another, of his having '*made many plausible motions abortive*.'[b]

---

[a] History of the Rebellion, b. iii. vol. i. p. 275, 8vo edition, 1705.[2]

[b] Commons Journals, 9th March 1620.

Since this sheet was sent to the press, chance has led me to a passage in the journals of the House of Commons, by which it appears, that even so late as the year 1675 the identity of the terms of the act of the House with those of the motion was not invariably preserved. I will state it at length, the rather as, while it exemplifies the deviation from that rule, it may also serve to exemplify and demonstrate the ill consequences of such deviation.

The whole passage is as follows:—'A debate arising in the House touching the ancient order and course of the House in the method of raising supplies, and concerning the precedency of the lesser sum;

The House, upon the question, did resolve and declare it an ancient order of the House, That when there comes a question between the greater and lesser sum, or the longer or shorter time, the least sum and longest time ought first to be put to the question.'[3]

Upon the face of this passage two propositions may be laid down as undeniable:—

1*st*, That the words of it are not all of them the same, without any variation, as those employed by the author of the motion which gave birth to it.

2*dly*, That if in any part of it such identity was preserved, it is impossible to say how far such part extends, it being impossible to say where it begins.

---

[1] Bentham 1791 adds after 'a committee': 'as alluded to on a former occasion'. There is no earlier reference to Lord Clarendon in Bentham's 1791 fragment.

[2] Edward Hyde (1609–74), Earl of Clarendon, was on 11 July 1641 elected to chair a Committee of the Whole House to discuss a Bill for the extirpation of episcopacy (the so-called 'Root and Branch Bill'). About the experience he wrote: 'When They were in the heat and passion of the Debate, they oftentimes were entangled in their questions; so that when He Reported to the House the work of the day, he did frequently Report two or three Votes directly contrary to each other, which, in the heat of their debate, they had unawares run into.' *The History of the Rebellion and Civil Wars in England, Begun in the Year 1641*, 3 vols., Oxford, 1705, i. 276 (not 275).     [3] *Commons Journals*, ix. 367.

*French Practice.—Provincial Assemblies.*

—What the practice has been in the French assemblies of old standing, such as the Provincial States and the Chambers of Parliament, does not appear, in a direct way, from any documents I have been able to meet with. The affectation of secresy, which, till the present auspicious period, has pervaded the whole system of French, as in general of monarchical government, keeps everything of this sort under a cloud.

The part that looks most like the authentic, and, if one may so say, the enactive part of it, is that which begins at these words: *'that when there comes a question between the greater and lesser sum . . .'*

But this cannot be taken for the beginning of the authentic part, for two reasons:—

1. Because these words, in order to make up, along with the succeeding one, a sentence capable of officiating in the character of an act of the House, require to be preceded by the word *resolved*, or (to use the phraseology that comes nearest to that word in the passage in question) by the words *resolved and declared*. But in this passage no such word or words stand immediately precedent to the words in question: nor can any form of words capable of answering that purpose be found in it, without going farther back, and that so far as to involve some words which upon the face of them could not have been the words of the author of the motion, could not have been the words of the House.

To get the complement of words necessary to make out an intelligible proposition, the least remote ones one can begin with are the words, 'The House upon the question did resolve and declare.' But these, it is evident, could not have been the words of the House, nor words given by the author of the motion as designed to be adopted by the House. They are not words of an act of the House, but words used by a third person in speaking of an act of the House.

2. Another reason why the part beginning at the words, *'that when there comes a question,'* cannot be taken as comprising all the words employed by the author of the motion, is, that between these words and the first words of the paragraph come others, the import of which forms an essential part of the import, whatever it be, of the act of the House; viz. those which speak of the antiquity of the regulation, the establishment of which was in view:—'*The House, upon the question, did resolve and declare it to be an ancient order of the House.*' These words, *'an ancient order,'* we see, are in their import inseparably interwoven with the preceding ones, which we have seen must have been words, not of the House, not of the author of the motion, but of a third person, the penner of the journals.

So far as to the fact of the uncertainty: now as to the ill effects of it. They consist in this, that as you cannot tell what part of the passage, if any, was in the words of the act of the House, you cannot tell to what cases the act of the House meant to extend itself. This we shall see immediately.

The first paragraph, not amounting of itself to an intelligible proposition—not amounting to a complete grammatical sentence, is inextricably interwoven with the second. They form two parts of the same sentence; and in both parts there is matter equally capable of being considered as representative of a part of the import of the act of the House. As you cannot tell where the language of the historiographer of the House ends, and where the language of the House itself begins,—it may be, that both paragraphs were expressive of the sense of the House; it may be, that only the latter was.

Now then comes the uncertainty and the mischief. The last paragraph gives the proposition generally, and without restriction: the former paragraph applies a restrictive clause. The last gives to understand, that in all cases where divers sums, meaning sums of

But of the general practice and notions on this head, the regimen prescribed to, or imagined by, the lately instituted provincial assemblies, affords pretty good presumptive evidence: and that evidence shows the practice in this respect to have been pretty much on a par with the English, at the time spoken of by Lord Clarendon; that is, about a century and a half ago.

money, are in question, it is the least sum that is to be put to the question first: the former paragraph contradicts this proposition in its character of an universal one, and says, that the only case to which this rule is to be deemed to extend, is that where the business upon the carpet is the business of supply—where the question is relative to '*the method of raising supplies.*' What is the consequence? That it is only in the case where the question is touching *the method of raising supplies,* that this passage in the journals affords any certain rule: and that, as to all other questions in which sums of money may be concerned, it not only affords no certainty, but presents a rule with which the certainty of any conclusion that can be formed relative to the subject is absolutely incompatible. The absence of all rule leaves the subject open to such other means of decision as the nature of it comports; but an ambiguous rule is mortal to all certainty while it lasts, and renders all true and regular decisions relative to that subject impossible.

Observe how subservient a rule, thus circumstanced, is to the purposes of disingenuous altercation.

A debate arises on a question not relating to supply. Does it suit your purpose to have the rule attach upon this question?—present the last paragraph alone. Does it suit your purpose to take the question out of the rule?—produce both paragraphs together.

Collateral considerations only make the confusion thicker: such lights as are to be collected from the situation of the legislators point one way; the interpretation given by subsequent practice points the other.

It is tolerably evident, that in the minds of the authors this rule had no other extent than what related to the single business of supply. Where money was concerned, the great object with them was how to keep their purses as close shut as possible against the swindler on the throne: it was no part of their purpose to sit down and frame a set of general principles, fit to enter into the composition of a regular code. How should it have been, when down to the present hour none of their successors have dared ever to harbour any such ambitious thoughts?

Besides that, the rule is given as an ancient one; and the farther back we go in the history of the House of Commons (setting aside the period of its short-lived tyranny during the civil wars) the less we find them have to do with money for any other purpose than the simple one of affording a temporary relief to the necessities of the Crown.

On the other hand, subsequent practice is in favour of the more general construction: in a question noways relating to the business of affording supplies to the crown, we shall find, in a succeeding chapter, a curious instance: and such, for aught I know, may be the practice in every other instance. Here, then, to increase the confusion, we have precedent against reason; and all for want of the observance of a rule of composition so simple in its conception, and so easy in practice.

To exhibit what ought to have been done, as well as what ought not to have been done, I will now give the order in question as it ought to have stood, and as it would have stood had it been penned on the same plan with others that precede and follow it in the same volume, and even in the same leaf. The words in brackets express the dubious parts, the retention or omission of which will give the different constructions of which the passage, as it stands in the journals, is susceptible:—

'The reports of the committees,' says an author who has given us a general account of the constitution, discipline, and proceedings of these assemblies,[a] 'the reports of the committees are made with a good deal of care. After having well settled the question, an account is given of the different opinions {*avis;*} of the effect produced by such and such an opinion {*opinion;*} of the number of persons who concurred in it; of those who differed from it, and why; of the reasons {*motifs*} which occasioned each proposition to be adopted or rejected, in part or in the whole; in short, of the opinions {*avis*} which prevailed generally, *or* of that which was adopted.'

'This method,' adds the author, 'ought always to be that of a committee. The assembly names them, not to pronounce a decision, but to elucidate an affair, and put the assembly in a way to judge.'

This elaborate and *careful* plan, which, according to the author's notion, *ought to be the plan of every committee,* affords a pretty strong presumption, that in those assemblies (supposing this account to be a just one) the simple principle of giving a determinate existence in writing to every proposition, and so proceeding, either to receive that proposition (with or without amendments,) or to reject it, was not known. The resolutions of the meeting, to judge from this account, are jumbled with the minutes of the proceedings, and the accounts of the debates: in the conception of the author, they are unquestionably.

As this is a subject of the first importance to the precision of the proceedings in the great national assembly to which it is my ambition to be of use, to the genuineness as well as clearness of the results, and to the efficacious development of their powers, it may be worth while to give this account a pretty minute consideration, for the purpose of comparing the proceedings as here described, with the standard above laid down.

1. '*After having well settled the question—{Après avoir bien posé la question.'*} What question? The question, meaning the motion or proposi-

| *The passage as it stands.* | *The resolution as it ought to have been given in by the author of the motion, and entered by the clerk.* |
|---|---|
| A debate arising in the House touching the ancient order and course of the House in the method of raising supplies, and concerning the precedency of the lesser sum; | Resolved, {and it is hereby declared to be an ancient order of the House,} that when {in matter of supply} there comes a question between the greater and the lesser sum, or between the longer and the shorter time, the least sum and the longest time ought first to be put to the question. |
| The House upon the question did resolve and declare it an ancient order of the House, that when there comes a question between the greater and lesser sum, or the longer or shorter time, the least sum and longest time ought first to be put to the question. | |

[a] Résultat des Assemblées Provinciales, p. 18.[1]

---

[1] Charles Marie, Marquis de Créquy (1737–1801), *Résultat des assemblées provinciales, à l'usage des états d'une province* [i.e. of Artois], Brussels, 1788.

tion in question, if delivered in, in writing, by the author himself, can neither require to be settled, nor admit of it. It has settled itself. It may require amending indeed; but that is a very different operation from settling.

2. 'After having well settled the question, *an account is given of the different opinions upon it—{on rend compte des différens avis.'}* What are these opinions?—these *avis?* They are not decisions upon the question: they are not votes given towards forming such decision. Each question, when put upon a single motion, can admit of but one of two decisions—adoption, or rejection: each vote can admit of but one of three modifications—for the question, against the question, or neuter.[a] *Avis* is perhaps, here, put for *argument*—argument used in course of the debate.

3. 'Account is given *of the effect which such or such an opinion produced—[de l'effet qu'a produit telle ou telle opinion:'}*—a further reason for supposing that *avis*, as well as *opinion*, here means argument. The effect that a decision produces, requires no account—no separate account: it produces the adoption of the resolution proposed, or the rejection of it: the resolution, if adopted, needs no account—it speaks for itself. It not only does not stand in need of any account—it admits of none: a composition given under that name, if it be in the same terms with those of the resolution, is not an *account* of that resolution, but the thing itself: if in different terms, then, so far as the difference extends, the account it gives is a false one.

A *vote*, if that were meant by *avis* and *opinion*, requires not, any more than the decision it has produced, or failed of producing, any *account:* it is given one way or the other, and the effect of it appears by the decision—by the adoption or rejection of the resolution proposed.

4. *Of the number of the persons that concurred in it* {in such opinion or argument}—*of those who differed from it, and why*—{de celles qui s'en sont éloignées, et pourquoi.} This *why*, this *pourquoi*, I must confess, I know not very well what to make of. I thought the *opinions* or *avis* had been themselves the *arguments*, and included the *reasons:* these *pourquois*, then, must have been the reasons of those reasons.

5. *Of the reasons* {motifs} *which occasioned a proposition to be adopted or rejected, in part or in the whole*—{des motifs qui ont fait adopter une proposition, en partie ou en total.}

The perplexity gets thicker and thicker: here we have not only reasons upon reasons, but reasons upon *them;* for *motifs* must surely here, as in French it does commonly, when spoken of with reference to an opinion, mean reasons—it cannot mean what in English we term *motives*. It can never have been meant, that, in these committees, the several members get up, and render an account of the motives that have given birth to their

[a] See Ch. XIV. *Of Voting*, p. 143.

respective votes; saying, one of them, it was patriotism; another, it was the love of reputation; another, it was sympathy for the proposer; another, it was antipathy to the opposers; another, it was the hope of gaining a personal advantage by it that determined me: as little is it likely that the penner of the report should have taken upon himself thus to answer for each man's motives.

6. *Lastly, Of the opinions* {avis} *which prevailed generally;* or *of that which was adopted*—{enfin, des avis qui ont prévalu généralement, *ou* de celui qui a été adopté.}

This is still more perplexing than before. What means this opposition between *prevailing generally*, and *being adopted?* and how is it that the opinions which may prevail generally are *several*, while the opinion that can be adopted is but *one?* If by *avis* is meant here *décisions*—decisions of adoption or rejection, on different questions you may have certainly as many decisions—in short, one or other of exactly twice as many decisions as there are questions. If by *avis* is meant here opinions given separately by the different members upon occasion of the same subject—discourses delivered, which if adopted by the assembly would have been so many *resolutions of opinion,*—these, if never put to the vote, are not acts of the meeting—acts of the body, but mere acts of the individuals. Yet after all, of this set of opinions there is (it seems, according to this author) one, and but one, which has been adopted. Has it, then, been adopted? It is then an act of the committee—a resolution of opinion passed by the committee. On the other hand, if only one of the set has been adopted, how is it that the rest,—which, since they are thus [contrasted][1] with that one, must, it should seem, have been opposite and contrary to it,—can have been *generally received?* A proposition cannot be said to have been generally received by a meeting of any kind, if it has not been received by a majority: and if it has really been received by a majority, how can it fail of having been adopted? An account like this puts one in mind of the grammatical history of the cake:—G got it, and yet H had it.[2]

Considering this confusion as the work of the anonymous author, it would not have been worth all this notice: but the practice, of which the *éloge* is thus given, must surely itself have been very confused, or it could scarcely have given birth to an account so perfectly confused.

Nothing like this is to be found in the reports of any English committee I ever met with or heard of. They do not report so much as their own

[1] Bowring 'constructed'. The preferred reading is taken from a correction made in Samuel Bentham's hand to his copy of the 1791 'Essay on Political Tactics' (in the University College London Bentham collection, shelfmark 2.E5).

[2] This is a reference to a children's rhyme designed to teach the alphabet. It is actually about an apple pie, not a cake. Part of the rhyme reads: 'G got it. H had it.' It is printed in *The Child's New Play-Thing: being a Spelling-Book intended to make the Learning to Read, a Diversion instead of a Task*, London, 1743.

*minutes;* much less do they report their own *debates:* no *opinion* is there given, which is not the opinion of the whole. Is a resolution of opinion proposed? If rejected, no traces of it appear; if adopted, it is given, not as the resolution of A or B, but as the resolution of the committee. Is a statement of any affair, or history of any transaction, given? One member, it is true, may have penned and proposed one part—another member another part; but neither the one part nor the other would have stood in the report, if they had not respectively been acceded to by a majority of the committee—if they had not, each of them, been the act of the whole.

Were a composition, like the one thus described, presented, under the name of the report of a committee, to a British House of Commons, what would they say? They would say, 'This is no report; you must go back again, and make one.' They would send it back to be *re-committed.* While A says one thing, and B, neither assenting to nor dissenting from what A has said, says another, this is no report of a committee: the report of a committee is what is said throughout by the major part of the committee, or by the whole.

But these, it may perhaps be observed, are but reports of *committees.* The committees, of which these are the reports, are very small assemblies, composed of a smaller number of members than what is commonly to be met with in the least numerous committees of a British House of Commons. The members may therefore be considered as acting in their individual capacity: and the reports, given under the name of such committees, may be considered as reports made by individuals. The reports of such committees as these may therefore be thus far informal, and yet the proceedings of the entire assemblies, to which these reports are made, be regular and exact.

Unfortunately, the account given in the same book of the method in which the decision of the assembly itself is formed (I should rather say, of the paper published as the decision of such assembly,) seems to indicate but too plainly, that the only simple and true method of forming such a decision is not less widely departed from in the one sort of meeting, than in the other.

'The opinion once formed by a plurality of voices (votes) {*voix,*}' says the author above quoted,[a] 'then comes the time for entering it (writing it) {*l'écrire*} upon the minutes. But this operation (drawing up) {*rédaction*}, *requiring a considerable time,* the assemblies name *committee-men* to perform it, and the meeting of the next day opens with the extract of the minutes of the day preceding. This regulation, highly beneficial as it is, *since it saves time,* may be productive however of a mischief.'

If this account be just, it is impossible that the principle of the identity between the motion and the act of the assembly, should have been

[a] Résultat, p. 27.

89

observed in these assemblies. For drawing up such act, no committee could have been either necessary, or of any use: no time could have been saved, but a great deal of time sadly wasted and consumed. The act, upon the only just and simple principle the nature of the case admits of, is already *drawn up* by him who moves it: to enter it upon the minutes is work—not for a committee, but for a copying clerk. Committee-men may be of use, to give a look occasionally to the journals, and see whether the secretary has done his business properly; that is, whether he has entered all the acts, and whether each of them be an exact copy of the original draught: but such occasional inspection is a very different thing from their doing of that business themselves.

The mischief here apprehended by the commentator is, that of the assemblies in general following, upon this occasion, the example which, in a passage which I have had occasion to quote elsewhere,[1] he takes notice of as having been set by the provincial assembly of Tours.[2] This assembly, it should seem, had conceived it proper to see what it was their committee-men had been making them say, and not to let the account thus given stand as definitive, till they, the assembly, had heard it read to them. The commentator, full of diffidence of the assembly itself, lest it should alter its own acts or pretended acts, is as full of confidence in their committee-men. It never occurs to him that, either through design or misconception, the latter can misrepresent, or upon just grounds be suspected of misrepresenting, an act which, under such circumstances it must be so difficult to represent at all, and which in truth can scarcely be said to have existence.

Turn to the journals of these assemblies, and, what is more, to the royal edicts published for the regulation of their discipline, and we shall find them confirm, in this respect, the account given of them by their commentator.

'In the case where divers opinions {*avis*} shall have manifested themselves, the assembly,' says the royal edict for Haute Guyenne,[a] '*shall be obliged* to reduce them to two; and that which has the plurality of votes {*suffrages*} shall form the act of the assembly {*la délibération.*'}

What *must* be done, is done somehow or other, however badly: and therefore, an assembly ordered by royal authority to reduce its *avis*

---

[a] Art. 9, page 14, of the journal of 1779.[3] This of Haute Guyenne is the second of the two original assemblies (Berri being the first,) the constitution of which was taken as a model for the others, since established all together in 1787.

[1] In Bentham 1791, the following footnote appears at this point: 'Essay IV, Ch. |    | Hours of sitting.' However, no reference to the provincial assembly at Tours appears in Chapter IV.

[2] See Créquy, *Résultat*, p. 27.

[3] *Collection des procès-verbaux des séances de l'Assemblée provinciale de Haute-Guienne, tenues à Villefranche, ès années 1779, 1780, 1782, 1784 et 1786; avec la permission du Roi*, 2 vols., Paris, 1787, i. 14.

(whatever is meant by *avis*) to two, will contrive to do so. But upon the principle of the identity of the terms of the motion and those of the resolution—and supposing only one motion upon the carpet at a time—and supposing the votes to be given upon that one, no assembly could contrive to do otherwise. *For* or *against* the motion—the motion adopted or rejected—there is no other alternative.

The truth is, that these different *avis*, which the royal penman considers as liable to be produced upon a given subject—these *avis*, as far as they can be said to be anything, seem to have been so many different propositions—so many different motions, which were to be going on and debating at the same time. They are not votes at least; for votes {*suffrages*} it is understood, are to be given upon them. Taking them for motions, why the number of them should undergo this reduction, is not by any means made apparent. If all are consistent, why not let them all pass into resolutions, if the assembly choose it? If any are inconsistent with others that are preferred, the assembly, one should think, might be trusted to for not passing them: if a man has not sense to keep him from falling into inconsistencies, it is not a royal edict that will give it him.

The assembly accepts this regulation,[a] adding an amendment, palliating in some degree the inconvenience arising from a fixed order of speaking, as hinted at on a preceding occasion,[b] and more fully developed a little farther on.

The case which I should suppose the penner of this edict to have had in view, is that of a number of motions started at the same time, like candidates on an election. In the English practice this can create no confusion; for the one first started must be first disposed of; the question can only be as to the adoption or rejection of that one: the others come on afterwards, as they are moved. I do not say but that this method admits of improvement: hereafter, a regulation will be seen proposed with that view. But, what is the great point, it thoroughly prevents that confusion which on the French method seems to be inevitable.

I set out with observing, that to exhibit as the act of an assembly a proposition which has not been put to the vote, and carried by the majority of votes in that assembly, is to commit a forgery. If credit may be given to an anonymous, but very intelligent author,[c] this forgery is in

---

[a] Procès-verbal de l'Assemblée de Haute Guyenne, 4to, 1779, p. 143.[1]

[b] Chap. IV.[2]

[c] Essai sur l'Histoire des Comices de Rome, des Etats-Généraux de la France, [et][3] du Parlement de l'Angleterre, 3 vols. 8vo, Philadelphie, (Paris) 1789, vol. ii. p. 195.[4]

[1] *Collection des procès-verbaux des séances de l'Assemblée provinciale de Haute-Guienne*, i. 143–4.

[2] Bentham 1791 'Essay IV.' The reference which Bentham had in mind appears not to have survived in the material for Chapter IV.                    [3] Bowring 'and'.

[4] Published anonymously, but by Paul Philippe Gudin de la Brenellerie (1738–1812).

France a matter of ordinary practice. It is where he has been speaking of the assembly of the States-General; and not only of that sovereign assembly, but of the particular preparatory assemblies collected for the purpose of sending deputies and instructions to that general one. Resolutions {*avis*} says he, are drawn up, frequently when nothing has been put to the vote. *On rédige les avis, et souvent on ne vote point.*

§4.—POINT III. *Unity of the subject of debate kept inviolate.*[1]

*Questions, with Answers exhibiting reasons.*

Why not suffer a second proposition to be started (except as excepted) till a former has been disposed of?

Answer: 1. That in the instance of such or such a particular proposition, the assembly may not, by *indecision* with respect to *that proposition*, be prevented from taking a course which, had its will been left free to exercise itself upon the subject, it would have taken.

This, we see, is what may be at any time the case, if a proposition, about which the assembly had begun to occupy itself, is thus permitted to be jostled, as it were, off the carpet, by another proposition different from the former, and incommensurable with it, before they are aware.

2. To prevent a degree of confusion, by which, for that time, the assembly may be deprived of the faculty of forming *any will* at all.

Without some such check, nothing is more likely to happen, even without design; and that in any assembly, much more in a new-formed and numerous one. And the endeavour to produce such an effect by design, is one of the most effectual plans that individual fraud or conspiracy can pursue. In this way a thousand propositions may be thrown out, which, had the assembly been left at liberty to occupy itself about them without interruption—in short, had it been left master of its own will,—must have passed.

A proposition (suppose) has been introduced: a debate arises, and in the course of the debate something is started, from which somebody catches, or pretends to catch, the idea of something else that would be very proper to be done. This something else happening to touch upon a more sensible fibre, the next speaker takes this for his theme. Affections grow warm, and crowding about this second subject, the first is insensibly departed from and forgotten. In the same manner, a third takes place of this second; and so on, till men's minds are effectually confused, and their whole stock of time and patience gone.

This divergency is what is the more liable to take place in any assembly, especially in any new-formed assembly, inasmuch as it is what scarce ever fails to take place in private circles. In this case, it is

---

[1] Dumont Chapter XV, 'Unité dans l'objet du débat', is based on this section.

productive of no sort of harm: for amusement, which is here the end in view, is better provided for by rambling freely from subject to subject, than by adhering to any one. But in the case of a political assembly, it is productive of the utmost harm which such an assembly, as such, is capable of suffering.

The more eligible in its nature, and the more likely to have been embraced by the assembly, any of these propositions may be in themselves, the greater is the mischief that may result from such an irregular introduction of it. Introduced singly, each at its proper time, each one might have been carried: introduced, one upon the back of the other, each stands in the other's way—each throws another out, and a confusion is raised to which they all of them fall a sacrifice at once.

The enforcing this law of unity, and guarding it as well from intentional and insidious, as unintentional violations, is one of the uses that concur to evince the importance of keeping the composition, which is the subject of debate, exposed to the view of the whole assembly—But of this in another place.[a]

*British practice.*—As to this point, so far as concerns as well the negative put by the general proposition to the introduction of extraneous matter, as the choice of the exceptions, the British practice is exactly conformable to the regulation above proposed. But in respect of the details relative to the mode of conducting the several businesses which form the matter of those exceptions, it has been deemed open to improvement, in a variety of particulars which will present themselves as we advance.

*French practice.*—Of the French practice relative to this point, some intimation has been given under the preceding head. What farther remains to be said of it, will more conveniently be referred to the next. The points themselves being so intimately connected, and the practice relative to each being a consequence of the same principle, it is next to impossible, upon any one of these topics, to avoid touching upon the rest.

§5. POINT IV. *The process of debating distinct from, and prior to, that of voting.*[1]

*Question, with Answers exhibiting reasons.*

Why not allow any vote to be given till the debate is finished?

Answer: 1. That the decision given may not prove an improper one, on the score of its having been built upon *insufficient* and partial *grounds*.

To *vote* for or against a motion, is to judge—to exercise the office of a judge: to *speak* for or against it, is to exercise the function of an advocate.

---

[a] See Chap. III. § 2, *Table of Motions.*[2]

---

[1] Dumont Chapter XVI, 'Séparation du débat et du vote', is based on this section.
[2] See p. 45 above.

To vote before any one else has spoken in the debate, is to judge altogether without documents—altogether without grounds: to vote while there still remains any one to speak, who has anything to say, is to judge without documents *pro tanto*. Is there any one member whose speech is to be looked upon as proper to be attended to in this view?—so, for the same reason, must that of every other: since, abstraction made of the differences in point of talent between individuals—differences of which no general rules can take cognizance, every man's speech presents just the same probability of affording useful lights, as that of every other.

2. That the decision given may not be exposed to the danger of proving an improper one, on the score of its being expressive of a will *different from the real* will of the majority of the assembly. Conceive a list of members, speaking in a fixed order, and each man giving his vote, as his turn comes, at the end of his speech, or without making any speech, as he thinks fit. The first upon the list, after having said what he thinks proper, gives his vote; all the others, down to the last, give their votes on the same side. The last, when it comes to his turn, gives a contrary vote, grounded on arguments which had happened to escape all the preceding voters, but which, when once brought to light, stamp conviction on their minds. What is the consequence? A decision is given, purporting to want but one voice of being an unanimous one: but, in fact, contrary to the unanimous will of all the members whose decision it purports to be.

*British practice.*—In all political assemblies, the idea of which would be presented by that name to an Englishman unacquainted with, or not thinking of, the state of things in France, the British practice agrees perfectly with the recommendation given by this article—so perfectly, that it is to the rule itself that he would probably stand indebted for the first conception of its being possible to depart from it.

The mode of proceeding in courts of justice on this head, might indeed, if considered in this point of view, furnish an exception to this rule: but in this point of view an Englishman would not be apt to consider it, the business of a court of justice standing upon a footing altogether peculiar in this respect, as will be seen hereafter.

*French practice.*—The French practice relative to this important point, is so inextricably interwoven with the practice observed in the same country in relation to the other less important points, of which the enumeration has been already made, that to touch upon any one of them, without encroaching upon the rest, is scarcely possible.

The process of speaking seems scarcely to have been distinguished from that of voting, or the thing called a *speech* from the thing called a *vote*, even in idea; the same terms, *opinion* and *avis*, being employed, as we have seen, to denote, indiscriminately, the one or the other, or both together. Not being distinguished in name, they would remain undistinguished in exercise; and each man, in making his speech, whether it consisted of ten words, or the amount of twice as many pages, would of course give his vote at the same time; and that perhaps without suspecting that in so doing, he was doing two different things at once.

But, whatever each man chose to say, whether barely enough to give that signification of his will which a bare vote would give, or enough to make a speech of two or three hours in length, it happened to be so ordered, that each man should say it in a fixed order, as between man and man; such a member, if present, always speaking first—such another second—and so on. *Precedence*—that is, the order of sitting—was carefully settled upon such principles as were thought the proper ones in such case; and *pre-audience*, including speaking and voting—pre-audience, as a matter of inferior importance, was made dependent on precedence. From this combination—of confusion in what required order, and order in what required none,—results an effect which it is difficult to state with any degree of seriousness. The chance a man has of gaining partisans to his opinion is proportioned, not to the cogency of his arguments, but to the fancied height of the place in which he sits. Conceive this regimen adopted by the States-General, consisting (suppose) of 1100 members: he who sits first may hope to persuade 1099; the hopes of his next neighbour are confined to number 1098; and so down to the lowest, who sees nobody on whom his eloquence can make any effective impression but himself.

On the other hand, the chance a man has of forming a right opinion, is exactly in the inverse ratio of the chance he has of gaining partisans to that opinion. He who has it in his power to govern everybody, has it not in his power to receive lights from anybody; he into whose lap the collected wisdom of the whole assembly is poured in a full tide, sees no one to whom he can give the benefit of illumination but himself. If the ingenuity of government had employed itself in considering by what means wisdom might be most effectually disjoined from power, no other method equally happy can possibly have been devised.

One glance more at the regulations of the Provincial Assemblies: they will afford an instructive example or two, of ingenuity and observation struggling against precedent and prejudice.

First comes Haute Guyenne. Strangers to the principle of the identity of the motion and the resolution grounded upon it, they had found themselves entangled, in manner as above noted, with a multitude of *avis*, opinions—things that were neither motions nor speeches, nor votes—but something betwixt all three, springing out of one subject. The king's provisional code had ordered the reduction of these *avis* to two; *viz.* the two which after one round of *avis* had found the greatest number of voices in its favour. The consideration of this article had suggested to the Guyenne committee an imperfect view of the inconvenience of this orderly method of proceeding: the *avis* of a member low in the scale of *opinans*, though it was *possible* it might be the better of the two, could not possibly have so many *suffrages* in its favour as that of a member higher in the scale might acquire. The remedy hit upon was—not to keep the processes of debating and voting separate—that was a step too wide from precedent and establishment to be thought of,—but to have two rounds of *avis*.[a] Then (say the committee,) a man who upon the first round has heard the *avis* given subsequently to his own, with the reasons that may have been produced in favour of them, *may*, upon the second turn, sacrifice his own to that of somebody else. That he *may*, is not to be disputed: but will he? Unfortunately, it is not quite so easy to human pride to adopt a right opinion after having avowed its opposite as before: and, if such be the case between equals, how must it be where the conversion cannot take place without mortifying the pride of rank, as well as the pride of wisdom?

This step towards reason was thought, it should seem, too bold. Seven years after this period, the Assembly of Orléans, though willing to do something, had not resolution, however, to venture quite so far.[b] It was settled, that 'for ordinary business there should be but one round of *opinions*, in which a man should be allowed to develope his *avis;* but that in matters that appeared to require discussion, the president, in conjunction with the first *opinans* of each order,[c] should judge whether the matter subjected to *délibération* required two rounds of *opinions*, and that this decision should precede the *délibération*.'[d]

One assembly there is, in which the process of debating; and that of giving the opinions, are distinguished and kept separate; and this is that of Picardy.[e] The province nearest to England has, on this important point,

---

[a] Haute Guyenne, I. 143; anno 1780.[1]      [b] Orléans, page 168; anno 1787.[2]

[c] By the first *opinans* of each order, I suppose was meant the first *parcel of opinans*: if so, pity but it had been expressed so.

*N. B.* The whole number of *opinans* stands, under this code of regulations, divided into parcels, four in a parcel, viz. one of each of the privileged orders, and two of the third estate. Of this see more under the next head.

[d] What is meant by the word *délibération* here—whether the *arrêté*—the act or resolution of assembly, which in the French nomenclature is frequently termed *délibération*—or the assemblage of acts whereby these *avis* are respectively exhibited by the individual members—is more than I can take upon me to say: I give the passage as I find it. The same confusion pervades the Berri code;[3] which has served as a sort of model to the rest, and which, in this respect, has been but too faithfully copied.

[e] Picardie, p. 184, 13 Décembre 1787; Règlement II. art. 5 and 6.[4]

---

[1] The reference is actually to the *Procès-verbal* of 1779.

[2] *Procès-verbal des séances de l'Assemblée provinciale de l'Orléanois, tenue à Orléans aux mois de novembre et décembre 1787*, Orléans, 1787.

[3] See *Collection des procès-verbaux de l'Assemblée provinciale du Berri*, i. 46–51.

[4] *Procès-verbal des séances de l'Assemblée provinciale de Picardie, tenue à Amiens en novembre et décembre 1787*, Amiens, 1788.

come over to the English practice.[a] This coincidence, however, can scarcely be reckoned other than fortuitous; it goes no farther: these *opinions* are the same indeterminate sort of thing, or nearly so, here as elsewhere: they are not mere speeches indeed, but they are something betwixt motions and votes; they are sorts of things of which an indefinite multitude are liable to start up, and which, in Picardy as in Haute Guyenne, require force to reduce the number of them to two.[b]

To wean a man completely from an error from which the chains of habit have rendered it difficult for him to break loose, no recipe is so effectual as the indication of its source. In the present instance, the cause of this entanglement of two processes, which in point of utility it is so necessary to keep distinct, may be traced pretty successfully in two circumstances. The one, which however may be looked upon as rather the effect than the cause, is the confusion of ideas indicated by the equivocal nomenclature already noticed: the other is the junction of the two processes in the practice of courts of justice, in which, as we shall presently observe, such a junction stands upon a very different ground, and is in some cases not productive of any inconvenience, and in none, of any degree of inconvenience approaching to that of which it is productive in the case of a political assembly of any other kind.

While no difference was as yet descried between *original motion, motion in amendment, argument,* and *vote;*—while men were as yet to learn how necessary the concurrence of all these objects is to the formation of a rational decision—how distinct they are in themselves, and how important it is to keep them so;—when the art of applying a correction to the original proposition, in such manner as to enable the assembly to choose between the proposition uncorrected and that which would be the result of the correction, was as yet unknown;—when, on offering a fresh proposition in the course of a debate, a man had not yet learnt so much as to ask himself what influence it would have, or what he meant it should have, on the fate of another that was already on the carpet;—what occasion, what warning, what motive should men have had for separating—in short, in this state of the progress of intelligence, what possibility of separating—argument from vote,—and that so perfectly as that all the arguments should be exhibited at one time, and all the votes at another? In common discourse, though the distinction equally exists, no

---

[a] . . . Après la proposition chacun pourra, à son tour, faire telles observations qu'il jugera convenables; . . .

La discussion de la proposition préalablement faite, . . . l'on ira aux opinions.[1]

[b] Picardie, Règlement II. art. 10.[2]

---

[1] Quotations from Articles 5 and 6 respectively, referred to at p. 96 n. above.

[2] See p. 185: 'Dans le cas où il s'élèveroit plusieurs avis, l'Assemblée seroit obligée de se réduire à deux.' On Haute Guyenne, see p. 90 above.

such separation usually takes place; and common discourse is not only the natural, but, till some particular reason presents itself to the contrary, the proper model for regular debate.

All objects present themselves at first appearance in the lump; discrimination and separate nomenclature are the tardy fruit of reflection and experience. In Europe, a dog and a horse are become different animals; at Otaheite, the first horse was a great dog.[1]

Not only in the unfettered intercourse of common conversation is this separation neglected, but the case is the same in the regulated practice of the species of political assemblies instituted for the purposes of justice. This practice is the model which the legislators of the modern provincial assemblies, and before them those of the ancient provincial states, would naturally have before their eyes; it is from this source that the spirit of their laws would naturally be drawn.

The mode of proceeding in the States-General, which ought naturally to have been the model for popular or pretended-popular assemblies, was too unsettled to serve as a model for anything, even for itself.

Courts of justice must have existed at all times, and everywhere; and everywhere and at all times, the members of them must have delivered arguments, and given votes.

That the regulations given provisionally to the provincial assemblies by royal authority, or those settled by the assemblies, had lawyers for their authors, we are nowhere told, as it is not natural that we should be. That matters of law should be given to a lawyer to draw up, is however nothing more than natural: but to a lawyer, the model of perfection is naturally the practice of his court.

That such should have been the regimen pursued by judges in courts of justice, is not to be wondered at: nor, in courts of justice, where the number of the judges is very small, and which confine their transactions to the business of administering justice, is it to be blamed. The principal courts of justice in France, the courts of parliament, though always abundantly too numerous for courts of justice, were at their first institution less so than at present: and it was at that early period that their practice in this particular must necessarily have been settled.

These judicial assemblies, and the sort of administrative bodies formed by the provincial assemblies, were so far analogous, that both sorts were assemblies of a political nature—both had propositions to decide upon,

---

[1] Bentham's source has not been traced. However, Captain James Cook, who first took the horse to Tahiti, brought back with him on the return of his second voyage in 1774 a Tahitian called Omai. J. Alexander, *Omai, Noble Savage* (1977) records that 'Omaisms' which appeared in print included 'great hog that carries people' as a description of a horse. Missionary reports from the 1820s (William Ellis, *Polynesian Researches, during a residence of nearly six years in the South Sea Islands*, 2 vols., 1829, vol. i, p. 149) state that Tahitians called the horse 'land-running pig' and 'man-carrying pig'. An error in the printing of Bentham's source ('dog' for 'hog') might explain this obscure reference.

resolutions to form, and votes to give. But there is one point in which the analogy totally fails; and this point, obvious as it appears when once started, seems totally to have escaped the observation of the man of law. In judicial assemblies, in as far as they act judicially, no resolution comes to be formed, no vote comes to be given—not even that of him who stands foremost upon the list, till after the question had undergone a full and elaborate discussion by advocates on both sides. But in political assemblies, in the narrower sense of the word, in assemblies legislative, administrative, or merely popular, there is no such distinct class of persons; at least none such has, anywhere that I recollect, made its appearance hitherto separate from the rest. In assemblies of these latter descriptions, each member unites in his single person the distinct, and in a certain sense opposite, characters of advocate and judge. By his vote he exercises the latter function; by the part he takes in the debate—by his speech, in a word—and in the case of the author of a motion, by the making of that motion—he exercises the former.

He who, standing first upon the list of speakers, gives his vote at the conclusion of his speech without hearing any of the others, acts exactly as a presiding judge would do, who should begin with giving an opinion in favour of the plaintiff or of the defendant, without hearing a syllable from the parties or their advocates on either side. I mistake; he acts still worse: he decides not *ignorantly*, without hearing anything from anybody; but *partially*, after hearing only on one side. A proposition of some sort or other is upon the carpet; it must have had somebody for its introducer: this introducer has been heard in favour of it; it is therefore upon this partial representation only that the vote of the member who stands first upon the list, must under this regimen be formed.

In the judiciary line, the French and British practice on this head are similar in appearance, without being so in effect. In both instances, each man's vote, it is true, follows immediately upon his speech; but in the British practice this usage is attended with no inconvenience: the senior judge, from being the first to speak and to give his vote, loses nothing in point of intelligence; the junior judge, from being the last, loses nothing in point of influence. Why? Because the speeches they make in public—the speeches they are *heard* to make, are not the speeches by which their judgments have been determined: in a word, their speeches are not debates. What debates may happen to take place among them, are always private; they are carried on in whispers, or out of court among themselves. Before any one begins to speak, every one of them knows the mind of every other: their speeches, accordingly, are addressed, not to one another, but to the parties and the audience. Their object in making these speeches is not to make proselytes of one another: that object is either already compassed, or recognised to be unattainable. Their object, if unanimous, is to instruct the audience, and plead, each man, in favour of the whole number;—if there be a difference of opinion (an incident, in South Britain at least, very rare) to defend and justify at the bar of the public, each man his own side.

How happens this? Because the smallness of their number renders this kind of concert practicable. In England, in ordinary cases, the number is not more than four; they sit close together: the whisper of a moment is sufficient to inform them whether the opinion of the three junior judges coincides with that of the chief; if it does not, an adjournment of the cause, to give them an opportunity of debating the matter over in private, is the constant consequence.

When the whole twelve form themselves into one court—an incident that does not take place perhaps so often as four times in a twelve-month—the small increase in number resulting from the junction makes, in this respect, no difference: here, as in the other case, the public declaration of opinions is constantly preceded by private conference.

In the court of justice composed by the House of Lords, the numbers, and other circumstances, being so widely different, the practice is accordingly different. The number who have a right to be present is very large; the number actually present is liable to prodigious fluctuation. The members of this large body are not collected together in one place— are not in the constant habit of living with one another, as are the members of that small brotherhood. Among the Lords there can be no general conference but in a formal debate: accordingly, among them the process of debating is as distinct from that of voting, when they act in their judicial capacity, as when they act in their legislative.

The French parliaments—at least the principal body of that denomina- tion, the parliament of Paris[1]—bear, in relation to the points in question, a much greater resemblance to the House of Lords than to the ordinary courts of justice in Great Britain, and particularly in England. The number commonly present in the House of Lords is scarcely equal to the number commonly present in the parliament of Paris, when all the chambers are assembled. When that body, stepping aside out of the track of justice, takes cognizance of business appertaining to the departments of legislation and administration, its numbers, instead of being less than on the other occasions, are commonly greater; both by the extraordinary affluence drawn by the importance of the business, and by the addition of the peers, whose presence on such great occasions is commonly requested. Yet in no instance, as far as I have been able to learn, does this assembly

---

[1] The thirteen *parlements*, or general courts, were the most significant of the many appeal courts in France which reported directly to the King. The *parlement* of Paris had a political as well as a judicial function, the most important feature of which was the duty of registering the King's edicts and other measures; the *parlement* also had the right to object against legislation. See the Editorial Introduction, p. xvi above.

ever depart from the judiciary usage of confounding the two processes of debating and voting, in manner above mentioned.

§6. —POINT V. *In debating, no fixed order of pre-audience.*[1]

*Question, with Answers exhibiting reasons.*

Why not admit of any fixed order of pre-audience in debate?

Answer: 1. Because a fixed order is unfavourable to the growth of that intelligence on which rectitude of decision in great measure depends; to wit, in as far as intelligence is the fruit of industry, excited by emulation.

A man who finds himself low upon the list, may, in ordinary cases, naturally expect to find his arguments forestalled; and the lower he is, the less will it appear to be worth his while to be at the pains of studying the subject, for so small a chance of distinguishing himself, or being of use. Should superior ability or perseverance now and then get the better of this obstacle, still it is an inconvenience in itself, and a disheartening circumstance to reflect on, that his arguments cannot be produced till after the attention of the hearers may have been exhausted, and their appetite palled.

In this line, as in every other, the less a man's faculties seem likely to be worth, either to himself or others, the less labour will be bestowed in cultivating them.

2. It tends to waste time by increasing the quantity of useless discourse.

What is lost in point of intelligence, may be made up in words. A man who stands high upon the list, standing in that conspicuous station, and finding himself perpetually called upon to speak, may fancy himself bound, as it were, to obey the summons, and speak at any rate, as it were in his own defence. Something he must every now and then say, to the purpose or not to the purpose, willing or unwilling, prepared or unprepared.—'For so many days together, nothing but a silent vote? This will never do: I must make something of a speech to-day, or people will begin to look upon me as nobody.'

Thus, while the able and willing are shoved out of the list of speakers with one hand, the ill-qualified and unwilling are dragged into it with the other.

3. It tends to diminish the measure of intelligence imparted to the assembly, and thence to diminish the chance in favour of rectitude of decision, in another way; viz. by preventing that concert between persons possessed of different talents—that casting of the different parts, which may be so necessary to the displaying of the strength of the cause on every side to the best advantage.

---

[1] Dumont Chapter XVII, 'Inconvénients d'un ordre fixe pour la parole', is based on this section.

One man, for instance, shall be fittest for the business of statement and narration:

Another man, who is capable of urging this or that argument with a superior degree of force, shall be unable to grasp the whole *compages*[1] of the business;

A third, who can begin nothing of himself, shall be excellent at improving a hint by another, or correcting an error, or supplying a deficiency:

A fourth, though sparingly endued with the power of invention, shall be good at summing the arguments offered by others, and putting each argument in its proper place.

A fixed order, with its blind inflexibility, shall chop and change all these parts, turn topsy-turvy the order designed by reason and by nature: the reasoner shall stand before the narrator, and the recapitulator before both.

Setting aside the case of previous concert, and supposing the order to be fixed anyhow, some error may be advanced by a man—say in matter of fact, say in matter of argument, which, as it happens, somebody of those who spoke before him is in a condition to correct, but no one of those who are to speak after him. What follows? That if the rule of fixed pre-audience be observed, the error must pass uncorrected, and be received for truth. So often as this happens to be the case—and there is no occasion on which it may not happen—truth and this rule are incompatible.

4. It tends to strengthen whatever hold might be obtainable by seductive influence; and thereby to throw discouragement in the way of sincerity and truth.

Every man having to say something in his turn, and to show the side he takes, by his vote at least, if not by a longer speech, those who stand lowest upon the list will be obliged, whether they will or no, to see, and it will be known that they see, the part that is taken by every man who stands above them. But of this more fully under the next head.

5. Considered in respect to its influence on the rights of individuals, it puts all the members upon an equal footing: and on this head at least, equality is justice. Whatever be the advantage of speaking before or after another man, no reason can be given why one member should enjoy it in preference to another: the consequence is, they ought all to have an equal chance for it.

In point of real importance, this last consideration ranks at a great distance behind the preceding ones. In those cases it is the interest of millions that is concerned: in this, it is the interest of units. But even this ought not to pass unnoticed; for millions are composed of units. And in the

---

[1] 'structure'.

present instance, it is the interest of the units that is the most palpable, and the most immediately at stake.

*British practice.*—The order in which members speak, is that in which they happen to present themselves for that purpose;[a] which they do by rising from their seats.[b] In case of doubt which person, out of a number, was up at first, it is the province of the Speaker to decide;[c] that is to say, provisionally; for ultimately nothing can be decided but by the House.[c] Upon each occasion, the race, if so one may term it, is renewed; by starting up second, on any occasion, a man does not acquire the right of being heard first upon a succeeding one.

This mode is liable to inconveniences, which a person not rendered insensible to them by habit, will not find it difficult to divine; and which will be considered, and a remedy endeavoured to be found for them, farther on. But these inconveniences are nothing in comparison of the advantage gained by the avoidance of those which, we have seen, are the inevitable result of every kind of fixed order whatever.

In the British practice, the fundamental principle is equality: and here, in prescribing equality, public utility concurs, as we have seen, with justice. In the particular course taken to enforce and apply the principle, injustice, or at least the danger or appearance of it, as we shall see hereafter, have insinuated themselves. But under the greatest practicable degree of injustice, its efficacy on this head can never fail of meeting with a powerful controul in the influence of chance—that incorruptible power, which in this, as in so many other instances, is the best guardian and firmest protector that equality can have. At the worst, it is but occasional injustice; and between occasional and constant injustice there is no comparison.

*French practice.*—In the English practice we have seen disorder at the surface—utility and justice at the bottom. In the French, we shall see order at the surface—inconvenience and injustice underneath: the private injustice palliated, or rather modified in different ways; but the public inconvenience remaining unaltered, and in full force.

In the code of regulations adopted by the first of the two pattern-assemblies, the provincial assembly of Berri, the following is the course laid down. The ecclesiastical members are to *sit* and *speak* in the order of their nomination to their respective benefices:[d] the noblesse, in the order of their age:[e] the third estate, according to an order which it is declared shall

---

[a] II. Hatsell.[1] Commons' Journals, 2d May 1604.        [b] Ibid. 76.
[c] Ibid. 76. Commons' Journals, 2d May 1604.
[d] Berri, Vol. I. anno 1778. Règlement pour la Convocation et la Formation de l'Assemblée, Sect. II. art. 5, p. 35.        [e] Ibid. III. 7, p. 37.

---

[1] See pp. 73–8.

be fixed as between the districts which they represent.[a] The monster equality being thus, by different processes, extirpated from the three different classes of citizens, order—good order, *bon ordre*, as doubtless it appeared—was established, and the duty of the legislator done.

The clergy, it is to be observed, stand first in dignity; after them the noblesse; the third estate in the rear. Accordingly, the clergy are placed all together at the right of the president; the noblesse on his left; and the third estate, below them on each side.[b] The important article of sitting being thus adjusted upon strict constitutional principles, the inferior businesses of speaking and voting admitted of a temperament. Accordingly, for the purpose of *opining*, the whole assembly, consisting, when full, of forty-eight members (exclusive of the two procureurs-syndics,)[1] is considered as distributed into parcels: twelve parcels, four in each parcel; the four consisting of an ecclesiastic, a noble, and two of the third estate. He who sits uppermost of the ecclesiastics is thus joined with him who sits uppermost of the noblesse, and with the two who sit uppermost of the third estate; and so downwards throughout the list.

If, by this expedient, the individuals concerned were satisfied, that was one great point gained. What was gained in the other points?

1. Nothing in point of emulation.

2. Nothing in point of saving time and words.

3. Nothing as to the convenience of casting the parts, or correcting mistakes.

4. A small matter as to the diminution of undue influence. This influence, as between men of different classes, is reduced in some degree: but the influence of man on man, in the same class, is left untouched.[c]

---

[a] Ibid. IV. 13, p. 40.   [b] Berri, Vol. I. anno 1778, 10. p. 31.[2]

[c] The small utility of the arrangement in this point of view, is more particularly observable in the instance of the ecclesiastical order; in which inequality of dignity is liable to be connected with subordination in point of power. When a bishop, for example, and a number of his diocesans, sit in the same assembly—a case exemplified, perhaps, in every one of these assemblies—none of these subordinates can open his mouth, till after the superior has declared his pleasure. If an historiographer of these assemblies is to be believed,[a] a bishop, in one of them, was explicit enough to declare, that an ecclesiastic ought always to be of the same opinion with his bishop. Admit this proposition, and a good deal of time might be saved from consumption, as well as a good deal of truth from violation. The multitude of the members, one of the most formidable rocks which the

[a] *Résultat des Assemblées Provinciales*, 8vo. 1788, p. 25.[3]

---

[1] The *procureurs-syndics* were officers of the assembly.

[2] i.e. Ch. 1, §I, Art. 10, pp. 31–2.

[3] Créquy, *Résultat*, writes: 'Les gens d'église n'adopteront pas la proposition de M. l'Évêque d'Amiens à l'assemblée provinciale de Picardie. Il disoit qu'*un ecclésiastique doit toujours être de l'avis de son Évêque*.'

5. Nothing in the article of equality. Where all have a right to be upon an equal footing, every scheme of preference is equally unjust.

In the second of these two original assemblies, that of Haute Guyenne, a fixed order is settled upon the same principles, with some little variation as to the details:[a] and, as a fruit of the experience gained in the two years that had elapsed between the institution of the two assemblies, and as a means of providing the more effectually against any violations of this good order, it is provided, in terms more positive than those employed in the Berri code, that no member shall give his *avis* till called upon by the secretary for that purpose.[b] The end in view was, I suppose, to prevent interruption: but the means employed are such as render the exercise of every member's right dependent upon their servant's pleasure.[c]

In the Assembly of the Notables of 1787,[1] another course was prescribed by royal mandate. The voices {*'voix'*}[d] were here to be

institution of the States-General is exposed to split upon, might be most happily reduced by giving, to every bishop chosen, the proxies of as many of his suffragans as are returned with him. I mention this only in the way of illustration, not as affording a specimen of a mode of thinking which can possibly be a general one. The anecdote, probably heightened, or grounded upon some hasty expression, would not have been given by the author from whom I take it, but for its singularity. It would be injustice to the nation, as well as to the order, to view it in any other light.

[a] Haute Guyenne, page 119; anno 1780, Sect. I, art. 15.[2]

[b] Ibid. Art. 21, page 121.

[c] Wherever the exercise of a right is deemed invalid till after some act has been performed by a particular individual, that individual, however insignificant in other respects, possesses thereby a negative upon the exercise of that right: and though he might not venture to exercise such a negative upon his own bottom, he might, when supported by a faction.

It was thus the French parliaments, and particularly that of Paris, from having in their custody the registers on which new laws were to be entered, acquired very happily a sort of negative in legislation. It is to some such circumstance, little heeded at its commencement, that arbitrary power owes in many instances its only checks. But in the same way may liberty be checked and fettered by arbitrary power.

[d] What do *voices* {*'voix'*} mean here? Speeches only, or votes only, or both together? The royal mandate does not say, and a stranger may be permitted not to know. In practice, I am inclined to think it was construed to mean votes, or at least the short and summary *opinions* given instead of votes. A debate must have preceded, if what I understand from good authority be true; and that carried on in a mode not only as irregular as the English, but rather more so. Half-a-dozen voices at a time, I am assured, was no uncommon concert; so natural is the connexion between bad government and anarchy.

To this arrangement the dignity of rank found, one may suppose, no great difficulty in reconciling itself. Montesquieu's story of the Spaniard and the Portuguese would naturally come to mind:[3]—'*No matter what the place, so it distinguishes me from you.*'

[1] See the Editorial Introduction, p. xvi n. above.

[2] The reference should be to the *procès-verbal* of 1779.

[3] See *De l'esprit des loix*, ii. 21. xvii, where reference is made to the establishment of a demarcation line between the colonial conquests of Spain and Portugal.

taken, not in the order of sitting, which we may be sure was the order of dignity, but in the reverse of that order. This course was directed to be observed as well in full assembly, as in the seven committees into which the assembly was immediately broken down.[a]

This plan, with all its impropriety, was no inconsiderable improvement. It was the least bad of all fixed orders that could be devised.[b] The influence of will on will is thus reduced to its *minimum;* as far as the quantum of influence is to be measured by the degree of dignity. Other advantages might be pointed out, were it worth while to spend words in measuring shades of inexpediency, with perfect expediency in full view.

### §7. —POINT VI. *Simultaneity of the Votes.*

#### *Question, with Answers exhibiting reasons.*

Why require the votes to be given all at once, rather than one after another, according to a predetermined order?

Answer: 1. To save time—of which, in a numerous assembly, the taking the votes one after another, though it were in the most expeditious mode possible, must occasion an enormous waste.

Imagine the States-General of France voting, in the order of regular succession, upon every motion, how much soever in course; and contrast this process with that observed in the British House of Commons, open, as I conceive it will be found to be, to further improvements. In the House of Commons, when there is no division, as is the case with perhaps ninety-nine motions out of a hundred, the business of taking the votes is the affair of two instants: one, in which the affirmative votes—the other, in which the negative votes, are called for. In the States-General of France, under the regimen supposed, that same business would be the affair of about eleven hundred such instants: that is, about five hundred times as much time would be consumed in the latter case as in the former. One might even say more: for when eleven hundred votes are given one after another, accounts must be taken, whatever be the eventual disparity, and a deal of time consumed, in taking care not to omit any man, nor count the same man more than once.

2. To lessen the efficacy of undue influence.

[a] Procès-Verbal, p. 78, in 8vo. Paris, 1788.[1]

[b] It puts one in mind of Solon legislating for the Athenians, and giving them—not good laws, but the best they could be brought to bear.[2] But since that day, national wisdom among our Athenians has made an immense shoot; and they are become ripe for good laws, if ever a people were.

---

[1] *Procès-verbal de l'Assemblée des Notables, tenue à Versailles, en l'année M.DCCLXXXVII,* Paris, 1788. Details of the royal mandate to which Bentham refers appear in fact on p. 93.

[2] Plutarch, *Life of Solon,* xv. 2.

I say only to lessen it; for if two men are absolutely and *bonâ fide* agreed to play the parts of master and slave, or pope and devotee, what possible means will there be of hindering them? Neither the process of crying *Aye* or *No*, nor that of holding up hands, can be rendered so exactly simultaneous, but that, if the slave is *bonâ fide* upon the watch, he may wait to observe the part taken by the master's voice or hand, so that his may take the same. But to the slave who feels an inward disposition to rebel, the practice of simultaneity may upon occasion furnish excuses that may stand a better or worse chance of being accepted:—'I beg a thousand pardons: I took another man's hand for your's.' 'If I have acted honestly for this once, it was through mistake: the matter appeared unfortunately so clear to me, that I made no doubt of finding your hand on the same side.'

Wherever a loop-hole offers itself at which probity may make its escape from the trammels of seductive influence, it is plain that too much care cannot be taken to leave it open. See the section on the cases where the secret mode of taking the votes is the proper one, viz. Chap. XIV. §2.

The concealment thus recommended is not that which forms the inconvenience, where there is any, resulting from the secret mode of voting. It is only the will of the seducer that is concealed, for the moment, from the knowledge of the voter—not the conduct of the voter that is concealed, at the long run, from the knowledge of the public.

The result of a decision given in this summary way may, it is true, come to be done away by another decision, given on the same question, in the exact and regular mode: but this latter opposes, or at least may be made to oppose, to improbity, other checks which are peculiar to itself: of which in another place.[a]

*British practice.*—The mode of voting pursued in the British practice accords thus far with the recommendation given by this theory. In the summary way, the voices given on each side are all lifted up promiscuously, and at the same instant. In the regular mode, on a division, all the feet move promiscuously, and as fast as they can. A division is not conceived to be either a procession or a dance.

In both cases, the practice is not free from particular inconveniences, which will be represented, and remedies proposed for them, in another place. In both cases, the outlines might be better filled up than they are; but the outlines themselves are just.

In point of diminution of undue influence, the advantage gained is perhaps no great matter. It is out of the question altogether in the regular

---

[a] See Chapter II. *On Publicity with regard to the proceedings of a political assembly.*[1]

[1] This was the original title planned by Bentham for Chap. II, p. 29 above.

mode, where the part taken by everybody being deliberate and conspicuous, must be observed by everybody: and in the summary mode, it cannot be expected to amount to much on those great questions of national importance, where party puts its shoulders to the task, and the part to be taken in the House is previously settled by most of the members at private or less public meetings. But still there are not wanting a multitude of occasions on which, under favour of this part of the discipline, probity may make its escape from undue influence. Let the advantage gained in this way amount to ever so little, it is so much got out of the fire.

*French practice.*—In the French practice, the speeches, where a man has anything to say, are made in a predetermined order, as we have seen; and as each man's vote comes immediately after, or instead of—in short, is confounded with—his speech,—hence vote follows after vote, as speech does after speech.

Speaking with an eye to the States-General, I have brought to view the enormous quantity of time which, upon this plan of regular succession, the mere operation of *voting* must of itself, in an assembly so numerous, unavoidably consume; but when to this one adds the process of *debating*, and the multitude of speeches which, in an assembly of eleven hundred persons, all picked men, selected for their talents by and out of four and twenty millions of people, may be extorted in a manner by the considerations above mentioned, the imagination starts at the idea.

In a company like the provincial assemblies, consisting of no more than eight and forty persons, this inconvenience might chance well enough not to rise to such a magnitude as to attract notice. But even in an assembly like that of the Notables of 1787, consisting of one hundred and forty-four, it seems already to have been apprehended. For this consideration must, at least, have been among the number of those, in virtue of which such haste was made to break down that assembly into seven committees of twenty or twenty-two each, as soon as formed. In the course of sixty-two days the *plenum* sat but six times: and on none of those days do the transactions, as represented by the *Procès-verbal*, seem to leave any room for a debate. In full assembly, nothing seems to have been done but hearing papers read, and speeches of ceremony pronounced.

Even in the provincial assemblies, consisting of but forty-eight members, it seems to have been a principle, to do the business as much as possible in committees, consisting of no more than a dozen members. In some of them, according to their historiographer,[a] a regulation is established, not to take into consideration any business in full assembly, that has not, in its passage from the committee in which it originated,

[a] Résultat des Assemb. Prov. p. 18.

gone through the other three. This he looks upon as 'necessary, in order to avoid as much as possible the noise and bustle to which debates carried on in numerous assemblies are exposed.'[a]

These observations, and many others that might be added, seem to bespeak a general apprehension of the impossibility of carrying on business in the French mode in *numerous* assemblies; that is, not only in such as would be esteemed numerous in England, but in assemblies, for example, consisting of half a hundred, or even so few as a quarter of a hundred persons. How must it fare then with the States-General, and its eleven hundred members? Is it to have no general will? Is it, like the first assembly of the Notables, to sit for no other purpose than to hear papers which would have been better read than heard, and speeches which might as well have been neither read nor heard?

Is no business to originate there?—nothing to be done but to pronounce definitively, and *in globo*,[1] upon some voluminous draught transmitted from some small and select committee? It is a fallacy, then, to speak of its having a will of its own—it is a fallacy to speak of it as possessing the power of the people. The real possessors of the power of the people are the members of this oligarchy, the select committee. But of this more fully in another place.[2]

*Observations.*—The circumstance that served us to account for the usage relative to the fourth point, will afford us a means equally natural of accounting for the practice relative to the present head.

Between the practices of speaking in succession, voting in succession, and confounding speech with vote, the connexion is not, it is true, a necessary one. Speeches *might* be made in turn, and yet votes given all at once. Speeches might be made in the order in which persons happened to rise to speak, or in any other uncertain order, while votes were given in a fixed order.

But the connexion, though not necessary, was natural. Why? Because it was natural that judicial assemblies should have served as a model: and in judicial assemblies it was as natural that the judges should speak in a fixed order, determined by the joint influence of rank and seniority, as that each man should speak and vote at the same time.

It was a natural course, which, as far as judicial practice is concerned, is sufficient here: whether, in the instance of that practice it be of all others the most expedient, is a question that belongs not to the present purpose.

---

[a] Ibid.

[1] 'As a whole'.
[2] See Chapter XV, §1, 'Of Special Committees', p. 153 below.

## CHAPTER VII.
## OF THE PROPOSAL OF MEASURES FOR ADOPTION.

THERE ought to be in every assembly one individual officially charged with the *initiative*, that is bound to commence the operations, and to propose the necessary measures. For if no member in particular ought to have a plan respecting the business to be considered, it may happen that there will be no plan,[+] and that the assembly will remain in a state of inaction.

It is not only necessary that there should be a plan upon each occasion, but there ought to be a train—a connexion, between the projects submitted. It is not enough to provide for the first sitting:[+] there ought to be a general plan, embracing all the requisite operations, disposing them in the best order, and leading them onward to their conclusion.

This *obligatory initiative* naturally belongs to those who convoke a political assembly, and who are best acquainted[+] with the wants of the state. The general distribution of labour is the duty of the administration: the ministers should propose—the assembly deliberate and resolve.

But the *right*[+] of initiation ought not to be the privilege of the executive exclusively:—each member ought equally to possess it. There are three principal grounds for this arrangement:—

1. That the intelligence of the whole assembly may be improved for the general good.[+]

There is as good a chance for obtaining the best advice from one party as from the other. To limit the right of proposing, is to renounce everything which might be expected from those who are excluded: it is to institute a monopoly mischievous in every respect, both because it extinguishes the emulation of those whom it reduces to merely a negative part, and because it may retain the greatest talents in a state of inaction. The most intelligent and clever[+] men may, under this exclusive system, be enchained by those who are greatly their inferiors in genius and knowledge.

2. That abuses may [be] reformed. If the right of proposing belong only to the administration, those abuses which are favourable to it would[+] be perpetual: the assembly would have no direct method of causing them to cease. This arrangement would give to the government a most commodious species of negative as against all measures which were unpleasant to it—a negative without noise and without debate.[a]

---

[a] In ancient times, the Scottish parliament was subject, as to the order of its labours, to a committee named by the King: the Lords of Articles alone had the initiative of all measures. They prepared beforehand everything which was to be presented to the Assembly, and consequently had an absolute negative, much more powerful than they

3. That the danger arising from the negative right, when it exists alone, may be prevented.[+] The assembly which should possess the power of rejecting alone, would be[+] tempted to abuse it; that is to say, to reject good measures, either from a feeling of pride, that it might show that it was not a mere nullity, that it might exercise its authority, or that it might constrain the hand of government, and lead it to concede one point that it may obtain another: for the right of refusal may be converted into an instrument of offence, and may be employed as a positive means of constraint. Such a system, instead therefore of producing harmony, would tend to produce[+] discord by creating a necessity on the part of the assembly for the adoption of an artificial conduct towards the executive power.[+]

But it may be said, if the direction of affairs ought to be confided to the officers of the executive power,—if they ought to propose those measures which the necessities of the state require:—how, then, can this agree with the desire which all the members may have of making propositions? For this right, if it be to be efficacious, supposes that the assembly has the power of entertaining them. But if it thus entertain them, the ministerial plan will be liable to be interrupted by incoherent, and even entirely subversive motions:[+] there will be no longer any regular progress; and there may even result from it general confusion in the government.

I can only answer this objection by supposing in the assembly an habitual disposition to leave to the ministers the ordinary exercise of the right of proposing.

The general privilege should be reserved for all the members without distinction; but the right of priority should be conceded by a tacit convention to the ministerial propositions.

It is here that it is proper to notice the conduct of the British parliament.

In the ordinary course of affairs, all eyes are fixed upon the minister: whether he present a plan, or speak in support of it, he is listened to with a degree of attention which belongs only to him. By a general, though tacit arrangement, important business is not commenced before he arrives.

He proposes all the principal measures—his opponents confine themselves to attacking them: in short, he is the director, the prime mover, the principal personage. Still he has not by right the slightest pre-eminence: there is no rule which secures to his motions, a preference above those of any other member;—there is no rule which gives him a right to speak

could have had after the debate.—Robertson's History of Scotland, Book I. Reign of James V. {They were not named by the King, but by the several Estates of the Parliament. *Ed.*}[1]

---

[1] Bentham's footnote is a summary of William Robertson's discussion of Scottish assemblies in *The History of Scotland, during the Reigns of Queen Mary and of King James VI*, 2 vols., London, 1759, i. 69–71.

first—it is an arrangement which exists only in virtue of its convenience and its utility.[+] Whilst the minister possesses the confidence of the majority, he is sure to preserve the right[+] of the initiative: when he loses this confidence, he cannot much longer remain minister, but must give place to another.

It may be well here to attempt to dissipate an error which may justly[+] be called popular, both on account of the little reflection which it discovers, and the number of those who adopt it. This error consists in concluding, that an assembly like the House of Commons is corrupt, because[+] in its ordinary course it is led by the ministers. This pretended proof of the corruption of the assembly, or its subjection, is, on the contrary, a real proof of its liberty and its strength. Why does the minister always take the lead in Parliament? It is because unless he had the power thus to lead, he would no longer be minister. The preservation of his place depends upon the duration of his credit with the legislative assembly. Were we to suppose all the members endowed with the most heroic independence, matters could not be better arranged than they are at present.[+]

## CHAPTER VIII.
## OF THE DIFFERENT ACTS WHICH ENTER INTO THE FORMATION OF A DECREE.

THOSE who pay only a superficial regard to a political assembly, may think that there is nothing more simple than a *motion*, a *debate*, a *decree*. What is there here which is the object of science or art? The ordinary affairs of life call us all to propose, to deliberate, to decide. There are scarcely any notions more familiar than these.

It is true, it is easy to form a conception of these operations, but it is difficult to describe them. In this respect, it is the same with the actions of the mind as with those of the body. To move the arms, requires but a moment: to explain this movement—to describe the muscles which perform it, requires great anatomical knowledge.

Let us trace the formation of a decree.[+]—The work which serves as its foundation, is a simple project proposed by an individual; when he presents this project to the assembly according to the prescribed forms, he makes what is called a motion.[+]

The original[+] motion having been made, every posterior motion with regard to it can only have one of two objects—either to *amend* or to *suppress* it. There are, therefore, two kinds of secondary motions:—

*Emendatory* motions.

*Suppressive* motions.

The first include all those which modify the original motion; since all these modifications may be considered as *amendments*—that is to say, ameliorations or corrections.

The second class will include all those which directly or indirectly tend to cause the original motion to be rejected; as by demanding priority in favour of some other motion, or by proposing an adjournment of the question for an indefinite time, &c.

In order to produce a decree, only three acts are absolutely necessary:—
1. To make a motion; 2. To vote; 3. To declare the result of the votes.

But before arriving at the conclusion, there are, in the ordinary course of things, many steps or intermediate acts proper to be taken.

We shall here set them down in chronological order:—
1. Previous promulgation of motions, projects of laws, and amendments.
2. Making the motion which exhibits the project.
3. Occasionally ordering it to be printed and published.
4. Seconding the motion.
5. Deliberating upon it.
6. Putting the question.
7. Voting summarily.
8. Declaring the result of the summary voting.
9. Dividing the assembly—that is, demanding distinct voting.
10. Collecting the votes regularly.
11. Declaring the result.
12. Registering all the proceedings.[+]


## CHAPTER IX.
## OF THE PROMULGATION OF MOTIONS—OF BILLS—OF AMENDMENTS, AND THEIR WITHDRAWMENT.

IT is proper that the assembly should previously have before its eyes a statement of the business with which it is to be engaged, that nothing may be left to chance, and that it may not be exposed to surprises. It ought to impose on all who wish to present any motions to it, the obligation of duly preparing them, and making them known. A discussion, the object of which has been previously made known, will be the result of more deliberation, and consequently shorter: the reasons for and against, having been the subjects of meditation, the debaters will have ascertained their strength, and taken up their positions accordingly.

This object may be accomplished by a single regulation. Let the secretary open three distinct registers—for Motions, *Bills* or projects of laws,[+] and Amendments; every member being allowed to present to him a motion to be registered; and all motions, after having been printed in a journal which should only have this object, should come before the assembly in the order in which they are registered, subject to the reservation of which we shall presently speak.

The journal of motions being published daily, those who wish to propose any amendments should be bound to make them known beforehand, by presenting them to the secretary, who should transcribe them in his register, and cause them to be printed in the journal of amendments.

The same steps should be followed with respect to bills: they should be inserted in a separate register, in the order of their presentation; but they ought not to be introduced into the assembly until three months after their inscription, unless upon special application this period should be shortened.[+]

Such ought to be the foundation of the arrangement for the table of occupations, which might be called, as in the British houses of parliament, The order of the day.[+]

But this inflexible order for motions and bills, this arrangement founded only upon the circumstance of anterior registration of accidental priority, would be liable to the most weighty inconveniences; it might prove destructive of real order, of that order which belongs to the train and connexion of matters, and thus prove incompatible with the liberty of the assembly. Because one motion has been placed upon the list before another, it does not follow that it deserves the preference: the last in date may be the first in importance.

It would even be impracticable to subject all motions to an absolute rule requiring previous registration. Unexpected incidents demand sudden measures; and in the course of its discussion, a subject may assume altogether a different appearance; a change made in one part of a project, may require an alteration in another—an unexpected breach must be repaired by sudden expedients.

The influence of a list of motions[+] is therefore reduced to this:—it would serve as a guide for the ordinary progress of the debates—it would present a general picture of the labours; but it would not restrain the liberty of the assembly, which ought to be able at any time to accelerate certain motions, or to receive new ones which have not been registered.

What has been said respecting motions is equally applicable to bills: but a bill admits of greater delay than a motion; and an interval of three months would not in general be too great between the presentation of a bill to the assembly, and its passing into a law.[+] If it have been possible to do without a given law during the course of past ages, it is possible to do without it at least three months longer. Besides, as soon as a law is proposed, the whole of the nation is more or less interested: the object is permanent; it ought therefore to be known to the public, and all the information possessed by the different parties in the kingdom ought to be collected concerning it; unless it be pretended that the deputies, by a miraculous concentration, not only possess all the judgment and know-ledge of the whole nation, but even of the world itself. Laws ought to be founded upon facts; but inasmuch as the facts are particular, they cannot be collected, unless the necessary time be allowed to the parties interested to present them to the legislators.

But in respect of bills as well as motions, an inflexible rule is not required: latitude must be left for unforeseen cases, and especially in favour of the government, which is charged to provide for urgent circumstances. If after an insurrection, or on the eve of an invasion, an interval of three months were required after introducing a bill before it were passed into a law,[+] the evil might have been consummated before it was possible to consider of the remedy. This would be to play the engines when the fire was extinguished.

It may be remarked, that the plan here proposed differs from that of the English parliament, every member having here the right to introduce a bill;[+] whereas in the English parliament a bill cannot be introduced without leave given by the House—a practice well calculated for preventing the consumption of time upon frivolous or dangerous projects of laws: but when a member moves for leave to introduce a bill, the House must consider whether it will admit or reject it. This power which it now exercises upon the motion, I propose that it should exercise over the bill at the moment in which it will be presented; that is to say, that the assembly should then decide whether it will entertain it or not; because it will then decide upon better grounds, as the bill will then have been published.

It is sometimes[+] the custom that bills should be printed before the debate; but this is not the case except upon special motion, which motion is sometimes rejected;—and, when printed, they are only distributed to members of parliament. In this respect[+] there is a fundamental error: the printing ought to be the rule, and also the public sale of such bills. Before the invention of printing, and when the art of reading was unknown to three-fourths of the deputies of the nation, to supply this deficiency, it was directed that every bill should be read three times in the House. At the present day, these three readings are purely nominal: the clerk confines himself to reading the title and the first words. But a most important effect has resulted from this antique regulation. These three readings have served to mark three distinct degrees—three epochs—in the passing of a bill, at each of which the debate upon it may be recommenced at pleasure.

Motions and bills being thus printed and published in journals destined to these objects alone, a regulation should be made, that amendments should be printed and published in the same manner. Why should they not be? If I wish to oppose a motion, ought my intention [to be] to come upon the assembly by surprise?[+]—ought its author to be deprived of the knowledge of my objections, and of leisure to prepare an answer to them?—ought I to be allowed to take advantage of him by an unforeseen attack? If I am only anxious for the success of my own schemes, the unforeseen amendment will best suit my purpose; but if I only desire the success of reason, I ought to make it known before the debate.[+]

If all the amendments are previously published, and presented all together, the assembly will have before its eyes a complete picture of the subject of discussion—a picture which will itself be a safeguard against the inconsistencies and contradictions which are so likely to be introduced into a composition of which all the parts are only considered successively. The more completely it is possible to present them simultaneously, the less is the exposure to this danger. This is the grand advantage of synoptic tables: the reciprocal dependence and union of all the parts is at once perceived: any incoherence strikes the eyes.

But the rule ought not to extend to the exclusion of amendments arising at the moment; for new ideas may spring out of the debate itself, and to reject a salutary amendment because its author had not foreseen it, would be an absurdity. All that can, and all that ought to be required of him, is to declare that the delay in the announcement of this amendment was not intentional—is not insidious; that he did not intend to take the assembly by surprise. The nature even of the amendment will indicate the motive which gave rise to it.[a]

[a] If it be necessary that motions should be composed beforehand, in order that they may be presented to the legislature, which is composed of the élite of the nation,—for a much stronger reason is this precaution indispensable with regard to popular assemblies, which are formed and dissolved in a day, and which can have little or no practice in the art of debate.

Such assemblies often take place in towns or counties in England, for the purpose of presenting petitions or addresses, either to the King or the Houses of Parliament.

If in these assemblies an individual propose a petition or address previously prepared, his antagonists seldom fail to draw from this circumstance an argument in its disfavour. There is indeed a term of ridicule for the designation of such previously prepared motions; they are called *pocket motions* and *pocket petitions*. By these terms an intention[+] is imputed to their author of surprising and deceiving the assembly, by causing his own personal ideas to be received as a public act.

There is in this suspicion a mixture of reason and error—of inadvertence and reflection.

The inadvertence consists in not considering that a motion, which is to be the act of all, must begin by being the act of one individual,—and that a writing of this kind, as well as every other writing, ought to be the better, precisely because it is the work of time and reflection.

But, on the other hand, it is an instinct of reason to distrust the ascendency which one individual may obtain over an assembly by proposing a measure which he had prepared at leisure, but upon which the assembly is called to decide at once, without having had time to examine its foundations and consequences.

What follows? Ought no one in a popular assembly to propose any motion previously

When a member has caused a motion, a bill, an amendment, to be inscribed in the register, he should not be allowed to withdraw or abandon it, without leave from the assembly. A simple prohibition alone is not sufficient in this respect: it ought to be an inflexible law. If the author of the act in question be not present on the day fixed, to support it—unless there be lawful reason for absence, he ought to incur the censure of the assembly, and his name should be inscribed in a separate book, having for its title, *List of the deserters of motions*, &c.

This rigorous law is requisite—1. In order to prevent thoughtless motions, and the confusion which would be produced by the false appearance of a great mass of business which would vanish at the moment in which it was touched.

2. To prevent the destruction of public confidence by accustoming the people to see that the motions which are announced are dropped by neglect.

3. To prevent the abuse which might be made of this instrument by announcing motions which there is no intention to support, either for the purpose of spreading alarm, or to affect the public funds; or for the purpose of preventing other parties from registering their motions or their bills, by an apparent monopoly of business; and because the evil which an individual could effect in this respect would be susceptible of the most alarming extension by means of combination among the members of a party.

# CHAPTER X.
## OF THE DRAWING UP OF LAWS.

W E proceed to consider the motions as compositions destined to become laws, and be presented to the examination of the assembly. In this respect it is desirable that they should possess that form which will allow them to be discussed in detail, and amended.

prepared? This certainly ought not to be the rule,—but the rather, that before the day of assembly, the motions intended to be made ought to be published.

There exist, in some assemblies of this kind, regulations which prohibit their convocation without a public declaration of the object of the meeting. This regulation ought to be universal; and there ought to be added to it, as a necessary condition, that the principal motion in its totality should be annexed to the act of convocation; that there should be a sufficient interval to allow of the publication of rival propositions, and that no motion should be presented to such assemblies, which had not been previously made known to the public. Will it be said, these are fetters and stumbling-stones for freedom. This would be a mistake: they are parapets upon the edge of precipices. Everything which renders reflection and order necessary in the proceedings of a free people is the assured safeguard of their rights.

Regulation cannot prescribe perfection in style;[+] but there are certain defects which it may prevent, certain conditions which it may impose, because every one may be subjected to them. The four following points may be prescribed:—

1. Brevity in the articles.
2. Simplicity in the propositions.
3. The pure expression of will.
4. The complete exhibition of all the clauses which the law ought to contain.

If these conditions are observed, whatever may be the extent of a motion, it will be of a manageable and ductile form; it will be easy to consider it in all its parts, and to amend it.

1. Brevity in the articles.—What is meant by an article is, so much matter as it is intended to put to the vote at one time. The longer the articles are, the more difficult is it to understand the whole together, and distinctly to see all the parts. But is it sufficient to recommend brevity? No: the force of a law ought to be given to this precept, by declaring that no project of a law, containing more than one hundred words for example, should be received, unless it were divided into numbered paragraphs, no one of which should exceed the above measure. This expedient, altogether singular as it may at first appear, is however the only one of absolute efficacy.[a] When it is necessary to present a long train of ideas, it is proper to assist the understanding by brevity of style. Each separate sentence forms a resting-place for the mind.

The paragraphs in a law ought to be numbered. There is no means more convenient and short for citation and reference.

Acts of parliament are exceedingly defective in this respect. The divisions into sections, and the numbers which designate them in the current editions, are not authentic. In the parchment original, the text of the law—the whole act, is of a single piece, without distinction of paragraphs, without punctuation, without figures. The word section[+] is not even met with there, nor anything which corresponds with it. How, then, is indication made of the termination of one article and the commencement of another? Always by repeating the same formula, the same introductory clause,—*and it is further enacted by the authority aforesaid*, or some other phrase to the same effect.

This is a species of algebra, but of an opposite character. In algebra, one letter supplies the place of a line of words; in this, a line of words very

---

[a] The longest paragraphs in the Code Napoleon do not exceed one hundred words, and there are very few of that length.[1]

[1] What became known as the Code Napoléon was first published as *Code civil des Français*, Paris, 1804. Although this is slightly overstated, the vast majority of the articles of the *Code Napoléon* are very brief.

imperfectly supplies the place of a single figure: I say very imperfectly,[+] for these words serve for the purpose of division, but they are of no use for the purpose of reference. Is it wished to amend or repeal one section in an act? As it is impossible to point out this section by a numerical reference, one is obliged to do it by circumlocutions, which produce repetitions[+] and obscurity. It is partly from this cause that acts of parliament are unintelligible compositions to all those who have not made them the object of long study.[a]

The first acts of parliament were passed at a period in which punctuation was not yet in use—in which the Arabian figures were not known. Besides, the statutes in their state of primitive simplicity and imperfection, were so short and so few in number, that the want of division could not produce any sensible inconvenience. These things have remained upon the same footing, partly from negligence and routine, but much more so from a secret interest on the part of the lawyers, who have found their advantage in this obscurity of the legal text, and who oppose to every reform the bugbear of innovation. Our forefathers lived for ages without the knowledge of commas, stops, and figures: why should they be adopted now? The argument amounts to this—Our forefathers lived upon acorns and mast;[+] corn is therefore a useless luxury.[+]

2. Simplicity in the propositions.—This is the principal point: the rule prescribed above respecting brevity, is established essentially on account of this.

*Every article ought to be reduced to a pure and simple proposition; or at least, an article ought never to include two complete and independent propositions, of such nature that the same individual may approve one and reject the other.*

Clearness would be carried to the highest point, if each article presented a complete sense, without reference to any other; but in a composition which has many parts, this species of perfection is impossible. The idea even of arrangement excludes that of independence.

A mathematical proposition is demonstrated by reference to propositions previously demonstrated;[1] and in every series of reasoning, the links are multiplied in proportion as they are removed from the first step.[+]

Among *conjunctions*, there are some which afford a mischievous facility for binding together an indefinite number of sentences into one. Of this kind are, in French, *d'autant que, considérant que;* in English, *whereas;* in Latin, *quandoquidem.*[2] The introduction of these phrases is a

---

[a] See *General View of a Complete Code of Legislation*, Chap. XXXIII. *Of the style of the Laws.*[3]

---

[1] See p. 136 & n. below.  [2] 'Since, seeing that.'

[3] See Dumont's recension of Bentham's writings, *Traités de législation civile et pénale*, 3 vols., Paris, 1802, i. 361–70 (Bowring, iii. 207–9).

principal fault in the style of the laws:[+] by means of them, a mass of confusion is created; objects which it is most desirable to keep apart, being thus without reason,[+] oftentimes coupled together.

But if the propositions ought not to be[+] independent one of another, they need not be made *complex*.

A complex proposition in matters of law, is one which includes two propositions, one of which may be approved, and the other disapproved.

The following question, proposed to the Notables in 1788,[1] may serve as an example: it referred to the composition of the States-General:— *Ought certain qualifications to be required of the electors and the persons eligible?* By the form of this phrase, two distinct propositions are presented, as if they formed only a single one.

Ought certain qualifications to be required of the electors?—

Ought certain qualifications to be required of the eligible?—

These are two questions, so distinct that each ought to be decided by different considerations, which may perhaps lead to a negative with regard to one, and an affirmative answer as to the other. But by uniting them in this manner, the mind is led into error: it is led to consider them as so connected together, that it is proper to give to them one common answer, either in the negative or affirmative.[a]

Suppose that a proposition, which is presented as a single one, really consists of two propositions—that you approve the one, that you disapprove the other: if it remains undivided, whatever may be the decision, one proposition will be passed in opposition to your will;—if it be divided, you are free to choose[+]—you can vote against the one without voting against the other; and this, which may happen to one individual, may happen to the whole assembly.

By means of complex propositions, an assembly free from all exterior constraint, may cease to be free by a species of internal constraint: a good law may be used as an instrument to compel the passing of a bad one.

Conjunctions may arise, in which an assembly may be compelled to sacrifice its most important rights. A certain law may be proposed to it, not only good in itself, but even necessary to its own preservation, or the preservation of the state; and to this law may be joined another, by which it may be deprived of some of its essential prerogatives. What can it do? It

---

[a] This sophism corresponds with that which in the logic of Aristotle is designated by the words—'*Secundum plures interrogationes, ut unam*—are honey and gall sweet?'[2] This is a *jeu d'esprit* for perplexing children, but it is often employed in legislation for deceiving men.

---

[1] See the Editorial Introduction, pp. xvi–xvii above.

[2] In *On Sophistical Refutations*, vi. 169[a]6, Aristotle discusses fallacies connected with 'the union of several questions in one'. This is the approximate translation of the Latin phrase quoted here.

is obliged to submit. It is in the situation of the patriarch, who, pressed with hunger, sold his birthright for a mess of pottage.[1]

This Machiavelism, it may be said, is a gratuitous supposition—a pure fiction. But it is not: history furnishes numerous examples of it. In the ancient republics, the *initiative* of the laws belonged exclusively to a senate: the people had no other alternative than that of approving or rejecting the whole together; the liberty of choice was not left to them;— their chiefs made them purchase a desired law, a necessary law, at the price of some other law unfavourable to their interests.[2]

3. Another principle of composition: *Employ only a pure and simple declaration of will, without intermixing therewith, reasons, opinions, or fancies, distinct from that same will.*

To assign the reasons for a law is a separate operation, which ought never to be confounded with the law itself. If it be desirable to instruct the people, it may be done in a preamble, or in a commentary which accompanies the law; but an imperative law ought only to contain the simple[+] expression of the will of the legislator. Intended to serve as a rule of conduct, it cannot be too simple, too clear, too free from dispute.[+] If reasons and opinions are intermingled with it, all those are ranged against the law, who do not approve the reasons or opinions which it expresses: instead of becoming stronger, it becomes more feeble; an instrument of attack is prepared for its adversaries, and it is delivered up to their disputes.

A single epithet is sometimes sufficient to alter the simple expression of the will. The same effect may result from the use of a term which implies blame or approbation, when it would have been proper to employ a neutral term—*heretic*, for example, instead of *dissenter*[+]—*innovation* instead of *change*—*usury* instead of *illegal interest*.

These eulogistic or dyslogistic terms[+] produce all the inconveniences which we have developed above: they include complex propositions; they not merely state a fact,[+] upon which all the world may be agreed, but also an *opinion*, which may be received by one party, and rejected by another.[+]

Let us give an example:—'It is decreed that no heretic shall be allowed to sit in this assembly.'

First proposition: 'It is decreed that no man who is not of the established religion of the state, shall be admitted to sit in this assembly.'

Second proposition: 'This assembly declares, that all those who

---

[1] Genesis 25: 29–34.

[2] At Sparta the people had no right to propose motions, but could only accept or reject motions laid before them by senators or kings (Plutarch, *Life of Lycurgus*, vi. 3–4). Nor did the people have the right to initiate laws at Rome, but magistrates and tribunes as well as the Senate could do so; Livy (*Ab urbe condita*, vi. 39) records an instance in 368 BC when the tribunes presented three proposals to the people to be voted on collectively or not at all. However, the *lex Caecilia Didia* of 98 BC stipulated that laws might only deal with a single subject (see Cicero, *De domo suo*, xx. 53).

profess any other religious opinions, merit the odious denomination of heretics.'

Here are two propositions altogether distinct and foreign to one another. The one declares a resolution relative to a fact;—the other declares the state of the opinions and affections of those who vote. The same individual might adopt the first, and reject the second.

Thus to unite into one proposition, two different things, is to commit a species of falsification, and to destroy$^+$ the freedom of voting, from which no benefit can result.

Hence, from inserting in the body of a law, opinions or reasons foreign to the law, the measure may be exposed to rejection, although conformable to the general wish of the assembly.

This may happen, because, although they may be agreed upon the measure, the voters may differ much with regard to the reasons which lead them to adopt it; and if the reasons which are assigned, are opposed to the opinions of the majority,$^+$ they will experience a very natural and just repugnance to profess opinions which they do not hold. To require them to pass such a law is, in fact, to exact a false declaration,$^+$ and make them tell a lie in the law.

Let us imagine the following proposition:—'Considering that there is no God, all penal laws relative to the divinity$^+$ are abolished.'

Even should all the members of the assembly be unanimous in favour of the abolition of these penal laws, there might not perhaps be found a single one who would not be shocked by this declaration of atheism, and who would not rather choose to reject the measure altogether, than to obtain it at this price.

It would seem that in a free assembly each proposer of a motion ought to observe this rule, if it were only as a measure of prudence, since an accessary of this nature can only tend to expose the principal motion to be rejected.

But the spirit of party does not reason thus. The more clearly a motion includes any clause offensive to its antagonists, the more clearly it proves the strength of those who cause it to pass: their triumph increases with the mortification of their antagonists.

We will give an example of this petty war of parties; we shall seek it in a remote period, although it would be easy to find specimens nearer to our own times; we shall see a motion produced in this spirit of hostility, applied in an opposite direction by the insertion of motives and opinions which presented it under an aspect altogether new.[a]

'A motion was made, and the question being proposed, that it be an instruction to the said committee that (in order to restore in some measure

[a] Journals of the House of Commons, Vol. XXI. p. 235, 24th February 1728.

the trade of this kingdom) they do consider of the proper means to take off the duties upon soap and candles (which are so very burthensome to the manufacturers, as well as the poor in general.')

The intention of the two phrases included in the parentheses is clear. The opposition wished to throw odium upon these two taxes, without considering that similar means might be applied to all the taxes without distinction.

The two clauses were first excluded by two very proper amendments. But this triumph was not enough: the ministerial party, wishing to throw out the motion by appearing to amend it, caused the following clause to be inserted:—

Taxes 'granted and made a security for several large sums of money advanced for the service of the public, upon parliamentary credit, the greater part of the surplus whereof belong to the sinking fund, appropriated to the discharging the national debt.'[+]

It need scarcely be added, that the motion[+] thus altered, no longer agreeable to the one party or to the other, was thrown out by common consent.

4. *A bill ought to contain a complete exhibition of all the clauses that the law ought to contain.*

This has reference to certain terms which are liable to be exchanged for terms of the same kind: for example, one quantity for another quantity, one number for another number, one portion of time for another portion of time, &c. *The imprisonment shall be{for a year.} The fine shall be {one tenth part of the parties' income.}*[+] *The reward shall be {twenty pounds sterling.}*[a]

In the projects of bills which were presented to the British parliament, the custom was to leave these points in blank between two crotchets thus: The imprisonment shall be {  ;} the fine shall be {  .}[+]

The points thus left in blank were those respecting which there is great latitude of choice. The author of the bill has no determinate reason for the choice of one term rather than another. The first debate turns rather upon the principle of the measure, without regard to these points. They are determined in committee upon the motion of some member. The journals of the House of Commons present many examples of cases in which it has been unwilling to receive bills, because the author, instead of leaving these blanks, had filled them up.

It was said, that liberty was thus better secured; so long as no term is fixed, there is greater latitude of choice.

I cannot perceive the force of this reason. Liberty exists upon this point as well as upon every other part of the bill.[+] It is lawful to propose the

---

[a] These exchangeable terms may be called[+] *congeneric competitors.*

smallest number in place of the greatest, one place instead of any other place, one quantity instead of any other quantity, and so of the rest.

On the other hand, the discussion cannot but be improved, when it has a determinate foundation upon all points. It is necessary at last that the blank should be filled up—that some one should propose a term; and who is better able to do this, than the author of the motion?—from whom can we expect greater knowledge of the subject?[a] If no one be obliged to think about the matter, is it not to be feared that these blanks will be filled up with indiscreet precipitation, as details of trifling importance.

This custom of leaving blanks most probably arose from the prudence of the framers of the laws. 'If,' they may have said, 'the term be left blank, the ideas of nobody will be hurt; but if a specific term be offered, which of course will not please everybody, the loss of a number of votes is risked upon this point alone.' This train of reasoning is not unfounded; since nothing is more common in political assemblies, than that want of candour which fixes upon the first objectionable matter of detail, which might easily be remedied, and converts it into a radical objection to the measure in which it appears.[b]

## CHAPTER XI.
## OF DEBATES.

### §1. *Of the Opening of a Debate.*

OUGHT a motion to require to be seconded?[+] A motion is not entertained by the House of Commons, until it is supported by some one besides its author; that is to say, until it is seconded.

This regulation is considered proper, in order to prevent the introduction of motions which would consume time without producing any fruit. Before occupying the time of the assembly, the proposer should consult a friend. If he cannot find a single approver, where is the evil of abandoning his motion?—what chance has he of persuading the majority, if he have not succeeded with the man of his choice?[+]

But this method has but little efficacy: it has none against party

---

[a] These blanks are now always filled up in a type of a character different from that of the other parts of the bill.—*Ed.*[1]

[b] For the other rules relative to the drawing up of laws, see also *General View of a Code of Laws*, Chap. XXXIII. *Of the style of the Laws.*[2]

---

[1] Thomas Erskine May, *A Treatise upon the Law, Privileges, Proceedings and Usage of Parliament*, London, 1844, p. 275: 'All dates, and the amount of salaries, tolls, rates, or other charges, were formerly required to be left blank; but the more convenient practice of printing such matters in italics is now adopted.'  [2] See p. 119 n. above.

motions—none against a man who in the assembly has a civil[+] or an easy friend—none against two fools or two madmen, who are determined to support one another.

Besides, it is only applicable to original motions, and not to incidental motions; that is, to those which arise in the course of the debate—to those amendments respecting which there is no opportunity of concert with any person.

It may be objected against this custom, that it tends to discourage those who have most need of particular encouragement—of isolated persons, jealous of their independence, not wishing to connect themselves with any party. Should a man of this temper, after two or three trials, find no one to second him, this would be sufficient to dishearten him. But he ought not to conclude that a motion is frivolous or absurd,[+] because at the first glance it has been rejected in this manner. How many other reasons, beside that of the demerit of the motion, may have operated to produce this refusal to second it! One may not have chosen to put himself forward; another have not liked to act the part of subaltern; a third have foreseen that it would not be successful; a fourth, that it would have made others his enemies. Many may have refused on grounds altogether foreign to the object[+] of the motion.

When a rule operates only as a restraint, if it be not useful it is mischievous.[+]

The House of Lords has never recognised this rule, and no one has found out that any inconvenience has resulted from the want of it.[+]

*Before the author of a motion is permitted to speak upon it, the motion ought to be read.*

The motion is the only subject to which his speech ought to apply. If its subject be unknown, the speech will lose a great part of its effect. It is impossible to judge of the force or weakness of the arguments, unless the object to which they refer is clearly present to the mind.

There is not a more efficacious rule than this for preventing useless discourses. If a member who had no motion to make were to begin to speak, he would find himself obliged at the first moment to give a justifying reason for so doing: if he had none, he would be reduced to silence.

In the House of Commons, the rule is, not to speak, but upon an admitted motion, or for the purpose of introducing one; but as it is not requisite to begin by presenting a motion, it sometimes happens that long speeches are made, which are not followed by a motion.

This is an example of those laws[+] which would be so good, so advantageous, provided only that they were observed.

In the English practice, the custom is to state beforehand to the House, more or less of the object of the motion, according to the supposed degree of its importance. But this statement is confined to a general indication: the whole motion is neither announced, nor reduced to writing. Is not this a defect? Is it not stopping half way? Certainly the same reasons which lead you to require that a motion should be announced beforehand, ought to make you desire that it should be presented complete. Is it not ridiculous to say to an assembly of legislators—'Divine, conjecture, imagine what the motion will be of which I have told you the title?'[+]—and to hold their curiosity in suspense, as if it were necessary to excite a dramatic interest, or to catch them by surprise?

The terms of the motion not being previously known, it is not possible to prepare amendments: hence, everything concerning them is a scene of precipitation. As they are proposed without plan, they are combated under the same disadvantage: they too frequently present vague and incoherent ideas, and are crude and indigested productions: but the greatest evil which arises, is that which it is not possible to see or to appreciate—the negative evil, the evil of privation; that is to say, the non-existence of the useful amendments which would have been offered,[+] if leisure for reflection had been afforded by a previous knowledge of the whole motion.

We have made one step. The motion being read, its author ought to be allowed the right of pre-audience.[+] It cannot be presumed that any other person can present the reasons for it, with more advantage than himself.

It is evident that no person ought to be heard against[+] a motion, before some one has spoken for[+] it. For if there be no argument to be produced in its favour, the combating the motion is loss of time. The arguments for,[+] ought to appear first, that those who oppose them may have a fixed point of attack, and not wander into vague conjectures.

In an assembly in which the members sit whilst they speak, it would be proper to agree upon a word—for instance, *dixi*[+]—which should mark the close of a speech.[+] This final word would prevent that species of preparation,[+] that indecent impatience, which is manifested in an assembly where those who wish to speak, watch all the accidental pauses of the speaker, and do not wait till he has finished before they begin.

If the member stand up whilst he speaks, the end of his discourse will be marked by his sitting down; and this gesture will more certainly reach the eye, than a word reaches the ear. The above rule would therefore be more necessary in an assembly in which the members sit whilst speaking, than in one in which they stand; but it would be useful everywhere, as a means of preserving the speaker from the fear of interruptions, and of conducting the debate with more propriety.

*In a large assembly, the person speaking ought to stand.* In this attitude, his lungs have more force, and his voice is more free[+]—he[+] exercises a

126

greater ascendency over the auditory—he more readily perceives the impression he produces. But this ought not to be made an absolute rule,[+] because it is not possible to fix the limits between a large and small assembly: besides, there are infirm persons who have sufficient strength for speaking, who are not able long to remain standing. A wounded officer ought not to be deprived of the right of speaking for his country. The last brilliant efforts of his eloquence were uttered by Lord Chatham, when he was feeble and languishing, and almost obliged to lie upon his seat.[1]

### §2. *Of free and strict Debate.*

There ought to be two kinds of debate: in one, replies should be allowed; in the other, not. The first of these I should call *free*, every member being allowed to speak as often as he pleases; the second I should call *strict*, every member, with a single exception, which will be shortly noticed, being allowed to speak only once.

The strict method may perhaps be necessary in large assemblies, where there are many who wish to speak. It becomes necessary, upon the principle of equality, to secure to each member the right of being heard: there would be a kind of injustice in allowing any one to speak twice, whilst there were others who had not once been heard. If, then, there be a superfluity of speakers—that is to say, more than can be conveniently heard, consistently with the speedy progress of business—the exclusion of replies becomes a necessary law.

But still the free method possesses great advantages. In an argument between two persons, the discussion is better followed—the reasoning is more connected, than when many persons are engaged. Each reply tends to increase the information received,[+] and to fortify the impression made. The debate becomes animated and more interesting: each one lends his attention to the argument—endeavours to understand it, and to foresee the reply it will call forth: no movement is either lost or retrograde—every step taken leads on to the conclusion. This interest is either weakened or disappointed whenever a new speaker interferes to disturb the thread of the debate, and to throw in altogether different ideas. Hence, the first feeling of men, their natural instinct, is altogether in favour of this manner of debating between two parties who alternately speak *pro* and *con*.

In the British parliament, both these methods are employed: the one when the assembly is said to meet as the *house*—the other when it meets in *committee*. When the house is assembled, the rule of speaking only once is strictly observed. In committee, it is the custom to allow of replies; and the discussion is frequently confined to a small number of individuals

---

[1] William Pitt the Elder (1708–78), 1st Earl of Chatham, made his final appearance in the House of Lords on 7 April 1778.

who have paid particular attention to the question. At all times[+] this is rather an indulgence than a rule; and thus it ought to be, for there are some obstinate speakers who will never have done; and replies have this inconvenience, that they often lead to personalities, which might make the debate degenerate into bitter and fruitless contentions.

In allowing the liberty of replies, you expose the debates to a duration incompatible with the transaction of business. This is the strongest objection against them. But first, the cases in which prompt decisions are necessary do not often arise in a legislative assembly; and in such cases it is always master of its own rules, and always at liberty to act according to circumstances.

Secondly, Can any time be considered as lost, which has been occupied in *bona fide* discussion, how long soever that discussion may have been? Is rapidity the principal object? Ought we to avoid a few moments of weariness, at the risk of many hours of repentance? Excess of examination need not be feared: bad laws are rather the results of inattention and precipitation. The general rule ought to be, to reject nothing which may enlighten the assembly: but how can it be decided beforehand, that an individual who wishes to speak has nothing useful to say?

In conclusion, it is doubtful whether the admission of replies would prolong[+] discussions. When a question is quite clear—when the two parties find[+] that their opposition is irremediable, the debate has reached its natural conclusion, and every one will be desirous of seeing it finished. Now, the liberty of reply has a direct tendency[+] to lead the discussion to this point. Two antagonists, engaged upon a question for which they have made preparation, will reply to each other with more strictness—they will go at once to the point without losing time in set phrases, exordiums, and apologies, as is done by each new orator, that he may give to his arguments the polish and ornaments of speech.

After all, the free method does not necessarily deprive any individual of the opportunity of speaking: it only retards the moment at which he obtains it. It is a simple transposition of time, which takes nothing from equality.

After this exposition of the reasons for and against these methods, every assembly must decide, according to circumstances, whether it will be proper to admit[+] the one or the other of these forms of debate.

But even when replies are not permitted, an exception should always be made in favour of the author of the motion. *He who opens the debate, should be allowed to speak last in reply.* He may naturally be presumed to be best acquainted with the strong and weak points of his cause, and if he were not allowed the right of reply, objections to which he only could reply, *might*[+] impose upon the assembly. In the British parliament, this last reply is frequently that which attracts the most attention. In this the speaker concentrates all his strength, and brings it to bear upon the essential points which ought to determine the judgment.[+] '*Videndum præcipue utrique parti ubi sit rei summa. Nam fere accidit, ut in causis multa dicantur, de paucis judicetur.*'[a]

### §3. *Of three Debates upon every proposed law.*[b]

The general rule in the English parliament is, that every bill shall be debated three times upon different days, and these days oftentimes distant from each other. These are called the[1] *three readings* of the bill. The bill may be thrown out on the first, the second, or the third reading; but it is not passed till it has been read three times.

This is not all. Between the second and third reading,[+] the bill is discussed in a *committee of the whole House.*

This general committee (which is spoken of elsewhere) admits of forms of discussion more free than those allowed in the regular debates.[+] A chairman is chosen for the occasion;—the details of the measure are discussed;—the same persons are permitted to speak several times upon the same subject; and the discussion is thus generally carried on by the individuals who possess the greatest knowledge of the particular question.

With regard to the *three readings*. The first is almost confined to the introduction of the bill, and general observations upon it;—the second is a debate upon its principles;—the third regards it as a whole, the terms of which have been considered and settled.[+]

The advantages of these reiterated debates are—1. Maturity in the deliberations, arising from the opportunities given to a great number of persons, of speaking upon different days, after they have profited by the information[+] which discussion has elicited; 2. Opportunity afforded to the public, to make itself heard—and to the members, to consult enlightened persons out of doors; 3. Prevention of the effects of eloquence, by which an orator might obtain votes upon a sudden impulse; 4. Protection to the minority of the assembly,[+] by securing to it different periods at which to state its opinions; 5. Opportunity for members absent during the first debate,[+] to attend when they perceive that their presence may influence the fate of the bill.

[a] Quint. V. 13.[2]

[b] In this chapter I have attempted to supply a subject omitted by Mr. Bentham, who makes frequent allusions to these reiterated debates, but who has not treated of them expressly.—*Dumont.*

[1] Bowring '*the*'.

[2] Quintilian, *Institutio Oratoria* v. xiii. 55. 'It is, however, specially important for both parties that they should see where the main issue lies. For it often happens that the points raised in pleading are many, although those on which a decision is given are few.' (Translation by H.E. Butler, Loeb edn., London, 1921.)

Every one knows by experience, that the strongest reasons alleged by two parties cannot be estimated at their true value the first time of hearing: they make either too much or too little impression;—too much, if they are developed with all the seduction of authority and eloquence—too little, if they are opposed by violent passions, interests, or prejudices.[+] After an interval of a few days, the mind becomes calm—public opinion has time to act—the effect of mere eloquence ceases to operate—reason resumes its sway. Very different views are often brought to the second debate, from those which were successful on the first,[+]—and the two parties approach each other with arguments matured by reflection and communication with the public.

Parties appear to have a necessary existence. If a single debate decide[+] the adoption of a law, each party has an extreme interest in employing all its means to secure the victory of the day—and great heat and animosity are produced by the debate.[+] But when it is known that a first victory is not sufficient—that the struggle must be renewed a second and a third time with the same antagonists,[+]—strength is reserved—it is tempered, that it may not injure the cause in which it is employed; no one dares to take an unlawful advantage,[+] because this would be to supply arms to his adversaries;—and the party in the minority, which gradually sees that its ultimate defeat approaches, gives way to it with the more moderation, inasmuch as it has been allowed every opportunity of preventing it.[+]

In the British parliament, independently of the *three readings* which are necessary, there are many other occasions in which it is possible to renew the debate during the *progress of a bill*—the technical term which comprises all the stages through which it must pass before its completion. It must, as I have already said, be *committed*—and it may be *recommitted*. It must be engrossed, that is, written on parchment, to become the authentic text.[+] It ought[+] at last to be transmitted to the House of Lords, and it may be sent back again to the Commons. Each of these stages are passed upon motion by a member, and each motion may become the occasion of a new debate. The *opposition* very rarely makes use of these different means for retarding the progress of a bill; but they are held in reserve for extraordinary occasions, when delay may produce important results.

It may be objected, that this plan occasions great delays,[+] and that circumstances may imperiously require that a law should be passed with rapidity. To this it may be replied, that in cases of necessity[+] the Houses of Parliament can suspend their usual orders, and that a bill may be made to pass through all its stages in both houses in one day.[+] An example of this kind occurred, if I am not mistaken, during the mutiny at the Nore in 1797;[1] but such extreme measures arise from urgent necessity,[+] which overcomes all opposition.

Those who consider the slowness of these forms as objectionable, do not perceive that their objection is directed against reflection—against that information which is often the fruit of time and study.[+] There may be repetitions; but a reasonable conviction[+] is not attained at once. The best argument requires to be presented at different times, and under many aspects. It is by these means that it becomes adapted to different minds, and is deposited in the memory.[+] Those men who are persuaded by a word, are lost as easily as they are gained. Allow of obstinacy in debate, and there will result from it perseverance in conduct. In France, the terrible *decrees of urgency*, the *decrees for closing the discussion*, may well be remembered with dread: they were formed for the subjugation of the minority—for the purpose of stifling arguments which were dreaded. The more susceptible a people are of excitement and of being led astray, so much the more ought they to place themselves under the protection of forms which impose the necessity of reflection, and prevent surprises.

A more direct answer may be given to this objection on the ground of delay:[+]—Three debates necessarily require intervals, but they do not tend to render the discussion longer upon the whole[+]—they have rather a contrary effect. Indeed, these three debates have different objects, and divide the deliberations in the most suitable manner. In the first, the question is, Shall the subject-matter be considered at all?[+] If its consideration be refused, there is a great saving of time, because no one has been engaged in the consideration of the details.[+] At the second reading, the question is, Shall the principle of the bill introduced be adopted? If its principle be admitted, it is then taken into consideration in committee, and each clause is considered by itself, and amendments, if necessary, proposed in it: when the whole has been thus considered, the bill is reported to the house.

At the time appointed, the project of the law, as thus prepared, undergoes a third debate: the whole of its parts and bearings being thoroughly understood, all are prepared to consider it in its principles and details; whilst those who wish again to propose their amendments can do so, if they hope to obtain the concurrence of the majority.[+]

---

[1] The mutiny at the Nore took place between 12 May and 16 June 1797. When the Admiralty refused to grant their demands for improved conditions of service, the mutineers planned a blockade of the Medway and the Thames. The collapse of the mutiny was effected by armed force and by 37 Geo. III, c. 70, which passed through all its stages on 5 June. See *Commons Journals*, lii. 635–6.

## §4. *Of the exclusion of Written Discourses.*

The rule for the exclusion of written discourses is strictly observed in the British parliament. It ought to be so in all deliberative assemblies.[a]

'The principal inconvenience of written discourses consists in their want of connexion—they have no relation to one another.

'It is easily perceived that a political assembly is not a society of academicians; that the principal advantage of a national senate, and of public discussion, arises from that activity of mind, from that energy of feeling, from that abundance of resources, which results from a large assembly of enlightened men who animate and excite each other, who attack without sparing each other, and who, feeling themselves pressed by all the forces of their antagonists, display in their defence powers which were before unknown to themselves.

'Attention is like the mirror, which concentrates the rays of the sun into one focus, and produces increase both of heat and light; but attention cannot be sustained except by connected discourse, and the kind of dramatic interest which results from it. When attention is excited,[+] nothing passes without examination: every truth tells—every error provokes refutation; a fortunate word, a happy expression, is more effective than a long speech;—and as these weapons cannot be wielded in debate except by the cleverest men, the assembly is spared from ennui, and saves its time. There is nothing useful in the plan of reading, except it be to procure for mediocrity the consolations of self-love, at the expense of the public good.

'Will it be said, that these prepared discourses will commonly have greater maturity, greater depth?—that the assembly by this means is less exposed to hear dangerous and ill-considered opinions? The effect is precisely opposite. It requires longer preparation and deeper meditation to be able to speak extempore than to write at leisure. To have completely mastered his subject—to have studied it under all its aspects—to have foreseen all objections—to be ready to answer every one:[+] such are the conditions necessary for a public speaker. But what ordinary man is not able to write upon a given subject any number of pages? One person employs writing for the purpose of facilitating meditation, to relieve his memory, to prevent the fatigue of retaining a series of ideas; another writes, that he may dismiss from his mind what he has committed to paper. It may therefore easily happen, that a man does not understand the

---

[a] Bentham does not appear to have discussed the above topic. The paragraphs which follow have been extracted from 'Le Courrier de Provence, No. 65.'—*Dumont*.[1]

---

[1] With the exception of the first sentence, which has been added by Dumont, the passage is from *Courier de Provence*, lxv, 11–12 November 1789, pp. 3–6.

subject upon which he has written; but he must always understand his subject, if he will speak well upon it.[+]

'If all those who have exhibited the talent of speaking in the National Assembly, had been asked why they were reduced to the reading of memoirs upon difficult and complicated subjects, they would[+] have accused the shortness of the time, the premature questions, the number and variety of the subjects: but they would thus have confirmed the opinion, that the plan of written discourses is bad in itself. It will never form powerful minds in a political assembly: it favours idleness of thought, and, like the habit of being carried, produces torpor and indolence.

'In England, as elsewhere, the distinguished talent for public speaking is concentered among a small number of individuals; but the plan of reading is not tolerated there, which multiplies speeches without multiplying ideas. Does it appear that there is any want of arguments in their discussion?—is there less vigour among their political combatants? As soon as the defender of a motion ceases to speak, does not the opposite party furnish an orator, who seeks, by his opposite arguments, to efface the impression which the first has made.'

Those who do not possess the talent of public speaking, may communicate facts and arguments to the habitual speakers. This is the best method of making them useful. These communications—these contributions of ideas, continually take place in the British parliament.[a]

## §5. *Other rules relative to Debate.*

The rules we are about to exhibit are not of the same importance as the preceding, but they all tend to prevent inconveniences, and to produce a better debate. The former were dictated by necessity, these by prudence.

1. *Address the president, and not the assembly in general.*

This custom, constantly followed in the House of Commons, is well adapted to a numerous assembly, it gives those who speak a fixed point of direction, and a common centre for all the speeches.

It is also natural that each should address himself to the individual who is officially to judge if he wander from the question, or if he fall into any irregularity prohibited by the rules of the assembly.

A speech addressed to the president of the assembly will be more grave and temperate, than if it were addressed to the whole assembly. An

---

[a] They occurred even[+] in the National Assembly. I have often seen M. de Mirabeau, in going to the tribune, and even in the tribune itself, receive notes, which he has glanced[+] at without interrupting his speech, and which he has sometimes interwoven[+] with the greatest art into the train of his discourse. A wit once compared him to those mountebanks, who cut a ribbon in pieces, chew it for a moment, and then pull the ribbon in one length out of their mouth again.[+]—*Dumont.*

excited individual addressing himself to an impartial magistrate, to a respected president, will feel the necessity of measuring his expressions, and repressing the movements of his indignation and wrath.

If the members speak directly to each other, the discussion will more easily degenerate into personalities.

There is no custom more useful in a political assembly, than that of treating the president with deference and respect; and there is nothing more likely to form this habit, than the considering him as the centre of the deliberations—as the assembly personified.

2. *Avoid designating the members of the assembly by their proper names.*

This rule, strictly followed in the House of Commons, renders it necessary to recur to circumlocutions in designating a member: *'The Honourable Member on my right,'* or *'on my left'*—*'the Gentleman in the blue ribbon'*—*'the Noble Lord'*—*'my Learned Friend,'*[+] &c. Most of these expressions are polite, without being insipid. The proper names would often be accompanied with a catalogue of complimentary epithets, of which we may see many examples in the speeches of Cicero pronounced in the Roman Senate:[1] but the real inconvenience is, that the mention of the name[+] in debate is a stronger appeal to self-love than every other designation. It is less offensive to say, 'the honourable member who spoke last has fallen into a gross mistake,' than to call him by his name: it is as though an abstraction were made of the individual, that he might be considered only in his political character. The observation of this rule is troublesome; and when the debaters are warm, it requires an effort to submit to it;—but this very circumstance proves that it is necessary.

3. *Never impute bad motives.*

This also is an absolute rule in British debate. You are at liberty to impute ignorance to a previous speaker—to tell him of his mistakes, his false representations of facts—but not to say one word inculpating his motives. Direct your energy against the mischievous effects of his opinions, or the measures he supports; show that they are fatal—that they tend to establish tyranny or anarchy; but never suppose that he foresaw or designed these consequences.

This rule is strictly founded on justice; for if it be difficult always to know our own true and secret motives, there is much more temerity in pretending to develope[+] those of others;—and from our own experience we ought to know how easy it is to be deceived in this respect. The reserve which this rule imposes, is useful to all. It is favourable to the freedom of opinion.[+] In political debate as in war, you ought not to employ any means which you would wish should not be employed against you.

But this maxim is especially conformable with prudence.[+] Is your

---

[1] See for example *De provinciis consularibus* I. i; *In Catilinam* I. viii. 21.

134

antagonist in error?—he may receive the truth you skilfully present to him:[+] but if you impugn his motives, you offend him—you provoke him—you do not leave him the quiet necessary for listening to you with attention: he becomes opposed to you: the fire communicates from one to another—his friends make common cause with him, and oftentimes resentments, which are prolonged beyond the debates, carry into political opposition all the asperity of personal quarrels. It is not enough to exclude personalities: it also is proper to proscribe all violent and bitter expressions; it is proper to proscribe them as signs of awkwardness, still more than as traits of passion.[+]

All who have watched political assemblies know that improper[+] expressions are the sources of the most tumultuous incidents and of the most obstinate wanderings.[a]

4. *Never mention the wishes of the sovereign or the executive power.*

This wish in itself proves nothing in regard to the fitness or unfitness of the measure: it can have no good effect, and can only be productive of evil.

The admission of this instrument would be incompatible with the liberty of the assembly, not only upon the particular occasion but upon every other; for if it may be alleged at one time, it will be alleged at all times; and if the least value be granted to a consideration of this nature, the power of the assembly is reduced to nothing: there is substituted for its will,[+] the will[+] of a superior.

If this wish,[+] when announced by one party, should be disputed or condemned by another party, it would follow that the head of the executive power would become the personal object of the debates—that its dignity would be compromised; and there would result a most fatal species of discord—that which leads on to civil war.

This rule has been long established and strictly followed in the parliamentary debates. The king's speech at the opening of the session only contains general recommendations; and besides this, it is only

---

[a] Mr. Fox,[1] the most distinguished orator of England, who attacked his adversaries with so close a logic, carried to the highest pitch the art of avoiding everything which might irritate them. In his most animated moments, when he was as it were borne onward by the torrent of his ideas, always master of himself, he was never wanting in the most scrupulous regard to politeness. It is true, that this happy quality was in him less a secret of the art of oratory, than the effects of the benevolence of his character—modest amidst its superiority, and generous in its strength. Still, however, no man ever expressed himself more courageously, or less ceremoniously. '*Les mots allaient,*' as says Montaigne, '*où allait la pensée*'.[2]

---

[1] Charles James Fox (1749–1806), Whig politician, Secretary of State for Foreign Affairs Mar.–July 1782 and Apr.–Dec. 1783.

[2] Michel de Montaigne (1533–92), essayist. 'J'ayme, entre les galans hommes, qu'on s'exprime courageusement, que les mots aillent où va la pensée', *Essais* III. viii (first published in 1588). See *Œuvres complètes de Montaigne*, ed. M. Rat and A. Thibaudet, Paris, 1962, p. 902.

considered as an act of the minister. It is therefore freely discussed without mention of the king, and the opposition attack it as they do any other ministerial measure.

5. *Never quote any justificatory piece, or means of proof, which has not been presented to the assembly in consequence of a motion made to that effect.*

*Omnis demonstratio ex præcognitis et præconcessis.*[1]

This rule is founded upon two manifest reasons:—

1. To secure the authenticity of the matter which is taken as a foundation for the decision.

2. To give every member an opportunity of being acquainted with it, and informed of the use which it is desired to make of it.

In consequence of neglecting this rule, the highest bodies in the state in France have sometimes fallen into errors with which the lowest official persons cannot be reproached in England.[+] The parliament of Paris, in its famous remonstrances of the 16th and 24th July 1787, enumerated Charles V and Henry IV among the kings who had assembled the States-General,[2] which is not true either of the one or the other.[a]

How often has the National Assembly passed decrees upon mere hearsay—upon facts said to be of public notoriety!—without thinking that there is nothing more deceitful than popular rumour, and that the more widely a fact was known, so much the more easily might proof be collected of it.

The legislative assembly transmitted articles of accusation against M. de Lessart[3] to the high national court, which contained only vague and declamatory imputations, without stating a single fact, and without having heard the accused.[b]

---

[a] This fact is drawn from L'Histoire du Gouvernement François, p. 147.[4]

[b] Every nation has its weakness and its endemic imperfections; and the greater the empire they have obtained, the greater the importance of knowing and guarding against them. Of all the faults with which French writers can be accused, inexactitude is the most

---

[1] 'Every proof must be based on what is known and accepted in advance.'

[2] Remonstrances were formal objections by a sovereign court to registration of new royal ordinances, edicts, or declarations. In this instance, the *Cour des Pairs*, a body consisting of the *parlement* of Paris with additional members, objected to the imposition of a stamp tax, and demanded the convocation of the Estates-General to approve a permanent tax, a task the *parlement* was not permitted to perform. See J. Egret, *The French Prerevolution 1787–1788*, Chicago and London, 1977, pp. 94–6. Charles V (1337–80) was King of France from 1364; Henri IV (1553–1610) was King of France from 1589.

[3] Antoine de Valdec de Lessart (1742–92), French Minister of Foreign Affairs 30 November 1791–17 March 1792. In March 1792 the National Assembly denounced him as an enemy of the Revolution, impeached him, and sent the case to the High Court at Orléans. There de Lessart argued that the accusations against him had been made precipitately. On 9 September 1792 he was killed at Versailles along with fifty-two other prisoners who were being brought to Paris for trial.

[4] Jean Pierre Papon, *Histoire du Gouvernement françois, depuis l'Assemblée des Notables, tenue le 22 février 1787, jusqu'à la fin de décembre de la même année*, London, 1788.

6. *Do not permit any motion which has been rejected, to be presented afresh during the same session, or before an interval {of three months.}*

This rule has for its object the repression of the obstinacy of parties, which would never leave off repeating questions which had been already decided against them, either from a hope of thereby keeping up the zeal of their partisans, or from a desire to embarrass the operations of the assembly.

This rule can only be strictly applied to motions which are identical. A party will never allow itself to be restricted by the prohibition to reproduce its motion. If it see any chance of success, it will not fail to present it again under a new form.

It is, however, always[+] well to insert this article in the regulations. It will follow from it[+] in ordinary cases, that a motion once rejected will not reappear in the same session.

A rule which should permit the definitive rejection of motions without return, would be the greatest possible attack upon liberty: it would be to seek to enchain one's self or one's successors.

### §6. *Of the Election of Debaters.*

I proceed to point out a mode of reducing the number of orators, in an assembly too numerous to allow the right of discussion to all.

It would, however, only be applicable to democratic constitutions; for with good regulations, six hundred persons at least might exercise the right of speaking without any occasion to limit it to a certain number.

The most simple method would be to elect in the first instance, twenty-four orators by name; 2dly, To choose one hundred other persons by lot, in order to give a chance to all parties; 3dly, To permit each of these to waive his right in favour of any other member of the assembly at pleasure.

marked—the most incontestible. If the English nation has any decided advantage over its rival, it is in the quality opposed to this defect that its cause should be sought for.

An historical work without authorities would be received in England very nearly as a plea without proofs, or as a romance. But in France, a great number of historians have considered it unnecessary to give references to original authorities: the condition[+] they impose upon their readers is to believe them on their word. But if the author had the original documents before him, why did he not cite them? Is it more difficult to make a reference than an extract? What reliance can be placed upon his judgment, if he have not felt that the confidence he demanded depends upon this exactitude? And if it arise either from negligence or trifling, that he has refused the labour necessary for furnishing his proofs, may it not with much stronger reasoning be presumed that he was incapable of taking the pains necessary for acquiring them?

There is a kind of maxim proverbial in France, that it is proper to regard the meaning[+] without weighing the letters—without quarreling about the words;—as if the meaning did not depend upon the words—as if correct ideas were not produced by correct words.[+] This pretext is the resource of feeble and careless heads, which would be thought strong; for there is no defect which has not attempted to employ itself as a mask.[+]

Those who did not possess the talent or inclination to speak, would then voluntarily surrender their places to such members of their own party as seemed best fitted to fill them. But it would be proper to reserve for all the members the right of making a motion—that is to say, a principal motion—and of explaining it.

## CHAPTER XII.
## OF AMENDMENTS.

AT first sight, it would appear scarcely possible to class amendments, since they may embrace every modification which the human mind can conceive with respect to a given motion. Upon calling analysis, however, to our assistance, we shall discover that this difficulty vanishes.

All amendments are necessarily relative to *the choice of terms*, or to *the mode of their connexion.*

Amendments which relate to terms, can only have for their object one or other of these three objects—to suppress, to add, or to substitute.[+] This last operation is effected by the union of the two first.

Amendments with reference to the connexion of ideas, can only have for their object—their *division*, their *union*, or their *transposition.*

Does the original proposition appear to me too complicated? I demand that it be divided,[+] with the intention of allowing the assembly the power of rejecting one part, without rejecting the other.

Does it appear proper that two propositions which are separated in the original project, should be considered together, or one following the other? I demand their union.[+]

Amendments which consist in transposing a certain word or phrase may have the effect of entirely changing the project: the word *only*, for example, placed in different situations, will[+] produce a meaning totally different.

Amendments are thus reduced to six kinds, and are capable of receiving clear and precise denominations:—

$$\text{Amendment} \left\{ \begin{array}{l} \text{Suppressive.} \\ \text{Additive.} \\ \text{Substitutive.} \end{array} \right.$$

$$\text{Amendment} \left\{ \begin{array}{l} \text{Divisive.} \\ \text{Unitive.} \\ \text{Transpositive.} \end{array} \right.$$

These technical terms appear necessary to prevent the confounding of ideas which only differ from each other by very slight shades. Things which are not classified, and which have no proper names, are always ill understood,[+] and cannot be designated but by periphrases which are often obscure.

A proper name is a great assistance to the understanding, to the memory, and to the communication of ideas. The greatest difficulty which can be alleged against new words is, that they are difficult to be understood; but those derived from more familiar terms are perfectly intelligible.

It frequently happens, that many amendments are offered upon one motion, and even amendments which refer to a previous amendment: this is what is called a *sub-amendment*. In what order ought they to be discussed? It is very difficult to give positive rules in this respect: each party will support the importance of his own, and seek to obtain priority. If a debate were always necessary to decide the matter, the principal question would be lost sight of, and the attention of the assembly exhausted upon these accessories.

These contests may be rendered more rare and short, by laying down as a general principle, that amendments upon the *connexion* shall always be taken into consideration first. What is their object? To place the objects to be discussed in the most suitable order: but this order, once formed, is that which most tends to produce a good discussion. Among this class of amendments, the divisive[+] ought to have the priority. Complex questions are the occasion of the most obscure and obstinate debates.

Among amendments as to the *choice of terms*, it might also be laid down as a general principle, that *suppressive* amendments ought to have the priority over the two others of the same kind. The suppression of a single term may remove the strongest objections, and that which is omitted is no longer the subject of debate: on the other hand, additive or substitutive amendments may be productive of sub-amendments of the same species.

The value of these observations will only be fully apprehended by those who have had experience in political assemblies. They will be aware how much confusion is produced by multiplied amendments, and how happy it would be, if without absolute rules some thread could be found[+] which would lead out of the labyrinth.

There remain many more difficulties upon this subject. When there are many additive amendments in concurrence, in what order should they be submitted to the vote? Ought they to be presented singly, or all at once? If they are presented singly, by deciding according to priority you do not give the others an equal chance. It is the same in elections. If you have to choose among many candidates, you do not treat them with equality if you put them to the vote one after another. He who is presented first, will in general have a great advantage; and if he be elected, the others would be rejected without having any chance of success. It is proper, therefore, to vote for[+] rival amendments after the elective manner. I see no other inconvenience than the length of the process. It would be proper always[+] to have recourse to this in cases of great importance. In ordinary cases, it may be allowed to the president to put amendments to the vote in the order which appears to him most suitable, it being understood, that if objection be made, it belongs to the assembly to decide.

It is scarcely necessary to say that amendments are only trials[+] which ought to admit of every possible variation. If the amendment pass, it does not follow that the clause amended shall be adopted. The motion, thus modified, becomes the object of debate, and may be rejected. That which has been suppressed, may be re-established: that which has been added, may be struck out. Words may be placed and displaced, as in the corrections of style, without deciding upon the value of the composition, which after this labour may be condemned or destroyed.[+]

One rule which ought to be absolute with respect to amendments, is— not to admit any which are insidious.[+]

I call these pretended amendments insidious,[+] which, instead of improving the motion, represent it as ridiculous or absurd, and which cannot be adopted without making the motion fall by means of the amendment itself.

Ridicule is useful for the overthrow[+] of an absurdity which does not deserve to be seriously attacked; but an epigram in the shape of an amendment is a piece of wit which is unbecoming the gravity and the design[+] of a political assembly. To propose an amendment, is to declare that one seeks to improve the motion, that it may become worthy of approbation: to propose an amendment which renders the motion ridiculous, is a species of fraud and insult, resembling that particular kind of impertinence which in society is called *jeering*.

Besides; these insidious amendments are altogether useless. They cannot pass unless the majority of the assembly be already disposed to reject the motion itself. It is therefore to go round about, in order to reach the end which may be attained by direct means. You only render necessary two operations instead of one. You begin by receiving the amendment which renders the motion absurd, and then reject the motion thus amended.

Let us apply these observations to the celebrated vote of the House of Commons in 1782—a vote which served as the foundation of a kind of revolution in the government:—

'It is declared, that the influence of the crown has increased, is increasing, and that it ought to be diminished.'[1]

---

[1] The motion was put by John Dunning (1731–83), 1st Baron Ashburton, on 6 April 1780 (not 1782). It was carried by 233 votes to 215.

Let us suppose that one of the opponents of the motion had proposed that it be adopted, upon the insertion of the word *necessary* before influence.

Here would be an example of the amendment insidious; since the insertion of this word would have rendered the motion contradictory, and even criminal; and the amendment having been admitted, the motion ought to be rejected.

Another example:—A motion having been made for the production of all letters written by the Lords of the Admiralty to an officer of marines,— it was proposed to add as an amendment, the words 'which letters may contain orders, or relate to orders not executed, and still subsisting.' The amendment having been adopted, the whole motion was rejected without a division.[1]

This mode of procedure united both the inconveniences I have mentioned: insult and derision were its object—cunning and tergiversation were its means. It was entirely opposed to the maxim—*suaviter in modo, fortiter in re.*[2]

## CHAPTER XIII.
## OF DILATORY MOTIONS, OR MOTIONS OF ADJOURNMENT.

*A motion made, and its proposer heard, it is lawful for any member, from this moment to the conclusion of the debate, provided he does not interrupt any speech, to propose a dilatory motion; and this shall take precedence of the previous motion.*

There are three kinds of dilatory motion:—

Indefinite adjournment . . . . . . . . . . . . . . . . . . . . . . . . . . . . . (*sine die.*)
Fixed adjournment . . . . . . . . . . . . . . . . . . . . . . . . . . . . . . . . (*in diem.*)
Relative adjournment . . . . . . . . . . . . . . . . . . . . . . . . . . . . (*post quam.*)

This latter motion consists in proposing to adjourn till after a future event: for example, till after the discussion of another motion, or of some bill already upon the order-book—or till after the presentation of a report,

---

[1] In the House of Commons on 12 March 1728, a motion was proposed for the production of all letters written between the Lords of the Admiralty and Commodore Edward St. Lo (?1682–1729) relating to British ships engaged in hostilities with the Spanish. See *Commons Journals*, xxi. 264. This example and the previous one were also cited by Romilly, in *Règlemens observés dans la Chambre des Communes pour débattre les matières et pour voter*, Paris, 1789, pp. 29–31 (*Tactique des assemblées législatives*, i. 320–1).

[2] i.e. 'gently in manner, forcibly in deed.' In a letter of December 1821 Bentham attributes this saying, albeit with the phrases reversed, to Philip Dormer Stanhope (1694–1773), 4th Earl of Chesterfield; see *The Correspondence of Jeremy Bentham*, vol. x, ed. S. Conway, Oxford, 1994 (*CW*), p. 461. Dumont also reverses the phrases.

which ought to be made by a committee, &c.—or a communication from the king, or expected petitions.

All these motions ought to be permitted, in order to secure to the assembly the exercise of its will; which would not be completely free, if any one of these modifications were excluded.

The relative adjournment, or *post quam*, is necessary as a preservative against the danger of coming to an unsuitable decision in the absence of the necessary documents.

Fixed adjournment, or *in diem*, may have the same object, the procuring of new documents upon a question which does not appear sufficiently clear; or it may be for the purpose of arresting a discussion which assumes too lively and passionate a character.

Precipitation may arise from two causes: from ignorance, when a judgment is formed without the collection of all the information required—from passion, when there is not the necessary calm for considering the question in all its aspects.

What may happen to an individual, may happen to an assembly. The individual may feel, that in the actual conjuncture he is not so sufficiently master of his passion, as to form a prudent determination, but he may be sufficiently so, not to form any—

'Quos ego. Sed motos præstat componere fluctus.' *Æn.* I. 139.[1]

'I would beat you,' said the philosopher to his slave, 'if I were not angry.'[2]

This faculty, of doubting and suspending our operations, is one of the noblest attributes of man.[+]

These two species of adjournment decide nothing as to the merit of the motion: but to demand an indefinite adjournment, is to cut short the debate by rejecting the motion itself. Ordinarily, the partisans of the original motion will be opposed to this adjournment, and they will employ all the arguments which they can advance in its favour, in opposition to the adjournment. In this case the debate will be less direct, but not shorter. But it may happen that they may themselves favour the indefinite adjournment, if they judge by the complexion of the debate that the chances of success are unfavourable, and that they can attempt their object with more success at a future time.

When an indefinite adjournment is adopted, it is probable that the original motion would have been rejected. The prompt termination of the debate is then an economy of time.

---

[1] Virgil, *Aeneid*, I. 135 (not 139); 'Whom I . . .! But it is better to calm the troubled waves.'
[2] A saying attributed to Plato by Diogenes Laertius, *Lives and Opinions of the Eminent Philosophers*, III. 39.

# CHAPTER XIV.
# OF VOTING.

## §1. *General Observations.*

THIS subject is both difficult and important. The freedom of an assembly resides in the expression of its will. It is necessary, therefore, so to proceed, that every one may give his vote in conformity with his real wishes, and that in the result we may be sure to have obtained the general wish.

The processes of voting are susceptible of divisions derived from many sources:—

1. Voting upon questions, or voting respecting persons.[+] The first takes place with reference to the adoption or rejection of a motion; the second with reference to the election of a person to an office.

There is no real difference between these two cases. To vote upon an election is to vote upon the question whether a certain individual shall be elected: to vote upon a question, is to vote upon an election whether the project shall be chosen or rejected.

2. A *simple* or a *compound vote.* The simple vote occurs when the question is so reduced that it is only necessary to say *yes* or *no*—such a project shall be adopted, or shall not—such person shall be elected or shall not.

The compound vote occurs, when many operations are to be performed;—when it is necessary to decide among many projects, to choose one person from among many candidates, or to nominate to many places.

With regard to motions, it is proper to reduce the question to the simple form, in which one side may vote by yes, and the other side by no.[+]

With regard to elections, the compound mode is often necessary. When a committee of twenty-four persons is to be chosen from among 1200, there will be 1200 persons eligible for each place, and twenty-four places for each of which it is necessary to choose out of 1200.

3. With reference either to motions or elections, the votes may be given *secretly* or *openly:* the secret mode is called ballot.[+]

4. The mode employed for obtaining a decision, may be either *dependent* or *independent* of human will.[+] Hence a new distinction— election by *choice*—election by *lot.*[+]

5. In conclusion, there is also regular and summary[+] voting. In the regular mode, all the votes are counted, and the exact number on each side known: in the summary mode, the president puts the question, and calls upon the assembly to express its will[+] by sitting down or rising up, or by holding up the hand, &c.; the president judging which party has the majority, and his decision being valid, unless objected to.

143

## §2. *Of open and secret Voting.*

*In general, it is very desirable that the voting should be open rather than secret.*

Publicity is the only means of subjecting the voters to the tribunal of public opinion, and of holding them to their duty by the restraint of honour.[a]

This supposes that publicity[+] is in accordance with the public welfare.

In general, this supposition is well founded. The opinion formed by the public is always conformable to what appears to be its interest; and in the ordinary course of things it sees its own interest, whatever it may be.[+] It is always opposed to misconduct; it always respects the probity, the fidelity, the firmness of its governors and judges.

Still, however, the opinion of the public may be incorrect, since all the members of this tribunal are men. If there be measures upon which the wisest men are not agreed, how is it possible that the public should agree, who are not all wise? If there be errors in morals and legislation, which have led the noblest minds[+] astray, how can the multitude, over whom prejudices have so great an empire, be secured?

It may therefore be said, that in those cases in which public opinion is erroneous, it is desirable that the legislators should vote in secret, that they may be withdrawn from unjust censure, and rendered more free in their votes.

This argument is unsound: for upon what is it founded? Upon the presumption that the opinion of a small number is more correct than the united opinions of a large number. This may be true; but a wise and modest man will be always unwilling to attribute to himself this superiority over his fellows—to pretend to make his opinion triumph over the general opinion. He will choose rather to submit his opinion to that which generally prevails in the nation, and especially will he not desire a victory obtained by clandestine votes, of which he knows the danger.

It follows, therefore, that recognizing the fallibility of the public, it is proper to act as though it were infallible; and that we ought never, under pretence of this fallibility, to establish a system which would withdraw the representatives of the public from its influence.

But may it not be apprehended that this publicity will render men too feeble—that is to say, disposed to sacrifice their real opinions to the general opinion? No: this plan tends in the long run to give greater strength and elevation to their characters. Experience will soon disclose the great difference between the opinion which arises out of a particular circumstance, and that which is formed after mature reflection—between the clamour of the multitude, which is dissipated in noise, and the

[a] See Chap. II. *Of Publicity.*

enlightened opinion of the wise, which survives transitory errors. Freedom of opinion conciliates the respect even of those whom it opposes, and mental courage is no less honoured in free states, than military bravery.

It is, therefore, in a correct knowledge of public opinion, that the means must be found for resisting it when it is considered ill founded: the appeal lies to itself—as from Philip misinformed, to Philip correctly informed.[1] It is not always[+] according to public opinion that an enlightened and virtuous man will decide,—but he will presume, in consulting general utility, that public opinion will take the same course; and there is no stronger moral probability in a country where discussion is free.

Such are the principles which may be advanced for the establishment of the general rule with regard to the publicity of voting.

This rule must be subject at all times[+] to widely extended exceptions.

The cases in which publicity would be dangerous, are those in which it exposes the voters to the influence of *seductive* motives more powerful than the tutelary[+] motives which it furnishes.

In judging whether a motive ought to be referred to the class of *seductive* or *tutelary*[+] motives, it is necessary to examine whether, in the case in question, it tend to produce more good or more evil—whether it tend to favour the greatest or the smallest number.

If, for example, a nobleman be called to decide between his own personal interest and the interest of the body of the nobility,—the motive, whatever it may be, which leads him to prefer this interest[+] to his own, deserves to be called *tutelary*. If this same nobleman be called to decide between the interest of the body of the nobility, and that of the total mass of the citizens,—this same motive loses its tutelary quality, and can only be considered as a seductive[+] motive.

Hence *l'esprit de corps*, a *social*[+] principle, when it leads to the sacrifice of the interest of the individual to that of the[+] particular society, becomes *anti-social*[+] when it leads to the sacrifice of the great interests of the public.[+]

The same observation is applicable to friendship. If this motive lead me to serve my friend at the expense of my own interest, it is social and tutelary: if it lead me to serve him at the expense of the general good, the same motive becomes anti-social and seductive.

From these considerations, it is proper to add to the general rule respecting publicity, a limiting clause:—

*Votes ought to be given secretly in all cases in which there is more to fear from the influence of particular wills, than to hope from the influence of public opinion.*

---

[1] A variation of the saying, 'appeal from Philip drunk to Philip sober', based on a passage in Valerius Maximus, *Facta et dicta memorabiles*, VI. ii. ext. 1.

What are these cases? To answer this question, it is necessary to distinguish two species of interest: the one *factitious*—the other *natural*.

Interest is purely factitious when the voter has nothing to gain or to lose in consequence of his vote, except when his vote is known.

Interest is natural when the voter may lose or gain in consequence of his vote, even should it remain unknown.

For example, the interest which results from the contract whereby I engage to sell my vote to a stranger, is a factitious interest.[+]

Secret voting[+] destroys the influence of factitious interest: it has no effect upon the influence of natural interest.

Under the régime of secresy, the buyer could have no sufficient security that the contract would be faithfully executed by the seller: an individual may be sufficiently dishonest to commit a fraud, but not to commit treason: the lesser crime is always more probable than the greater.

The system of secresy has therefore a useful tendency in those circumstances in which publicity exposes the voter to the influence of a particular interest opposed to the public interest.

Secresy is therefore in general suitable in elections. Are the votes given openly?—no one can tell to what extent friendship, hope, or fear, may take away the freedom of voting.

It would be a great evil, if in elections, especially popular elections, the effect of secresy were to destroy all influence. This idea of absolute independence in the voters[+] is absurd. Those whose situation does not permit them to acquire political knowledge, have need of guidance from more enlightened persons; but happily the secret mode of election does not diminish the influence of mind on mind:[+] all other things being equal, the most deserving individual in elective assemblies will have the ascendency over the more obscure member;[+]—the man distinguished by his services will have more votes than he who does not rise above the common level. The opulent proprietor, the employment of whose fortune presents a spectacle to the observation of the multitude, will be more readily taken as a model for imitation, than the individual who moves in a narrower circle. This preponderance of the aristocracy is as natural as it is just and necessary. The advantages of wealth and rank suffice, in case of equilibrium in other respects, to turn the balance: but if the one of the candidates had exposed himself to public contempt, whilst the other, rising from obscurity, had acquired the general favour, the illusion[+] would be broken;—and if the votes were free, merit would be preferred to fortune.

It is proper to observe, that the secret mode does not prevent those who desire it, from making known their sentiments. A constrained and universal secresy in elections would be a bad measure: this servile silence would be in contradiction to freedom of action. Each candidate ought to have his friends—his defenders—to cause his claims to be duly estimated by the assembly, to dissipate false imputations—in a word, to enlighten the decision of his judges. Since to proceed to an election is to proceed to try the candidates with the intention of bestowing a reward,—to exclude previous *vivâ voce* discussion, is to decide the cause of the candidates and that of the public, without allowing the interested parties an opportunity of being heard.[+]

It is true that these public debates—these manifestations of party— may sometimes, in popular elections, produce a tumultuous ferment; but this is a small evil, compared with that of restraining the expression of the public feeling. It is by this freedom that the people are interested in persons and things, and that the firmest bonds are formed between the electors and the elected. Even in England, where these periods rarely return,[+] the fear of this species of popular assize exercises a marked influence over those who devote themselves to the career of politics.

With this mixture of publicity, secret voting appears to me, then, most suitable for elections; that is to say, the most suited to prevent venality, and to secure the independence of the electors. In political matters, I do not see any other case in which it can be recommended as a general rule. But it is proper to observe here, that a nation may find itself in particular circumstances, which will demand the same system upon other points. It may be, for example, that at the period when secret suffrages were introduced at Rome[+] the change was desirable. Cicero thought otherwise.[1]

The adoption, however, of one of these methods, does not exclude the other. There are cases in which it is advantageous to combine them, by making them follow upon the same question. The result of these two operations, whether they coincide or whether they differ, would always furnish very instructive indications.

I find a very singular example in the latter days of Poland, when she made a last and generous effort to withdraw herself from the dominant influence of Russia.

The permanent Council, the depositary of the executive power, exercised the supreme power during the interval of the Diets: this Council, intimidated or corrupted, was only the instrument of the will of Russia. It was proposed to raise an army to cause the territory to be respected,—it was proposed to place this army under the orders of a commission, independent of this Council. On the 16th October 1788, they voted upon this proposition:—publicly collected, the votes showed a majority of 80 against 60 for the negative. The secret vote reduced this majority to 7.[a]

[a] Courrier de l'Europe, 22d Nov. 1788.[2]

---

[1] Cicero's opposition to the secret ballot appears in *De legibus*, III. iii. 10, xv. 33–xvii. 39.

[2] By this date the *Courier de l'Europe* had been renamed the *Courier de Londres*. In fact the report said that under open voting the majority was 'de 50 à 60 voix', reduced to seven in the secret ballot.

On the 3d of November, the same proposition was discussed again:— the open vote gave for the independence of the commission 114, against it 148; but the secret vote turned the majority on the other side—for the independence 140, against it 122. Thus, among 262 votes, this change of method had made a difference of 52.[a]

When secret voting is established, it ought only to be when circumstances render a hidden influence suspected; and even then, it is proper that it should be preceded by open voting. Publicity ought to be the ordinary plan.

Secresy ought only to be admitted as a kind of appeal. To demand a ballot, is to appeal from the apparent to the real wish of the assembly.

To take the opposite direction—that is to say, to proceed from secret voting to open voting—would be wrong.[+] The natural order is to pass from the false, or what is suspected to be false, to the true.[+] The real wish once ascertained, what good purpose would be served by taking another vote, which would not be the real vote if it differed from the former?

That these two methods may have their highest effect, they ought to be carried to the highest possible pitch. In secret voting, the secresy cannot be too profound: in public voting, the publicity can never be too great. The most detrimental arrangement would be that of demi-publicity—as if the votes should be known to the assembly, and should remain unknown to the public. Individuals would thus be exposed, in all their votes, to every seductive influence, and would be withdrawn from the principal tutelary influences. This is the system which it would be proper to establish, if we would secure punishment to probity, and reward to prevarication.

In governments in which there are public assemblies, acting in conjunction with a powerful monarch whose influence is feared, it has been thought that the secret mode ought to be the ordinary plan, that the members might be withdrawn from the factitious[+] interest which the monarch might create by his threats or his rewards.

If the monarch can act upon the assembly by means of force, imprisonments, or depositions[+]—security does not exist—liberty is but a name. The intimidated members would find in secret voting an asylum against public opinion.

In relation to the modes of seduction, those which are public may be arrested by laws excluding from the assembly those individuals who hold certain employments at the nomination of the sovereign.

---

[a] Gazette de Leide, 5th December 1788.[1]

---

[1] *Nouvelles extraordinaires de divers endroits*, xcviii. The journal was often referred to as the 'Gazette de Leyde' after the city in which it was published. The report actually stated that the numbers under open voting were 114 for and 149 against; these are also the figures given by Dumont. Thus the change from open to secret voting made a difference of 53 votes.

With regard to clandestine favours, or what may be called corruption,[+]—the danger can never be equal, in a numerous assembly, to the grand antiseptic effect of publicity. The number of persons who could be reduced to dependence by such means will never be large: the majority will be restrained by the dread[+] of shame; a still larger number by the fear[+] of being removed in an assembly liable to change.

Should a sovereign grant perpetual favours,—he would most frequently purchase ingratitude.[+] Should he grant his favours periodically,—these secret negotiations would be too disgraceful and perilous to be frequent. Does one kind of honour enjoin the observation of a clandestine bargain?—another kind of honour directs the breach of it, at least in the case when it cannot be observed without openly offending public opinion.[+]

### §3. *Of summary and distinct Voting.*

Every numerous political assembly which has many operations to perform, has soon been led, by the necessity of economizing time, to ascertain its votes in a summary manner[+]—contenting itself with knowing them by approximation in cases in which the result is manifest, or in which it is not of importance to ascertain the respective numbers with precision. This is the case with regard to the greater number of motions relative to current affairs.

It is better to take the votes by a visible sign, rather than by acclamation, especially if the assembly be numerous: the sense of sight is a more correct judge than that of hearing. The raised hands, or the persons standing up, are always distinct: voices are more easily mistaken. Are the proportions doubtful?—the operation by standing up and sitting down may be repeated or prolonged without inconvenience: prolonged or reiterated exclamations would be equally ridiculous and inconvenient.

Besides, the voice is a deceptive witness: strength of lungs or party feeling may give to a small number an apparent majority, or at least render the result more often doubtful, and distinct voting necessary.

Acclamations ought to be avoided for another reason: they have a contagious quality, which tends to inflame the mind, and to produce quarrels. In matters which excite a lively interest in the parties, they are a sort of *war-cry*.[+]

The plan of rising and sitting down discovers the voters—the plan of acclamation hides them in a crowd: it may be employed for stifling all opposition, for oppressing liberty, and causing falsehood to triumph.

Indeed, to say that anything has passed by acclamation, is to wish to make it be believed that it has passed unanimously; but if this unanimity were real, more would be gained by proving it by distinct voting.

*The votes should not be taken successively, but all at once, as far as it is possible.*

Reference is here made to those cases in which the votes are taken openly. This mode of taking the votes simultaneously is not only recommended as summary—it is also recommended[+] as tending to weaken the influence of party and authority, at least in those cases in which there has been no pre-concerted arrangement.

Distinct or regular voting is that in which all the votes are taken and counted:—this operation is called *dividing* the assembly.

It may be effected by various methods: by lists, upon which each member inscribes his vote—or by counters—or by a simple change of place on the part of the voters. The choice depends on circumstances, or the nature of the assemblies. Precautions ought to be taken against all possible frauds, either on the part of the voters, lest they should give many votes; or on that of the scrutineers, lest they should falsify the votes.[+]

Each member ought to have the right of demanding it by a simple formula[+] delivered to the president,—*I require the division.*[a] For it is not proper to deprive any member of the right of knowing whether the decision be really conformable to the wish of the assembly, or of that of appealing to public opinion, by making known those who vote for or against a measure.

He who demands a division[+] can only have the one or other of two objects in view. Is the disproportion manifest?—he desires to make known the relative force of the two parties—or he wishes to subject the voters to the law of publicity. In this case, it is a species of appeal to the people against the decision of the majority—or, to speak more strictly, it is a demonstration of the votes.[+]

If this privilege were abused by the frequency of divisions for slightly[+] important objects, it might be remedied by requiring the concurrence of a certain number of individuals in a requisition for distinct voting. But such an abuse is scarcely probable. One individual would not often desire to divide the assembly solely to show that he alone was opposed to all the rest.

The mode used in the House of Commons appears to me liable to several inconveniences.

[a] The form used in the House of Commons is not so simple, nor so conformable to truth. The Speaker declares the majority in favour of the *ayes*—*The ayes have it.* It is necessary, in order to divide the House, that a member of the other party should deny the truth of this report, and say, *The noes have it,* even in the case when he may be found voting alone in opposition to hundreds. I am well aware that this assertion, founded upon ancient usage, is neither understood as giving the lie to the Speaker, nor as expressing the opinion of him who makes it. But wherein consists the propriety or utility of a legislative assembly employing a form which, beside other inconveniences, is everywhere[+] else an indecorum and a lie?

150

All business is suspended—the assembly is in a state of confusion, whilst the account is taken of the votes of those who leave the House, and of those who remain. This tumultuous movement of parties, and this interruption, which often last half an hour, has none of the dignity which ought to characterize a legislative assembly.

But this is the least evil. As this derangement is agreeable to no one, a regular division is often foregone in order to prevent the inconvenience; and as it is particularly disagreeable to those who are subjected to temporary expulsion, it is often a subject of controversy to determine upon whom the inconvenience ought to fall. For determining this controversy, a rule has been required; but this rule itself has furnished a crop of the most abstruse metaphysical questions: a volume might be filled with the difficulties which have arisen from this branch of parliamentary jurisprudence. This[+] great assembly has been occupied in discussing points altogether as clear in themselves as the famous question of the schoolmen: *Utrum*[1] *chimæra bombilans in vacuo posset comedere secundas intentiones.*[a]

These useless creations of science have for their common effect the restraint of liberty and the concealment of truth.[+] The majority of individuals recoil with affright from the aspect of this labyrinth, and allow themselves implicitly to be led by those who are willing to purchase, at the price of a dry and disgustful study, the privilege of domination. Here, as elsewhere, mystery opens the door to imposture.

To create the world out of nothing was the work of divine power: to create a science out of nothing, and for nothing, has often been the employment of human folly.

From a train of these subtleties, one circumstance still more extraordinary has arisen in English voting: it is, that a member may be forced to vote against his will, and that the legislative assembly should commit an act of falsehood. If the members have, from inattention or any other circumstance, neglected to go out before the door is shut, it is no longer at

---

[a] The general rule which has served as the foundation of all this ridiculous science is, 'That those that give their votes for the preservation of the orders of the House, should stay in; and those that give their votes otherwise, to the introducing of any new matter, or any alteration, should go out.'[+]—*Journals of the House of Commons*, 10th December 1640; Hatsell, Edit. 1818, II. 187.[2+]

---

[1] 'Questio subtilissima, *Utrum Chimera in uacuo bombinans possit comedere secundas intentiones?* et fuit debatuta per decem hebdomadas in concilio Constantiensi.' ('The very subtle question, whether a chimera purring in the void could eat second intentions, was debated for ten weeks at the council of Constance.') Rabelais, *Pantagruel, roy des dipsodes, restitué à son naturel, avec ses faictz et prouesses espoventables: composez par feu M. Alcofribas abstracteur de quinte essence*, 1532, Ch. vii. See F. Rabelais, *Œuvres complètes*, ed. M. Huchon and F. Moreau, Paris, 1994, p. 238.

[2] Reference altered in Bowring. Bentham's own source would have been the 1785 edition of Hatsell, ii. 134, which Dumont cites.

their option to vote as they wish—they are counted as voting with those who remain in the House, although it be known that their vote is contrary to their known and avowed inclination.—*Hatsell*, Edit. 1818, II. 195.[1]

This mode of voting is an ancient custom, established when printing was not invented, and when the art of writing was not common. In ancient Rome, the Senate voted nearly in the same manner:—'*Manibus*[2] *pedibus-que descendo in sententiam vestram.*'[a]

I shall only say one word concerning the French practice—it has been spoken of elsewhere.[3] In the National Assembly, the summary mode takes place by *sitting* and *standing*. The regular mode takes place by *calling over the names*—a method so long, so fatiguing, so little favourable to individual independence, that one is almost tempted to believe that the governing party has preserved it as a means of intimidating the weak. It is true, that silence is imposed upon the galleries—that signs of approbation or disapprobation are prohibited: but the sovereign people often mutiny against these prohibitions.[+]

In regular voting, every member ought to be required to give his vote. This obligation is founded upon the nature of his office,[+] as we have seen more in detail in treating *of absence*. He cannot, as appears to me, neglect this duty, except from indifference, pusillanimity, or corruption.

'No,' says a wise man, 'I shall not vote because I am not sufficiently enlightened upon the question: I am equally afraid of error in declaring myself for or against.'

Indecision is a possible state. The mind is as susceptible of this modification as of the two others. To require an affirmative or negative answer from a man who is in doubt, is to substitute constraint for liberty—is to oblige him to tell a lie. The ancient Romans, in penal matters, had seized the distinction of these three states of the mind, and had found formulas for their expression: *absolvo—condemno—non liquet*. The jurisconsults and legislators, who have drawn so many absurd and atrocious laws from Roman jurisprudence, have never thought of adopting this simple arrangement—this religious homage to truth.

I propose, therefore, a new form of voting. There have hitherto been

---

[a] The inutility of this form is clearly shown by the circumstance, that when the same individuals in the same number call their assembly a committee of the whole House,[+] this expulsion does not take place. In this case, they have discovered that the two sides of the House are as sufficient to mark the separation of the two parties, as two different rooms. It may perhaps happen in the long run, that they will profit by this discovery.

---

[1] Reference altered in Bowring; the passage in question is actually at p. 196, not 195. Bentham's own source would have been the 1785 edition of Hatsell, ii. 141, which Dumont cites.

[2] i.e. 'With my hands and feet I agree with your opinion.' In the Roman Senate, when there was a division, opposing factions moved to different sides of the house. See Pliny the Younger, *Epistulae*, VIII. xiv.

[3] See pp. 94–101 above.

only two lists, or two ballots—the one for the *ayes*, the other for the *noes;* I would establish a third, for the *neuters.*[+]

But it may be asked, why require a man to vote, whilst he is permitted to give a vote which will have effect neither on the one side nor the other?

It is replied, that a *neuter* vote subjects the individual who gives it to the judgment of public opinion. By abstaining from voting, he may escape observation, or he may excuse himself upon divers grounds. But admit a *neuter* vote[+] in a case in which the public interest is manifest, the voter cannot withdraw himself from censure—it will exhibit either his crime or his incapacity in as clear a manner as if he had decidedly taken the wrong side.

In cases which admit of honest doubts, the number of neuter votes would serve to enlighten the assembly, by showing that its deliberations had not yet reached maturity.[a]

# CHAPTER XV.
## OF COMMITTEES.
### §1. *Of Special Committees.*

THE more numerous an assembly is, the less is it fitted for certain labours. By dividing itself into committees, it multiplies itself—it resolves itself into many parts, each one of which is better calculated to attain a certain object than the whole body would be.

Each committee may be engaged with a different matter. The labour is distributed—progress is accelerated—a degree of attention may be given to all the details of each new project, of which a large assembly would be incapable. This formation of committees, or *bureaux,*[+] is absolutely necessary for the collection of documents—for engaging in those preparatory researches which require that a great number of persons should be heard—for the verification of accounts,—&c. &c.

It is there frequently that the preparation of a law is completed—a species of labour, for which a large assembly is very ill adapted, and which, if attempted in such an assembly, would be attended with a considerable loss of time.

---

[a] It would seem that this form, very applicable to *facts*, is less so to the *making of laws*. He who is undecided ought to be for the negative, for he sees no sufficient reason for making the law.

If *doubtful, wait,*[+]—is more applicable to matters of legislation than to any others.

Should the neuters[+] be the greater number, what ought to be done? Ought not indecision in this case to have the force of a negative?

In a general committee, the *neuter* vote might be admitted for the purpose of better judging whether the deliberation ought to be continued or adjourned: but it is not necessary: the motion for adjournment supplies its place. All who are undecided have only to support it,[+] in order to obtain leisure for the acquisition of new information.

Ought these committees[+] to be named for the whole session, or upon each occasion? The correct answer will depend upon the circumstances and the object in view. In matters of finance, of commerce, of political economy, there will be in a permanent committee greater coherency in their proceedings, more experience and special knowledge.

Occasional committees have the advantage of being[+] composed of members who, having made the object in question their particular study, may be considered as better acquainted with it;[+] and who, as they are only charged with a single operation, may give more application[+] to it, that they may better justify the choice of the assembly.

The great difficulty lies in the manner of naming committees. The best mode, perhaps, would be to begin by a free nomination—each member being allowed to name a certain individual as a candidate, and from this list to make nomination according to the relative majority of suffrages.

But whatever may be the merit of these committees, it is not proper that the assembly should so far rely upon them, as to dispense with any one of its opportunities of debate.[+] By so doing, it would be in danger of insensibly transferring the power of the whole body to a small body of individuals, naturally exposed to secret influences.

## §2. *Of Committees of the whole House.*

In relation to all[+] legislative measures, the two Houses of Parliament are accustomed to resolve themselves into Committees of the whole House, that there measures may be discussed more freely than in the course of a regular debate. The following are the points of difference between these two methods:—

| IN THE HOUSE. | IN COMMITTEE. |
|---|---|
| 1. The motion or bill is considered as a whole. | 1. The motion or bill is considered article by article. |
| 2. A member can only speak once, except for purposes of explanation. | 2. Upon each article each member may speak as often as he pleases. |
| 3. The Speaker is the president in the House. | 3. The Committee has its own president, chosen for the occasion. |
| 4. Each motion requires to be seconded. | 4. A motion does not require to be seconded. |
| 5. Upon a division,[+] one of the parties remains in the House, the other goes into the lobby.[a] | 5. Upon a division, the two parties go to different sides of the House. |

[a] Upon a division, both parties now leave the House.—*Ed.*[1]

---

[1] The resolution determining the new method of forming a division was passed on 18 February 1836. *Commons Journals*, xci. 54.

6. The motion may be avoided, by moving the previous question.

6. The previous question is not admissible.

Some of these distinctions appear useful; others are altogether arbitrary:—

1. It is highly proper that bills and motions composed of a series of articles, should undergo two different discussions—first as a whole,[+] and afterwards article by article.[+] This subject has already been considered in Chapter XI. §3, '*Of three Debates.*'

2. It is highly proper, that upon important subjects there should be two forms of debate: the strict debate, in which each member may speak, but speak only once—and the free debate, in which he has the liberty of replying.

3. With regard to the change of the president, the inconveniences of allowing the president of the assembly to take part in its discussions have been elsewhere pointed out: he is a judge, and as a judge ought not to be exposed to the danger of being infected with party spirit.

## CHAPTER XVI.
## OF FORMULAS.

FORMULAS are models of what ought to be said upon each occasion by the individual to whom it is prescribed that he should express himself in a certain manner. It can scarcely be determined beforehand, how many formulas an assembly may require: they will be many or few,[+] according to the number of the members, and according to the nature of its powers.

It is proper, for example, that the president always take the votes in the same manner, employing the same expressions—that the members make use of the same terms in presenting their motions, in requiring the exercise of any of their rights,—&c. &c.

Everything unnecessary in such formulas is pernicious. *Clearness* and *brevity:*—such are the essential qualities: to attempt to ornament them at the expense of precision, is to disfigure them.

Formulas not only save words: they have a superior utility—they prevent variations which may have a concealed object—and, above all, they prevent disputes.

In England, the royal sanction is always expressed by the same words: *Le Roi le veut;* and if he reject a bill, the formula of refusal is equally determined: *Le Roi s'avisera.*[1]

Judicial formulas have too often merited the reproach which has been

---

[1] See Hatsell ii. 247; *Lords Journals*, xv. 733.

almost everywhere thrown upon them, of being at the same time vague and prolix—of sinning by omission and by excess.

Their prolixity is easily accounted for in all cases in which lawyers have been able to find, in the multiplication of words, a pretext for their services, and the increase of their price. And when the spirit of revenue has been introduced into procedure, and a traffic has been made of words, increase of length has been given to the formulas, that more profit might be derived from them.

It has in certain cases been thought right to proportion the number of words to the importance of the subject. To dismiss a grave matter in two or three words, it has been considered, was not to form a sufficiently high idea of it—not to treat it with a sufficient dignity. This is the error of a little mind. The most sublime thoughts are often expressed by a single word.

# APPENDIX[1]

## Motion-Table—General Idea.

Nº 3

By the *changeable Promulgation-Table*, or *conspicuous Motion-Table*, or, for shortness, *Motion-Table*, I mean a very simple apparatus, contrived for the purpose of giving to Motions, and other such compositions as are liable to be taken for the subjects of debate, a mode of promulgation equally conspicuous and effectual, with that which may be afforded to the *standing* regulations of the Assembly, by the *fixed Promulgation-Tables* spoken of in the preceding[2] chapter.[a]

1. Motion-Table, what.

A general idea of the contrivance may be thus formed: a more particular detail will be found in a separate paper.[3]

2. General idea of the contrivance.

Conceive a *door*, such as the cloth-doors used in houses for warmth; but composed of two surfaces of cloth, without any wood between them, except what is necessary to serve as a frame for stretching them.

A set of *types* are provided, each consisting of a letter, mounted on a wire, in the manner of the pins used for ornament in womens' head-dresses. These, in order to form words and lines upon the Motion-Table, are stuck upon it, as pins upon a pin-cushion. The cloth behind, by detaining the pins towards the point, will serve to prevent their turning over and dropping out. The letters are of such a size, as that the words formed of them shall be legible at the farthest part of the room where any Member may have occasion to sit.

## Uses and Necessity of the Motion Table.

Nº 4

1. Placed in the most general point of view, the use of such an implement is, so to Order Matters, that no Man can avoid for a Moment knowing what the Question is, that he is to vote upon: an Article of Knowledge, which cannot be impressed with Certainty by any other means.

1. General Considerations evincing the Necessity of such an implement as the *Motion Table*.

It is the *purport*, it is true, and not the *Tenor*, of every discourse that

---

[a] Were an implement of this sort ever to come into use, it might naturally enough come to be stiled, the *Carpet*, partly from its physical resemblance to that article of furniture, partly in conformity to the well-known figurative phrase.

---

[1] The Appendix reproduces the only surviving fragment of text for 'Political Tactics'. The manuscripts (Dumont MSS 72) have a wrapper bearing the following inscription, in Morellet's hand: 'Bentham. Pratiques utiles à une assemblée deliberante. Pratiques utiles à une assemblée Deliberante Par Bentham.' For further details see the Editorial Introduction, p. xxxix above.

[2] Marginal note: 'That chapter was not thought necessary to accompany these papers.' This is a personal note to Morellet.

[3] Marginal note: 'See Nº. 8'. See pp. 170–5 below.

is really of importance; the Spirit and not the letter. But it is only by the letter that the Spirit can be ascertained. Mistake but a single word, and you may mistake most compleatly the whole tendency of the Discourse. So many Instants as the Discourse in question fails of being present to the Mind, in any single article, so many instants is a man in danger of falling into mistakes. But neither to this danger, nor to any other, should any Man be left exposed, while every Man can be freed from it, with the utmost certainty.

In no point of view, can this Article of Knowledge cease to be indispensable; it is requisite at any rate to ground a Man's *own* Vote as founded on his *own* conception of the Subject: to enable him to make a proper Application of the *Arguments* he hears *from others*: and if he *himself* speaks, to enable *him* to form such Arguments, as he has to present *to* others. It is essential to a Man in the judicial Capacity in which every member acts as often as he gives his Vote: It is still more essential to him, if, by taking a part in the Debate, he acts in the Character of an Advocate.

If an Individual had a Book or Paper of any kind to examine and give a deliberate Opinion upon, in his Study, he would choose surely to have it lying open before him. Though alone and free from every kind of interruption he would hardly think proper to trust the Subject altogether to his Memory, while he could have it before his Eyes. To this mode of possessing himself of the Contents, he would hardly think of preferring that of giving the Paper to a Third person, to read over to him once or twice, with a degree of celerity he could not regulate, and at periods not depending upon his Choice.

2.[1]

Particular Utilities that would result from the Use of it

This general use, when considered in a nearer point of view will be found to include, and branch out into, a Multitude of more particular ones.

1. It would save the unremitted stretch of Mind otherwise necessary.

1. An help of this Sort would save a Man the Effort and Tension of Mind necessary to keep a discourse of any kind unaltered in his Memory; much more a discourse which he has had no other means of possessing himself of, than what has been afforded by the hasty glympse he can have caught in the instant of it's passing through the lips of another Man. This Strain of the Mind bears a part, that can not surely be deemed an inconsiderable one, in the production of that weariness which is incident to a long attendance.

2. And the time which is wanted to be employed in reflection and invention.

2. The Saving of this *labour* saves a Man a great deal of that *time*, which on these occasions he may have so much need of employing in other ways. Without this help a Man is employed in chaining down the

[1] There is an additional, different sequence of numbers in the margin of this section. This has been omitted for clarity, as occasionally have other misleading extra series of numbers in these manuscripts.

Subject as it were in his Memory, when he ought to be looking out for Reasons *pro* and *con* to ground the decision he will have to make upon it.

3. It would save the whole Assembly, whatever time would otherwise be consumed in *vivâ voce* readings. Establish a durable source of information, and those evanescent ones become as superfluous as they are insufficient.

3. It saves repeated readings.

[4.] If a Man takes upon him to speak, it saves him from the danger of falling into that hesitation and confusion, which are the natural Accompaniments of Uncertainty. Hesitation is but too apt to attend the Search for Arguments: but to what degree must it not be encreased, where the very Subject is unknown?

4. It would save hesitation and Confusion.

5. It saves a Man from undesigned misconceptions, and thence from misrepresentations equally undesigned. But from misrepresentations, if *un*noticed by other Speakers, may follow misguided Votes, erroneous decisions,—if *noticed,* then time and Toil are to be consumed in Accusation, defence, recrimination or apology.

5. It would prevent undesigned Mis-conceptions and Mis-statements of the question.

6. It cuts off all hopes of Success in Wilful Misrepresentations. At present under Cover of the Clouds raised in the heat of Debate, Misrepresentations are heaped on Mis-representations by the disingenuous, as calumnies are heaped on Calumnies, in hopes that some, at least, may stick and serve the Cause. And wilful misrepresentations are protected by the impossibility of distinguishing them from undesigned ones.

6. It would render wilful misrepresentations of it impossible.

Against misconstruction of the Words, whatever they are, it affords indeed no certain or immediate remedy: but nothing can give greater Scope or advantage to Mis-construction of the meaning of words, than the uncertainty of the Words themselves.

7. By keeping a Motion or other Subject of criticism held up in constant view, before the Eyes of the whole Assembly, it affords such an opportunity of thinking of Amendments, as never can be presented by a fugitive and momentary glance.

7. It would facilitate Amendments.

8. It saves a Man from the unpleasant circumstance of being interrupted by his Neighbour, to ask what the question is?—and from the almost equally unpleasant Circumstance of finding one's self obliged to attempt to give others that sort of interruption. But this is an interruption that must be occasioned by every Man who does not come in till after the Motion is read, on pain of his remaining in utter ignorance.

8. It would save interruptions given by asking what the Question is.

9. By affording the means, to every Man who is willing to embrace it, of forming his own Judgment on his own Grounds, it exempts him from the necessity of acting blindfold, and pinning his Faith, in each instance, on the sleeve of Party; an operation which at present affords a ready, and the only, solution to all Doubts and difficulties.

9. It would save Men from the Necessity of acting Blindfold and going by Party.

159

10. It would afford a restraint from voting for bad measures.

**10.** It not only saves a Man from the *necessity* of voting for a bad measure, merely because his party have adopted it, but affords a strong *check* to *restrain* him from so doing. He can no longer plead ignorance either to himself or others. If the Motion be improper, the Motion with its improprieties stares him in the Face; and (what is the material thing in this point of view) its doing so is seen by every body else.

11. It would save short Memories from being discouraged and acting under a disadvantage.

**11.** It saves the Assembly from losing the Services of many a Member whose assistance might have been of Use. It is well enough known that neither Soundness of Judgment, nor even fertility of invention, are in any necessary proportion to the Strength of Memory.

In Talents as in virtue, the less quantity every Business requires, the less it stands in danger of falling Short of the necessary Complement.[a]

12. It tends to enure Men to Habits of Accuracy & self determination.

**12.** It would operate by degrees to the generation and Enforcement of good habits, intellectual and Moral, and to the Suppression of bad ones. It would weaken the Habits of Misrepresentation and blind adherence to Party: it would strengthen the Habits of precision and close reasoning.

13. It would afford the only practicable means of enforcing the Rule against digressions: Viz: naming the Rule, or pointing to the Motion.

**13.** Lastly, In case of a wandering from the Subject, a failing which, from Strength of Passion, looseness of Attention, or Weakness of Judgment, may always happen to a Man, though he has the Subject before his Eyes, it affords the only means of giving, to Regulations made on the view of Repressing that Inconvenience, the sort of enforcement they are capable of, to any tolerable Advantage. All that prohibitive Regulations can do on this head, is to say, *You shall not wander from your Subject.* But suppose a Man does? How to stop him?

At present there is no Remedy, but what is worse than the disease. Another Member gets up, and interrupts the one that is speaking, charging him with a breach of the Rule. The latter, irritated with the interruption, of course defends himself right or wrong. This introduces, instead of a debate on the Motion, a Debate on the pertinency, or impertinency of the Argument: and, in half the time, the Wanderer, if let alone would have finished either his excursion or his Speech. Yet even this inconvenient remedy, bad as it is, cannot be dispensed with: for, though bad as a curative Remedy, it is necessary as a punishment: If the apprehension of being called to Account for impertinence were altogether removed, matters would be still worse.

But the Exhibition of the Motion, on the Motion Table in view of every one at once, affords a Remedy, which not only must in its Nature

---

[a] If I may be allowed to take, for an Example on this point, the Person of all others with the State of whose faculties, I have the best opportunity of being acquainted, I do not suppose that, unless by the help of rhyme or measure, there ever was that Discourse of which he was able to recollect five lines together. And though most others have undoubtedly the advantage over him in this particular, yet I have every now and then found reason to think this is not the Case with every one.

be more efficacious than the other, but, whatever be its efficacy, is not purchased by any Inconvenience. The instant the Offence is conceived to manifest itself, the President, without interrupting the Speaker, or saying a Word, glances a look on the Motion Table, or points to it with his Wand. The superior efficacy of this Remedy does not admit of doubt, occasioning neither interruption, nor the irritation, of which Interruption cannot fail to be productive, it affords no incitement to persevere; it is a *Sedative*, not a *Stimulant*; an Admonition, not an accusation; the Act not of an Adversary, but of the Judge.

[14.] In this way, and upon this condition, but upon this condition only, the President may be expected to interfere of himself, for the purpose of enforcing such a Rule. In this way he need not fear the giving the Admonition, as often as the want of it appears to be incurred. In any other way, such Admonitions cannot be given with any tolerable frequency, without his committing his dignity by frequent and sometimes long continued altercations: for an absolute interruption cannot be given without some reason; nor the Member interrupted be debarred the liberty of defending himself, either *eo nomine*,[1] or on pretence of apology or explanation.

*14. It is only when thus assisted, that the President can be expected to interfere for such a purpose.*

Even supposing an interference in this way to do no good, at any rate it will do no harm. But it will do more good than will be seen. The Orator thus admonished, will not give any signs, perhaps, of express and immediate submission; he will not stop short and acknowledge himself in the wrong; but he will come back to his Subject as soon as he can do so, without appearing to have been forced; and he will be upon his guard against straying from it in future. He knows that it is not only the President that is judging him, but the whole Assembly, to whom the President by that Judgment appeals, and whose Eyes have been turned on him with that view.

[15.] It is obvious that in many Cases the expedient of *Printing* might be employed; and that as often as it can be employed, it will answer the purpose of the Motion Table in some degree. But, not to mention the Expence, it can neither be employed in every Case in which the Motion Table may be made use of, nor, when it is employed, will it answer the purpose equally well in every particular.

*15. Printing is not an adequate Succedaneum.*

1. Printing could never be applied to Motions discussed the same day they were penned.

2. Bending down, to find out the Passage in Question on a Printed Paper, may in some cases occasion a Man some interruption. During that interval, if he is speaking, he must cease to speak; if hearing only, he must cease to hear: looking at the Motion Table, to which all Eyes will be generally directed, and to which they can always be

---

[1] i.e. 'expressly, overtly.'

turned, without Change of Posture, or turning leaf over leaf, can occasion none.

3. But for preventing wilful departures from the Subject, or wilful Misrepresentations of it, the great point is, not merely that he who is speaking should himself *be* rightly possessed of the Motion, but that he should be *known* and *seen*, by every body else so to be. This point is compleatly accomplished by the contrivance of the Motion Table; and it is *not* accomplished by ordinary printing.

4. Lastly, a still more important Use of the Motion Table is, the Means it affords, by being pointed to, of giving the Law against digressions a degree of enforcement hitherto looked upon as impracticable: in which particular an ordinary printed paper will not answer the purpose.[1]

N° 5.

*Of the British Practice in this particular.*

1.

British Commons —Rules against digression.

In the Discipline of the House of Commons Rules against departure from the Subject are not wanting;[a] nor would their inefficacy be now a matter of Complaint, if the Efficacy of a Law depended upon the frequency of its repetition.

2.

Their natural inefficacy.

To give a Law to Debaters, saying to them *You shall not quit your Subject*, without letting them see what that Subject is, is as Edifying as a Law to Travellers would be, saying *You shall not quit your road.* A better Way would be, to set up Direction-Posts.

3.

Means made use of for giving information of the Subject of debate.
1. Two readings of course.

To Travellers in the Road of Debate, the only Direction-Post that can be given, is the Motion Table above described. For want of this visible and permanent source of information, the British Assemblies have naturally enough confined themselves to the transient and momentary resource of *vivâ voce* readings.

In the House of Commons, the President (the Speaker) when a Motion has been handed up to him, gives it a Second Reading, after the one, which it will naturally have had from the Member who proposed it.[2] This is all the Means the Members have of possessing themselves of the Contents. They must catch it flying, and get it by Heart, as it flies.

4.

2. Occasional readings upon Requisition.

Indeed if any Member will get up and desire to have it read anew, the Speaker, it is said, must, as often as such desire is repeated, even by the same person, give the Motion a repeated reading.[3] This faculty of apprehending for an instant what a Man is to give his Vote for

---

[a] See Journals 14th 17th & 19th April 1604: 19th May 1604: 10th Nov.r 1640: and II Hatsell 166.

---

[1] Marginal note: 'See the following paper, N° 5.'
[2] Marginal note: 'II Hatsell 82.'
[3] Marginal note: 'ibid.', i.e. a further reference to Hatsell, *Precedents and Proceedings*, ii. 82.

adopting or rejecting for ever, it may well be imagined is not much made use of. A Man will hardly choose to put the Business to a Stand, and draw on himself the attention of the whole House, for so trifling a purpose as the affording information, and that perhaps but momentary, to his own private conscience. He will not choose to put himself into any such conspicuous situation, unless it be at the time when he is speaking, or about to Speak, in order to give to the Arguments he is about to use their due weight and application. It is not for his *own Information* then, that a Man will commonly, one may almost say, will ever—call for this intelligence; but for his own *support* and *justification*, and for the information of his Hearers. Of the Assistance thus provided, one may therefore venture to say, that it is scarce ever given, but at the requisition of those, who do not stand in need of it, or at least do not conceive themselves so to do.

As to the Case of a 'Member speaking beside the Question'—if such a contingency happen, 'it is the duty' (it seems) 'of the Speaker to interrupt him', 'and the House' (it is said) 'ought for their own Sake to support the Speaker in such an interposition'.[1] That such is the duty of that Officer, I am not disposed at all to dispute; but it has been seen how unpleasant an one, and how unlikely on the present footing, to be fulfilled, with any degree of constancy, as matters stand at present. If, supposing such an Account capable of being taken, I should find the Rule thus enforced, so often as once in 500 of the Instances in which it had been infringed, I should be much surprized.

5. The Rule against digression cannot conveniently be enforced by the President.

I do not believe it is enforced so often. In general when this duty is fulfilled, it is fulfilled, not by the Speaker, but by some Member, that is, by some Member, to whose person or to whose friends or party the digression is obnoxious. If the digression is checked or attempted to be checked, it is not then because it is a *digression*, but because it is an Offensive one. So long as the Offence confines itself to the mere Waste of time, a Man will hardly find a motive strong enough to give birth to the effort necessary for reclaiming the execution of the Law, at the expence of his exhibiting himself in such an invidious Situation. Neither Zeal for the Execution of the Law, nor a Sense of the value of time, nor any other motive less powerful than Enmity, will naturally be sufficient for this purpose.[a] So long as the Effect is produced what

6. Inconveniences that attend the Enforcement of it by Members.

[a] When the Offence does not go beyond the length of frivolousness and irrelevancy, a gentler and less invidious course is fallen into by individuals, of repressing it, or at least of putting themselves out of the way of being affected by it. A General cold pervades the House; or each Member finds himself under an indispensable necessity of communicating something to his Neighbour; or a pressing occasion of quitting the

[1] Marginal note: 'II Hatsell 77.'

the motive is, which it is produced by, is, it is true, a Matter in itself as unimportant as it is unascertainable. But the Case is, that when this motive is not called forth into Action, there the Law will be without Assistance: and it is in this way, that the consideration of the motive becomes worth attending to.

7. *Evidence of the inefficacy of these Rules. 1. From a publication by the Clerk of the House.* That this practice amongst others unfavorable to Order, prevails in that Assembly to a very inconvenient degree, may safely be averred, upon the Authority of a very respectable and old Experienced Officer of the House;[1] who in a work designed for the instruction of his Masters, would hardly take upon him to charge them, with this or any other Species of misbehaviour, without Cause.

'It is very much to be wished,' says Mr. Hatsell[2] 'that the Rules which have been from time to time laid down by the House for the preservation of . . . Order . . . could be enforced and adhered to more strictly than they have been of late Years. It certainly requires a Conduct on the part of the Speaker full of resolution, yet of delicacy. But as I very well remember that Mr. Onslow[3] did in fact carry these rules into execution, *to a certain point*, the fault has not been in the want of Rules, or of authority in the Chair to support those rules, if the Speaker thought proper to exercise that Authority.'

'The Neglect of these Orders' (continues Mr. Hatsell) 'has been the principal cause of the House sitting so much longer of late Years, than it did formerly; Members . . . assume liberty of speaking beside the question . . . And though' (continues he) 'as is said on the 10th of November 1640 any Member "*may*" yet Mr. Speaker "*ought*" to interrupt them.'[a]

But though Mr. Onslow, 'did carry these rules into execution *to a certain point*' yet even that venerable Magistrate, with all his Authority, and though as Mr. Hatsell 'but too well remembers he endeavoured to preserve them with great strictness' could not so far succeed, as that Mr. Hatsell could 'pretend to say that his Endeavours had always their full Effect'.[4]

Room. But these Admonitions (which are only casual, and which are some of them troublesome, to those who concurr in giving them) can seldom be timely, and are not always effectual: and when they do attain the Effect proposed by them, it is at the Expence of a violation, not only of the Rules of the House, but of the Laws of Decency.

[a] He had begun with reporting the rules above referred to.—p. 1. of this | |.[5]

---

[1] i.e. Hatsell.

[2] Marginal note: 'II Hatsell 167'. The emphasis in this passage has been added by Bentham.

[3] Arthur Onslow (1691–1768), Speaker of the House of Commons 1728–61.

[4] Marginal note: 'ib. 171.', i.e. Hatsell, ii. 171.

[5] Bentham clearly means the first sheet of the current section, 'Of the British Practice in this particular'. The rules are referred to at p. 162 n. above.

Since the days of that celebrated veteran, the enforcement of these Rules, (as his Panegyrist, sitting all the while at the feet of his Successors, has been informing us) has been endeavoured at, either less strenuously, or at any rate, with less effect: and the view that has been given of the difficulties attending such interference can hardly have left much ground for wondering at its inefficacy.

That in the present State of Things, however unequal the Authority of the *presiding* Member may be to the task, that of the *House*, that is, of other Members getting up and interposing in manner above mentioned, may again be asserted to be still more incompetent, upon the Authority of the same experienced and intelligent Officer, who, in speaking of 'the interposition of the House' for such purposes, adds '*which in calling to Order, seldom produces anything but disorder.*'[1]

The Employment of such means for such a purpose, puts one in mind of the controversy about Jansenism, in which one of the Parties, we are told, wrote Books upon Books, to prove that it was time for both parties to have done.[2] The pointing to the Motion Table, if it *saved* no breath, would at least *consume* none.

While writing as above, in comes the Newspaper of the Day, in which, in an Account of a Debate of the 11th of February 1789, the first words I happen to alight upon are as follows.[3] 'Mr. Bo——[4] was going to speak, and was called to Order by

Mr. D——,[5] who said when those things that had been alluded to had passed in the House' (it was 5 years before) 'Gentlemen on both sides were very warm . . . He wished they would adhere to the point before them;

Mr. Bu——[6] began with the disgrace and degradation of Parliament, alluding to what had been advanced.' (as above)

'He was called to Order by Mr. T.'[7]

'Sir J.J.[8] said, *he did not know what the question was*, and begged the Chairman to read it.

8.
From the Debates
of the Day.

---

[1] Marginal note: 'II Hatsell 75.' The emphasis in this quoted passage has been added by Bentham.

[2] François Marie Arouet, usually known as Voltaire (1694–1778) gave an account of the notorious disputes that raged around the doctrines of Cornelius Jansen (1585–1638) during the late seventeenth and much of the eighteenth centuries. Voltaire writes that the two sides printed 'volume sur volume, lettres sur lettres'. See *Le siècle de Louis XIV*, 2 vols., Berlin, 1751, ii. 295.

[3] The following passages are taken from a debate on the Regency Bill which was reported in *The Times*, 12 February 1789. Bentham himself abbreviates the names of the MPs and adds the emphasis.

[4] William Bouverie (1732–1806), MP for Salisbury.

[5] George Dempster (1732–1818), MP for the Forfar and Fife Burghs.

[6] Edmund Burke (1729–97), the celebrated statesman, orator, writer, and MP for Wendover 1765–74, Bristol 1774–80, and Malton 1780–94, Paymaster-General 1782, 1783.

[7] *The Times* here reads 'Mr. Sumner'. George Holme-Sumner (1760–1838), MP for Ilchester.

[8] Sir James Johnstone (1726–94), MP for Dumfries Burghs.

The Chairman of the Committee said, he thought it his duty to inform the Committee, that there was *no question at all*, before the House.'

NB. This is an incident that occurs not unfrequently; The House continue debating the Question for Hours, and at last, to the Surprize of every body, they discover that there is none. For this mischief at least, the Motion Table would afford a pretty effectual cure.

9.
Superior Grounds of apprehension for the States General in this respect.

If such is the difficulty of preserving Order without a Check of this kind, in a Nation so much remarked for Sobriety and Phlegmaticalness as the British, and in an Assembly so antient and so broken into discipline as the British House of Commons, what may not be apprehended in a newformed Assembly of the French Nation, and in point of effective numbers, more than twice as numerous?

10.
The Exhibition of the *Regulation-Tables*, would be necessary to compleat the Plan of enforcement presented by the *Motion Table*.

☛ NB. To compleat this plan of Enforcement a Copy of the most material of the Rules of the Assembly ought to be hung up in Characters as universally legible, and in a situation as universally conspicuous, as those of the Motion Table. Accordingly the Plan and beneficial Effects of such fixed Tables are discussed in a preceding Chapter.[1] But this part it will be hardly worthwhile to subjoin at present; partly because what can be offered on that head may now be pretty well conceived, and partly because the Regulations themselves can only be the work of the Assembly, and because whenever they are fixed on, the giving them this sort of promulgation will not require an Apparatus of new contrivance, or any thing that would be a Work of time.

Nᵒ 6

## *Purposes to which the Motion-Table is applicable.*

1.
Instances of other Compositions, for which the Motion-Table may be equally requisite. Documents serving as Grounds of proceeding: such as *King's Messages* and *Answers*.

I have given the Sort of Table in question the Name of The Motion-Table, because Motions are the Objects with respect to which, on Account of their Shortness, its Capacity of being applied with advantage is most obvious and most incontestable.

But it is manifest, that in point of Subject, the contrivance is just as applicable to one Species of discourse as to another; nor does its application, admit of any other limits, than what are imposed by the circumstances of *time* and *space*.

It is accordingly applicable, for example, not only to discourses designed of themselves to become Acts of the Assembly, but to any documents which are of a Nature to be made use of, as grounds for such Acts, and which, by their importance require to be subjected, for a

---

[1] No other manuscript on Regulation-Tables has survived, but see Ch. III, §4, p. 50 above.

166

length of time, to the Consideration of the Assembly; for instance *King's Messages*, and *King's Answers* to *Addresses*.

Nor need the length of any Subject be any Objection to its being submitted to discussion under this advantage; For, be it long or short, more of it cannot be discussed at a time, than can be exhibited upon such a Table. The only point that can require Consideration is, how to manage so as that, where the Subject is of considerable length, and not likely to receive, in every part of it, an examination of equally long continuance, the Number of Tables requisite may be made to succeed one another, with a degree of celerity sufficient to keep pace with the examination. *The length of the composition need be no Objection.*

Accordingly Bills (*Projets de Loix*), of any length, may be entered upon the Table; the several Articles being thus successively exhibited in the Order in which they are to be submitted to discussion. *2. Instance the Draught of a Law.*

In general it is supposed the contents of one such Table will hardly be done with, before there has been time for another to have been composed. Should the Affirmative in any instance be the Case, either more Tables and more Compositors will be necessary, or the Assembly must wait now and then for the completion of a Table, or they must proceed *for a while*, as, without such Assistance, they must have done to the end of the debate.

Still however, whatever limits the Nature of the Contrivance may be found to set to the employ of it, such Limitation will afford no Argument against its Utility, so far as it can be employed. Whatever be the discourse under Consideration, a Motion, Message, Answer, Draught of a Law, Draught of an Address, the same dilemma militates in every Case in its favour. *3. In every Instance the Operation will be practicable in proportion as it is necessary.*

If the Examination of the Subject, takes up a certain length of time, there the Subject will always be; if that examination does not take up that length of time, the case appears to be of the number of those in which the employment of the Motion Table may be dispensed with, without much inconvenience. The greater the importance of the Subject, whatever it be, the surer the Examination of it is, of receiving this Assistance.

Take time enough, or Compositors enough, and you may give the Benefit of it, to every Subject without exception, that can come before the Assembly.

*On the Promulgation of Motions.*

*Rules.*

**1.**
Rule 1. Motion to
be read before the
Speech is made.

1. Every Motion shall be read either by the Member who proposes it, or by the Secretary, before any one, even the mover, is at liberty to say any thing upon the Subject of it.

**2.**
Rule 2. Entry on
the Table, but the
Business not to
wait.

2. Every Motion, immediately as soon as read, shall be handed over to the Compositor, to be by him with all possible Expedition entered on the Motion-Table: but business shall not wait for such Entry to be made.

*Questions with Answers, by way of Reasons.*

**3.**
Questions with
Answers by way
of Reasons.
Quest. 1. Why
Motion before
Speech?

Question 1$^{st}$ Why read before the Mover is at liberty to speak in favour of it?

[Answers.] 1. Because the Motion is the Subject which the Speech made in its behalf, ought to have to apply to. For want of such application, a great part of the Effect of the Speech may be lost. Neither the strength of the Argument, if strong, nor the Weakness of it, if weak, can be duly judged of, unless the Subject, to which it applies is already in view.

2. Because the interval occupied by the Speech of the Mover, or so much of it as is necessary, will be of use, in affording time, for the Entering of the Motion upon the Motion Table.

3. Because a Regulation to this Effect, will save many useless and improper Speeches from being made. In general, when no Motion is on the Carpet, no Speech ought to be made, but to introduce one. Require the Motion to be produced first, and if a Man, who has none to make attempts to Speak, he finds himself obliged, in the first Instance, to give a particular Account, *why* he does so; If he has no such Account to give, he will not attempt speaking; or if he does, the Calling of the Rule, will put him immediately to Silence.

According to a Rule of the House of Commons, unless a Motion is already on the Carpet, no Speech is to be made without a Motion. But as it does not require the Motion to be Exhibited first, the Remedy does not begin to act, till after the Mischief is at an End. This is one of those Laws one hears so much of, that are so good and so wise, and would be so beneficial, if people would but execute them.

On the 9$^{th}$ of February 1789 in the House of Commons, a Mr R.——[1] gets up and makes a long Speech, the whole of it contrary to an acknowledged Rule of the House. After he has done, and when another

---

[1] John Rolle (1750–1842), MP for Devonshire.

Member is getting up to answer him, the Speaker interposes and says, 'if he had known how Mr. R.——'s Speech was to have ended, he would have interrupted him at the first word; but from the Circumstance of his holding a printed Paper in his hand, he imagined his Speech was to conclude with a formal Motion.'[1]

The Speech in Question was an infringement of two rules: the one, against allusions to the contents of a former debate: the other, against Speaking without a Motion to refer to.

The second Rule (which is that we are here concerned with) is so well contrived, that the violation of it, we see, enables a man to get the better of the first.

The Newspaper containing an Account of the Debate alluded to, it was supposed the mention of the Debate was a preface to a Motion of Censure upon the Newspaper.

Question 2. Why *every* Motion? seeing that of the Motions which the Course of Business requires to be made, the greater part will be so much in course, as not to admit of any debate.

4.
Question 2. Why *every* motion.

Answer. Because it is not possible to ascertain before-hand, which Motions *will* give rise to debate, and which will *not*; nor respecting those that do, what will be the length of each debate. But so long as the Business is not made to wait, the universality of the requisition can never occasion the smallest inconvenience.

The Compositor, as soon as a Motion is handed up to him, begins entering it: if the Motion is decided upon before the Entry is finished, there is no harm done. He leaves off his Work, and either breaks it up immediately, or leaving it standing for the present, takes a fresh Table, according as he finds leisure.

The need which the Memory has of this Assistance is in proportion, *cæteris paribus*, to the length of the debate. If the Debate is so short as not to afford time for the entering of the Motion on the Table, the necessity of such Entry cannot be very great: if the time admits of such Entry, there the Motion is, in the view of every one.

But in general no Motion which is of any particular importance, and which, as such, is likely to give occasion to debate, will be presented, without such previous notice, as will afford ample time for the entering of it upon the Table.[2]

---

[1] Bentham appears to have paraphrased reports in several newspapers of 10 February 1789. The printed paper to which he refers seems to have been a newspaper containing a report of a previous day's debate. This report was uncomplimentary to Rolle. For details of Rolle's speech see the *Morning Chronicle* of 10 February 1789.

[2] Marginal note: 'vide infra Ch: |    |'. See pp. 113–14 above.

*Details concerning the Motion-Table, and the manner*
*of making use of it.*

1. The Table itself may be in the *form* of a *door*, and of the *size* of a very
Table—its form—<br>materials—and<br>structure. large one. Of the manner of encreasing the number, if necessary, see
below.[1] It is to be formed by two parallel surfaces of cloth, strained
upon a wooden frame. That the surfaces may be even, and not sink in
the middle, at least that which presents itself to the spectators, they
must, of course, be strained very tight and smooth. See paragraph 3.

2. The size of the *letters* must depend on the size and shape of the *room*
Letters—their size. in which the table is placed; as *that* must upon the number of spectators
that are to be accommodated. I found by observation that a table
composed of letters of $\frac{3}{4}$ of an inch in height was perfectly legible at the
distance of 52 Feet, to an ordinary eye. At what greater distance, I can
not say: the observation being made on a table that was fixed in a
Church. Among the letters used in printing-presses for Play-Bills, and
other such papers as are printed to stick up against walls, are some
sizes equal or superior to the above.

3. The *letters* may be formed by a square, or rather by an oblong,
Letters—Materials<br>—colour—and<br>form. *button*, with a pin or streight wire, instead of the *shank*, run through it,
as it were, in the middle. The cloth of the Table being *black*, the ground
of the buttons may be of the same colour, covered with a black varnish:
the part which forms the letter being a little raised, and gilt. The
coarsest kind of Japan-work seems well enough adapted to this
purpose. The Table, which formed the subject of the observation
mentioned in the preceding paragraph, was composed of gold letters
on a black ground. Black letters on a white ground, as in a printed
paper, would not answer so well, on account of the soiling. I found by
various observations, that the legibility depended, even more than I
should have expected, on the degree of illumination. Perhaps the letters
would appear the more distinct, if the brilliancy were confined to the
characters themselves, and the varnish composing the ground were
deprived of its gloss. At night the Table might receive the light from a
reverberating lamp. At the above-mentioned distance of 52 feet, lines
composed of gilt letters no more than $\frac{3}{4}$ of an inch in height, in a
Church, were a great deal more legible than some lines composed of
letters of exactly twice the height, black upon white marble, were at
twice that distance, even in the open air.

The oblong character seems preferable to the square. By the
contraction thus given to them in breadth, a greater number might
be included in a line, without prejudice to their legibility.

---

[1] See p. 172 below.

The length of the pin should be no more than sufficient to prevent it from upsetting and falling out; when the point, for farther security, has been passed through the other cloth behind. The proper height will depend therefore upon the size and weight of the button. The shorter the pin, the better; as it would be the less liable to break or bend. Possibly *one* surface of cloth might be found to give the pins sufficient hold: in which case the hinder surface might be spared. If *two* should be found necessary, the most convenient length for the pin, and consequently the most convenient distance between the two cloths, might easily be found by experiment; by straining them each on a separate frame, and connecting the two frames at a variable distance, by screws at the four corners.

The streightness of the lines, and the uniformity of their distance, might be effectually ensured by lines traced in the cloth, and which might be made perceptible to the Compositor, without being so to the Spectators. The letters being placed in contact with one of these traced lines at bottom, and in contact with each other at the sides, it would be still more easy to ensure uniformity to lines thus composed, than to those of a printed page. 4.<br>Streightness and uniformity of the lines.

A Table of this sort should turn on an axis, in the manner of a door. The Compositor, when at his work, presents his side to the Spectators with the Table before him; and then it is as if the door were open: when the work is finished, he quits his station, presents the Table to the Spectators; and then it is as if the door were shut. 5.<br>Manner of composing and presenting the Table.

For the convenience of shifting, it should be made to hook off and on, by means of two hooks or pins, one at top, the other at bottom: which hooks, when inserted into so many *eyes* or small rings projecting from an upright pillar, will serve as axes for the door to turn upon.

It may be convenient to have two of these Tables close together, and in the same line, by the side of each other; like the two leaves or doors of a pair of folding-doors; except that it will be better that the axes on which they turn should be close together, as in a pair of *back-gammon* or *trick-track-tables*, than on opposite sides, as in the sort of doors just-mentioned. It will be more convenient for the stationing of the Compositors, of whom one may be at work on each leaf at the same time. On this plan the appearance of the two Tables will be exactly like that of the two pages of an open book: except that the former will form one even surface, without any hollow in the middle. 6.<br>Double Tables, like folding-doors.

*Amendments* to Motions may be thus exhibited. The original Motion stands enter'd upon a Table of this kind, occupying one or more leaves according to its length. 7.<br>Amendments—how to be exhibited.

{ For a *defalcative* amendment, place *brackets*, as thus, {at the} beginning and ending of the clause proposed to be omitted:} adding } on the outside, for the better guidance of the eye, brackets of a larger kind, inclosing the line or lines, as here.

{ For an *insertive* amendment, put a caret ⌃ at the place in question,} (with an outside bracket to the line, as before): and exhibit the proposed insertion, on the same level, in a separate Table, placed as close as may be to the former.

For a *Substitutive* amendment, include in brackets the clause proposed to be omitted, and exhibit on the *Amendment-Table*, as before, the clause proposed to be inserted in its room.

8.

Figures, to facilitate reference.

To facilitate the referring in the course of debate, to this or that line, it will be convenient to place figures, in the margin, at every five lines, expressive of the number of the lines, as here:[1] an expedient sometimes made use of in books.

9.

Multiplication of the number of Tables.

These Tables, it is evident, may be multiplied, according as they are wanted. There are no other limits to their multiplication than what may be set by the expence. It need not be limited by the size of the Gallery allotted to the exhibition of them: for all above what are in actual use may be kept in an adjacent room. Being made to shift off and on, they need never be in each other's way.

10.

Quantity of matter capable of being exhibited at once.

It may be a satisfaction to form a general notion of the quantity of discourse capable of being exhibited at one view upon a pair of tables of this sort. Supposing each table 9 feet high and six wide, it is supposed, upon a rough calculation, the two together might contain a quantity of letters nearly equal to four pages of the closest letter-press used in the 8$^{vo}$ edition of the *Procès-Verbal* of the *Notables*[2] of 1787.[a] But the type employ'd in those pages is remarkably small, and the lines

---

[a] In the sample mentioned in paragraph 2,[3] each line was in length six feet and an inch.  }  Feet. I.  } 6 — 1

In that space were contained the following eighteen words.

*'That by and out of the same they should cause the railing round the family vault to be . . .'*  }  Words  } 18

|  | Inches |
|---|---|
| Total space occupied by nine such lines in depth . . . . . . . . . . . . . . . . . . . | 19 |
| Which gives for each line a depth of a little more than . . . . . . . . . . . . . . | 2 |

In the Procès-Verbal.

| | |
|---|---|
| Number of the words, (where they happen to be short as in the specimen above mentioned) contained in a line . . . . . . . . . . . . . . . . . . . . . . . . . . . . | 12 |
| Number of *lines* in a page . . . . . . . . . . . . . . . . . . . . . . . . . . . . . . . . . . | 42 |
| Number of such *words* in a page . . . . . . . . . . . . . . . . . . . . . . . . . . . . . . | 504 |
| Number in 4 pages . . . . . . . . . . . . . . . . . . . . . . . . . . . . . . . . . . . . . . . . | 2016 |

---

[1] In the MS, Bentham inserts the numbers 5, 10, 15, 20, and 25 at appropriate places in the margin.

[2] *Procès-verbal de l'Assemblée des Notables, tenue à Versailles, en l'année M.DCCLXXXVII.*

[3] i.e. paragraph 2, p. 170 above.

proportionably close: insomuch that one of them would probably be found to contain at least double the quantity of matter most usually found in an 8$^{vo}$ page. One may therefore venture to set down the quantity of matter, that can be commodiously exhibited on a double Motion-Table, as equal to half a sheet of ordinary letter-press, and that in such manner as to be legible with facility at 52 feet distance.[a]

If the Tables are made of the breadth of 6 feet, as above proposed, it would be proper to divide them each into two columns; that the length of the lines may not occasion difficulty and confusion in passing from one line to another.

11.
Two *columns* in each Table.

Of the *time* that it might take to compose a given quantity of letter[s] upon this plan, I can not at present speak with any precision. Some conjecture may be formed from the time employ'd in composing in the ordinary way for the press.

12.
Expedition—what degree practicable.

In several respects this new mode of composition would have the advantage, in point of celerity, over the old one.

1. The detail of *blanks* and lines and all the contrivances for filling up the interstices (a detail of which I can not pretend to speak) would here be spared.

2. *Errata* would be much less liable to occurr; as the letters would be out of danger of being mistaken, one for another; partly by reason of their presenting themselves in the natural instead of the reversed form; partly by reason of their size.

3. It is scarce necessary to observe, that the operation of the press,

In the Table referred to as a Specimen.

F I

| | |
|---|---|
| N° of words in a line of 6- 1 long . . . . . . . . . . . . . . . . . . . . . . . . . . . . . . . . . | 18 |
| N° of lines that may be placed in a height of 9 feet, at 2 inches to a line . . | 54 |
| N° of words that would be contained at that rate in a single leaf of the Motion-Table . . . . . . . . . . . . . . . . . . . . . . . . . . . . . . . . . . . . . . . . } | [972][1] |
| N° of words in the two leaves . . . . . . . . . . . . . . . . . . . . . . . . . . . . . . . . . . . | 1944. |

[a] Since writing the above, I have formed a calculation, which for want of time, has been but a loose one, of the greatest distance between two Members' seats, supposing the number of Members to be 1100, and the room of the form which reduces that distance within the narrowest limits, upon the principle mentioned in N° 2.[2] And I have the mortification to find it rather over than under *double* the 52 feet distance mentioned in the text. It would therefore probably be necessary to double the length of the letters, or else to have *two* Motion-Tables, one at each end of the room.

So much for *seeing*.—But what is to be done for *hearing*? See once more N° 2.—Two speakers to speak the same speech at the same time, is not quite so feasible as two Motion-Tables to exhibit the same Motion.

[1] MS '974'.

[2] A reference to Essay III, Chapter II, '*Rules* relative to the *construction* of such an Edifice', which appears in Bentham's plan of the contents of the projected 'Essays on Political Tactics'. See Table I, p. 176 below, and Ch. III, §1, p. 44 above.

which consumes so much time in the common mode of typography, would have no place here.

13.
*Magazine for sup-plying the letters.*

For a magazine for supplying the characters, let the Compositor have by his side, a Table of the same dimensions as one leaf of the Motion-Table, stuck *full* of the several sorts of characters required, in groupes following each other in determinate order, and in numbers proportioned to the relative frequency of their occurrence: a matter well known to Printers and Letter-founders. In the Church-Table above-mentioned, (par[s]. 2 and [3])[1] the void spaces occupied $\frac{5}{8}$ of the whole extent, without reckoning breaks, or distances between words. A surplus to this amount would contain a fund, which, it should seem, would be amply sufficient to provide against the utmost variety to which the relative proportions could be liable.

Possibly what is called in England the *logographical* principle (or as it might more properly be termed the *holo-epic*)[2] the principle of printing by whole words, might be applied to this purpose with some advantage in the way of saving time.

14.
*Conjectures relative to the expence.*

As to the expence, according to the calculation below, it may be computed at about £680 for two double tables, with the magazine above-mentioned, and the whole apparatus compleat.[a]

[a] Expence of the Types.
N° of types required to cover compleatly without interstices a Table of 6 feet wide by 9 in height, the types being supposed to be $\frac{3}{4}$ of an inch each in height, and, upon an average, $\frac{1}{2}$ an inch in width—19440

| | |
|---|---:|
| 19440 types = 1620 dozen, at 2ˢ per dozen, for a single Table . . . . . . . . . . | £162 |
| For a double Table—Doz: 3240 . . . . . . . . . . . . . . . . . . . . . . . . . . . . . . | £324 |
| For two double Tables. Doz: 6480 . . . . . . . . . . . . . . . . . . . . . . . . . . . . | £648 |

Expence of the Tables.
For a single Table, 4 Yards of black cloth at 12ˢ 1$\frac{1}{2}$ yard wide—for the front surface . . . . . . . . . . . . . . . . . . . . . . . . . . . . . . . . . . . . . . . . . } £ 2- 8
4 d° coarse for the hinder surface at 2ˢ-6ᵈ . . . . . . . . . . . . . . . . . . . . . . . . 0-10
For a double Table . . . . . . . . . . . . . . . . . . . . . . . . . . . . . . . . . . . . . . . . 5-16
Frames and Pillar for d°—say . . . . . . . . . . . . . . . . . . . . . . . . . . . . . . . . 4- 4

Total expence of one double Table . . . . . . . . . . . . . . . . . . . . . . . . . . . 10-[0]
Expence of two double Tables . . . . . . . . . . . . . . . . . . . . . . . . . . . . . . . . £20- 0
Expence of two double Magazine Tables
32 Yards of coarse cloth at 2-6 £ 4- 0
2 Pillars and 4 Frames—say 8- 0

£ 12- 0

Total expence of Tables for 2 double Motion-Tables . . . . . . . . . . . . . . . . £ 32
Types for d° . . . . . . . . . . . . . . . . . . . . . . . . . . . . . . . . . . . . . . . . . . . . £648

Total expence of types and Tables. £680

---

[1] MS '10'. See p. 170 above.
[2] From the Greek ὅλος (whole) and ἔπος (word).

This expence, even if doubled, would be of no great consideration for an object of such magnitude: such a sum would pass without observation, if consumed in useless decorations.

A more material expence is that of the Salaries of the Compositors, of whom there could not well be fewer than *two*. But, under the name of Clerks, the expence of two additional hands would hardly be thought worth notice.

Previously to the bespeaking of the types, it might be deemed proper to ascertain by experiment, the largeness of type suited to the dimensions of the room and the number of the spectators. An experiment in this view might be made at a very trifling expence.

15.
Cheaper apparatus for making previous trials.

To represent the *ground* or *Table*, take a sheet of *sail-cloth* or any other kind of canvas, no matter how coarse, so it be tolerably white: hang it up in the manner of a map: strain it either on a frame, or by ropes.

For the letters, print, on one side, with types of the size thought most eligible, such a number of sheets as will furnish a stock of letters sufficient to cover the abovementioned ground. Paste the letters on paste-board: then cut them out, and run through each a common pin of a proportionable size.

To make the experiment fairly, the spectator ought to be placed at the greatest distance at which any Member can take his seat: and he should rather be a man of weak than strong sight. Near-sighted persons, it is evident, are out of the question. They must relieve themselves as they can, in this case as in others.

The fundamental experiment would be to fix the diameter of the *sphere of audibility*: that is, the greatest distance at which an ordinary voice could be clearly and constantly heard, with no greater degree of exertion than it would be capable of maintaining for hours together. A *weak* voice should be taken for the standard, rather than a *strong* one. To make the experiment conclusive, something of an assembly should likewise be collected, in order that such kinds and degrees of noise, as are inseparable from the best-disciplined assembly, may be taken into the account. This distance being thus ascertained in the best manner that the uncertainty inseparable from the subject will admit of, the problem of the *sphere of legibility* will admitt of a solution much more satisfactory. Suppose the speech or other composition sufficiently well *heard* at the distance of a *hundred* feet: it remains only to be seen, what magnitude of type will be *legible* at that distance. Happy would it be for the rectitude and genuineness of the decisions of numerous assemblies, if the ear were capable of receiving assistance equally sure and effectual, with that which by these means may be given to the eye.

# TABLE I

## HEADS TREATED OF IN A WORK

### ENTITLED

## ESSAYS on POLITICAL TACTICS,

### OR

ENQUIRIES *concerning the* DISCIPLINE *and* MODE *of* PROCEEDING *proper to be observed in* POLITICAL ASSEMBLIES:

Principally applied to the Practice of the BRITISH PARLIAMENT, and to the Constitution and Situation of the NATIONAL ASSEMBLY of FRANCE.

# TABLE II

# TABULA ATAXIOLOGICA:

### OR,

## SYNOPTICAL TABLE,

Giving an Analytical Sketch of the several Heads of INCONVENIENCE corresponding to the several ENDS proper to be kept in View, in framing a System of TACTICS for the Use of a POLITICAL ASSEMBLY.

N.B. This Table may be made to serve as a *Test* of the Propriety of all manner of Rules and other Institutions, proposed or proposable for the Regulation of Proceedings in a Political Assembly. Every legitimate Reason, given as operating in *favour* of any such Rule or Institution, consists in the Allegation of its Tendency to *prevent* the taking place of some one or more of the Inconveniences therein exhibited. Every legitimate Reason, given as operating in *disfavour* of any such Rule or Institution, consists in the Allegation of its Tendency to *give birth* to some one or more of those Inconveniences.

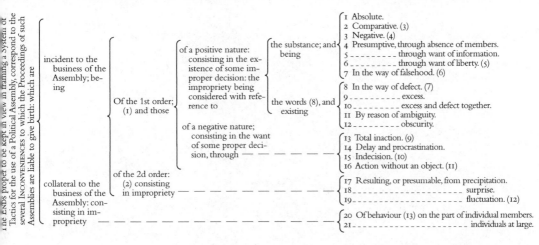

The ENDS proper to be kept in view in framing a System of Tactics for the use of a Political Assembly, correspond to the several INCONVENIENCES to which the Proceedings of such Assemblies are liable to give birth: which are

incident to the business of the Assembly; being

Of the 1st order; (1) and those

of a positive nature: consisting in the existence of some improper decision: the impropriety being considered with reference to

the substance; and being
1 Absolute.
2 Comparative. (3)
3 Negative. (4)
4 Presumptive, through absence of members.
5 — — — — — — — through want of information.
6 — — — — — — — through want of liberty. (5)
7 In the way of falsehood. (6)

the words (8), and existing
8 In the way of defect. (7)
9 — — — — — — — excess.
10 — — — — — — — excess and defect together.
11 By reason of ambiguity.
12 — — — — — — — obscurity.

of a negative nature; consisting in the want of some proper decision, through — — — — —
13 Total inaction. (9)
14 Delay and procrastination.
15 Indecision. (10)
16 Action without an object. (11)

of the 2d order: (2) consisting in impropriety — — — — —
17 Resulting, or presumable, from precipitation.
18 — — — — — — — — — surprise.
19 — — — — — — — — — fluctuation. (12)

collateral to the business of the Assembly: consisting in impropriety — — — — —
20 Of behaviour (13) on the part of individual members.
21 — — — — — — — — — — individuals at large.

## NOTES.

(1) {*Of the 1st order,*} viz. Inconveniences which are so in themselves.

(2) {*Of the 2d order,*} viz. Inconveniences which are so, only in virtue of their tendency to give birth to some inconvenience or inconveniences of the 1st order.

(3) {*Comparative,*} viz. The decision in question being compared with some other, the formation of which has been prevented by it.

(4) {*Negative,*} viz. The decision being of no use.

(5) {*Want of liberty.*} Want of liberty may here be considered as capable of resulting not only from physical force or fear, but from the action of any principle of seduction of the alluring class; bribery, for instance.

(6) {*Falsehood,*} viz. Where along with, or instead of, some *declaration of will,* which is the proper and principal business of a Political Assembly, the decision in question is such as conveys some *false allegation* relative to a matter of fact.

(7) {*Defect,*} viz. By reason of the want of certain words.

(8) {*The words.*} In all motions in *amendment,* the decision originally proposed is considered as chargeable with impropriety in this point of view.

(9) {*Inaction,*} viz. Not meeting: or meeting without motion or debate.

(10) {*Indecision,*} viz. Motion or debate without decision.

(11) {*Action without an object.*} Instance: Debate or conversation, without motion previous or consequential.

(12) {*Fluctuation,*} *i.e.* The successive formation of *opposite* decisions: of which (circumstances remaining unaltered) one or more must accordingly have been *improper.*

(13) {*Impropriety of behaviour.*} For the several possible varieties of improper behaviour, see the Analysis of the several possible modifications of *Delinquency,* given in an Introduction to Morals and Legislation, 1789, Ch. 16.[1]

{*Division of offences.*} Any instance of such misbehaviour, in as far as its tendency is to give birth to *absence of members, want of information, want of liberty, inaction, delay, indecision, precipitation, surprise,* or *fluctuation,* may be regarded in this respect as an inconvenience of the *third* order. For those inconveniences, considered in themselves, are but inconveniences of the second order. Of all the inconveniences to which the nature of such an Assembly is capable of giving birth (those excepted which are merely collateral to the business of it), the only radical ones are, the formation of some bad decision, or the non-formation of some good one. Suppose all the requisite good decisions formed, and no bad ones, all the other incidents marked as attended with inconvenience would either cease to exist, or cease to be attended with that effect.

Most of the above causes of inconvenience possess, over and above their particular tendencies, a sort of common tendency to produce an inconvenience of a more remote and general nature: viz. the bringing a degree of *discredit* on the proceedings and general character of the Assembly. Acts of this tendency may be considered as so many *offences against the reputation* of the Assembly. *Want of liberty,* decisions chargeable with *falsehood,* and frequent *misbehaviour* on the part of the members, may be particularly noted in this view. What life is to an individual, reputation is to a Political Assembly. An offence against the reputation of such an Assembly, committed by the Assembly itself, is a sort of approach to suicide.

[1] See *An Introduction to the Principles of Morals and Legislation,* ed. J.H. Burns and H.L.A. Hart, London, 1970 (*CW*), p. 195.

# ENDNOTES

*Note*: The endnotes draw attention to significant discrepancies between the present text and the 1816 edition of 'Tactique des assemblées politiques délibérantes'; variations and additions in the 1822 edition are also noted. See the Editorial Introduction, p.xxxviii above.

In the first column, the first figure refers to the page number(s), the second figure to line number(s): hence 15, 17 refers to page 15, line 17.

| | |
|---|---|
| 15, 17 | nuire au |
| 16, 14 | plusieurs |
| 16, 16 | Les élus |
| 16, 20 | actuellement |
| 16, 25 | *conditions* |
| 16, 27 | moins attachés au maintien de l'ordre établi, |
| 16, 39 | peuvent avoir des intérêts particuliers et faire des lois contre l'intérêt général. |
| 16, 40 | *1822* la majorité |
| 16, 47 | l'autorité des électeurs sur leurs députés, |
| 16, 49 | *1822 adds* Il y a trois autres conditions nécessaires pour constituer un gouvernement représentatif: la publicité des séances, la liberté de la presse, et le droit de pétition. |
| 17, 11 | les unes. |
| 17, 16 | bien |
| 17, 26 | Longueurs. |
| 17, 33 | fond. |
| 18, 16 | *Longueurs.* |
| 18, 18 | longueurs, |
| 18, 19 | longueurs |
| 18, 21 | dans l'ordre judiciaire. |
| 18, 22 | longueurs |
| 19, 2 | n'ont même que trop de tendance |
| 19, 5 | n'est qu'un assemblage |
| 19, 19 | justesse |
| 19, 24 | *Décision vicieuse par rédaction.* |
| | Une rédaction vicieuse est celle qui pèche non par le fond, mais par la forme; |
| 19, 30 | *adds* Je renvoie les lecteurs à ce qui a été dit sur le *style des lois*, dans les *Traités de législation*. T.1, p.341.[1] |
| 19, 31 | *Décision vicieuse par le fond.* |
| 19, 38 | son vœu est de conformer ses décisions à l'utilité publique, |
| 20, 12 | depuis le commencement de ses opérations jusqu'à leurs derniers résultats; |
| 20, 13 | de sa police |
| 20, 24 | au lieu de s'affoiblir et de s'embarrasser par le nombre, |
| 20, 28 | le despotisme ou le démagogisme. |
| 20, 38 | *Corps politique* |
| 20, 40 | des métaphores, |
| 21, 3 | *assemblée,* |

---

[1] For the chapter entitled *Du style des Lois*, see *Traités de législation*, i. 361–70 (not 341).

| | |
|---|---|
| 21, 24 | du sein |
| 21, 28 | *concours de plusieurs membres dans un même acte.* |
| 21, 35 | la possibilité |
| 22, 2 | destinés |
| 22, 19 | *adds* mais cette unanimité étant comme impossible, |
| 22, 19 | vœu |
| 22, 20 | vœu |
| 22, 22 | vœu |
| 22, 25 | sans qu'on ait besoin de donner |
| 23, 23 | *corps politique* |
| 23, 38 | soit pour abréger, soit pour tempérer l'aridité du sujet, |
| 23, 40 | et même on y est souvent forcé |
| 24, 3 | impropre, |
| 24, 3 | ne s'accorde plus |
| 24, 12 | efficacité |
| 25, 1 | Leurs |
| 25, 23 | réduit à la négative |
| 26, 2 | de brider la précipitation et de prévenir les surprises. |
| 26, 8 | qui ont à faire valoir quelque intérêt: |
| 26, 16 | *1822 adds* c'est-à-dire, pour obéir aux passions du jour. |
| 26, 38 | le danger de la démagogie |
| 27, 4 | premier |
| 27, 26 | *représentative* |
| 27, 29 | toutefois |
| 27, 37 | elle craint les affaires comme les procès, |
| 28, 32 | les limites de son autorité très-peu déterminées, |
| 28, 37 | la Noblesse même |
| 29, 24 | *1822 adds* Premier avantage de la publicité: |
| 30, 25 | Second avantage de la publicité: |
| 30, 35 | *1822* excitera, dans certaines circonstances, |
| 30, 41 | vous enlevez au mécontentement toutes les armes qu'il auroit pu tourner contre vous. |
| 30, 43 | ses couleuvres se nourrissent de venin dans les cavernes, l'éclat du jour leur est mortel. |
| 31, 8 | hommes d'État, |
| 31, 13 | *ce qui* |
| 31, 16 | après un combat entre les deux partis |
| 31, 33 | échoue contre |
| 31, 34 | *1822 adds* on ne se décourage point, parce qu'on peut mesurer ses progrès; |
| 31, 38 | dans les clubs, dans les groupes, dans les assemblées inférieures |
| 32, 13 | [*Sentence omitted.*][1] |
| 32, 16 | le régime |
| 32, 33 | qu'on ne donne que par nécessité |
| 32, 35 | le bien même échoue, |
| 32, 36 | qu'on a heurté |
| 32, 38 | Par exemple, en 1780, dans l'affaire des Catholiques. |
| 33, 2 | *1822* [*Sentence omitted.*] |

[1] Thus in the Bowring edition, Dumont's five 'Raisons justificatives' become six 'Reasons for Publicity'. Dumont provides numerals for only the first two reasons.

| | |
|---|---|
| 33, 5 | *1822* Troisième avantage de la publicité: *Ménager aux électeurs la faculté d'agir avec connaissance de cause.* |
| 33, 13 | *1822* Quatrième avantage de la publicité: |
| 33, 20 | *1822* la fonction de faire des lois? |
| 34, 12 | un bien. |
| 34, 13 | un bien tout réalisé: |
| 34, 15 | me paroît suffisant à lui seul pour élever le bonheur d'une nation qui en jouit fort au-dessus de celui des nations qui ne le connoissent pas. |
| 34, 17 | *1822* plus généralement recherchés: |
| 34, 32 | Faut-il en chercher la cause dans des vices, |
| 35, 14 | la fantaisie |
| 35, 20 | la publication des pièces, |
| 35, 33 | Ce n'est pas à la troisième: |
| 35, 40 | la source, |
| 36, 5 | parce que vous êtes incapables |
| 36, 13 | à chaque instant, |
| 36, 15 | le régime |
| 37, 9 | ce Supérieur, |
| 37, 10 | *1822* la protection de l'opinion publique; la bienveillance générale devient son égide. |
| 37, 11 | La précaution des délibérations secrètes |
| 37, 12 | ce Supérieur, |
| 37, 16 | ce Supérieur, |
| 37, 17 | un prétexte. |
| 37, 33 | *1822* sans pouvoir être convaincus de malversation. |
| 37, 35 | Que reste-t-il donc pour surmonter tous ces motifs dangereux qu'à créer un intérêt d'une force supérieure? |
| 38, 27 | prochain. |
| 40, 26 | seront, dès le lendemain, imprimés en seize colonnes in-folio d'un petit caractère, |
| 40, 31 | *adds* ou plutôt qu'elle en est la condition essentielle. |
| 40, 32 | soupçonner |
| 40, 34 | et qu'il se passe dans l'Assemblée beaucoup de choses |
| 41, 13 | fournissoient |
| 41, 16 | de rien rapporter de ce qui s'y sera passé, |
| 41, 19 | treize |
| 41, 24 | Cette doctrine de la publicité paroîtra bien paradoxale à nos Gouvernements Helvétiques. Les Conseils représentatifs établis dans presque tous les Cantons, c'est-à-dire dans tous ceux qui n'ont pas conservé le régime démocratique, non-seulement n'admettent point d'externes à leurs séances, mais encore ne publient point de procès-verbaux de leurs délibérations. L'admission du public se présenteroit à eux sous l'aspect d'une nouveauté tout-à-fait dangereuse: on en craindroit une fermentation continuelle dans l'esprit public; on se croiroit exposé à des rapports tronqués, insidieux ou calomnieux. Ce seroit, diroit-on, ouvrir un spectacle à des oisifs, qui acquerroient bientôt une activité malfaisante, et provoquer une perte de temps pour ceux qui ne subsistent que par leur travail. En un mot, la publicité seroit bientôt suivie de quelque révolution. |

Je ne me dissimule pas les inconvénients.—Mais en même temps je vois avec regret nos Gouvernements renoncer aux avantages qui résultent de la publicité. Ils font des lois dont les raisons ne sont connues que de ceux qui ont suivi les discussions des Conseils. Le public les ignore, et ne pouvant rien connoître, il reste dans un état d'infériorité qui établit une disproportion fâcheuse entre les gouvernants et les gouvernés.

Il est vrai que la *représentation* est beaucoup plus forte par rapport à la population de chaque Canton, qu'elle ne l'est dans des États tels que la France et l'Angleterre. C'est là une différence réelle et qui diminue les dangers de la non-publicité. La classe moyenne, étant beaucoup mieux représentée, a bien plus de motifs de confiance dans ses députés, en même temps qu'elle a moins à craindre de la part du gouvernement, qui n'a pas à sa disposition les moyens de les séduire. On doit bien convenir aussi que si la salle des délibérations étoit ouverte au public, il en résulteroit le danger des rapports partiaux et infidelles, à moins qu'il n'y eût un journal exact des débats.

Je pense toutefois que dans chaque Canton, on pourroit accorder l'admission dans le Conseil représentatif à un certain nombre de personnes, sans inconvénient et avec de grands avantages. On pourroit donner ce droit de présence, 1.º à ceux des candidats auxquels il n'auroit manqué qu'un petit nombre de suffrages pour être élus députés; 2.º à ceux qui seroient sortis par la loi de l'amovibilité et qui peuvent rentrer par une nouvelle élection; 3.º aux jeunes élèves qui étudient le droit et qui sont destinés aux magistratures; 4.º à des employés publics, aux ecclésiastiques, aux directeurs des établissements de charité, etc. etc.

Voilà des hommes qui ont une responsabilité, un attachement naturel au maintien de la constitution, un intérêt particulier à connoître les raisons qui ont servi de base aux lois et aux actes publics. Leur admission auroit l'heureux effet d'associer un plus grand nombre d'individus à la chose publique, de faire cesser la jalousie et le mécontentement que l'exclusion peut inspirer, et d'augmenter ainsi la confiance générale.

*1822 adds* Si ce moyen ne paraissait pas admissible, il y en aurait d'autres qui produiraient en partie le même effet, tels que l'impression des rapports officiels, des comptes rendus, et surtout d'un procès-verbal circonstancié, comme celui de la chambre des pairs en France.

La diète helvétique fait imprimer son *recez*, c'est-à-dire le journal de ses opérations: mais on se borne à en distribuer à chaque canton un exemplaire. N'est-ce point la suite d'une vieille idée aristocratique qui fait envisager toutes les affaires publiques comme le patrimoine exclusif de ceux qui gouvernent? La publicité du recez donnerait un grand intérêt à la diète et à ses discussions. Rien ne serait plus propre à étendre ce sentiment de nationalité, qui est trop faible en Suisse et trop dominé par l'esprit cantonnal. Est-ce la faute des citoyens s'ils ne connaissent pas une patrie qui ne se montre point à eux, qui ne les associe point à ses pensées, qui ne les entretient jamais de leurs affaires communes, et qui leur laisse même ignorer le bien qu'on leur fait? Depuis le nouveau pacte fédéral, il n'est point de session de la diète qui n'ait été signalée par de sages mesures d'administration générale, et par une tendance vers l'utilité commune: mais pour apprécier ses services il faut les connaître, et la nation ne connaît ni ses hommes publics ni ses intérêts généraux. Il résulte de ce manque absolu de publicité que la politique étrangère est la seule pâture de la curiosité nationale. Est-ce là un système juste, légitime, conforme à la nature de nos gouvernemens, à l'esprit du siècle, aux besoins actuels des hommes?

42, 2    *Votes.*
42, 9    *Journaux de la chambre.*
42, 10   Ces journaux sont donnés à chaque Membre, et ne sont point vendus au public.
42, 15   *1822 omits* d'un membre.

42, 19    *1822* les vrais principes de liberté
42, 21    les principes d'un gouvernement libre étoient encore si peu connus qu'on ne voit aucune réclamation générale contre une conduite qui tendoit à détruire
42, 25    *adds* ils ont cessé d'être en vigueur, et
42, 29    les innovations insensibles
42, 30    *adds* par indulgence
42, 31    *adds* ou deux cents
42, 34    le cas d'exception
44, 1     un emplacement plus commode;
44, 14    *adds* par l'art. 32,
44, 19    *1822* L'absence du public
44, 20    *1822* La publicité leur est plus nécessaire qu'aux députés,
44, 24    ou devant être
44, 25    les propositions inconsidérées
44, 27    contre-sens
44, 29    gouvernement.
44, 41    si peu flatteur pour eux,
44, 42    *1822 adds* La chambre des pairs a tellement reconnu l'infériorité de sa position relative, par cette obligation des *délibérations secrètes*, qu'elle a cherché tous les moyens de s'en affranchir sans violer le texte de la constitution.

    Elle ordonne l'impression des rapports et de la plupart des discours. Elle fait publier officiellement dans les journaux le procès-verbal très-circonstancié de ses délibérations.

    Ce procès-verbal n'énonçant pas les noms des divers orateurs, elle a permis d'y suppléer dans l'impression officielle par des notes qui désignent nominative-ment.

    Enfin la chambre a admis la publicité pour les débats lorsqu'elle procède comme *cour judiciaire*, et on a pu juger dans le procès de l'année dernière sur la conspiration d'août 1820, tout ce que la publicité pouvait lui faire acquérir en considération et en confiance.[1]

45, 2     la promptitude du service.
45, 14    peut être
45, 23    *1822 adds* et qu'il soit vu de l'orateur;
45, 27    la commodité du service.
45, 33    *adds* dans un tableau,
45, 36    *adds* pendant toute la durée de la délibération,
45, 38    *adds* réservant un article séparé pour une description plus détaillée.[2]
46, 9     *1822* qui la transcrivent sur ce tableau, et qui la présentent
46, 21    *1822* les termes précis de la proposition
46, 32    tous ceux qui sont venus trop tard pour l'entendre,
47, 25    un plaidoyer sur la compétence de ses arguments.
47, 31    *1822* des admonitions fréquentes,
47, 36    une apostrophe
48, 1     *tableau*
48, 4     *1822* pour apprécier la justesse des expressions.

---

[1] In August 1820, there was an unsuccessful attempt by Bonapartists and republicans to overthrow the Bourbon Restoration of 1814. Of the many who were tried by the Chambre des Pairs, only six were punished, and those with light prison sentences. For a report of the proceedings of the Chambre des Pairs in this case, see *Archives parlementaires de 1787 à 1860, deuxième série (1800 à 1860)*, Paris 1879–1913, XXXIII. 327–551.

[2] Presumably a reference to § 3, p.49 above.

48, 6     à plusieurs reprises,

48, 19    moins le service en exige, moins on est en danger d'en manquer.

48, 28    On ne se baisse point pour lire sans cesser d'écouter ou de parler,

49, 19    l'autre,

49, 21    si

49, 30    Je l'ai trouvé ainsi par une espèce de calcul approximatif.

49, 35    *adds* en Angleterre

50, 14    l'impéritie

50, 39    manier

51, 9     *1822 adds* du mal

51, 15    d'un *costume*

51, 33    éclairer

51, 34    autour d'eux.

52, 6     Ce Juge si fameux

52, 14    *1822 adds* à son choix,

52, 22    longueurs,

52, 28    la vérité seule a tout à gagner dans ce concours.

52, 37    se sont naturellement placés

52, 39    *banc de la Trésorerie,*

53, 9     dans leur *place,* ont droit à cette *place,* au moins pendant la durée de ce Parlement,

53, 15    à en juger par le local,

53, 25    *1822* qui ont si misérablement absorbé l'attention des assemblées politiques,

54, 25    doit

54, 27    est

54, 40    et qui est dérouté quand il est appelé à juger

55, 8     où

55, 9     où

55, 12    *1822 adds* La tribune, telle qu'elle est établie dans la chambre des députés de France, est sujette à d'autres objections. Le président est placé derrière l'orateur: dès lors une des règles essentielles ne peut pas être observée, celle d'adresser la parole au président et à lui seul.

         Cette position offre un autre inconvénient. Si l'orateur s'écarte de la question ou de l'ordre, le président ne peut pas l'interrompre ou s'en faire entendre, sans agiter sa bruyante sonnette. Ce mode d'avertissement, désagréable en lui-même, provoque l'amour-propre et l'irrite tout autrement que ne ferait un signe ou un mot de la part du chef de l'assemblée.

55, 14    Toutefois il faut observer

55, 27    car il doit être admis qu'on laisse achever un discours commencé.

55, 42    aspirant à la décision,

57, 18    *adds* ou, pour mieux dire, l'*absentation*

57, 31    *contre*

57, 38    et à se faire un avis à soi,

58, 17    *quota*

58, 31    *Moyens préventifs.*

58, 34    *adds* (50 liv.)

58, 36    *adds* (50 liv.)

58, 42    ce n'est pas là une objection,

59, 1     *s'exécutent d'elles-mêmes.*

59, 20    et plus doux.

59, 21    Cet expédient même ne suffiroit pas.

# ENDNOTES

59, 40    V. Théorie des Peines et des Récompenses. T. II. Ch. IV.
60, 13    presque seul
60, 24    Les deux tiers de cette Assemblée
61, 4     dans le cas d'un appel spécial (*a Call of the House*),
61, 12    Et peut-on s'attendre qu'un Corps politique fasse des lois efficaces pour prévenir
          un abus dans lequel chacun trouve son compte?
61, 14    qui auroit perdu toute autre Assemblée,
62, 1     la suspension des affaires est-elle autre chose qu'une peine infligée
62, 14    vœu
62, 20    des moyens tout particuliers
62, 36    des hommes qui s'énivrent de la popularité du moment;
63, 3     bons esprits.
63, 4     qu'il ne l'eût été par
63, 13    pourroient
64, 5     je répugnois
64, 8     sauroit
64, 13    la justesse
64, 16    premier
64, 19    mouvement
64, 30    On avoit observé
65, 4     *Un Président—unique,—permanent,—toujours subordonné à l'assemblée,—n'y*
          *exerçant d'autres fonctions que celles de son office,—élu par elle seule,—amovible*
          *par elle seule,—*je vais développer et justifier ces différents points.

          Je ne m'arrête pas à prouver qu'il faut un Président pour mettre l'assemblée en
          activité, poser la question, recueillir les votes, parler en son nom, et y maintenir
          l'ordre.

          Il est de l'essence de toute assemblée délibérante de faire naître à chaque
          moment des contestations. Les règlements sont faits pour y obvier; mais quand
          les contestations s'élèvent, il faut une personne autorisée pour faire l'application
          des règlements, et terminer sur-le-champ des difficultés qui interromproient le
          cours des affaires, s'il falloit en appeler à l'assemblée même.
66, 5     Ce Président unique
67, 6     *adds* Craindroit-on qu'au moyen de cette permanence, il n'acquît trop d'ascen-
          dant? Mais plus cet ascendant seroit grand, plus il tourneroit au profit général, si
          d'ailleurs le règlement lui ôte tout moyen d'acquérir une influence indue sur
          l'ordre des motions, et sur la manière de recueillir les votes.
67, 9     *adds* Ce Président doit être unique.
67, 20    *adds* Des membres très-éclairés du Parlement Britannique, que j'ai consultés sur
          ce point, ne sont pas, en ceci, de l'avis de M. Bentham. Ils pensent qu'il y auroit
          beaucoup d'inconvénients à admettre des substituts. Des affaires infiniment
          multipliées et reprises à divers intervalles, seroient exposées à des irrégularités
          de formes, si elles passoient par différentes mains. Mais le plus grand danger
          seroit celui d'une diversité de décisions, d'où il résulteroit des antécédents
          contradictoires. Un seul juge conserve mieux l'uniformité des règles.—Il faut
          savoir, pour apprécier cette objection, que les règlements parlementaires ne sont
          point écrits, qu'ils n'existent que par tradition, et ne sont fondés que sur les
          *précédents* ou décisions antérieures; ce qui les expose à varier. Cet inconvénient
          n'auroit pas lieu pour une assemblée qui auroit un règlement écrit.[1]
67, 24    *Juge*

---

[1] It was not until 1853 that a resolution was passed which permitted the chairman of the Committee
of Ways and Means to take the Speaker's chair in the event of the unavoidable absence of the Speaker.

67, 25 *Agent*

67, 26 dans les autres opérations de son ministère.

68, 18 en possession de toute cette confiance

68, 19 l'acquiescement

68, 21 *adds* et impartial

68, 23 par son devoir même,

71, 12 Le règlement de la Présidence

71, 16 ont été presque partout méconnues.

110, 8 si aucun Membre en particulier n'étoit tenu d'avoir un plan, il se pourroit qu'il n'y en eût point,

110, 12 *adds* il faut pourvoir à toute la session.

110, 16 à celui qui a convoqué l'Assemblée, et qui connoît le mieux

110, 19 droit

110, 23 *L'avantage de tourner au profit commun l'intelligence de toute l'Assemblée.*

110, 30 capables

110, 33 pourroient

111, 2 *Le danger du droit négatif, quand il existe seul.*

111, 3 pourroit être

111, 10 pourroit bien ne tendre qu'à

111, 12 une conduite artificieuse contre le pouvoir exécutif.

111, 20 voilà le plan ministériel sujet à être interrompu par des motions incohérentes, et même entièrement bouleversé.

112, 2 adds c'est le résultat de l'expérience et de la réflexion.

112, 3 privilège

112, 6 dans tous les sens de ce mot,

112, 9 de cela seul que

112, 17 *adds NOTE sur la présence des Ministres dans l'Assemblée.*

M.<sup>r</sup> Bentham n'a pas insisté sur la nécessité de la *présence* des Ministres dans l'Assemblée Législative, parce qu'il l'a supposée comme une règle admise et nécessaire, d'après l'usage immuable du Parlement Britannique, où il n'est jamais venu dans l'esprit de personne de les en exclure.

Cette idée, vraiment anarchique, prévaloit tellement en France, à l'époque des États-Généraux, que les Ministres qui les convoquèrent ne pensèrent pas même à s'y placer; ils ne prirent l'initiative sur rien, ils abandonnèrent l'Assemblée à elle-même, sans aucun plan, sans aucun travail préparé, se tenant en-dehors de tout, comme pour soumettre l'autorité royale à ne recevoir que des ordres du vainqueur. C'étoit déjà une abdication virtuelle.

Les hommes judicieux, qui étoient en grand nombre dans cette Assemblée, quoiqu'ils ne fussent pas la majorité, s'aperçurent bientôt des inconvénients de ce manque de connexion entre le Corps Législatif et le Pouvoir Executif. Il y avoit peu de séances qui ne fournît des preuves de ce désaccord. Un journal qui se publioit sous le nom du Comte de Mirabeau, (quoiqu'il n'eût aucune part à sa composition,) dès le mois de septembre [1789],[1] mit dans le plus grand jour la nécessité de les faire marcher de concert, en donnant aux Ministres séance et voix consultative dans l'Assemblée. La citation de ce passage n'est point étrangère ici. (Courrier de Provence, N.º 41.)

'En vain une politique étroite et soupçonneuse prétendoit-elle que l'indépendance du Corps Législatif souffriroit de cette réunion dont un État voisin offre l'exemple, et dont les bons effets sont prouvés par l'expérience. En vain

---

[1] Dumont '1807'.

l'opiniâtre et présomptueuse ignorance de quelques hommes rejette-t-elle toute induction tirée de la constitution de ce peuple que notre esclavage nous fit si long-temps envier, et que notre sottise méprise aujourd'hui. Jusqu'à ce que notre constitution ait subi l'épreuve du temps, les hommes sages admireront toujours dans cette Angleterre des résultats-pratiques supérieurs aux sublimes théories de nos Utopiens: ils ne cesseront de penser qu'une correspondance directe et journalière entre les Ministres et le Corps Législatif, telle qu'elle a lieu dans le Parlement Britannique, est non-seulement juste et utile, mais nécessaire et sans inconvénient.

'Elle est *juste*. Les Ministres sont citoyens comme les autres Français; et s'ils ont le vœu des Bailliages, on ne sauroit voir pourquoi l'entrée de l'Assemblée Nationale leur seroit fermée.

'Elle est *utile*. Le Corps Législatif s'occupe des mêmes objets que le Pouvoir Exécutif; toute la différence consiste en ce que l'un *veut* et que l'autre *agit*. On ne sauroit attendre de la législature des résultats sages, adaptés aux circonstances, tant qu'elle ne s'aidera pas des lumières que l'expérience, l'habitude des affaires, et la connoissance des difficultés fournissent continuellement au Pouvoir Exécutif.

'Cette correspondance paroîtra surtout *nécessaire*, si l'on fait attention à l'excessive diversité des objets qui entrent dans la législation, au caractère national, à l'impatiente ardeur qui nous dévore pour mettre en avant nos idées, pour opérer sous le nom d'améliorations des changements dans la partie qui nous est connue, sans trop nous soucier des rapports qu'elle peut avoir avec celle que nous ne connoissons pas, à l'effrayante activité que cette disposition recevra de la composition de l'Assemblée, et de son renouvellement biennal.

'Les *inconvénients* ne nous frappent point. De quelque manière qu'on les exprime, ils reviennent tous à ces deux mots: influence royale, influence ministérielle . . . . . Vains fantômes avec lesquels on effraie les esprits foibles, mais qui ne doivent point détourner des hommes raisonnables d'une mesure nécessaire. Sans doute l'influence, soit royale, soit ministérielle, est à craindre; mais c'est lorsqu'elle est indirecte, lorsqu'elle agit dans l'ombre, lorsqu'elle mine sourdement, et non quand elle se montre à découvert dans une Assemblée où chacun parle en liberté, où chacun discute, où le Ministre le plus éloquent et le plus adroit peut trouver son supérieur ou du moins son égal.

'La voie des Comités, à laquelle l'Assemblée a été forcée de recourir pour correspondre avec les Ministres, est nécessairement vicieuse, outre qu'elle fournit à l'influence ministérielle des développements plus sûrs, des armes que rien ne peut combattre. Elle tend à tirer en longueur les arrangements les plus simples, et souvent les plus provisionnels. Elle ne pourvoit d'ailleurs qu'imparfaitement à l'instruction de l'Assemblée.—Que de choses un Comité n'osera jamais demander au Ministre, et que ce Ministre n'oseroit pas refuser dans l'Assemblée, même sur la réclamation d'un seul Membre? Enfin, ces Comités ne sont jamais établis que pour des objets isolés, et il n'y a point de séance de l'Assemblée où la présence, sinon de tous les Ministres, au moins de quelqu'un d'eux, ne fût indispensable.

'Qu'on se figure une séance où les Ministres siégeroient à leur place comme tout autre Député, où ils donneroient leurs avis, fourniroient leurs éclaircissements; où ces avis, ces éclaircissements seroient débattus par eux et avec eux. Une telle séance ne seroit-elle pas tout à-la-fois plus utile à l'Assemblée, plus fructueuse pour la chose publique, que vingt séances où les Ministres n'auroient point assisté, et où, faute d'information nécessaire, l'Assemblée aurait pu commettre quelqu'une de ces erreurs qui discréditent toujours la législation aux yeux du peuple.

'Qu'on se figure enfin quelle révolution produiroit dans les esprits cette habitude que contracteroient les Ministres, de déposer leur morgue viziriale dans l'Assemblée de la Nation, d'y exposer non-seulement leurs principes politiques, mais leur vrai caractère, et jusqu'à leurs défauts; d'abjurer enfin cette étiquette, ces réserves astucieuses qui si long-temps composèrent tout l'art ministériel, pour revêtir les formes candides, franches et loyales des États Républicains.'[1]

Les Ministres, n'étant pas admis à siéger dans l'Assemblée, furent réduits à un rôle aussi singulier que dangereux. Recevant des décrets et des masses de décrets pour être soumis à la sanction royale, ils furent dans la nécessité de suspendre cette sanction dans plusieurs circonstances, et de présenter à l'Assemblée des mémoires, des notes, des observations, des remontrances où ils sollicitoient des explications et des modifications dans ces décrets. Il falloit, dans un tel conflict, ou que la dignité royale fût compromise, ou que l'Assemblée Nationale fît l'aveu d'une erreur. Mais un Corps Législatif ne se soumet guère à recevoir des leçons; et les Ministres étoient souvent mandés à la barre et réprimandés pour avoir osé remplir le premier devoir de leur place.

Le 6 novembre 1789 (Courrier de Provence, N.º [63]),[2] M.ʳ de Mirabeau fit une motion expresse pour donner aux Ministres une voix consultative, et requérir leur présence dans l'Assemblée. Ses arguments étoient les mêmes que ceux que nous venons de citer, en y joignant toutes les insinuations oratoires qui pouvoient flatter l'orgueil de ceux qu'il vouloit convaincre.

'Dira-t-on que l'Assemblée nationale n'ait nul besoin d'être informée par les Ministres? Mais où se réunissent d'abord les faits qui constituent l'expérience du Gouvernement? N'est-ce pas dans les mains des agens du Pouvoir exécutif? Peut-on dire que ceux-ci qui exécutent les lois, n'aient rien à faire observer à ceux qui les projettent et qui les déterminent? Les exécuteurs de toutes les transactions relatives à la chose publique, tant intérieures qu'extérieures, ne sont-ils pas comme un répertoire qu'un Représentant actif de la Nation doit sans cesse consulter? Et où se fera cette consultation avec plus d'avantage pour la Nation, si ce n'est en présence de l'Assemblée? Hors de l'Assemblée, le consultant n'est plus qu'un individu auquel le Ministre peut répondre ce qu'il veut, et même ne faire aucune réponse. L'interrogera-t-on par décret de l'Assemblée? Mais alors on s'expose à des délais, à des lenteurs, à des tergiversations, à des réponses obscures, à la nécessité, enfin, de multiplier les décrets, les chocs, les mécontentemens, pour arriver à des éclaircissemens qui, n'étant pas donnés de bon gré, resteront toujours incertains. Tous ces inconvéniens se dissipent par la présence des Ministres. Quand il s'agira de rendre compte de la perception et de l'emploi des revenus, peut-on mettre en comparaison un examen fait en l'absence du Ministre, avec un examen qui sera fait sous ses yeux? S'il est absent, chaque question qu'il paroîtra nécessaire de lui adresser, deviendra l'objet d'un débat; tandis que dans l'Assemblée, la question s'adresse à l'instant même au Ministre par le Membre qui la conçoit. Si le Ministre s'embarrasse dans ses réponses, s'il est coupable, il ne peut échapper à tant de regards fixés sur lui; et la crainte de cette redoutable inquisition prévient bien mieux les malversations, que toutes les précautions dont on pourroit entourer un Ministre qui n'a

---

[1] *Courier de Provence*, xli, 11–14 September 1789, pp.1–5.
[2] Dumont '45'.

jamais à répondre dans l'Assemblée. Où les Ministres pourront-ils combattre avec moins de succès la liberté du peuple? Où proposeront-ils avec moins d'inconvéniens leurs objections sur les actes de législation? Où leurs préjugés, leurs erreurs, leur ambition, seront-ils dévoilés avec plus d'énergie? Où contribueront-ils mieux à la stabilité des décrets? Où s'engageront-ils avec plus de solennité à leur exécution? N'est-ce pas dans l'Assemblée nationale?'[1]

Les objections furent toutes tirées de la crainte de l'influence ministérielle. On eût dit que ces hommes qui venoient de faire une révolution, alloient tous devenir tremblants et timides, s'ils avoient à parler en présence d'un Ministre du Roi. M. de Noailles[2] fit un tableau burlesque du Parlement Britannique, où il représenta le Chancelier de l'Échiquier, au milieu de la troupe qu'il a enrôlée, distribuant les fonctions, assignant les postes, prescrivant la parole ou le silence, observant de l'œil qui l'on doit récompenser, qui l'on doit punir, dirigeant à son gré toutes les évolutions de sa bande mercenaire.

L'un des Membres les plus distingués, M. de Clermont-Tonnerre, fit un dernier effort pour soutenir la motion du Comte de Mirabeau. 'On oppose à l'admission des Ministres le nom de *liberté*: mais il ne faut pas regarder le Pouvoir exécutif comme l'ennemi de la liberté nationale. Je ne vois que des avantages à admettre les Ministres dans l'Assemblée, avec voix consultative (car la voix délibérative n'appartient qu'à ceux qui la tiennent de leurs commettans). Nous avons gémi longtemps sous des ministres ineptes, qui sont le fléau le plus humiliant pour une nation: mais des Ministres ineptes, appelés à soutenir l'épreuve et l'éclat des délibérations publiques, seront chassés dans quatre jours. Leurs palais sont les asyles de leur ignorance; ils ont là mille moyens d'en imposer et d'échapper aux regards des citoyens: ils sont entourés de flatteurs, de commis, de protégés qui se croient honorés d'un coup-d'œil: mais au milieu de l'Assemblée nationale, ils verront des hommes; ils seront forcés de savoir et de faire eux-mêmes leur métier de ministres: s'ils ont des talents et des vertus, ils ne sont point à craindre; s'ils ont des talents et des vices, ils seront démasqués ici par des talents égaux. Quant aux brigues, à l'influence, aux traités secrets, tout ce trafic honteux est dangereux dans l'Assemblée et dans le silence du cabinet. Le mal qu'on ne voit pas est toujours le plus funeste. La présence des Ministres, loin d'ajouter à ce danger, le diminue.'[3]

Un Député Breton[4] proposa une motion directement contraire; non content que celle de Mirabeau eût été rejetée, il demanda qu'aucun Membre de l'Assemblée ne pût parvenir au ministère durant la présente session. Le bruit s'étoit répandu que le Roi vouloit appeler M.ʳ de Mirabeau dans son Conseil; et la question, de politique qu'elle étoit d'abord, étoit devenue purement personnelle. On peut voir, dans le Courrier de Provence, la réponse que fit le Député d'Aix au Député Breton. C'est un modèle d'esprit, de raison, de sarcasme; mais les passions étoient enflammées, et l'exclusion fut prononcée.

Je me suis permis cette longue digression, parce qu'il m'a paru nécessaire de mettre, dans le plus grand jour, la faute essentielle de l'Assemblée Nationale, et de la constitution qu'elle donna au peuple français,—le défaut de concert entre le Pouvoir Exécutif et le Pouvoir Législatif. On ne sauroit trop insister sur la

---

[1] *Courier de Provence*, lxiii, 6–7 November 1789, pp.32–4.

[2] Louis Marie, Vicomte de Noailles (1756–1804).

[3] *Courier de Provence*, lxiii, 6–7 November 1789, pp.43–4. Stanislas Marie Adelaïde, Comte de Clermont-Tonnerre (1757–92), was the president of the Assemblée Nationale at this time.

[4] Jean Denis, Comte de Lanjuinais (1753–1827). For a report of the debate, see *Archives parlementaires de 1787 à 1860, première série (1787 à 1799)*, Paris, 1879–1913, IX. 710–16.

nécessité de mettre l'initiative habituelle des opérations entre les mains du ministère. Ceux qui ne comprennent pas cette nécessité, n'entendent rien à la véritable Tactique d'une Assemblée politique, et ne sont que des ouvriers d'anarchie.

112, 31   *décret.*

112, 34   *motion.*

112, 35   *originaire*

113, 23   adds *Décret, arrêté, résolution.* Ces trois mots sont souvent employés comme synonymes pour désigner l'acte définitif de l'Assemblée. Ils présentent le même sens intellectuel, mais ils sont dérivés de différents types physiques.

Quand on dit *arrêté,* on s'est peint les idées comme flottantes ou comme passant en succession dans l'esprit: il en choisit une, et s'y *arrête. Décret* offre à peu près la même idée: on a vu et considéré divers objets, on a discerné celui qu'on juge le meilleur, et on s'y fixe.

Quand on dit *résolution,* on s'est représenté une question comme un nœud à délier.

Ceci est un exemple de la manière dont on pourroit expliquer les termes fondamentaux d'une science par l'étymologie. On remonte à l'archétype, au premier type physique, à l'image qui a servi de modèle pour imposer des noms aux choses intellectuelles. Ce travail seroit très-propre à entrer dans la composition d'un dictionnaire.

Les Français se servent très-souvent du mot *délibération,* comme synonyme de *décret.* En voici la preuve dans l'acte constitutionnel de 1795. *Chaque Conseil pourra se former en Comité genéral et secret, mais seulement pour discuter et non pour délibérer.*[1] C'est un contresens grammatical. Qui délibère est indécis. Tant que la délibération continue, il n'y a point de résolution prise, point d'acte commun, point d'arrêté produit. Le type de *délibération* est *librare,* tenir en balance.

*Amendement* vient du latin *menda,* faute. Amender, c'est ôter une faute.

*Motion* est un terme générique pour exprimer toutes les propositions soumises à l'Assemblée. Le mot avoit été adopté en France; mais les souvenirs révolutionnaires l'ont rendu odieux, et l'ont fait bannir. Un scrupule de cette nature n'a pas dû m'empêcher de me servir d'un mot technique, usité en Angleterre, et beaucoup plus propre à exprimer ce qu'on veut dire que *proposition.* Mais il faut observer qu'on auroit besoin d'un terme particulier pour désigner les *projets de loi.* La langue française n'en a point. On avoit essayé d'introduire le mot anglais *bill,* qui n'a pas réussi, quoiqu'il fût très-propre à devenir technique. Le mot est dérivé par contraction de vieux mot latin *libellula,* diminutif de *liber,* un livre. Ce qui rend cette distinction nécessaire, c'est que les *projets de loi* étant par leur nature d'une importance supérieure à la plupart des motions, requièrent des précautions plus grandes, soit dans leur promulgation antérieure au débat, soit dans les divers degrés de discussion auxquels il convient de les soumettre.

113, 39   adds *Bill,* terme technique: projet de loi.

114, 12   à moins d'une délibération expresse pour hâter ce terme.

114, 15   ce qu'on appelle l'*ordre du jour.*

114, 30   *liste des motions*

---

[1] *Constitution de la République Française du 5 Fructidor an III,* Paris, [1795], article 66: 'Sur la demande de cent de ses membres, chaque conseil peut se former en comité général et secret, mais seulement pour discuter, et non pour délibérer'.

| | |
|---|---|
| 114, 38 | entre l'enregistrement d'un bill et sa présentation à l'Assemblée. |
| 115, 12 | pour introduire un bill, |
| 115, 17 | dans le plan que je propose, chaque Membre auroit le droit d'introduire un bill; |
| 115, 27 | Il est d'usage que |
| 115, 30 | *adds* on l'ose dire, |
| 116, 1 | mon intention doit-elle être de la présenter à l'Assemblée par surprise, |
| 116, 6 | *1822 adds* Il y a un autre avantage à publier d'avance les amendemens; c'est un moyen de les réduire et de les simplifier. Tous ceux qui ne diffèrent pas essentiellement peuvent se réunir en un seul; et leurs auteurs seront d'autant plus disposés à cette concentration, qu'en agissant de concert, ils auront beaucoup plus de chance de succès qu'en s'attaquant les uns les autres pour obtenir la préférence. |
| 116, 34 | une intention secrète |
| 118, 1 | *1822* Le règlement ne peut pas enseigner la logique de la rédaction et de la liaison des idées, ni prescrire les perfections de style; |
| 118, 31 | *section* |
| 119, 1 | *très imparfaitement,* |
| 119, 5 | beaucoup de longueurs |
| 119, 20 | nos pères ont vécu de gland, |
| 119, 20 | *1822 adds* Ces deux paragraphes sont empruntés du chapitre cité dans la note précédente.[1] |
| 120, 1 | c'est le poison du style des lois; |
| 120, 3 | en accouplant les objets qu'il importe le plus de tenir séparés. |
| 120, 4 | ne peuvent pas être |
| 120, 25 | *adds* vous votez pour l'une sans voter pour l'autre, |
| 121, 17 | pure |
| 121, 18 | trop au-dessus de toute contestation. |
| 121, 27 | *non-catholique,* |
| 121, 29 | Ces termes passionnés |
| 121, 31 | *fait* |
| 121, 32 | qui peut être reçue par les uns et rejetée par les autres. |
| 122, 8 | nuire à |
| 122, 16 | choquent leurs sentiments, |
| 122, 18 | C'est, dans le fait, exiger d'eux une déclaration fausse; |
| 122, 21 | la nature de la Divinité, |
| 123, 15 | Impôts qui ont été accordés pour servir de sûreté à différents emprunts, et dont le produit appartient au fonds d'amortissement destiné à payer la dette nationale. |
| 123, 16 | les motions |
| 123, 25 | (la dixième partie du revenu); |
| 123, 29 | *l'emprisonnement durera* { }*; l'amende sera* { }. |
| 123, 41 | motion. |
| 123, 42 | L'auteur appelle ces termes commuables |
| 124, 22 | *Doit-on exiger qu'une motion soit secondée?* |
| 124, 30 | auprès d'aucun homme de son choix? |
| 125, 1 | complaisant |
| 125, 13 | il ne faut pas conclure qu'une motion soit frivole ou absurde, |
| 125, 19 | nature |
| 125, 22 | un mal. |

[1] i.e. *Traités de législation*, i. 361–70.

125, 24    *adds* Au reste, les raisons pour et contre sont très-foibles.
125, 40    *adds* dont on entend parler avec tant d'éloges,
126, 7     dont je ne vous donne que le titre;
126, 17    auroient pu être offerts,
126, 21    *son auteur doit être admis à parler le premier,*
126, 23    *contre*
126, 24    *pour.*
126, 25    *pour*
126, 29    1822 *j'ai dit:*
126, 30    Il faudroit convenir d'un mot qui marquât la fin du discours, *dixi:*
126, 31    cette espèce d'âpreté,
126, 43    *1822 adds* plus variée;
126, 43    *1822* l'orateur
127, 2     on ne peut pas en faire une règle absolue,
127, 26    répandre la lumière,
128, 1     Toutefois
128, 21    doive prolonger
128, 22    Dès que la question est éclaircie, ou que les deux partis reconnoissent
128, 24    une tendance
128, 36    chaque Assemblée peut juger des circonstances où il lui convient d'admettre
128, 42    pourroient
129, 2     C'est là où l'Orateur concentre toutes ses forces, et ramène toute sa cause au
           point essentiel qui doit déterminer le jugement.
129, 11    Entre la première et la seconde lecture, ou entre la seconde et la troisième,
129, 14    *adds* On n'y décide rien d'une manière définitive.
129, 22    La seconde est le vrai champ du débat. La troisième n'est guère que pour la
           forme.
129, 26    lumières
129, 30    *adds* c'est-à-dire, le parti le plus foible,
129, 32    de donner l'éveil aux Membres qui ont été absens dans un des premiers débats,
130, 5     si elles attaquent des passions, des intérêts ou des préjugés violents.
130, 9     de celles qu'on avoit à l'issue du premier;
130, 13    peut décider
130, 15    vous produisez tout au moins une grande chaleur, et peut-être une grande
           animosité dans le débat.
130, 17    qu'il faudra lutter une seconde fois, et même une troisième contre ses
           antagonistes,
130, 19    *adds* dans une première occasion,
130, 23    tous les moyens de se défendre.
130, 30    Il doit, comme on l'a déjà dit, être soumis à un Comité de la Chambre
           (*commitment* et quand l'opération se répète, *recommitment*). Il doit être transmis
           sur un parchemin pour devenir le texte authentique (*engrossment*).
130, 30    doit
130, 37    longueurs,
130, 39    *1822* d'une évidente nécessité,
130, 41    Je réponds à cette objection que, dans ces cas de nécessité, les trois lectures d'un
           Bill peuvent se faire dans le même jour et dans les deux Chambres.
131, 2     il faut, pour en venir à ces moyens extrêmes, une urgence évidente
131, 5     ne s'aperçoivent-ils pas que leur objection porte contre la réflexion, contre les
           informations, qui ne sont souvent que le fruit du temps et de l'étude?
131, 6     Il y aura des répétitions. Mais une conviction raisonnée

131, 9   *adds* Un Membre expérimenté de la Chambre des Communes disoit: *a truth in the House of Commons requires a great deal of soaking.* Ce mot présente le progrès de la vérité sous l'image d'une étoffe qui doit tremper long-temps dans la couleur pour s'en imbiber.

131, 20  longueurs.

131, 21  dans sa totalité.

131, 24  *1822* Dans le premier, on se borne à considérer la convenance ou la disconvenance du projet de loi, sous un point de vue générale.

131, 26  Et, en effet, à quoi serviroit-il d'en examiner en détail toutes les clauses, et de proposer des amendements! Ce seroit ôter les taches d'un habit que peut-être on va jeter au feu. Le projet de loi est-il admis comme convenable en lui-même et dans son principe? il passe alors au second débat: et c'est là qu'on prend en considération, l'une après l'autre, chaque clause de la loi, qu'on propose des amendements, ou qu'on renvoie, dans l'intervalle d'une séance à l'autre, à un Comité particulier, chargé de rédiger toutes les corrections de détail, espèce de travail auquel une assemblée nombreuse n'est guère propre. Les votes qu'on prend dans ce second débat n'ont rien de définitif. Ces votes ne sont qu'une manière de terminer la discussion sur chaque article, et de pressentir le vœu de l'Assemblée.

Après un intervalle nécessaire pour laisser reposer l'esprit, et pour revoir de sang-froid ce projet de loi, ainsi amendé, on arrive au troisième débat avec une connoissance approfondie de la loi; on en reprend l'examen dans sa convenance générale et dans toutes ses clauses particulières. Ceux qui ont proposé des amendements les reproduisent s'ils ont obtenu l'assentiment de la majorité, et ne les reproduisent pas dans le cas contraire. Plus une Assemblée sera exercée, plus la matière sera éclaircie dans les deux premiers débats, et le troisième, en général, sera très-rapide. Le premier, qui roule sur la convenance ou la disconvenance de la loi, peut être fort long, mais le plus souvent il est presque nul.

131, 36  *1822 adds* En France, les lois proposées par le roi ne sont soumises qu'à deux débats: l'un sur la convenance ou la disconvenance; c'est là où se succèdent sans se rencontrer les orateurs à discours écrits: l'autre qui se fait article par article, et où l'improvisation commence. Par rapport à toutes les dispositions particulières de la loi, c'est un débat unique. Peut-on s'étonner de la vivacité, de la violence avec laquelle on cherche à s'arracher les décisions? Souvent un amendement improvisé dans la séance même, changeant toute l'économie de la loi, a été enlevé de prime-assaut. Dans les lois telles que celles des finances, où la remise n'est pas possible, la chambre des pairs ne peut point offrir de remède à cette précipitation. Elle a été obligée de le reconnaître, et elle a signalé à cet égard son impuissance.

Cependant on avait reconnu la convenance d'une marche plus mesurée, et le règlement a imposé les trois débats, mais dans le cas où ils étaient le moins nécessaires. Pour les *propositions de loi faites par un membre*, on a adopté les trois lectures (art. 46); la discussion est ouverte après chacune d'elles (art. 47).[1] Or, en quoi diffère d'une proposition individuelle, l'amendement qui va changer du tout au tout la *proposition royale*, et pour lequel on se borne à un débat? Si la lenteur était nécessaire dans le premier cas, comment justifier la précipitation dans le second?

---

[1] The articles referred to are from the *Règlement* adopted by the French Chamber of Deputies on 27 June 1814. See *Procès-verbal des séances de la Chambre des Députés des départemens, qui ont eu lieu du 4 juin au 30 juillet 1814*, Paris, 1814, pp.129–30.

132, 17 Alors

132, 31 être en état de faire face à tout,

133, 2 ce qu'on a *écrit*; mais ce qu'on veut *dire*, il faut le *savoir*.

133, 5 *adds* tous

133, 37 de même

133, 38 parcouroit de l'œil

133, 39 enchâssoit

133, 42 *adds* M. Benj. Constant, dans ses *Principes de politique* (Ch. VII. de la discussion), a traité ce sujet avec autant de raison que d'esprit. Je ne puis me refuser au plaisir d'en citer quelques passages.

'Quand les Orateurs se bornent à lire ce qu'ils ont écrit dans le silence de leur cabinet, ils ne discutent plus, ils amplifient: ils n'écoutent point, car ce qu'ils entendroient ne doit rien changer à ce qu'ils vont dire; ils attendent que celui qu'ils doivent remplacer ait fini. Ils n'examinent pas l'opinion qu'il défend, ils comptent le temps qu'il emploie et qui leur paroît un retard. Alors il n'y a plus de discussion; chacun reproduit des objections déjà réfutées; chacun laisse de côté tout ce qu'il n'a pas prévu, tout ce qui dérangeroit son plaidoyer terminé d'avance. Les Orateurs se succèdent sans se rencontrer: s'ils se réfutent, c'est par hasard; ils ressemblent à deux armées qui défileroient en sens opposé, l'une à côté de l'autre, s'apercevant à peine, évitant même de se regarder, de peur de sortir de la route irrévocablement tracée . . .'

'Voulez-vous que nos Assemblées représentatives soient raisonnables? imposez aux hommes qui veulent y briller la nécessité d'avoir du talent. Le grand nombre se réfugiera dans la raison, comme pis-aller; mais si vous ouvrez à ce grand nombre une carrière où chacun puisse faire quelques pas, personne ne voudra se refuser cet avantage. Chacun se donnera son jour d'éloquence et son heure de célébrité. Chacun pouvant faire un discours écrit ou le commander, prétendra marquer son existence législative, et les Assemblées deviendront des Académies, avec cette différence que les harangues académiques y décideront du sort et des propriétés, et même de la vie des citoyens.

'Je me refuse à citer d'incroyables preuves de ce désir de faire effet aux époques les plus déplorables de notre révolution. J'ai vu des Représentants chercher des sujets de discours, pour que leur nom ne fût pas étranger aux grands mouvemens qui avoient eu lieu: le sujet trouvé, le discours écrit, le résultat leur étoit indifférent. En bannissant les discours écrits, nous créerons dans nos Assemblées ce qui leur a toujours manqué, cette majorité silencieuse qui, disciplinée, pour ainsi dire, par la supériorité des hommes de talent, est réduite à les écouter, faute de pouvoir parler à leur place; qui s'éclaire, parce qu'elle est condamnée à être modeste, et qui devient raisonnable en se taisant.'[1]

*1822 adds* Il y a quelque chose de plus fort encore que tous ces raisonnemens; c'est ce qui se passe sous les yeux du public dans la chambre des députés à Paris. Dès qu'un orateur déploie à la tribune le terrible rouleau, ou même lorsqu'il ne montre qu'une feuille de manuscrit pour tromper un auditoire qu'on ne trompe plus, c'est le signal du bruit et de l'alarme; quelquefois on parvient à le faire taire; mais plus souvent, il manifeste un courage héroïque contre les murmures; alors les conversations particulières s'établissent; les uns quittent

[1] Henri Benjamin Constant de Rebecque (1767–1830), *Principes de politique, applicables à tous les gouvernemens représentatifs et particulièrement à la constitution actuelle de la France*, Paris, 1815, pp.124–5, 127–8. Dumont has reproduced Constant's text closely, although there are some differences in punctuation and spelling.

leur place, d'autres lisent, personne n'écoute, un bruit confus remplit la salle, le discours est complètement perdu pour tout le monde, et ne se retrouve que dans les journaux. Si deux ou trois orateurs-lecteurs se succèdent à la tribune, on n'y tient plus et on appelle de toutes parts cette *clôture de la discussion*, cette clôture si contraire à la liberté et à la justice que l'assemblée doit à tous ses membres. C'est donc aux discours écrits qu'on peut attribuer en grande partie les fâcheuses habitudes d'inattention, de tumulte et d'impatience qui troublent si souvent ses débats.

134, 15  *adds* (en parlant d'un homme de loi),
134, 20  *Nom*
134, 37  démêler
134, 40  *adds* elle est la sauve-garde commune.
134, 42  Mais surtout cette maxime est conforme à la prudence.
135, 2   la vérité que vous lui présentez en le ménageant:
135, 10  *1822 adds* 'L'art de persuader, dit Pascal, consiste autant en celui d'agréer qu'en celui de convaincre.' Le même auteur fournit une règle de prudence non moins importante que celle-ci, mais qu'on ne peut pas convertir en loi. 'Quand on veut reprendre avec utilité, dit-il, et montrer à un autre qu'il se trompe, il faut observer par quel côté il envisage la chose, car elle est vraie ordinairement de ce côté-là, et lui avouer cette vérité; il se contente de cela parce qu'il voit qu'il ne se trompait pas, et qu'il manquait seulement à voir tous les côtés. Or, on n'a pas honte de ne pas tout voir; mais on ne veut pas s'être trompé, et peut-être que cela vient de ce que naturellement l'esprit ne se peut tromper dans le côté qu'il envisage, comme les appréhensions des sens sont toujours vraies.' *Pensées de Pascal.*[1]
135, 11  peu ménagées
135, 22  vœu
135, 23  ce vœu du Prince,
136, 15  des erreurs qu'on n'auroit jamais eu à reprocher en Angleterre aux Officiers les plus subalternes.
137, 12  toutefois
137, 13  *adds* du moins
137, 32  La première condition
137, 40  l'esprit
137, 42  comme si la justesse dans les idées ne produisoit pas la justesse dans les termes.
137, 44  il n'est aucun défaut qui n'ait réussi à se faire un masque.
138, 15  *supprimer, ajouter,* ou *substituer.*
138, 20  qu'on la *divise,*
138, 24  la *réunion.*
138, 27  peut
139, 1   mal connues;
139, 21  *divisifs*
139, 33  combien il seroit heureux de trouver, sinon des règles absolues, du moins un fil
140, 1   sur
140, 2   toutefois
140, 7   des tâtonnements et des essais
140, 14  condamnée au néant.

[1] Blaise Pascal (1623–62), religious philosopher and mathematician. The *Pensées* were first published in 1670. In an edition published in London in 1785, with notes by Voltaire, the first passage quoted here is numbered i.2, and the second i.5.

140, 16    *insidieux.*
140, 17    *insidieux.*
140, 21    pour faire ressortir
140, 24    la bonne foi
142, 24    *1822* [*Sentence omitted.*]
143, 11    Le *vote sur les questions,* le *vote sur les personnes.*
143, 26    par *oui* d'un côté et par *non* de l'autre.
143, 32    *scrutin* ou *balotte.*
143, 34    dépendant de la volonté des hommes, ou indépendant.
143, 35    *par sort* ou *par lot.*
143, 36    votation *régulière* et votation *sommaire.*
143, 39    vœu par oui ou par non,
144, 7    l'opinion publique
144, 10    tel qu'il est.
144, 17    meilleurs esprits,
145, 7    toutefois
145, 13    Toutefois
145, 16    *tutélaire*
145, 18    motifs séducteurs ou des motifs tutélaires,
145, 23    cet intérêt général
145, 27    *séducteur.*
145, 28    social
145, 29    cette
145, 30    anti-social
145, 31    le sacrifice des intérêts de la grande société du public.
146, 8    *adds* L'intérêt qui me porte à voter pour procurer à mon père ou à mon fils une place lucrative, est un intérêt naturel et préétabli.
146, 9    Le *secret* dans les suffrages
146, 23    dans les votes
146, 26    *adds* il ne porte que contre l'influence de volonté sur volonté.
146, 28    l'homme constitué en dignité aura, dans les Assemblées électives, plus d'ascendant qu'un citoyen obscur;
146, 37    prestige.
147, 7    *adds* Ceci dépend des circonstances. Les citoyens de Genève procédoient à l'élection de leurs magistrats dans une Église, sans que personne eût le droit de faire un discours. Mais dans un si petit État, où les hommes publics étoient sans cesse sous les yeux de tous, une discussion publique eût été plus dangereuse qu'utile.

           Depuis que Genève a recouvré son indépendance, les élections des magistrats se font par un Conseil représentatif. On n'y a point admis de discussion sur le mérite des candidats, et par la même raison. L'exemple de l'Angleterre ne paroît pas applicable en ceci à des gouvernements de famille.
147, 14   et même, en Angleterre, où ces époques reviennent rarement,
147, 23   la République Romaine,
148, 13   un contre-sens.
148, 14   la recherche du vrai.
148, 29   *factice*
148, 32   destitutions,
149, 2    ce qu'on appelle la corruption,
149, 5    frein
149, 6    frein

149, 8   *1822 adds* Le lord North,[1] après une longue expérience ministérielle, définissait la reconnaissance *un sentiment très-vif des faveurs à venir*. Aussi par une place donnée, on tient tout au plus un individu, mais on en tient cent qui l'espèrent.

149, 13   *1822 adds* Dans la chambre des députés de France, on cumule les deux modes de votation. On procède d'abord publiquement par assis et levé. On passe ensuite au scrutin. (Art. 52 et 53 du règlement.)[2]

La France est-elle dans ces circonstances extraordinaires qui justifient la votation secrète? Non sans doute. Le scrutin qui succède au vote par assis et levé n'est donc qu'une perte de temps. C'est une opération puérile et oiseuse si le résultat doit être le même que dans le vote public; et si le résultat était différent, cette opposition entre les deux votes serait la honte du corps où un pareil scandale se serait manifesté.

149, 17   *par un mode sommaire*

149, 35   cri de guerre.

150, 5   *adds* comme étant plus favorable à la liberté des suffrages,

150, 16   *adds* La votation distincte est nécessaire pour deux raisons: 1.° pour vérifier une première déclaration de pluralité, si elle est exposée au moindre doute; 2.° pour assurer l'exécution de la loi de la publicité.

150, 18   formule signée,

150, 23   *division*

150, 28   c'est une dénonciation des votants.

150, 29   peu

150, 44   qui seroit partout

151, 14   *adds* et dans cent occasions,

151, 19   nuire au vrai savoir.

151, 35   nouvelle matière doivent sortir.

151, 36   *1822 adds* Ceux qui seraient curieux de se faire une idée des différentes questions sur lesquelles tantôt les oui, tantôt les non, doivent sortir, peuvent consulter le *Manuel du droit parlementaire* par M. Jefferson, traduit par M. Pichon. *Vid. section.* XXXIX.[3]

152, 16   [*Except for the first sentence, paragraph in past tense.*]

152, 18   mandat,

152, 35   *Comité général,*

153, 2   *indécis.*

153, 8   un vote d'*indécision*

153, 25   Bureaux

153, 36   *adds* Cette maxime de Confucius

153, 37   *indécis*

153, 42   *indécis* ne peuvent manquer de l'appuyer,

154, 1   Comités ou Bureaux

154, 6   de pouvoir être

154, 8   comme des *Experts.*

154, 9   *adds* et d'émulation

154, 17   des *trois débats;*

[1] Frederick North (1732–92), second Earl of Guilford, styled Lord North 1752–90, Chancellor of the Exchequer 1767–82, First Lord of the Treasury 1770–82.

[2] See *Procès-verbal des séances de la Chambre des Députés des départemens*, p.131.

[3] Baron Louis André Pichon (1771–1850), *Manuel du droit parlementaire, ou Précis des règles suivies dans le parlement d'Angleterre*, Paris, 1814. This is a translation of *A Manual of Parliamentary Practice. For the use of the Senate of the United States*, Washington, 1801, by Thomas Jefferson (1743–1826).

# ENDNOTES

154, 21  grandes
154, 36  Quand on *divise,*
155, 6   *in globo,*
155, 7   *article par article.*
155, 22  *adds* selon sa constitution,

# 1791 COLLATION

Collation: Jeremy Bentham, 'Essay on Political Tactics', (London, 1791).

*Note.* The collation prints the variants between the present edition of 'Political Tactics' and Bentham's 1791 'Essay on Political Tactics', some copies of which included part of Essay V as well as Essay VI. The collation includes variations in punctuation, italics, and capitalization of initial letters. References to the present edition are given in the left hand column by page and line numbers: hence 65, 1 refers to page 65, line 1; 1791 variants are given in the right hand column. Major differences are also indicated in editorial footnotes to the text. The following variants are not recorded: variations in the size of capital letters and in the form of footnote markers in the text; the capitalization of the initial letter of the words 'Assembly(ies)', 'Bill(s)', 'Committee(s)', 'King(s)', 'Member(s)', 'President(s)' (which Bowring normally renders in the lower case); and the appearance as two words of the terms 'anybody', 'anyone', 'anything', 'anywhere', 'everything', 'everywhere', 'nowhere', 'somehow' (which Bowring combines).

| | |
|---|---|
| 65, 1–5 | ESSAY V. CHAPTER I. Of the Office of PRESIDENT.—*Rules.* I. *Number and Supply.* |
| 65, 6 | RULE 1. |
| 65, 6 | Assembly there ought, |
| 65, 6 | times, |
| 65, 9 | offers, |
| 65, 11 | were confined |
| 65, 13 | *Speaker* |
| 65, 14 | different and |
| 65, 15 | name; and |
| 65, 16 | debate it |
| 65, 17 | *Member* |
| 65, 18 | *viz.* |
| 65, 19 | involves contradiction: |
| 65, 20 | slipt |
| 65, 21 | present, |
| 65, 21 | *speeches* |
| 65, 21 | all other |
| 65, 22 | view it |
| 65, 23 | etymology generally |
| 65, 23 | *not speaking;* |
| 65, 23–24 | ut *lucus* |
| 65, 25 | *Orator {Orateur}* |
| 65, 25 | *Speaker* |
| 65, 26 | Presidency |
| 65, 27 | Orders |
| 65, 27 | Diet |
| 65, 28 | Speaker, |
| 65, 29 | supplication; supplication |
| 65, 29 | *pliancy,* |

| | |
|---|---|
| 65, 30 | Presidents, |
| 65, 32 | *Chairman* |
| 66, 1 | RULE 2. |
| 66, 1 | assembly that |
| 66, 3 | number that, |
| 66, 5–7 *omitted* | |
| 66, 8 | *Speaker* and *Orator*. |
| 66, 8 | confined: |
| 66, 12 | *Chairmen* |
| 66, 12 | *you.—* |
| 66, 12 | *Chairman* |
| 66, 12 | a *President* or a *Porter?* |
| 66, 13 | is denoted in |
| 66, 13 | Diet, |
| 66, 14 | Orders |
| 66, 14 | name, |
| 66, 14 | Provincial |
| 66, 15 | Noblesse instituted |
| 66, 15 | years throughout |
| 66, 16 | Empire. |
| 66, 16 | inexpressive, |
| 66, 17 | German it |
| 66, 17 | or less |
| 66, 18 | or a groom— |
| 66, 20–21 | King, was |
| 66, 21 | a great military |
| 66, 23 | *Marshal,* |
| 66, 23 | *General,* |
| 66, 23 | denote in |
| 66, 23–24 | Europe the |
| 66, 24 | militarily is |
| 66, 25 | Diet, |
| 66, 25 | Nobles, |
| 66, 25 | Marshal, |
| 66, 26 | Crown, are |
| 66, 26 | or hold |
| 66, 26 | Soldier |
| 66, 27 | left, |
| 66, 27 | Commander |
| 66, 28 | Adolphus, |
| 66, 29 | words that |
| 66, 29 | be, devised, |
| 66, 30 | Assembly which |
| 66, 31 | *Marshal* |
| 66, 32 | *Presidents* |
| 66, 32 | Assemblies, |
| 66, 33 | *Marshal,* |
| 66, 37 | been to |
| 66, 38 | *Marshal,* |
| 67, 1–6 *omitted* | |
| 67, 7 | RULE 3. |

| | |
|---|---|
| 67, 7 | President no |
| 67, 8 | *officiate* |
| 67, 9–12 *omitted* | |
| 67, 13 | RULE 4. |
| 67, 13 | ought |
| 67, 14 | *present* |
| 67, 14 | at a time. |
| 67, 15–20 *omitted* | |
| 67, 21 | II. *Functions competent and incompetent.* |
| 67, 22 | RULE 5. |
| 67, 23 | *Judge,* |
| 67, 24 | *Agent* |
| 67, 24 | Assembly: as Judge, |
| 67, 25 | Agent, |
| 67, 27 | RULE 6. |
| 67, 27 | Judge, |
| 67, 27 | instance to |
| 67, 28 | *appeal,* |
| 67, 30 | RULE 7. |
| 67, 30 | Agent, |
| 67, 31 | Assembly: |
| 67, 31–32 | in face of |
| 67, 34 | RULE 8. |
| 67, 34 | controul, in any degree, |
| 67, 36 | question: |
| 67, 36 | decision resulting from the numbers |
| 67, 37 | votes: |
| 67, 37 | subordinates: |
| 67, 37 | individuals: or in |
| 68, 1 | RULE 9. |
| 68, 1 | *numerous* |
| 68, 2 | *Member.* |
| 68, 3 | right, |
| 68, 5–36 *omitted* | |
| 68, 39 | Boards of Administration and |
| 68, 40 | Courts of Justice |
| 68, 40 | Boards |
| 69, 1–24 *omitted* | |
| 69, 25 | III. *Choice.* |
| 69, 26 | RULE 10. IN |
| 69, 27 | ought, in every case, |
| 69, 29 | RULE 11. |
| 69, 30 | *absolute* |
| 69, 31 | RULE 12. |
| 69, 31 | Assembly, |
| 69, 33 | RULE 13. IN |
| 69, 35 | in |
| 69, 36 | ought not determine |
| 69, 37 | has a |
| 69, 38 *adds* | For the method of reducing a comparative majority to an absolute one, see Essay VI. |

| | |
|---|---|
| 70, 1 | *natâ,* |
| 70, 2 | claim however |
| 70, 2 | stand, in that instance, |
| 70, 4 | RULE 14. |
| 70, 4 | business, |
| 70, 4 | Assembly which, |
| 70, 6 | GENERAL OBSERVATIONS. |
| 70, 7 | A VERY |
| 70, 9 | obtain in |
| 70, 10 | purity the |
| 70, 12 | end every thing |
| 70, 16 | *animorum*: |
| 70, 17 | Encyclopedist, |
| 70, 17 | successors. To |
| 70, 17 | *Nature,* |
| 70, 18 | her:—to soothe upon occasion the |
| 70, 19 | parturition:— |
| 70, 19 | produce in |
| 70, 19 | time the |
| 70, 19 | offspring:— |
| 70, 19 | it; |
| 70, 21 | Officer |
| 70, 22 | If in |
| 70, 22 | instance a |
| 70, 24 | possesses |
| 70, 28 | Assembly, and |
| 70, 31 | King, |
| 70, 31 | State, |
| 70, 34 | Thus in |
| 70, 34 | Presidency |
| 70, 35 | Sheriff, |
| 71, 3 | President we |
| 71, 5 | Judge |
| 71, 6 | eye: complaint, |
| 71, 6 | judgment, and execution, |
| 71, 8 | if in |
| 71, 9 | delay, simplicity |
| 71, 10 | of observation, |
| 71, 11 | of the law |
| 71, 12–23 *omitted* | |
| 72, 1–4 | ESSAY VI. On the Mode of proceeding in a POLITICAL ASSEM-BLY in the Formation of its Decisions. CHAPTER I. *Introductory Observations.* |
| 72, 7 | intricate and |
| 72, 13 | system is |
| 72, 23 | lost as it were in |
| 72, 27 | what as |
| 72, 27 | learn has |
| 72, 28 | points too, |
| 73, 1 | work: |
| 73, 4 | bye corner an |

| | |
|---|---|
| 77, 10 | V. |
| 77, 10 | *debating* NO |
| 77, 11 | VI. |
| 77, 12 | *Points.* |
| 77, 13 | Assembly that |
| 77, 18 | As |
| 77, 18 | *Orders* and *Resolutions* |
| 77, 19 | *Laws;* |
| 77, 19 | *Addresses,* |
| 77, 19 | Declarations |
| 77, 19 | *Resolutions* |
| 77, 20 | practice), |
| 77, 20 | *Reports.* |
| 77, 21 | Whether |
| 77, 21 | *motion,* |
| 77, 22 *adds* | See Essay I. |
| 77, 32 | By |
| 77, 32 *adds* | Of the difference between a *comparative* and an *absolute* majority, see *infra*, Ch. . . . |
| 77, 34 | intitled |
| 77, 34 *adds* | See this question discussed in Essay IV. |
| 78, 3 | received, until |
| 78, 4 | of no |
| 78, 5 | purposes: |
| 78, 16 | preaudience |
| 78, 20 | CHAPTER III. Principal Points continued—Motion written, and *in Terminis.* |
| 78, 21 | *Reasons.* |
| 78, 22 | QUESTION I. WHY |
| 78, 24 | ANSWER. |
| 78, 24 | words, |
| 78, 26 | BRITISH PRACTICE. FROM |
| 78, 26 | Lords made |
| 78, 27 | proposition: I, |
| 78, 28 | draught following to |
| 78, 28 | act of the assembly. |
| 78, 28 | A.M. |
| 78, 29 | N.B. Then |
| 78, 29 | Order, Resolution, Address, Report, Bill, |
| 78, 32 | Chapter I |
| 78, 32 | shew |
| 78, 33 | it immediately |
| 78, 36 | Chapter, |
| 79, 4 | officer, |
| 79, 4 | Clerk |
| 79, 5 | Journals, |
| 79, 5 | officer, (the Speaker) under |
| 79, 12 | vote and |
| 79, 16 | *Ordered,* |
| 79, 16 | *Resolved,* |
| 79, 22 | antient |

| | |
|---|---|
| 79, 23 | form |
| 79, 24 | custom (says Mr. Hatsell) I |
| 79, 29 | suppose, is, |
| 79, 31 | Lords |
| 79, 31 | Lords |
| 79, 31 | 14 Dec. |
| 79, 31 | 23 Feb. |
| 79, 31–32 | 20 May, |
| 79, 33 | Commons |
| 79, 33 | 27 Jan. |
| 79, 34 | Commons |
| 79, 34 | 22 March, |
| 79, 34 | 7 April, |
| 79, 34 | 3 Feb. |
| 79, 34 | 21 Feb. |
| 79, 36 | Observations by |
| 79, 37 | Esq; |
| 80, 1 | name?— |
| 80, 1 | Clerk |
| 80, 1–2 | him:—Whence |
| 80, 7 | Melchisedeck, |
| 80, 8 | that, |
| 80, 10 | House, that |
| 80, 11 | Members, must, |
| 80, 13 | such: |
| 80, 14 | and, |
| 80, 15 | periods, |
| 80, 17 | House, orders, |
| 80, 17 | rules, nobody |
| 80, 22 | purpose any |
| 80, 26 | instance; |
| 80, 27 | done, nothing |
| 80, 30 | what: say, |
| 80, 34 | House, therefore, |
| 80, 38 | recognized. |
| 80, 38 | November, |
| 80, 40 | together; Mr. |
| 80, 41 | privilege; |
| 80, 41 | Minister), |
| 81, 1 | first; Mr. |
| 81, 4 | settle, who |
| 81, 5 | first, Mr. Wilkes or |
| 81, 6 | QUESTION |
| 81, 7 | ANSWER. |
| 81, 9 | ascertained, |
| 81, 12 | QUESTION |
| 81, 14 | ANSWER. |
| 81, 15 | can.— |
| 81, 17 | person, |
| 81, 24 | time.— |
| 81, 25 | on: this |

| | |
|---|---|
| 81, 28 | place, |
| 81, 29 | while in business |
| 81, 32 | house; |
| 81, 33 | do, as |
| 81, 33 | on, |
| 82, 2 | instance, corrected |
| 82, 4 | QUESTION |
| 82, 6 | ANSWER. |
| 82, 8 | House.—The composition, |
| 82, 9 | composition, |
| 82, 9–10 | those whose |
| 82, 11 | have voted |
| 82, 17 | else, the Secretary |
| 82, 18 | President, differs |
| 82, 23 | BRITISH PRACTICE. In |
| 82, 30 | House: |
| 82, 30 | this (adds he) has |
| 82, 30 | discontinued: |
| 82, 31 | present, |
| 82, 35 | *amendment*, |
| 82, 39 | authors, two |
| 83, 2 | Chairman |
| 83, 2 *adds* | as alluded to on a former occasion, |
| 83, 2 | suspect that |
| 83, 15 | Journal |
| 83, 18 | in of |
| 83, 20 *adds* | Essay V.—Hist. |
| 83, 20 | B. III. |
| 83, 20 | edition. |
| 83, 20 *adds* | 1705 |
| 83, 21 | March, 1620. |
| 83, 22 | Journals |
| 83, 23 | appears that |
| 83, 25 | length; |
| 83, 27 | follows: 'A |
| 83, 33 | undeniable: |
| 83, 34 | 1st, |
| 83, 36 | 2dly, |
| 84, 1 | FRENCH PRACTICE. |
| 84, 3 | States, |
| 84, 5 | secrecy, |
| 84, 9 | words:— *that* |
| 84, 10 | *sum* .... |
| 84, 11 | part for |
| 84, 11 | reasons: 1. |
| 84, 14 | *Resolved*, |
| 84, 15 | *Resolved*, |
| 84, 26 | words '*that* |
| 84, 27 | by author |
| 84, 30 | *viz.* |
| 84, 31 | view. '*The* |

| | |
|---|---|
| 84, 32 | words 'an |
| 84, 35 | Journals. |
| 84, 36 | Now |
| 84, 36 | it, they |
| 84, 40 | proposition, not |
| 84, 45 | begins, it may be that |
| 84, 46 | be that |
| 85, 2 | Provincial |
| 85, 3 | shews |
| 85, 8 | says that |
| 85, 12 | Journals |
| 85, 22 | question? Present |
| 85, 23 | rule? Produce |
| 85, 32 | been; |
| 85, 36 | wars), |
| 85, 39 | no ways |
| 85, 41 | Here then, |
| 85, 49 | Journals, |
| 85, 49 | susceptible. |
| 86, 1 | Reports |
| 86, 2 | discipline and |
| 86, 3 | Reports |
| 86, 5 | {*avis*}; |
| 86, 5 | such or such |
| 86, 6 | {*opinion*}; |
| 86, 11 | method (adds the author) ought |
| 86, 15–16 | presumption that |
| 86, 18 | proceeding either |
| 86, 18 | proposition, |
| 86, 19 | amendments) |
| 86, 24 | Assembly, |
| 86, 26 | developement |
| 86, 27 | consideration for |
| 86, 28 | proceedings, |
| 86, 29 | *question*' |
| 86, 30 | *question*}. |
| 86, 35 | House}, |
| 87, 6 | *avis*}. |
| 87, 7 | opinions? these |
| 87, 9–10 | decisions; adoption, |
| 87, 10–11 | modifications: for |
| 87, 12 | *argument*; argument |
| 87, 12 | in the course |
| 87, 14 | *opinion*}:' |
| 87, 15–16 | argument: the |
| 87, 16 | account, no |
| 87, 18 | account: it |
| 87, 19 | account, it |
| 87, 26–27 | decision; by |
| 87, 28 | *it*, |
| 87, 29 | argument} *of* |

| | |
|---|---|
| 87, 29 | *why*: {de |
| 87, 30 | pourquoi.} |
| 87, 32 | been, themselves, |
| 87, 32–33 | *pourquois* then must |
| 87, 35 | *whole*: {des |
| 87, 38 | *them*: |
| 87, 40 | reasons; it |
| 87, 40 | *motives*: it |
| 87, 43 | See ch. &#124;   &#124; Voting. |
| 88, 8 | adopted {enfin |
| 88, 9 | adopté}. |
| 88, 11 | *generally* and |
| 88, 13 | *décisions*, decisions |
| 88, 15 | decisions, in short one |
| 88, 15–16 | decisions, as |
| 88, 17 | Members, |
| 88, 17 | subject, discourses |
| 88, 18 | which, |
| 88, 18 | Assembly, |
| 88, 19 | *opinion*; these, |
| 88, 20 | meeting, acts |
| 88, 21 | opinions, |
| 88, 21 | Author) |
| 88, 22 | adopted.—Has it then been |
| 88, 25 | rest, which, |
| 88, 26 | it, can |
| 88, 30 | adopted?— |
| 88, 36 | Reports |
| 89, 2 | given which |
| 89, 6 | part, another |
| 89, 11 | Report |
| 89, 12–13 | *This is no Report; you must go back again, and make one.* |
| 89, 18 | Reports |
| 89, 19 | Reports, |
| 89, 23 | Reports, |
| 89, 25 | Reports |
| 89, 26 | Reports |
| 89, 28 | Unfortunately the |
| 89, 30 | Assembly), |
| 89, 34 | {*voix*},' |
| 89, 35 | Author |
| 89, 41 | impossible the |
| 90, 1 | act no |
| 90, 2 | necessary or |
| 90, 2 | use. No |
| 90, 6 | Clerk. |
| 90, 7 | use to |
| 90, 7 | Journals, |
| 90, 8 | Secretary |
| 90, 8 | properly: |
| 90, 12 | Commentator |

| | |
|---|---|
| 90, 14 | passage I have |
| 90, 14 *adds footnote* | Essay IV, Ch. \|     \| Hours of sitting. |
| 90, 15 | Provincial |
| 90, 19 | Commentator, |
| 90, 21 | that either |
| 90, 22 | misconception the |
| 90, 23 | circumstances, |
| 90, 26 | Journals |
| 90, 26 | and what |
| 90, 27 | Edicts |
| 90, 28 | confirm in |
| 90, 28 | respect the |
| 90, 31 | Royal Edict |
| 90, 33 | {*suffrages*}, |
| 90, 33 | *délibération*}. |
| 90, 35 | therefore an |
| 90, 36 | Journal |
| 90, 37 | first), |
| 91, 3 | resolution, and |
| 91, 3–4 | time, and |
| 91, 7 | is that |
| 91, 7 | Royal |
| 91, 8 | subject, these |
| 91, 10 | propositions, so |
| 91, 12 | {*suffrages*}, |
| 91, 13 | reduction is |
| 91, 15 | chose it? |
| 91, 17 | them; |
| 91, 18 | Royal Edict |
| 91, 19–20 | palliating, in some degree, |
| 91, 26 | of: |
| 91, 28 | say, |
| 91, 30 | confusion, |
| 91, 32 | that, |
| 91, 35 | is, |
| 91, 36 | 4°, 1779. |
| 91, 37 | Essay IV. |
| 91, 38 | & du |
| 91, 39 | II. |
| 92, 1 | France, |
| 92, 2 | Sovereign |
| 92, 5 | {avis}, |
| 92, 6 | *avis, & souvent* |
| 92, 7 | CHAPTER IV. Principal Points continued. POINT III. *Unity of the Subject of Debate kept inviolate.* |
| 92, 8 | *Reasons.* |
| 92, 9 *adds* | QUESTION I. |
| 92, 9 | WHY |
| 92, 11 | ANSWER. |
| 92, 12 | not by *indecision,* |
| 92, 15 | proposition about |

| | |
|---|---|
| 92, 17 | carpet by |
| 92, 24–25 | fraud, or conspiracy, |
| 92, 29 | proposition, suppose, |
| 92, 29 | arises: and, |
| 92, 30 | debate, |
| 92, 32 | else, |
| 92, 35 | manner a |
| 92, 40 | case it |
| 93, 10 | introduced one |
| 93, 11 | way, each |
| 93, 16 | Assembly: but |
| 93, 18 | BRITISH PRACTICE. As |
| 93, 24 | particulars, |
| 93, 25 | FRENCH PRACTICE. OF |
| 93, 31–2 | CHAPTER V. Principal Points continued. POINT IV. *The* PRO-CESS *of* DEBATING *distinct from, and prior to, that of* VOTING. |
| 93, 33 | *Questions,* |
| 93, 33 | *Reasons.* |
| 93, 34 *adds* | QUESTION I. |
| 93, 34 | WHY |
| 93, 35 | ANSWER. |
| 93, 37 | judge, to |
| 93, 39 | See Essay III. |
| 94, 2 | documents, altogether |
| 94, 5 | view? So, |
| 94, 7 | individuals, differences |
| 94, 12 | Assembly.— |
| 94, 23 | BRITISH PRACTICE. IN |
| 94, 26 | article; so |
| 94, 29 | Courts of Justice |
| 94, 32 | Courts of Justice |
| 94, 34 | FRENCH PRACTICE. THE |
| 94, 34 | practice, |
| 94, 35 | observed, |
| 94, 36 | country, |
| 95, 1 | exercise: |
| 95, 4 | that, |
| 95, 9 | first, such |
| 95, 10 | second, and |
| 95, 10 | *Precedence*, that |
| 95, 10 | sitting, was |
| 95, 12 | case: |
| 95, 12 | voting, pre-audience, |
| 95, 14 | combination, of |
| 95, 15 | none, results |
| 95, 16 | partizans |
| 95, 18 | sits.— |
| 95, 19 | consisting, suppose, |
| 95, 22 | impression, |
| 95, 28 | of the illumination |
| 95, 29 | Government |

| | |
|---|---|
| 95, 31 | could possibly |
| 95, 33 | two of |
| 95, 38 | opinions, things |
| 95, 39 | votes, but |
| 96, 1 | proceeding; |
| 96, 5 | separate; that |
| 96, 6 | of—but |
| 96, 7 | Committee), |
| 96, 11 | Unfortunately it |
| 96, 14 | rank as |
| 96, 16 | period the |
| 96, 17 | resolution however to |
| 96, 24 | debating and |
| 96, 25 | opinions are |
| 96, 27 | I, 143; |
| 96, 31 | parcel; |
| 96, 31 | *viz.* |
| 96, 32 | Orders, |
| 96, 31–32 | Third Estate. |
| 96, 33 | here.—Whether |
| 96, 33 | *arrêté,* |
| 96, 34 | french |
| 96, 35 | *délibération,* or |
| 96, 36 | members, is |
| 96, 36 | say; |
| 96, 39 | II, Art. 5 & 6. |
| 97, 1 | coincidence however can |
| 97, 5 | votes: |
| 97, 11 | which, |
| 97, 17 | is, |
| 97, 17 | cases, |
| 97, 24 | decision, how |
| 97, 34 | separating, argument |
| 97, 34 | vote— |
| 97, 40 | II, Art. |
| 98, 2 | but till |
| 98, 6 | Europe a |
| 98, 7 | Otaheite the |
| 98, 11 | Provincial |
| 98, 12 | Provincial States, |
| 98, 15 | States General, |
| 98, 18 | Justice |
| 98, 19 | every where, |
| 98, 20 | arguments and |
| 98, 21 | Provincial |
| 98, 25 | lawyer the |
| 98, 27 | Judges |
| 98, 27–28 | Courts of Justice, |
| 98, 28 | at; |
| 98, 28 | Courts |
| 98, 29 | Judges |

| | |
|---|---|
| 101, 5 | WHY |
| 101, 6 | ANSWER. |
| 101, 7 | intelligence, |
| 101, 7 | depends: |
| 101, 10 | forestalled: and, |
| 101, 21 | encreasing |
| 101, 29–31 | *For so many days together nothing but a silent vote? This will never do: I must make something of a speech to-day, or people will begin to look upon me as nobody.* |
| 101, 38 | talents, that |
| 102, 7 | an hint given by |
| 102, 17 | man, say |
| 102, 20 | him.—What follows?— |
| 102, 22 | case,— |
| 102, 23 | happen,— |
| 102, 27 | shew |
| 102, 41 | And, |
| 103, 3 | BRITISH PRACTICE. THE |
| 103, 6 | up first, |
| 103, 23 | Chance: that |
| 103, 25 | Equality |
| 103, 25 | worst it |
| 103, 28 | FRENCH PRACTICE. In |
| 103, 29 | surface, utility |
| 103, 30 | surface, inconvenience |
| 103, 35 | Ecclesiastical Members |
| 103, 36 | Noblesse, |
| 103, 37 | Third Estate, |
| 103, 38 | Commons |
| 103, 38 | May, |
| 103, 39 | Ibid. |
| 103, 39 | Ibid. Commons Journals, 2d May, 1604, |
| 103, 40 | vol. |
| 103, 40 | Convocation & |
| 103, 41 | Art. 5. |
| 103, 41 | 7. |
| 104, 2 | Equality |
| 104, 3 | order, good |
| 104, 4 | appeared, was |
| 104, 4 | Legislator |
| 104, 5 | Clergy, |
| 104, 6 | Noblesse; |
| 104, 6 | Third Estate |
| 104, 6 | Clergy |
| 104, 7 | Noblesse, |
| 104, 7–8 | Third Estate, |
| 104, 8 | them, |
| 104, 9 | adjusted, |
| 104, 11–12 | 48 Members, |
| 104, 12 | Procureur-Syndics) |
| 104, 13 | 12 |

| | |
|---|---|
| 104, 13 | 4 |
| 104, 13 | parcel: |
| 104, 14 | Ecclesiastic, |
| 104, 14 | Noble, |
| 104, 14 | Third Estate. |
| 104, 15 | Ecclesiastics |
| 104, 16 | Noblesse, |
| 104, 17 | Third Estate; |
| 104, 28 | 13. |
| 104, 28 | Ibid. I. 10. p. 31. |
| 104, 30 | Ecclesiastical |
| 104, 31 | Bishop, |
| 104, 35 | Bishop, |
| 104, 35 | Ecclesiastic |
| 104, 36 | Bishop. |
| 104, 40 | 1788. *p.* 25. |
| 105, 3 | Haute-Guyenne, |
| 105, 10 | Secretary |
| 105, 16 | Bishop |
| 105, 22 | 1780. |
| 105, 22 | Art. |
| 105, 29 | Parliaments, |
| 105, 34 | '{*voix*}' |
| 105, 35 | Royal |
| 105, 39 | Half a dozen |
| 105, 43 | mind. |
| 105, 43 | *No* |
| 105, 43 | *you.* |
| 106, 11 | CHAPTER VII. Principal Points continued. POINT VI. SIMUL-TANEITY *of the* VOTES. |
| 106, 12 | *Questions,* |
| 106, 12 | *Reasons.* |
| 106, 13 | WHY |
| 106, 15 | ANSWER. |
| 106, 15 | time:— |
| 106, 18 | States General |
| 106, 24 | one in |
| 106, 24 | votes, the other in |
| 106, 25 | States General |
| 106, 34 | in—8vo, |
| 106, 35 | them not |
| 106, 36 | day national |
| 107, 9 | accepted;— |
| 107, 9–13 | *I beg a thousand pardons; I took another man's hand for yours.—If I have acted honestly for this once, it was through mistake: the matter appeared unfortunately so clear to me, that I made no doubt of finding your hand on the same side.* |
| 107, 14 | itself, |
| 107, 16–17 | See, in another Essay, the Chapter on the cases where the secret mode of taking the votes is the proper one. |
| 107, 21 | voter; |

| | |
|---|---|
| 107, 28 | BRITISH PRACTICE. THE |
| 107, 32 | promiscuously and |
| 107, 33 | procession, |
| 107, 34 | cases the |
| 107, 36 | cases the |
| 107, 40 | See the Essay on *publicity* with regard to the proceedings of a political assembly. Essay II. |
| 108, 1 | every body, |
| 108, 2 | mode it |
| 108, 3 | much, on |
| 108, 4 | importance where Party |
| 108, 5 | settled, |
| 108, 5 | members, |
| 108, 8 | Probity |
| 108, 8 | Undue Influence. |
| 108, 11 | FRENCH PRACTICE. IN |
| 108, 11 | practice the |
| 108, 12 | seen: |
| 108, 13 | after—or |
| 108, 14 | speech, hence |
| 108, 16 | States General, |
| 108, 18 | must, |
| 108, 24 | Provincial |
| 108, 30 | Committees, |
| 108, 31 | 20 |
| 108, 31 | 22 |
| 108, 31 | 62 |
| 108, 33 | *Procès-Verbal,* |
| 108, 34 | assembly nothing |
| 108, 36 | Provincial |
| 109, 2 | avoid, |
| 109, 2 | possible, |
| 109, 3 | exposed. |
| 109, 6 | assemblies: |
| 109, 8–9 | an hundred |
| 109, 9 | States General, |
| 109, 14 | Nothing |
| 109, 16 | fallacy then to |
| 109, 17 | own: it |
| 109, 19 | oligarchy; |
| 109, 21 | OBSERVATIONS. |
| 109, 21 | THE |
| 109, 25 | connection |
| 109, 30 | connection, |
| 109, 32 | Judges |
| 109, 36 | practice, |

# COMPARATIVE TABLE OF CONTENTS

*Note.* The table shows the relation between the chapter headings of the three versions of 'Tactics'. There are four chapters in Dumont which do not relate to Bentham's 1791 plan: Chapters IV, 'Division du Corps législatif en deux Assemblées'; VII, 'De l'Initiative d'obligation et du Droit de proposer commun à tous'; VIII, 'Des divers Actes qui entrent dans la formation d'un Décret'; and XXXIV, 'Des Formules'. These became Chapters I §5; VII; VIII; and XVI in the Bowring edition.

<table>
<tr><td>

*Bentham*, 'Heads treated of in a Work entitled Essays on Political Tactics', 1791.

</td><td>

*Dumont*, 'Tactique des assemblées politiques délibérantes', 1816.

</td><td>

*Bowring* edition, 'An Essay on Political Tactics'.

</td></tr>
</table>

| *Bentham* | *Dumont* | *Bowring* |
|---|---|---|
| ESSAY I. GENERAL CONSIDERATIONS. CHAP. 1. *General View* of the Subject. | Ch. I. Sujet de l'ouvrage. | Ch. I. *General Considerations* §1. General View of the subject. |
| CHAP. II. *Ends* that ought to be kept in view in a Code of Regulations relative to this Head. | Ch. V. Inconvénients à éviter. | §2. Ends that ought to be kept in view in a code of regulations relative to this head. |
| CHAP. III. Of *Political Bodies* in general. | Ch. II. Notion des Corps politiques. II. *Des Corps permanents.* | §3. Of political bodies in general. §4. Of permanent bodies. |
| CHAP. IV. Of the *three rights* incident to a *Member* of a Political Assembly, as such: viz. *proposing, debating*, and *voting*. | | |
| CHAP. V. Nomenclature, Phraseology, and Analytical Views. | | |

217

218

# COMPARATIVE TABLE OF CONTENTS

# COMPARATIVE TABLE OF CONTENTS

| Bentham | Dumont | Bowring |
|---|---|---|
| CHAP. V.<br>— 4, The process of *Debating* distinct from, and prior to, that of *Voting*. | Ch. XVI.<br>Séparation du débat et du vote. | §5. Fourth point—The process of debating distinct from, and prior to, that of voting. |
| CHAP. VI.<br>— 5, In debating, *no* fixed Order of *Pre-audience*. | Ch. XVII.<br>Inconvénients d'un ordre fixe pour la parole. | §6. Fifth point—In debating, no fixed order of pre-audience. |
| CHAP. VII.<br>— 6, *Simultaneity* of the Votes. | | §7. Simultaneity of the votes. |
| PART II.<br>CHAP. VIII.<br>Of the *Penning* of Draughts of Motions, &c. | Ch. XI.<br>De la rédaction. | Ch. X. *Of the drawing up of Laws.* |
| CHAP. IX.<br>Of the *previous Promulgation* of *Motions*. | Ch. IX.<br>Promulgation des motions,—des bills des amendements. Ordre du travail. | Ch. IX.<br>*Of the Promulgation of Motions—of Bills—of Amendments, and their withdrawment.* |
| CHAP. X.<br>Of the previous Promulgation of *Bills*. | " | " |
| CHAP. XI.<br>Of the previous Promulgation of *Amendments*. | " | " |
| CHAP. XII.<br>Of the *extemporaneous* Promulgation of *Motions*. | " | " |
| CHAP. XIII.<br>Of the *extemporaneous* Promulgation of Amendments. | " | " |
| CHAP. XIV.<br>Of *Debates*. | Ch. XIV.<br>Du débat libre et du débat strict. | Ch. XI. *Of Debates.*<br>§2. Of free and strict debate. |

# COMPARATIVE TABLE OF CONTENTS

[1] These chapters cover, albeit briefly, all the subjects of Bentham's planned Chapters XIX–XXV.

# COMPARATIVE TABLE OF CONTENTS

[1] This subject is dealt with in Dumont's Chapter XXI, 'Des amendements', and Bowring's Chapter XII, *Of Amendments*, although in neither case is there a subtitle equivalent to Bentham's heading.

[2] This subject is dealt with in Dumont's Chapter XIII, 'De l'ouverture du débat', and in Bowring's Chapter XI, *Of Debates*, §1, 'Of the opening of a debate', although in neither case is there a subtitle equivalent to Bentham's heading.

# INDEX OF SUBJECTS

*Note.* References to Bentham's notes and to editorial notes are given by means of the page number(s) followed by the letter 'n'. Page numbers in italics refer to material written by Dumont.

The symbol 'v.' is used to indicate 'as distinct from' or 'as opposed to'. Other abbreviations for frequently occurring words and phrases are as follows:

| | |
|---|---|
| ass. | assembly(ies) |
| Brit. | British |
| Engl. | English |
| Fr. | French |
| govt. | government(s) |
| H. of C. | House of Commons |
| H. of L. | House of Lords |
| leg. | legislative |
| mem. | member(s) |
| parl. | parliament(s) |
| pol. | political |
| pres. | president(s) |

ABSENCE: in case of, whether rights of individual mem. of pol. ass. transmissible to another, 17; decision precipitated by taking advantage of, of many mem. of ass., 18; cause when ass. wanders from public utility, 19; continually changes identity of ass., 23; inconveniences of, of mem. of ass., 57–8, 177; deduction made from deposit for every day mem. absent from ass., 58–9; every legitimate excuse for, from ass. admissible as ground of exemption from punishment, 59; every case of, from ass. should be specified in register, 60; mem. absenting themselves from Brit. H. of C., 60–1; with good regulations against, no necessity for requiring certain number to form a House, 61; in ass. general advantage in case of, on side of executive power, 62; case of, of pres. of pol. ass., 66, 67; if author of act not present to support it he ought to incur censure of ass., 117; in Engl. parl. reiterated debates afford opportunity for mem. absent during first debate to attend, *129*

ABUSE(S): distribution of powers produced by division of leg. body source of perpetuity for, 25; very imperfect security against, of power results from public opinion, *26*; division of leg. body presents obstacles to reform of, *27*; cannot be expected that pol. body will make efficacious laws for prevention of, unless compelled by public opinion, 42; if right of proposing in pol. ass. belong only to administration, favourable to it perpetual, 110; of privilege of demanding division of ass. scarcely probable, 150

ACT(S): power of agreeing in same intellectual, constitutes principle of unity in body, 21 & n.; in ass. same force given to, of majority as to that of total number, 22; no, of ass. results if numbers equal on each side, 22; number necessary for rendering, of ass. legal, 23; publishing number of voters on each side may weaken authority of, of ass., 38; Votes of the House with mass of private, form Journals of the House, 42 & n.; principal points to be attended to in mode of proceeding relative to formation of, of pol. ass., 77–109; of different, which enter into formation of decree, 112–13; motion which is, of all must begin by being, of one individual, 116n.; of parl. defective in respect of numbered paragraphs, 118–19; king's speech at opening of session of Brit. parl. considered as, of minister, 135–6. *See* RESOLUTION(S)

227

ADJOURNMENT(S): in Engl. practice two, necessary as every bill read three times, 56; of dilatory motions or motions of, 141–2; in general committee motion for, supplies place of neuter vote, 153n.

ADMINISTRATION: efficacy of publicity extends to, 37; general distribution of labour duty of, 110

ADMIRALTY: motion in H. of C. on letters written by Lords of, 141

ADVOCATE: mem. of ass. acts as, or as judge, 46, 93–4, 99, 158

AGENT: functions belong to pres. (of ass.) in capacity of *judge* or of, 67 & n.

AMBASSADORS: proper to keep certain places for visitors to ass. in reserve for, and strangers, 62–3

AMBITION: advantage of presenting fixed and precise career to, *29*; peers least exposed to danger of popular, 44n.

AMENDMENT(S): table of motions and, 48, 49, 159, 171–2; proposition once received no other motion shall be made unless to offer, 78; and identity of terms of motion and resolution, 82 & n., 86, 87; while no difference descried between motion in, and vote, 97; and the formation of decree, 112–13; of promulgation of, 113–17; ministerial party wishing to throw out motion by appearing to amend it, 123; requirement that motion be seconded not applicable to, 125; if terms of motion not previously known not possible to prepare, 126; in Brit. parl., may be proposed when bill considered in committee or in third debate, *131*; all, relative to *choice of terms* or *mode of connexion*, 138–40; absolute rule not to admit insidious, 140–1

AMERICA: quarrel with American colonies, 33–4; American Congress represented all resolutions as unanimous, 39

AMOVEABILITY: condition requisite to inspire nation with confidence in ass., 16n.; until a system of removability established leg. ass. only responsible to public opinion, *26*; immoveability of peers weakens motives of emulation, 44n.; pres. ought to remain removable by ass. at its pleasure, 69

AMUSEMENT: should present essay afford half an hour's, to half an hundred thinking individuals, 4; among advantages of publicity, which results from it, 34; in private circles, end in view, 92–3

ANARCHY: every cause of disorder prepares for approach of, 20; law of unanimity produces frightful, 22; natural connexion between bad govt. and, 105n.; in pol. ass. measures which establish, 134

APPEAL: second ass. a tribunal of, from judgment of first, *26*; division of ass. is, to people against decision of majority, 150

APTITUDE AND INAPTITUDE: inaptitude for corporeal exercises partly cause and partly effect of studious disposition, 45; no better pledge of aptitude for labour than pleasure which accompanies it, 58

ARGUMENT(S): in ass. ought not to be necessity of seeking for words when already much to do in seeking for, 46; while no difference descried between, and vote, 97; everywhere and at all times mem. of courts of justice delivered, 98; impossible to judge, of motion unless it is clearly present to mind, 125, 168; best, requires to be presented at different times, *131*; is there any want of, in discussions of Engl. parl., 133; partisans of motion opposed to adjournment employ, in its favour, 142; in ass., and knowledge of motion, 158, 159; in pol. ass. debate on motion v. debate on pertinency of, 160; mem. of H. of C. desires to have motion read anew in order to give weight to his, 163

ARISTOCRACY: *See* NOBILITY

ARMY: word tactics may serve to designate art of directing evolutions of, 15; ass. not meant for, or puppet-show, 66n.; in Poland proposed in Council to raise, to cause territory to be respected, 147

ART: word tactics signifies, of setting in order, 15; of legislator limited to prevention of everything which might prevent development of liberty and intelligence of ass., 15; duty and, of pres. of pol. ass. is duty and, of *accoucheur*, 70; what is there which is object of, in operations of pol. ass., 112

ASSEMBLY: *See* POLITICAL ASSEMBLY(IES)

ATHENS: had deliberative ass., *11*; Solon gave Athenians not good laws but the best they could bear, 106n.

BALLOT(S): secret mode of giving votes called, 143; to demand, is to appeal from apparent to real wish of ass., 148; hitherto only two, 152–3

BERRI: modern provincial ass. instituted in, 76 & n., 90n., 103–5; code served as model to rest of provincial ass., 96n.

BILL(S): in England projects of laws before passed by parl. called, 42; in England every, must be read three times, 56, *129–31*; proposition *i.e.* whether motion or, 77–8; at commencement of session upon return of Commons from H. of L., read by clerk, 79–81; of promulgation of, 113–17; ought to contain complete exhibition of all clauses that law ought to contain, 118, 123–4; adjournments to motion and discussion of, already upon order-book, 141; considered in house v. considered in committee, 154–5; if king reject, formula of refusal determined, 155; may be entered upon motion table, 167

BLAME: in pol. ass. spirit of party strips, of its nature, 30; pol. ass. subjects itself to sovereign's influence exposing itself to public, 37

BREVITY: in articles prescribed for motions in ass., 118–19; clearness and, essential qualities of formulas, 155

BRITTANY: provincial state of ancient institution, 75 & n.

BURGUNDY: provincial state of ancient institution, 75 & n.

CAPABILITY: admission of less capable individuals inconvenience of absence of mem. of ass., 57, 58

CAPRICE: without publicity election or rejection of deputies guided only by, 33

CHAIRMAN: word, free from inconvenience attached to use of words *speaker* and orator, 65–6n.; Lord Clarendon's account of exploits in character of, of committee, 83; in Engl. parl., chosen for general committee, *129*

CHOICE: people who only elect electors not connected with deputies by affection of, 16n.; in ancient republics liberty of, not left to people, 121; author of bill and, of one term rather than another, 123; election by, v. election by lot, 143

CITIZENS: relation of ass. to, belongs to its pol. constitution, 15; at provincial ass. of Berri equality extirpated from different classes of, 103–5; nobleman called to decide between interest of nobility and that of mass of, 145

CLASS(ES): no approximation of superior and inferior, 16n.; interests of particular, v. interests of nation, 24; diversity of ranks spreads emulation among different, of society, *28–9*; two, in ass.—those paid for functions and those who paid for not fulfilling them, 59; generosity of superior, promises to France constitution which may be object of envy, 74; at provincial ass. of Berri equality extirpated from different, of citizens, 103–5; bribery a principle of seduction of the alluring, 177

CLERGY: better to give to their deputies a separate ass., *27*; nobility and, in Denmark held commons in nullity, *28*; clergyman excluded from national representation, 34 & n.; order of speaking of ecclesiastical members in provincial ass. of Berri, 103–4

CODE NAPOLÉON: longest paragraphs in, do not exceed one hundred words, 118n.

COLONIES: quarrel with American, 33–4

COMMITTEE(S): less numerous body detached from great body is, 21; in Brit. H. of C., *26*, 56, 57, 88–9, 123, 127–8; contiguous rooms for, of pol. ass., 45; Lord Clarendon's account of exploits in character of chairman of, 83; of Fr. provincial ass., 86–8, 89–90; Ass. of

our perceiving true sources of evil, 71; powerful talents and public-spirited dispositions comprise utmost good which best possible constitution can produce, 74; that intelligence of ass. may be improved for general good, 110; in respect of bills inflexible rule might cause evil to be consummated before remedy considered, 115; evil of announcing motions which there is no intention to support, 117; good law may be used as instrument to compel passing of bad one, 120; if proposer cannot find approver where is evil of abandoning motion, 124; greatest evil of precipitation concerning amendments, 126; reading in debate procures consolations for mediocrity at expense of public good, 132; wish of sovereign or executive power can only be productive of evil, 135–6; to judge whether motive is seductive or tutelary necessary to examine whether it produce more good or more evil, 145; great evil if in elections secresy destroyed all influence, 146; ferment a small evil compared with that of restraining expression of public feeling, 147; lack of dignity of division of H. of C. least evil, 151; motion table operates to generation of good habits, 160; laws that are so good and would be so beneficial if people would but execute them, 168; of all inconveniences in pol. ass. only radical ones formation of bad decision or non-formation of good one, 177

GOVERNMENT(S): all, need to understand art of deliberation, 5; in many branches of, end is of negative character, 15; relation of ass. to, belongs to its pol. constitution, 15; science of, to have reference to greatest happiness of society, 17; in which leg. body subject to law of unanimity an extravagance, 22; relief which superior chamber gives to, in eyes of people, *28*; conducted secretly v., conducted openly, 31–2; elected possess all general and local knowledge which function of governing requires, 33; publicity and governors, 34–5; regulated by ass. founded upon disposition to conformity with wish of majority, 38; secresy ought not to be system of regular, 39; in England principles of free, so little known, 42; England's escape from aristocratic, resembling that of Venice, 43; have great progress to make before they attain prudence in public matters, 51; public opinion in representative, disposed to conform itself to wish of ass., 58; if granting of tickets of admission to public seats in ass. in hands of, 63; affectation of secresy which has pervaded whole system of Fr. as in general of monarchical, 84; if ingenuity of, employed itself in considering by what means wisdom be disjoined from power, 95; natural connexion between bad, and anarchy, 105n.; if right of proposing in pol. ass. belong only to administration, would be given most commodious species of negative, 110; ass. which should possess power of rejecting alone tempted to reject good measures that it might constrain, 111; general confusion in, may result from right of all mem. to make propositions, 111; in respect of bills latitude must be left especially in favour of, 115; vote of H. of C. which served as foundation of revolution in, 140–1; in which secret mode of voting ought to be ordinary plan, 148

GREAT BRITAIN: rules necessary to every ass.: rules actually observed in ass. of Brit. legislature, 1; in rules of Fr. Ass. no indications that Brit. practice met with attention, 3–4; Brit. parl. a compound body, 21; rules as if non-existing in Brit. parl., 50; Brit. practice relative to mode of proceeding in pol. ass., 77n., 78–81, 82–3, 93, 94, 103, 107–8; France promised constitution which may soon be object of envy to, 74; Brit. practice in judiciary line, 99–100; Fr. parl. bear greater resemblance to H. of L. than to courts of justice in, 100; ministers in Brit. parl., 111–12; table of occupations in Brit. houses of parl., 114; projects of bills presented to Brit. parl., 123–4; in Brit. parl. both free and strict method of debate employed, 127–8; in Brit. parl. last reply in debate attracts most attention, 128–9; in Brit. parl. many occasions in which it is possible to renew debate during progress of bill, *130–1*; rule for exclusion of written discourses strictly observed in Brit. parl., 132–3; absolute rule in Brit. debate never to impute bad motives, 134–5; rules against digression in ass.: Brit. practice, 162–6. *See* ENGLAND, HOUSE OF COMMONS, HOUSE OF LORDS

history of several of their, 75 & n.; Commons and king's speech at commencement of every session, 79–80, 135–6; mem. who is up to speak in H. of C. speaks not to business offered to House by, 80; Mr. Grenville starts up with message from, 80–1; royal edicts published for regulation of discipline of Fr. provincial ass., 90–1, 98; in Provincial Ass. of Haute Guyenne king's provisional code, 95–6; royal mandate for Ass. of Notables, 105–6; Scottish parl. subject as to order of labours to committee named by, 110–11n.; popular ass. in England present addresses to, 116n.; parl. of Paris enumerated Charles V and Henry IV among, who assembled States-General, 136; adjournments of motion and communication from, 141–2; in England royal sanction always expressed by same words, 155; motion table applicable to king's messages and king's answers to addresses, 166–7. *See* CROWN, MONARCHY, SOVEREIGN

KNOWLEDGE: legislation requires variety of local, 16n.; division of leg. body deprives each ass. of, 24 & n.; in ass. elected by people publicity necessary to enable electors to act from, 33; elected possess all general and local, which function of governing requires, 33; utility of table of motions is that no one avoids knowing upon what motion he ought to vote, 46–7, 157–8; voting if according to, supposes debate, 71n.; most intelligent men in pol. ass. may be enchained by those greatly their inferiors in, 110; pretended that deputies possess all, of nation, 115; from whom can we expect greater, of subject than from author of motion, 124; in Engl. parl. in general committee discussion carried on by individuals who possess greatest, of question, 129; in correct, of public opinion that means must be found for resisting it when ill founded, 145; voters whose situation does not permit them to acquire pol., 146

LANGUAGE: figurative, and pol. bodies, 23–4; of proudest despots v. that of popular ass., 41

LANGUEDOC: provincial state of ancient institution, 75–6

LAW(S): prepossession in favour of Engl., among our nearest neighbours, 2–3; small *junta* of legislators may have particular interests in making, opposed to general interest, 16n.; constitutional, v. tactics, 16–17; useless decision an evil by augmenting mass of, 18; govt. in which leg. body subject to, of unanimity, 22; agreement of two ass. necessary to authority of, 24; refusal of popular, will expose deputies of nobility and clergy to judgment of nation, *27*; bad, prevented and good, rejected by H. of L., *28*; greater force conferred on, when nobility have concurred in sanctioning them, *28*; of publicity fittest, for securing public confidence, 29; public deliberations respecting, 31; publicity in pol. ass. not established by, 32; riot proper to make, of publicity absolute, 39; Votes of the House with mass of public, form Journals of the House, 42 & n.; projects of, 42, 56, 113, 115, 118, 167; improvement in England regarding publicity of ass. accomplished through violation of, 42; only reasons presented to public in authentic form are those opposed to, 43; can have no effect except as it is known, 50; when, which condemns is before eyes no one tempted to violate it, 50; distinctive dress for mem. of ass. might attain end of sumptuary, 51; in ass. gradations of affronts regarded with more respect and defended with more obstinacy than most important, 54; evil of absence of mem. of ass. sufficiently great to justify, of constraint, 57; which execute themselves, 58–9; necessary to add coercive punishment to give effect to, 59; men are what, make them to be, 60; not possible to expect that tribunal will be severe when all judges are interested in contravention of, 61; in distribution of places for visitors to ass. proper to allow particular seat for students of, 62; how could judges fix attention with impartiality upon point of, 69; happy the suitor if instead of complication and delay simplicity and celerity taken for standard and model by founders of, 71; pres. of pol. ass. to apply remedies in case of contravention of, of ass., 71n.; principles by which propriety of regulations tried and reasons deducible from principles are open to researches of invention in demesnes of, 73n.; acts *i.e.* as well permanent and general, 77 & n.; proposition once received no other motion shall be made unless to reclaim execution of, of order, 78; source of spirit of, of Fr. provincial ass., 98; that matters of, should be given to lawyer to draw up is nothing more than natural, 98; Fr. parl. had registers on which new, were to be entered, 105n.; Solon gave Athenians not good, but the best they could bear, 106n.; interval of three months between presentation of bill to ass. and its passing into, 114–15; rigorous, requisite against abandonment of motions, 117; of the drawing up of, 117–24; which would be so good provided only that they were observed, 125, 168; if superfluity of speakers in ass. exclusion of replies necessary, 127; bad, results of inattention and precipitation, 128; of three debates upon every proposed, 129–31; public modes of seduction arrested by, 148; he who demands division of ass. wishes to subject voters to, of publicity, 150; legislators who have drawn so many absurd, from Roman jurisprudence, 152; in making of, he who is undecided ought to be for negative, 153n.; preparation of, frequently completed in committee, 153; against digressions in pol. ass., 162, 163–4; no complaint if efficacy of, depended upon frequency of repetition, 162

LAWYERS: regulations given to French provincial ass. had, for authors, 98; secret interest on part of, 119; find in multiplication of words pretext for services and increase of price, 156

LEGISLATION: topics that fall to be treated under this head of, 4; requires variety of local knowledge and not susceptible of direct responsibility, 16n.; in, indecision corresponds to denial of justice, 18; efficacy of publicity extends to, 37; necessity of appeal in judicial matters not of same importance as in, 38; Fr. parl. acquired a sort of negative in, 105n.; errors in morals and, which have led noblest minds astray, 144; in, he who is undecided ought to be for negative, 153n.; in relation to all leg. measures Houses of Parl. accustomed to resolve themselves into Committees of whole House, 154–5

LEGISLATIVE ASSEMBLY(IES): composition of, better in proportion as interest similar to that of community, 15–16; govt. in which legislative body subject to law of unanimity an extravagance, 22; division of legislative body into two ass., 24–5, *25–9*; until system of free election and removability established, only responsible to public opinion, *26*; individual who first laid transactions of, before public deserves reward, 34 & n.; decisions of judges v. decisions of, 38; of what concerns mem. of, 51–64; in numerous, pres. ought not to be mem., 68–9; in, pres. ought to be chosen by ass. over which he is to preside, 69; in, no class of advocates, 99; preservation of minister's place depends upon duration of his credit with, 112; cases in which prompt decisions necessary do not often arise in, 128; transmitted articles of accusation against M. de Lessart to high national court, 136; wherein consists utility of, employing form which is indecorum and lie, 150n.; division of H. of C. has none of dignity which ought to characterise, 151; in Engl. voting extraordinary circumstance has arisen that, should commit act of falsehood, 151–2. *See* POLITICAL ASSEMBLY(IES)

LEGISLATIVE BODY: *See* LEGISLATIVE ASSEMBLY(IES)

LEGISLATOR(S): art of, limited to prevention of everything which might prevent development of liberty and intelligence of ass., 15; small *junta* of, may have particular interests in making laws opposed to general interest, 16n.; tribunes of people v., 36; practice of courts of justice model which, of provincial ass. have before their eyes, 98; at provincial ass. of Berri duty of, done, 104; facts cannot be collected unless time allowed to parties to present them to, 115; imperative law ought only to contain simple expression of will of, 121; ridiculous to say to, 'Divine what motion will be', 126; in cases in which public opinion erroneous it is desirable that, vote in secret, 144–5; who have drawn so many absurd laws from Roman jurisprudence, 152. *See* LEGISLATIVE ASSEMBLY(IES), LEGISLATURE

LEGISLATURE: rules necessary to every ass.: rules actually observed in ass. of Brit., 1;

advantages of wealth and rank suffice to turn balance, 146; in matters of finance greater coherency in permanent committee, 154

MORALS: errors in, and legislation which have led noblest minds astray, 144

MOTION(S): proposer of, not present in ass. in which objections made against it, 24 & n.; publicity and, of pol. ass., 38; Votes of the House contain, 42; in England printing of bills ordered upon special, 42; table of, exhibits to ass., on which they are deliberating and voting, 45–7, 157–61; simple reading sufficient for seizing spirit of, 48; printing of, v. motion table, 48, 161–2; rapidity of, in Constituent Ass. of France, *48–9n.*; in H. of C. principal, announced beforehand, 61; in numerous leg. ass. pres. ought not to possess right to make, 68–9; celerity with which, oftentimes made, 72; proposition *i.e.* whether, or bill, 77 & n.; nothing deemed act of ass. that has not been proposed in ass. by, written and *in terminis*, 78–92; in debating no mem. after author of, shall have right of speaking before any other, 78 & n., 126; to vote for or against, is to judge, 93–4; identity of, and resolution, 95–6; in ass. of Picardy opinions something betwixt, and votes, 97–8; by making of, mem. of pol. ass. exercises function of advocate, 99; voting on, in H. of C., 106; ministerial plan interrupted by incoherent and subversive, 111; in Brit. parl. no rule which secures to, of minister a preference above those of any other mem., 111–12; to make, is act necessary to produce decree, 112–13; of promulgation of, 113–17, 168–9; as compositions destined to become laws and be presented to examination of ass., 117–24; not entertained by H. of C. until it is seconded, 124–5; before author of, permitted to speak upon it, ought to be read, 125–6; evident that no person ought to be heard against, before someone has spoken for it, 126; when replies not permitted exception made of author of, 128–9; in Brit. parl. each stage during progress of bill passed upon, by mem., *130*; in Engl. parl. as soon as defender of, ceases to speak opposite party furnishes orator, 133; never quote justificatory piece which has not been presented to ass. in consequence of, to that effect, 136; once rejected not to be presented afresh during same session, 137; and amendments thereupon, 138–41, 171–2; of dilatory, or, of adjournment, 141–2; voting with reference to, 143; votes ascertained in summary manner in, relative to current affairs, 149; in committee, for adjournment supplies place of neuter vote, 153n.; considered in house v. considered in committee, 154–5; proper that mem. of ass. use same terms in presenting, 155; in H. of C. Speaker gives, second reading, 162; capacity of motion table of being applied with advantage: most obvious with respect to, 166; when, under consideration limitation of motion table affords no argument against its utility, 167; inaction is meeting without, 177. *See* MEASURE(S), PROPOSITION(S)

MOTION TABLE: *See*: TABLE OF MOTIONS

NATION(S): pol. ass. selected from whole body of great, 1; temper and modes of thinking prevalent in Fr., 2–3; composition of leg. ass. better in proportion with greater number of points of contact with, 15; conditions requisite to inspire, with confidence in ass., 16n.; interests of particular class v. interests of, 24; refusal of popular law will expose deputies of nobility and clergy to judgment of, *27*; continual transfusion of noble families among body of, *29*; tribunal of the public unites all wisdom and all justice of, 29; in pol. ass. let it be impossible that any thing be done which is unknown to, 30; public deliberations operate upon spirit of, in favour of govt., 31; order which reigns in discussion of pol. ass. forms by imitation the national spirit, 31; too numerous to act for itself obliged to entrust powers to deputies, 33; pleasure sufficient to increase happiness of, 34; which suspends judgment, 35; decisions of leg. ass. regulate interests of whole, 38; in England conduct which destroys influence on part of, 42; cause of Fr. Chamber of Peers too feeble to sustain observation of, 44n.; establishment of particular dress for mem. of ass. point upon which it would not be proper to wound national customs, 51; ambassadors and strangers would carry from exhibition of ass. advantageous

persons, 31; rich would not be indisposed to acquire honourable, 59; of, of Pres., 65–7; if pres. of ass. is mem. he will have different kind of ambition from that which belongs to his, 68; for sake of ass. that institution of, of pres. is necessary or proper, 70; voting respecting persons takes place with reference to election of person to, 143; obligation for mem. of ass. to give vote founded upon nature of, 152–3

OPINION(S): act of ass. announces, or will, 21; if deputies of nobility and clergy act separately responsibility of, will rest upon their own heads, *27*; sound, more common among a people accustomed to public ass., 31; publicity in pol. ass. places public in situation to form enlightened, 32; all, freely debated in Engl. newspapers, 34; class of public which does not form own, v. class of public which furnishes, 35; class of public which judges directs, 35–6; quality of votes has influence on, 39; H. of L. gives to one set of, publicity, 43; secresy takes more from influence over, than was given in superiority of rank, 44n.; those in pol. ass. who do not hear obliged to decide upon borrowed, 45; mem. of Constituent Ass. of France not able to form, *48–9n.*; those mem. of ass. who have announced, fear to render themselves suspected by change of, 56; if two pres. of ass. whenever there arises difference of, there will be no decision, 67; acts *i.e.* as well declarations of, 77 & n.; in reports of committees of Fr. provincial ass. account given of different, 86, 87, 88; in reports of Engl. committee no, given which is not, of whole, 88–9; in Fr. ass., formed by plurality of voices then entered upon minutes, 89–90; in Fr. ass. divers, reduced to two, 90–1, 95–7; under regimen of precedence in pol. ass. chance of forming right, 95; not easy to human pride to adopt right, after having avowed its opposite, 96; public declaration of, by judges in Engl. court preceded by private conference, 100; principle of composition of laws: employ simple declaration of will without intermixing, 121–3; in Engl. parl. reiterated debates secure to minority of ass. periods at which to state its, *129*; ass. by means of prepared discourses less exposed to dangerous, 132; in pol. ass. rule never to impute bad motives favourable to freedom of, 134; publicity in accordance with public welfare as, formed by public conformable to its interest, 144. *See* PUBLIC OPINION

OPPOSITION: distribution of powers produced by division of leg. body source of undue, 25; absurd to create body of nobles solely for purpose of opposing wishes of deputies of the people, *27 & n.*; in pol. ass. individual almost always secure of suffrages of one party in, to the other, 30; assists authority, 31; legal, to unpopular measures prevents illegal resistance, 31; improvement produces shock when opposed to inclinations of people, 32; personal interests of mem. of ass. often in, to interests confided in them, 37; illegal v. legal, to acts of ass., 38; in Brit. parl., rarely makes use of means for retarding progress of bill, *130*; oftentimes resentments carry into pol., asperity of personal quarrels, 135; attack king's speech at opening of session of Brit. parl. as they do any other ministerial measure, 135–6; voting by acclamation may be employed for stifling all, 149

OPPRESSION: oppressive laws press upon legislators themselves, 16n.

ORATOR: the word by which *speaker* rendered in general language of Europe, 65n.; word Chairman free from inconvenience attached to use of words *speaker* and, 65–6n.; Mr. Fox the most distinguished, of England, 135n.

ORDER: word tactics signifies art of setting in, 15; individuals who cannot offer pledge of property less attached to established, 16n.; England's beautiful pol., *29*; which reigns in discussion of pol. ass. forms by imitation the national spirit, 31; in ass. system of insults increasing from last to first place called, 53; attention of pres. of ass. principally directed to maintenance of form and, 68–9; useful in general to facilitate conception, 72n.; good, at provincial ass. of Berri and Haute Guyenne, 103–4, 105; of sitting in Ass. of Notables, 105–6; in pol. ass. there ought to be general plan disposing requisite operations in best, 110; inflexible, for motions and bills might prove destructive of real, 114; everything which renders, necessary in proceedings of free people is safeguard of their rights,

might permit mem. to make short explanations without quitting his place, 55; proper to keep certain places for visitors in reserve at disposal of, 62–3; of, and vice-pres. belonging to pol. ass., 65–71; in Ass. of Orléans, 96; of provincial ass. of Berri, 104; in ass. those who speak should address, 133–4; may put amendments to vote in order which appears to him most suitable, 140; and summary mode of voting, 143; in the House v., of committee, 154–5; proper that, always take votes in same manner, 155; uses motion table as remedy for digressions, 160–1; in H. of C., gives motion second reading, 162

PREVARICATION: facility of, inconvenience of absence of mem. of ass., 57; demi-publicity proper if reward to, to be secured, 148

PRINTING: in England bills not printed under general rule but upon special motion, 42; in H. of L. protests are printed in opposition to regulations, 43; of motion v. motion table, 48, 161–2; act which enters into formation of decree: occasionally ordering motion to be printed, 113; and public sale of bills ought to be rule, 115; relative frequency of occurrence of letters: matter well known to printers, 174; logographical principle: principle of, by whole words, 174

PROBITY: exclusion from pol. power of those incapable of exercising power with, 16n.; in pol. ass. internal censure will not be sufficient to secure, without assistance of external censure, 30; makes escape from undue influence, 108; public respects, of its governors and judges, 144; demi-publicity proper if punishment to, to be secured, 148

PROCEDURE: theory of mode of, most proper to be observed in pol. ass., 1; delays in deliberations correspond with useless delays in, 18; with pace of tortoise v. rapid as lightning, 50; *nullo modo* gives form of, of Fr. national ass., 75; spirit of revenue introduced into, 156

PROCEEDING(S): minutes of, work performed with utmost exactness in H. of C., 4; order to be observed in, of pol. ass., 15; public an incompetent judge of, of pol. ass., 35; publicity may expose to hatred mem. of ass. for, which deserve other treatment, 36; publicity of, of pol. ass. in monarchy, 37; Votes of the House a history of its, 42 & n.; system of tactics which in form of, ass. may happen to embrace, 74; if, of States-General had been attended with any effect we should have seen mode in which they proceeded, 75; regimen established in modern provincial ass. gives latest mode of, known in France, 76 & n.; principal points to be attended to in mode of, relative to formation of acts of pol. ass., 77–109; registering, act which enters into formation of decree, 113; test of propriety of rules proposed for regulation of, in pol. ass., 177

PROCRASTINATION: *See* DELAY

PROPERTY: eligibility and general distrust of individuals who cannot offer pledge of, 16n.

PROPOSITION(S): right of proposing v. right of deciding upon, already made, 16–17; want of activity may arise if ass. can only act upon, presented to it by executive power, 17–18; those who have principal conduct of affairs will carry all important, to ass. which has more influence, 25; desire of popularity may suggest dangerous, to mem. of ass., 36–7; in Fr. Chamber of Deputies obtained popular favour, 44n.; what is of most importance to be known is sense not tenor of, 46; consider as surprise every, the success of which resulted from absence, 58; in case of equality, which has not had majority of votes is rejected, 69; in pol. ass. identity of terms of, with those of act proposed, 77–8, 82–92; in pol. ass. second, not to be started till former disposed of, 92–3; art of applying correction to original, in pol. ass., 97; both judicial ass. and provincial ass. had, to decide upon, 98; in pol. ass. introducer of, has been heard in favour of it, 99; right of all mem. of pol. ass. to make, 111; right of priority conceded to ministerial, 111; simplicity in, prescribed for motions in ass., 118, 119–21; complex, which state fact and opinion, 121–2; in pol. ass. and amendments, 138. *See* MEASURE(S), MOTION(S)

PROPRIETY: principles by which, of regulations tried and reasons deducible from principles are open to researches of invention in demesnes of law, 73n.; test of, of rules proposed for regulation of proceedings in pol. ass., 177

PROTESTS: declarations by minority in H. of L. of reasons for dissent from measures adopted by majority, 43

PROVINCIAL ASSEMBLIES: of noblesse throughout Russian empire, 66n.; publication of journals of Fr., *8–9*, 75–6; modern, in France, 76, 84–6, 89–92, 95–7, 98–9, 103–5, 108–9

PRUSSIA: resistance that would not have been made to king of, 66n.

PUBLIC: and conduct of deputies of nobility and clergy, *27*; tribunal of, 29–30, 35, 38, 144–5; ass. forms internal, which serves as restraint upon itself, 30; will repay with usury confidence reposed in it, 30; publicity in pol. ass. places, in situation to form enlightened opinion, 32; publicity provides ass. with means of profiting by information of, 33–4; individual who first laid transactions of leg. ass. before, deserves reward, 34 & n.; publicity secures governors against injustice of, 34; incompetent judge of proceedings of pol. ass., 35; publicity and distinguishing of, into three classes, 35–6; mem. of ass. possess all means of serving themselves at expense of, 37; very easily misled by false reports, 39; names of voters in ass. ought to be published so that, know principles of deputies, 39; authentic publication of proceedings of ass. made with slowness which would not give, satisfaction, 40; success of non-official journals depends upon avidity of, 40; admission of, to sittings of ass., 40–1, 42–4, 62–4; in England journals of House formerly given to each mem. but not sold to, 42 & n.; only reasons presented to, in authentic form are those opposed to laws, 43; in respect of preventing interruption to unity of plan in ass. party interests same as those of, 52; effect on, of mem. of ass. speaking from tribune, 54; to talk to no purpose in ass. before, which judges, 56; if the part (of ass.) absent greater than that which is present, knows not to which to adhere, 58; responsibility of ass. with regard to, 62; pol. liberty depends upon manifestation of public will, 73; without discipline public spirit stands as poor a chance in numerous ass. as valour in the field, 73; greater instrument of public felicity, 74; success with which, is served depends upon use which each man makes of own powers, 74; in secret mode of voting conduct of voter not concealed from knowledge of, 107; as soon as law is proposed it ought to be known to, 114–15; no motion should be presented to popular ass. which had not been made known to, 117n.; taxes made security for money advanced for service of, 123; in Engl. parl. reiterated debates afford opportunity to, to make itself heard, *129*; in second debate parties approach each other with arguments matured by communication with, *130*; principal advantage of public discussion, 132; reading in debate procures consolations for mediocrity at expense of public good, 132; National Ass. passed decrees upon facts said to be of public notoriety, 136; *l'esprit de corps* an anti-social principle when it leads to sacrifice of interests of, 145; secresy in voting useful when publicity exposes voter to interests opposed to public interest, 146; in election to exclude discussion is to decide cause of, without allowing interested parties to be heard, 147. *See* PEOPLE, PUBLICITY, PUBLIC OPINION

PUBLICATION(S): conjuncture which gave rise to, of present essay, 1–2; of proceedings of ass. in London v. in Paris, 4; authentic and non-authentic, on proceedings of ass., 39–40; numerous, give account of debates and voters in H. of C., 43; of journals of ass. of ancient Fr. provincial states, 75–6. *See* JOURNALS

PUBLICITY: deliberations of pol. ass. to be public, 17; law of, in pol. ass. fittest law for securing public confidence, 29; reasons for, 29–34; objections to, 34–7; points to which, should extend, 38–9; exceptions to the rule of, 39; means of, 39–41; state of things in England relative to, 41–4; and Fr. Chamber of Peers, 44n.; essential connexion between liberty and, 53; giving tickets of admission to public seats in ass. to mem. would restrict prerogative of, 63; act which enters into formation of decree: occasionally ordering

proceed to election is to proceed to try candidates with intention of bestowing reward, 147; punishment to probity and reward to prevarication, 148; monarch might create factitious interest by rewards, 148; remedy for digressions in pol. ass. necessary as punishment, 160

RIDICULE: seductions of eloquence and, most dangerous instruments in pol. ass., 64; and amendments to motions in pol. ass., 140–1; prolonged exclamations in summary voting would be ridiculous, 149

RIGHT(S): of mem. of pol. ass., 16–17; mem. of privileged body have certain, which other citizens do not possess, 21; claim of, of Commons to proceed, 79–80; at ass. of Haute Guyenne exercise of mem.'s, dependent upon servant's pleasure, 105 & n.; of initiation ought not to be privilege of executive exclusively, 110–12; everything which renders order necessary in proceedings of free people is safeguard of their, 117n.; conjunctions of laws may arise in which ass. compelled to sacrifice its most important, 120–1; wounded officer ought not to be deprived of, of speaking for his country, 127; mode of reducing number of orators in ass. too numerous to allow, of discussion to all, 137–8; each mem. ought to have, of demanding division of ass., 150; proper that mem. of ass. use same terms in requiring exercise of, 155

RIOTS: caused by govt. acting with precipitation, 32 & n.

ROME: had deliberative ass., *11*; Roman senate, *11*, 21n., 56n., 60, 63, 134, 152; history of, furnishes examples of violent parties, 19; Roman emperor proposed reward for individual who invented new pleasure, 34; in ancient republics popular ass. subjected to demagogues, 45; in ancient republics initiative of laws belonged exclusively to senate, 121; secret suffrages introduced at, 147; ancient Romans in penal matters seized distinction of three states of mind, 152

ROYALTY: *See* CROWN, KING(S), MONARCHY, SOVEREIGN

RULE(S): observed in ass. of Brit. legislature, 1; in, of Fr. Ass. no indications that Brit. practice met with attention, 3–4; single ass. may have best, and disregard them when it pleases, *26*; constant subjection of H. of C. to, which it prescribes to itself, *28*; made for state of calm and security, 39; in H. of C., relative to publicity, 41–2; arrangements for execution of good, in ass., 50–1; rich might glory in infraction of, when punishment only pecuniary fine, 59; of pres. and vice-pres. belonging to pol. ass., 65–71; without, power of ass. evaporates or becomes prey to obstinate, 73; starting up pretending to be acts of the House, 80; ambiguous, mortal to all certainty, 85n.; no general, can take cognizance of differences in point of talent between individuals, 94; truth and, of fixed pre-audience in pol. ass., 102–3; impracticable to subject all motions to absolute, requiring previous registration, 114; in respect of bills inflexible, not required, 115; imperative law intended to serve as, of conduct, 121; when, operates only as restraint if not useful it is mischievous, 125; efficacious, for preventing useless discourses in pol. ass., 125; in H. of C., is not to speak but upon admitted motion, 125; upon word which should mark close of speech in pol. ass., 126; that in large ass. person speaking ought to stand, 126–7; in Brit. parl., of speaking only once, 127–8; leg. ass. always master of its own, 128; general, to reject nothing which may enlighten ass., 128; general, in Engl. parl. that every bill debated three times, 129; for exclusion of written discourses strictly observed in Brit. parl., 132–3; relative to debate, 133–7; with respect to amendments in pol. ass., 139, 140; general, with regard to publicity of voting, 144–6; relating to division of H. of C., 151 & n.; against digressions in pol. ass., 160–1, 162–6; relating to promulgation of motions, 168–9; test of propriety of, proposed for regulation of proceedings in pol. ass., 177. *See* REGULATION(S)

RUSSIA: *Marshal* the appellation by which pres. designated in provincial ass. of noblesse throughout Russian empire, 66n.; Poland made last and generous effort to withdraw herself from dominant influence of, 147–8

# INDEX OF NAMES

*Note.* The following is an index of names of persons and places appearing in the introduction, text, and notes; the last (whether Bentham's or the editors') are indicated by 'n.' Under Bentham's name only references to his other works are indicated.